Front cover
Dome of the Rock, interior decoration, detail, Jerusalem.

Museum With No Frontiers *Exhibition Trails*

ISLAMIC ART IN THE MEDITERRANEAN | PALESTINIAN TERRITORIES

Pilgrimage, Sciences and Sufism

Islamic Art in the West Bank and Gaza

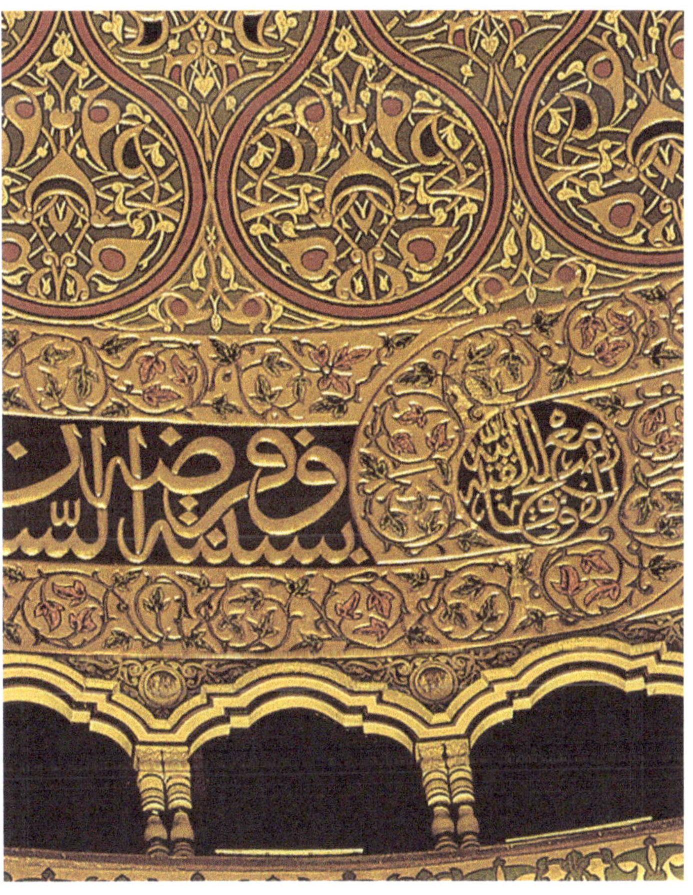

Museum With No Frontiers

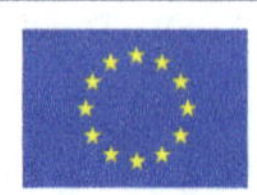

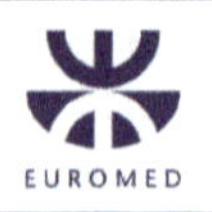

EUROPEAN UNION
Euromed Heritage

The realisation of the MWNF Exhibition Trail
PILGRIMAGE, SCIENCES AND SUFISM: Islamic Art in the West Bank and Gaza
has been co-financed by the **European Union** within the framework
of the **Euromed Heritage** programme
and has received the support of the following Palestinian and international institutions:

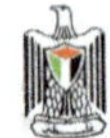

Ministry of Culture
Directorate of Cultural Heritage
Palestinian Authority

Ministry of Culture, Directorate of Cultural Heritage, Palestinian Authority

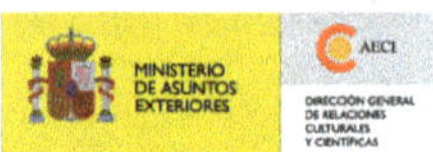

Ministry of Foreign Affairs and Cooperation,
Spanish Agency for International Development Cooperation, Spain

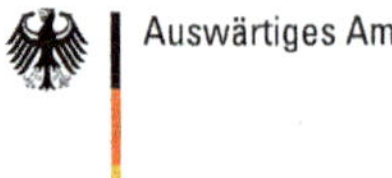

Federal Foreign Office, Germany

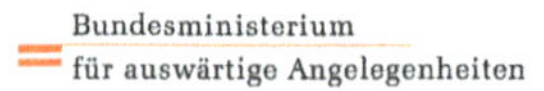

Federal Ministry for European and International Affairs, Austria

ISBN: 978-3-902782-10-6

Information
www.museumwnf.org
www.mwnfbooks.net

Museum With No Frontiers
Idea and overall concept
Eva Schubert

Head of Project
Walid Sharif, Ramallah

Coordinator
Curatorial Committee
Mahmoud Hawari

Curatorial Committee
Mahmoud Hawari, Jerusalem
Yusuf Natsheh, Jerusalem
Nazmi al-Ju'beh, Jerusalem
Marwan Abu Khalaf, Ramallah
Mu'en Sadeq, Gaza

Catalogue

Introductions
Yusuf Natsheh, Jerusalem
Nazmi al-Ju'beh, Jerusalem

Presentation of Itineraries
Curatorial Committee

Revision
Anne-Marie Lapillone, Marseille

Technical texts
Sa'd al-Nimr, Ramallah
Jihan Barakat, Ramallah

Editing of the Arabic text

Chief Editor
Yusuf Natsheh

Scientific editing
Mahmoud Hawari
Nazmi al-Ju'beh

Proofreading
Rushdi al-Ashhab

Illustrations

Photographer
Issa Freij, Jerusalem
Garo Nelbendian, Jerusalem

Iconographic Research
Diana Phillips, London

General maps and sketches
Sa'd al Nimr, Ramallah
Sergio Viguera, Madrid

Monument plans
Sergio Viguera, Madrid

English Translation
Cornelia al-Khaled, London

Copy editor and revision of the English edition
Mandi Gomez, London

General introduction
Islamic Art in the Mediterranean

Texts
Jamila Binous, Tunis
Mahmoud Hawari, Jerusalem
Manuela Marín, Madrid
Gönül Öney, Izmir

Maps
Şakir Çakmak, Izmir
Ertan Daş Izmir
Yekta Demiralp, Izmir

Layout and design
Augustina Fernández,
Electa España, Madrid
Christian Eckart,
MWNF, Vienna (2nd edition)

Local coordination

Production Manager
Sa'd al-Nimr, Ramallah

Production Assistant
Jihan Barakat, Ramallah

International coordination

Overall coordination
Eva Schubert

Curatorial committees, translations, editing and production of the catalogues (1st edition)
Sakina Missoum, Madrid

Acknowledgements

We thank the following institutions for their support:

Ministry of Culture, Directorate of Cultural Heritage, Ministry of Culture, Ramallah
Ministry of Tourism and Antiquities, Department of Development and Planning, Ramallah
Ministry of Planning and International Co-operation, Ramallah
Ministry of Waqf and Religious Affairs, Ramallah
Ministry of Labour, Ramallah
Ministry of Local Government, Ramallah
Municipality of Nablus
Municipality of Gaza
Municipality of Hebron
Municipality of Jericho
European Commission Technical Assistance Office to the West Bank and Gaza Strip, Jerusalem
Khalil Sakakini Cultural Center, Ramallah

Photographic references
See page 5 and
Ann & Peter Jousiffe (London), page 20 (Aleppo)
Oronoz Photographic Archive (Madrid), page 23 (Alhambra, Granada)

Map references
Ettinghausen R., and Grabar O. (Madrid, I, 1997), page 26 (Mosque of Damascus)
Sönmez Z. (Ankara, 1995), page 27 (Mosques of Divriği and of Istanbul) and page 28 (Madrasa of Sivas)
S. Viguera (Madrid), page 28 (Minarets typologies)
Blair S. S. and Bloom J. M. (Madrid, II, 1999), page 29 (Mosque and Madrasa Sultan Hasan)
Ettinghausen R. and Grabar O. (Madrid, I, 1997), page 30 (Qasr al-Khayr al-Sharqi)
Kuran A. (Istanbul, 1986), page 31 (Sultan Khan, Aksaray)

Preface

In 1996 Museum With No Frontiers (MWNF) initiated a comprehensive programme to research, document and increase knowledge and public awareness of the history and cultural legacy of Islam in the countries surrounding the Mediterranean basin. This book is one of the outcomes of this programme, which involves hundreds of scholars and is carried out in cooperation with institutions from all the countries concerned. Important initial funding from the European Union made it possible to set the basis for a sustainable network of public and private partners implementing attractive projects in the field of culture, education and tourism.

When the MWNF programme was first launched, the topic of Islamic art and architecture was familiar only to experts and there was an implicit understanding that cultural heritage in the Mediterranean meant the legacy of the classical civilisations. Thanks to the launch coinciding with the establishment at the end of 1995 of the Euro-Mediterranean Partnership, a joint initiative of the European Union and its Mediterranean neighbours, the MWNF programme took off quickly and became a pioneering venture to disseminate knowledge about the world contribution of Islam.

The initial focus on the Mediterranean region was determined by its place at the centre stage of Islamic history and the economic and cultural interdependence of its shores throughout that history. However, we look forward to extending the programme to other areas of the Islamic and Arab world.

In connection with our Exhibition Trails and related thematic guides, MWNF also offers the possibility to participate in themed tours organised in cooperation with specialised local travel agencies in each country. For further details and virtual tours to the Exhibition Trails please visit *www.mwnftravels.net*.

Our Virtual Museum – *www.discoverislamicart.org* – offers access to a large collection of Islamic artefacts and monuments, with descriptions for all items regularly updated in Arabic, English, French and Spanish. A series of Virtual Exhibitions enables visitors to locate the topics of the Exhibition Trails within the relevant regional context.

All MWNF publications are compiled, written and illustrated by scholars and photographers from the country concerned and convey the cultural and historical context of the featured sites from a local perspective. 'We appreciate only what we see and we understand only what we know.' It was with this idea in mind that our Egyptian colleagues who designed the visit and wrote the text for this book paid particular attention to providing information that usually remains undisclosed to tourists.

On behalf of the whole MWNF team I wish you an enjoyable visit to the Palestinian Territories and look forward to meeting you soon in another part of our Euro-Mediterranean museum with no frontiers.

Eva Schubert
Chairperson and CEO
Museum With No Frontiers

Advice

Transliteration of the Arabic

We have retained standard spelling for Arabic words in common usage and accepted by the English dictionary. We have maintained the phonetic transcription of names and Arabic words in accordance with Palestinian standards. For all other words, we have simplified the transcription. We do not transcribe the initial *hamza* nor do we distinguish between long and short vowels, which have been transcribed as *a, i, u*. The *ta' marbuta* has been transcribed as *a* (in its absolute), and as *at* (when followed by a genitive). The transcription for the 28 Arabic consonants is as follows:

ء	'	ح	h	ز	z	ط	t	ق	q	ه	h
ب	b	خ	kh	س	s	ظ	d	ك	k	و	u/w
ت	t	د	d	ش	sh	ع	'	ل	l	ي	y/i
ث	th	ذ	dh	ص	s	غ	gh	م	m		
ج	j	ر	r	ض	d	ف	f	ن	n		

Words in italic in the text without an accompanying translation or explanation can be found in the glossary.

The Muslim Era

The Muslim era began with the exodus of the Prophet Muhammad from Mecca to Yathrib. Then the name was changed to *Madina,* "The City" or "the town of the Prophet". With his small community of followers (70 people including members of his family) recently converted to Islam, the Prophet undertook the *al-hijra* (literally "the emigration") and the new era began.

The date of the emigration is the first of the month of *Muharram* in year one of the *Hijra*, which corresponds to the 16th July of the year 622 of the Christian era. The Muslim year is made up of 12 lunar months, each month having 29 or 30 days. Thirty years form a cycle in which the 2nd, 5th, 7th, 10th, 13th, 16th, 18th, 21st, 24th, 26th and 29th are leap years having 355 days; the others are normal years with 354 days. The Muslim lunar year is 10 or 11 days shorter than the Christian solar year. Each day begins immediately after sunset, i.e. at dusk rather than after midnight. Most Muslim countries use both the *Hijra* calendar (which marks all the religious events) and the Christian calendar.

Dates

Dates are given according to the *Hijra* calendar followed by their equivalent date in the Christian calendar after an oblique stroke. The *Hijra* date is not indicated in references derived from Christian sources, European historical events or those that have occurred in Europe, Christian dynasties, or dates proceeding the Muslim era or subsequent to the British Mandate of Palestine (1917–1948).

Exact correspondence between years in one calendar and another is only possible when the day and month are given. To facilitate reading, and even when it may have been recommended, we have chosen to avoid intermediate years and, in the case of *Hijra* dates falling between the beginning and end of a century, both centuries are mentioned.

Dates before the Christian era are denoted by the abbreviation BC.

Abbreviations:

AD = Anno Domini; BC = before Christ; b. = born; d. = died; r. = reigned.

Practical Advice

The present catalogue was written in 2001. As a consequence of the political developments in the region after that date, some descriptions provided by this catalogue might differ from the effective situation the visitor is likely to meet in the field.

The mention of Palestine as the definition of the country refers in this catalogue to the territories under the Administration of the Palestinian Authority according to International Conventions currently in force. In addition this catalogue includes three itineraries in East Jerusalem.

Visitors should hold a passport that is valid for at least six months, whereby they are permitted to stay in Palestine for three months. It is possible to enter Palestine either by way of the joint boarders with Egypt and Jordan or by air through the airports of Gaza (Palestinian Authority) and Tel Aviv (Israel):

Gaza Airport

Shuttle buses and taxis are available to Gaza City, from where individual and collective taxies run regularly to Jerusalem and most Palestinian cities; Gaza–Jerusalem 80 km.

Tel Aviv Airport

Shuttle buses are available from the airport to Jerusalem (Damascus Gate); 35 km.

Through Jordan

From King Hussein Bridge, individual and collective taxies are available to Jerusalem and most Palestinian cities; King Hussein Bridge–Jerusalem 30 km.

Through Egypt

From the Raffah border crossing, a number of shuttle buses and taxis leave to Gaza City.

The official language is Arabic whereby many Palestinians communicate also in English.

During their stay in Palestine, visitors could use American dollars, Jordanian *dinars* or Israeli *shekels*, since all these currencies are valid. Euros have begun to circulate as well, and can be exchanged at Banks and with moneychangers in all Palestinian cities. Major credit cards are accepted all over the country. Cash withdrawal is possible at several banks in the main cities.

Accommodation in hotels from three to five stars is available in the major cities, most of them offering bed and breakfast or half-board arrangements. Advance reservations can be made through the Arab Hotel Association, website: www.palestinehotels.com.

The most suitable way to visit the itineraries, monuments and sites integrating the Palestinian MWNF exhibition is by car, whereby the hotel will be delighted to provide assistance in hiring a car. Alternatively, on the main routes, the visitor can make use of the relatively well-developed network of Palestinian public transportation or can take a collective taxi. For private taxis, one-day or half-day arrangements will depend on the extension of the itinerary. The hotel will gladly provide further assistance and advice about travel on request.

The use of an up-to-date road atlas and street maps of cities is advisable. It is also recommended that each itinerary be followed in the suggested order so as to explore a route planned along a natural succession of themes and monuments. Visitors are advised to wear comfortable clothes while travelling in Palestine. When visiting holy places, suitable clothing according to local standards is recommended. Women may be asked to cover their heads with a veil in order to enter religious monuments.

The mosques, *madrasa*s and *khanqa*s are religious buildings in which prayers are held five times a day: at dawn, *al-fajr*; at midday, *al-duhr* (winter 12:00 and summer 13:00); during mid-afternoon, *al-'asr* (winter 15:30, summer 16:30); at sunset, *al-maghrib*; and at night, *al-'isha'*. The best times for visiting are before midday prayer, and between midday prayer *(al-duhr)* and mid-afternoon prayer *(al-'asr)*.

Official holidays in Palestine are the religious ones, and the day of occurrence (*Hijra* calendar) varies every year (Christian calendar). Further holidays are New Years Day and Labour Day (1st May).

During the month of Ramadan, Moslems fast from sunrise to sunset. Shops will be closed around sunset. Restaurants, except those in hotels, will be closed during the day and open only after sunset. We advice the visitor not to eat, drink, or smoke in public places in order not to offend those people that are fasting.

Museum With No Frontiers is not responsible for any variations to the information given in this catalogue, or for inconvenience, loss or personal injury that may be caused during travel in Palestine and to the specific sites suggested by MWNF.

We wish you an enjoyable stay in Palestine.

The Palestinian MWNF Team

INDEX

ISLAMIC DYNASTIES IN THE MEDITERRANEAN

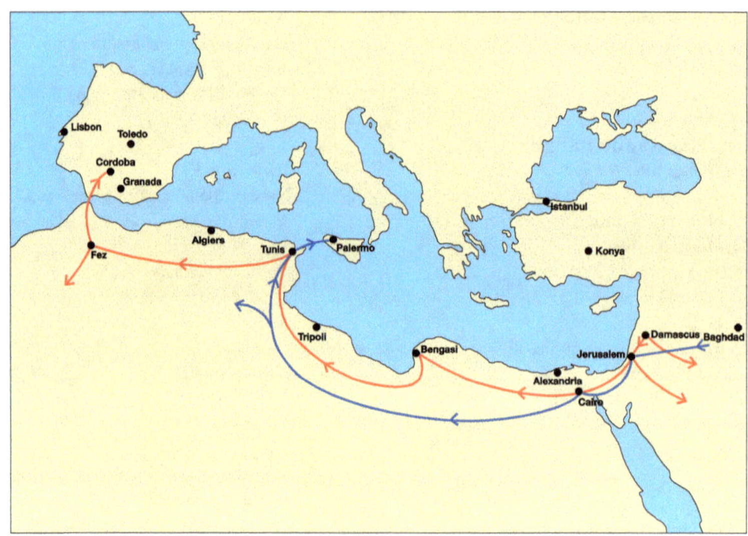

The Umayyads (41/661-132/750) Capital: Damascus
The Abbasids (132/750-656/1258) Capital: Baghdad

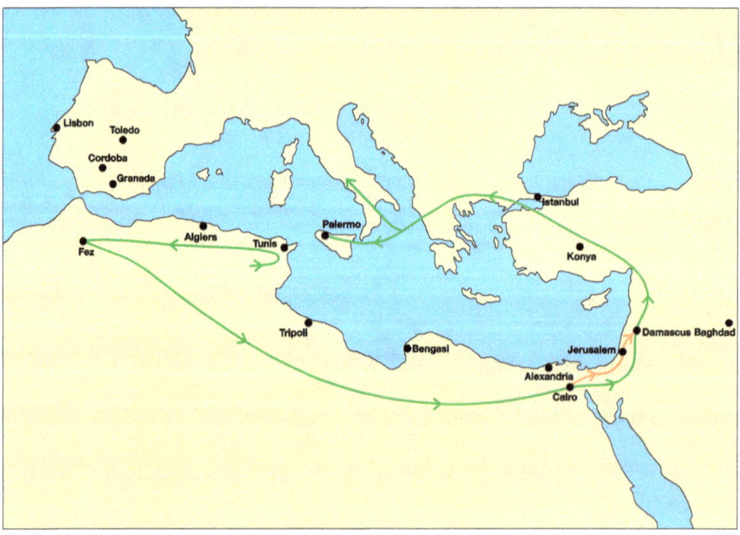

The Fatimids (296/909-567/1171) Capital: Cairo
The Mamluks (648/1250-923/1517) Capital: Cairo

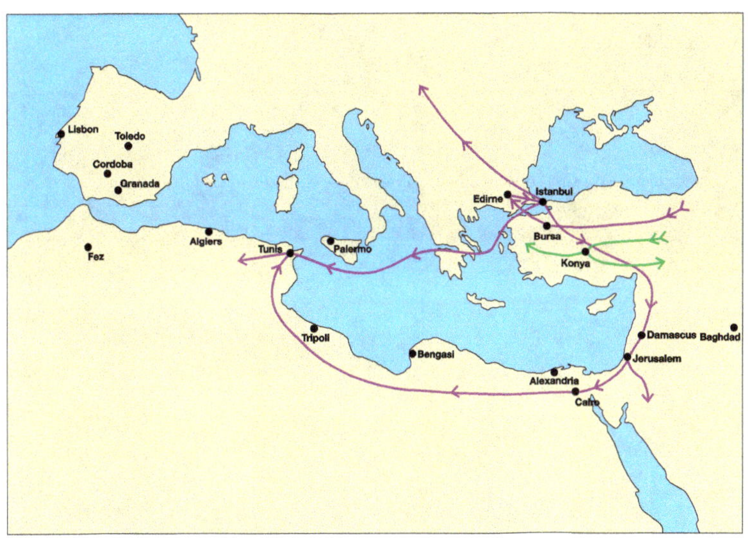

The Seljuqs (571/1075-718/1318) Capital: Konya

The Ottomans (699/1299-1340/1922) Capital: Istanbul

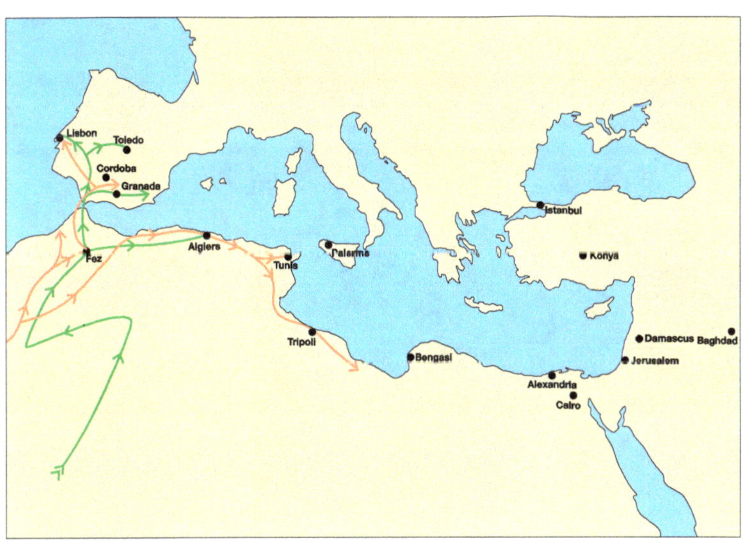

The Almoravids (427/1036-541/1147) Capital: Marrakesh

The Almohads (515/1121-667/1269) Capital: Marrakesh

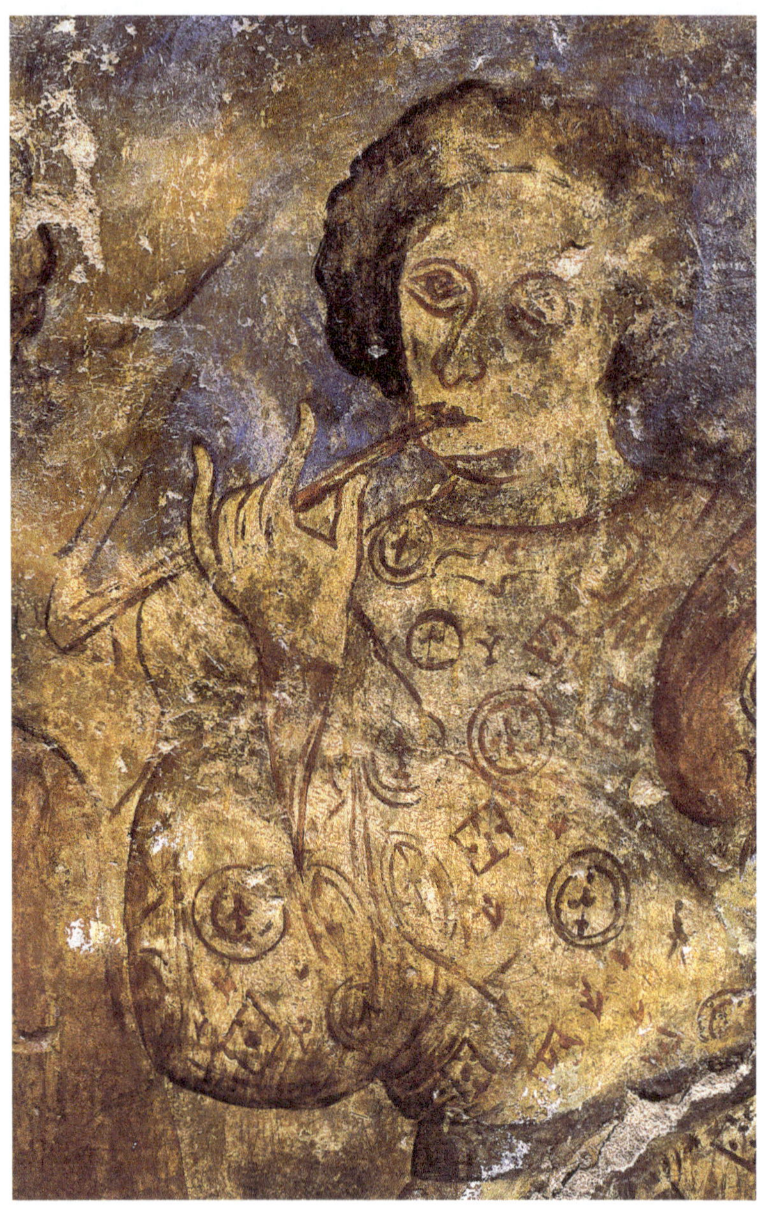

Qusayr 'Amra, mural in the Audience Hall, Badiya of Jordan.

ISLAMIC ART IN THE MEDITERRANEAN

Jamila Binous
Mahmoud Hawari
Manuela Marín
Gönül Öney

The Legacy of Islam in the Mediterranean

Since the first half of the 1st/7th century, the history of the Mediterranean Basin has belonged, in remarkably similar proportion, to two cultures, Islam and the Christian West. This extensive history of conflict and contact has created a mythology that is widely diffused in the collective imagination, a mythology based on the image of the other as the unyielding enemy, strange and alien, and as such, incomprehensible. It is of course true that battles punctuated those centuries from the time when the Muslims spilled forth from the Arabian Peninsula and took possession of the Fertile Crescent, Egypt, and later, North Africa, Sicily, and the Iberian Peninsula, penetrating into Western Europe as far as the south of France. At the beginning of the 2nd/8th century, the Mediterranean came under Islamic control.

This drive to expand, of an intensity seldom equalled in human history, was carried out in the name of a religion that considered itself then heir to its two immediate antecedents: Judaism and Christianity. It would be a gross over-simplification to explain the Islamic expansion exclusively in religious terms. One widespread image in the West presents Islam as a religion of simple dogmas adapted to the needs of the common people, spread by vulgar warriors who poured out from the desert bearing the *Qur'an* on the blades of their swords. This coarse image does away with the intellectual complexity of a religious message that transformed the world from the moment of its inception. It identifies this message with a military threat, and thus justifies a response on the same terms. Finally, it reduces an entire culture to only one of its elements, religion, and in doing so, deprives it of the potential for evolution and change.

The Mediterranean countries that were progressively incorporated into the Muslim world began their journeys from very different starting points. Forms of Islamic life that began to develop in each were quite logically different within the unity that resulted from their shared adhesion to the new religious dogma. It is precisely the capacity to assimilate elements of previous cultures (Hellenistic, Roman, etc.), which has been one of the defining characteristics of Islamic societies. If one restricts one's observations to the geographical area of the Mediterranean, which was extremely diverse culturally at the time of the emergence of Islam, one will discern quickly that this initial moment does not represent a break with previous history in the least. One comes to realise that it is impossible to imagine a monolithic and immutable Islamic world, blindly following an inalterable religious message.

If anything can be singled out as the *leitmotiv* running through the area of the Mediterranean, it is diversity of expression combined with harmony of sentiment, a sentiment more cultural than religious. In the Iberian Peninsula – to begin with the western perimeter of the Mediterranean – the presence of Islam, initially brought about by military conquest, produced a society clearly differentiated from, but in permanent contact with Christian society. The importance of the cultural expression of this Islamic society was felt even after it ceased to exist as such, and gave rise to perhaps one of the most original components of Spanish culture, Mudejar art. Portugal maintained strong Mozarab traditions throughout the Islamic period and there are many imprints from this time that are still clearly visible today. In Morocco and Tunisia, the legacy of al-Andalus was assimilated into the local forms and continues to be evident to this day. The western Mediterranean produced original forms of expression that reflected its conflicting and plural historical evolution.

Lodged between East and West, the Mediterranean Sea is endowed with terrestrial enclaves, such as Sicily, that represent centuries-old key historical locations. Conquered by the Arabs established in Tunisia, Sicily has continued to perpetuate the cultural and historical memory of Islam long after the Muslims ceased to have any political presence on the island. The presence of Sicilian-Norman aesthetic forms preserved in architectural monuments clearly demonstrates that the history of these regions cannot be explained without an understanding of the diversity of social, economic and cultural experiences that flourished on their soil.

In sharp contrast, then, to the immutable and constant image alluded to at the outset, the history of Mediterranean Islam is characterised by surprising diversity. It is made up of a mixture of peoples and ethnicities, deserts and fertile lands. As the major religion has been Islam since the early Middle Ages, it is also true that religious minorities have maintained a presence historically. The Classical Arabic language of the *Qur'an,* has coexisted side-by-side with other languages, as well as with other dialects of Arabic. Within a setting of undeniable unity (Muslim religion, Arabic language and culture), each society has evolved and responded to the challenges of history in its own characteristic manner.

The Emergence and Development of Islamic Art

Throughout these countries, with ancient and diverse civilisations, a new art permeated with images from the Islamic faith emerged at the end of the 2nd/8th century, which successfully imposed itself in a period of less than 100 years. This art, in its own particular manner, gave rise to creations and innovations based on unifying regional formulas and architectural and decorative processes, and was simultaneously inspired by the artistic traditions that proceeded it: Greco-Roman and Byzantine, Sasanian, Visigothic, Berber or even Central Asian.

The initial aim of Islamic art was to serve the needs of religion and various aspects of socio-economic life. New buildings appeared for religious purposes such as mosques and sanctuaries. For this reason, architecture played a central role in Islamic art because a whole series of other arts are dependent on it. Apart from architecture a whole range of complimentary minor arts found their artistic expressions in a variety of materials, such as wood, pottery, metal, glass, textiles and paper. In pottery, a great variety of glaze techniques were employed and among these distinguished groups are the lustre and polychrome painted wares. Glass of great beauty was manufactured, reaching excellence with the type adorned with gold and bright enamel colours. In metal work, the most sophisticated technique is inlaying bronze with silver or copper. High-quality textiles and carpets, with geometric, animal and human designs, were made. Illuminated manuscripts with miniature paintings represent a spectacular achievement in the arts of the book. These types of minor arts serve to attest the brilliance of Islamic art.

Figurative art, however, is excluded from the Islamic liturgical domain, which means it is ostracised from the central core of Islamic civilisation and that it is tolerated only at its periphery. Relief work is rare in the decoration of monuments and sculptures are almost flat. This deficit is compensated with a richness in ornamentation on the lavish carved plaster panelling, sculpted wooden panelling, wall tiling and glazed mosaics, as well as on the stalactite friezes, or *muqarnas*. Decorative elements taken from nature, such as leaves, flowers and branches, are generally stylised to the extreme and are so complicated that they rarely call to mind their sources of origin. The intertwining and combining of geometric motifs such as rhombus and etiolated polygons, form interlacing networks that completely cover the surface, resulting in shapes often called arabesques. One innovation within the decorative repertoire is the introduction of epigraphic elements

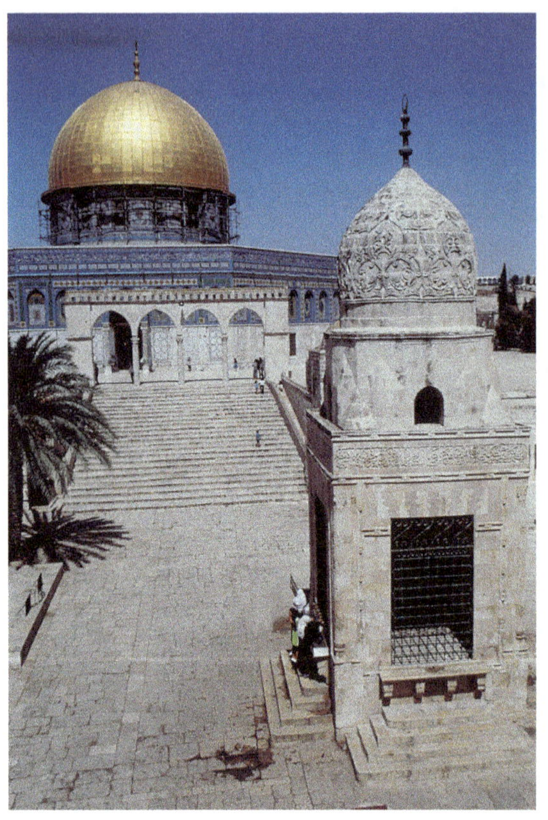

Dome of the Rock, Jerusalem.

in the ornamentation of monuments, furniture and various other objects. Muslim craftsmen made use of the beauty of Arabic calligraphy, the language of the sacred book, the *Qur'an,* not only for the transcription of the Qur'anic verses, but in all of its variations simply as a decorative motif for the ornamentation of stucco panelling and the edges of panels.

Art was also at the service of rulers. It was for patrons that architects built palaces, mosques, schools, hospitals, bathhouses, *caravanserais* and mausoleums, which would sometimes bear their names. Islamic art is, above all, dynastic art. Each one contributed tendencies that would bring about a partial or complete renewal of artistic forms, depending on historical conditions, the prosperity enjoyed by their states, and the traditions of each people. Islamic art, in spite of its relative unity, allowed for a diversity that gave rise to different styles, each one identified with a dynasty.

The Umayyad Dynasty (41/661-132/750), which transferred the capital of the caliphate to Damascus, represents a singular achievement in the history of Islam. It absorbed and incorporated the Hellenistic and Byzantine legacy in such a way that the classical tradition of the Mediterranean was recast in a new and innovative mould. Islamic art, thus, was formed in Syria, and the architecture, unmistakably Islamic due to the personality of the founders, would continue to bear a relation to Hellenistic and Byzantine art as well. The most important of these monuments are the Dome of the Rock in Jerusalem, the earliest existing monumental Islamic sanctuary, the Great Mosque of Damascus, which served as a model for later mosques, and the desert palaces of Syria, Jordan and Palestine.

When the Abbasid caliphate (132/ 750-656/1258) succeeded the Umayyads, the political centre of Islam was moved from the Mediterranean to Baghdad in Mesopotamia. This factor would influence the development of Islamic civilisation and the entire range of culture, and art would bear the mark of that change. Abbasid art and architecture were influenced by three major traditions: Sassanian, Central Asian and Seljuq. Central Asian influence was already present in Sassanian architecture, but at Samarra this influence is represented by the stucco style with its arabesque ornamentation that would rapidly spread throughout the Islamic world. The influence of Abbasid monuments can be observed in the buildings constructed during this period in the other regions of the empire, particularly Egypt and Ifriqiya. In Cairo, the Mosque of Ibn Tulun (262/876-265/879) is a masterpiece, remarkable for its plan and unity of conception. It was modelled after the Abbasid Great Mosque of Samarra, particularly its spiral minaret. In Kairouan, the capital of Ifriqiya, vassals of the Abbasid caliphs, the Aghlabids (184/800-296/909) expanded the Great Mosque of Kairouan, one of the most venerable congregational mosques in the Maghrib. Its *mihrab* was covered by ceramic tiles from Mesopotamia.

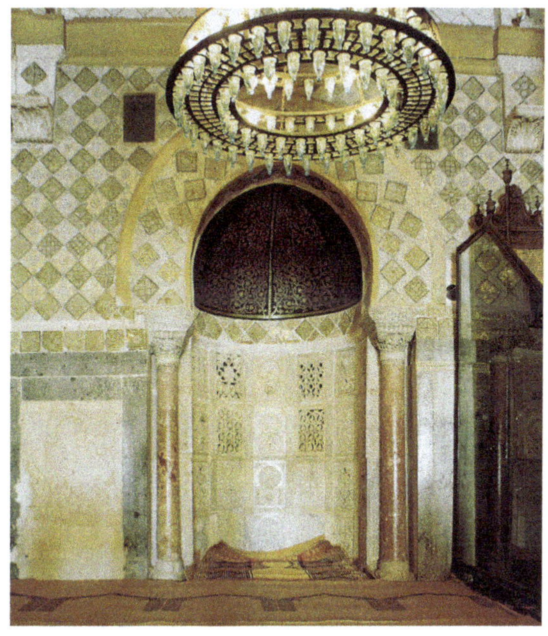

Kairouan Mosque, mihrab, Tunisia.

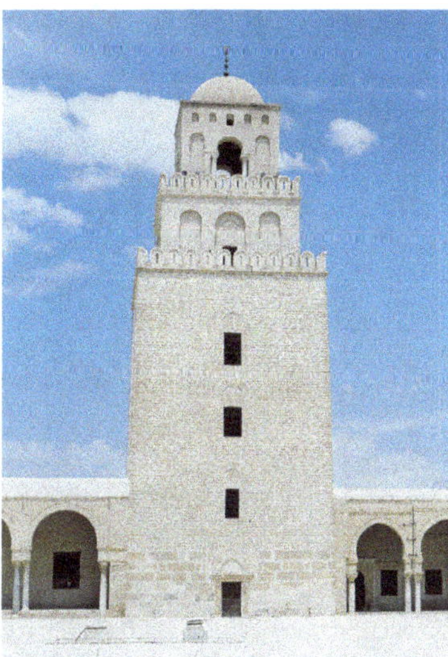

Kairouan Mosque, minaret, Tunisia.

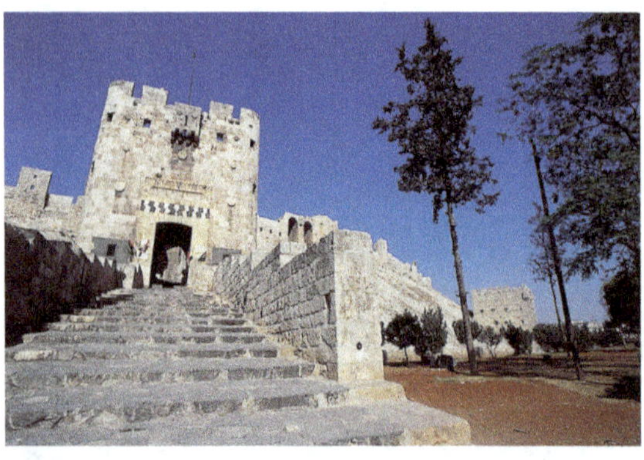

Citadel of Aleppo, view of the entrance, Syria.

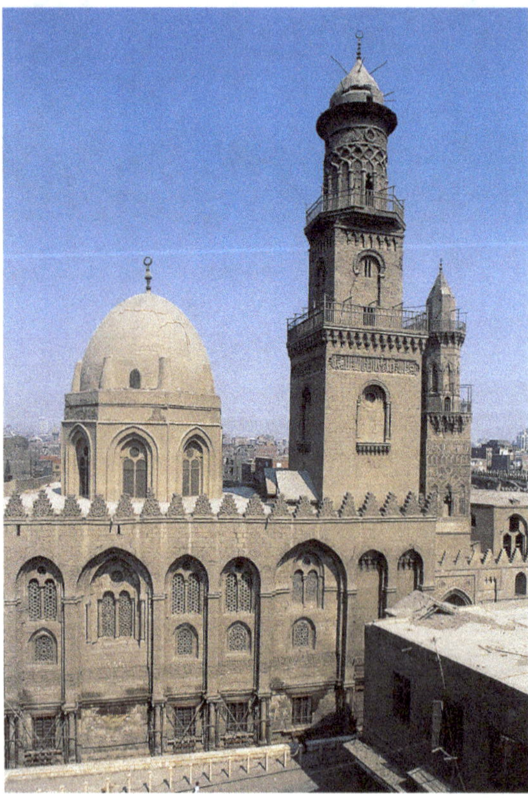

Complex of Qaluwun, Cairo, Egypt.

The reign of the Fatimids (297/909-567/1171) represents a remarkable period in the history of the Islamic countries of the Mediterranean: North Africa, Sicily, Egypt and Syria. Of their architectural constructions, a few examples remain that bear witness to their past glory. In the central Maghrib the Qal'a of the Bani Hammad and the Mosque of Mahdiya; in Sicily, the Cuba (*Qubba*) and the Zisa (*al-'Aziza*) in Palermo, constructed by Fatimid craftsmen under the Norman King William II; in Cairo, the Azhar Mosque is the most prominent example of Fatimid architecture in Egypt.

The Ayyubids (567/1171-648/1250), who overthrew the Fatimid Dynasty in Cairo, were important patrons of architecture. They established religious institutions (*madrasas, khanqas*) for the propagation of *Sunni* Islam, mausoleums and welfare projects, as well as awesome fortifications pertaining to the military conflict with the Crusaders. The Citadel of Aleppo in Syria is a remarkable example of their military architecture.

The Mamluks (648/1250-923/1517) successors of the Ayyubids, successfully resisted the Crusades and the Mongols, achieved the unity of Syria and Egypt and created a formidable empire. The wealth and luxury of the Mamluk Sultan's court in Cairo motivated artists and architects to achieve an extraordinarily elegant style of architecture. For the world of Islam, the Mamluk period marked a rebirth and renaissance. The enthusiasm for establishing religious foundations and reconstructing existing ones place the Mamluks among the greatest patrons of art and architecture in the history of Islam. The Mosque of Hassan (757/1356), a funerary mosque built with a cruciform plan in which the four arms of the cross were formed by four *iwans* of the building around a central courtyard, was typical of the era. Anatolia was the birthplace of two great Islamic dynasties: the Seljuqs (571/1075-718/1318), who introduced Islam to the region; and the Ottomans (699/1299-1340/1922), who brought about the end of the Byzantine Empire upon capturing Constantinople, and asserted their hegemony throughout the region.

Selimiye Mosque, general view, Edirne, Turkey.

A distinctive style of Seljuq art and architecture flourished with influences from Central Asia, Iran, Mesopotamia and Syria, which merged with elements deriving from Anatolian Christian and antiquity heritage. Konya, the new capital in Central Anatolia, as well as other cities, were enriched with buildings in the newly developed Seljuq style. Numerous mosques, *madrasas, turbes* and *caravanserais*, which were richly decorated by stucco and tiling with diverse figural representations, have survived to our day.

As the Seljuq Emirates disintegrated and Byzantium declined, the Ottomans expanded their territory swiftly changing their capital from Iznik to Bursa and then again to Edirne. The conquest of Constantinople in 858/1453 by Sultan Mehmet II provided the necessary impetus for the transition of an emerging state into a great empire. A superpower that extended its boundaries to Vienna including the Balkans in the West and to Iran in the East, as well

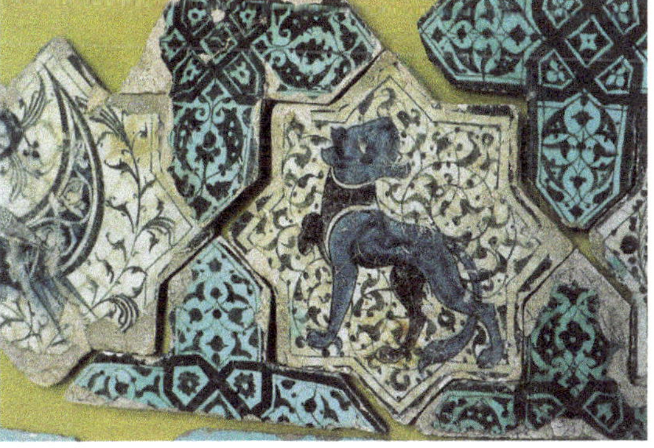

Tile of Kubadabad Palace, Karatay Museum, Konya, Turkey.

Great Mosque of Cordoba, mihrab, Spain.

Madinat al-Zahra', Dar al-Yund, Spain.

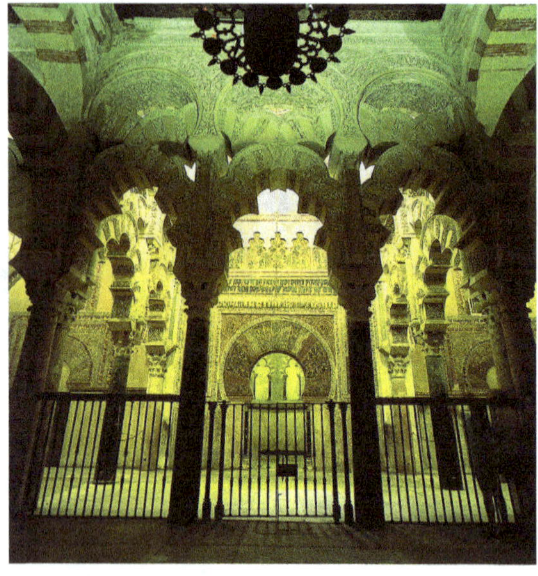

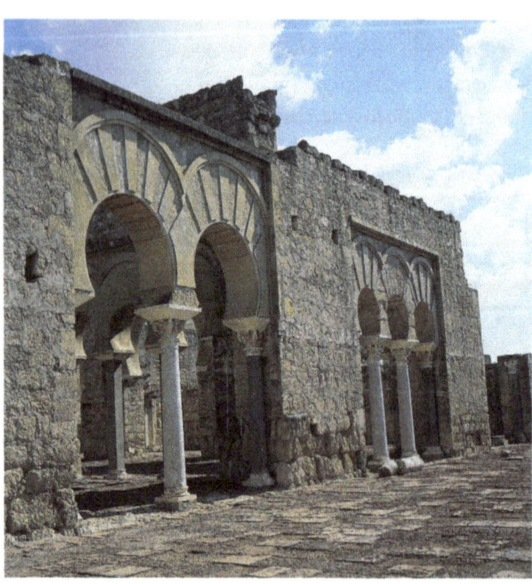

as North Africa from Egypt to Algeria, turning the Eastern Mediterranean into an Ottoman sea. The race to surpass the grandeur of the inherited Byzantine churches, exemplified by the Hagia Sophia, culminated in the construction of great mosques in Istanbul. The most significant one is the Mosque of Süleymaniye, built in the 10th/16th century by the famous Ottoman architect Sinan, it epitomises the climax in architectural harmony in domed buildings. Most major Ottoman mosques were part of a large building complex called *kulliye* that also consisted several *madrasas*, a *Qur'an* school, a library, a hospital (*darussifa*), a hostel (*tabhane*), a public kitchen, a *caravanserai* and mausoleums (*turbes*). From the beginning of the 12th/18th century, during the so-called Tulip Period, Ottoman architecture and decorative style reflected the influence of French Baroque and Rococo, heralding the Westernisation period in arts and architecture.

Al-Andalus at the western part of the Islamic world became the cradle of a brilliant artistic and cultural expression. 'Abd al-Rahman I established an independent Umayyad caliphate (138/750-422/1031) with Cordoba as its capital. The Great Mosque of Cordoba would pioneer innovative artistic tendencies such as the double-tiered arches with two alternating colours and panels with vegetal ornamentation which would become part of the repertoire of al-Andalus artistic forms.

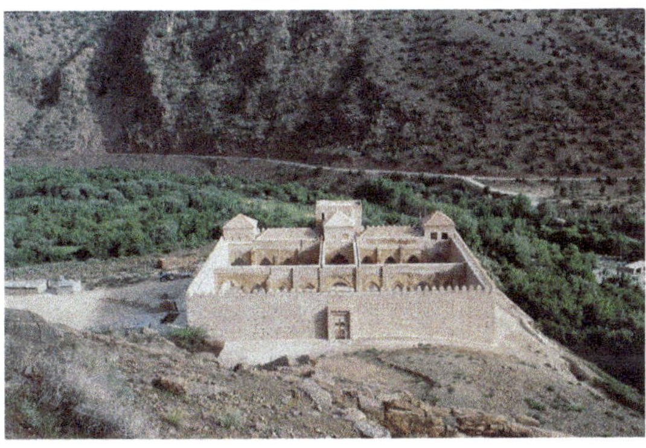

Tinmal Mosque, aerial view, Morocco.

In the $5^{th}/11^{th}$ century, the caliphate of Cordoba broke up into a score of principalities incapable of preventing the progressive advance of the reconquest initiated by the Christian states of the Northwestern Iberian Peninsula. These petty kings, or Taifa Kings, summoned the Almoravids in 479/1086 and the Almohads in 540/1145 in order to repel the Christians and re-established partial unity in al-Andalus.

Through their intervention in the Iberian Peninsula, the Almoravids (427/1036-541/1147) came into contact with a new civilisations and were captivated quickly by the refinement of al-Andalus art as reflected in their capital, Marrakesh, where they built a grand mosque and palaces. The influence of the architecture of Cordoba and other capitals such as Seville would be felt in all of the Almoravid monuments from Tlemcen, Algiers to Fez.

Under the rule of the Almohads (515/1121-667/1269), who expanded their hegemony as far as Tunisia, Western Islamic art reached its climax. During this period, artistic creativity that originated with the Almoravid rulers was renewed and masterpieces of Islamic art were created. The Great Mosque of Seville with its minaret the Giralda, the Kutubiya in Marrakesh, the Mosque of Hassan in Rabat and the Mosque of Tinmal high in the Atlas Mountains in Morocco are notable examples.

Ladies Tower and Gardens, Alhambra, Granada, Spain.

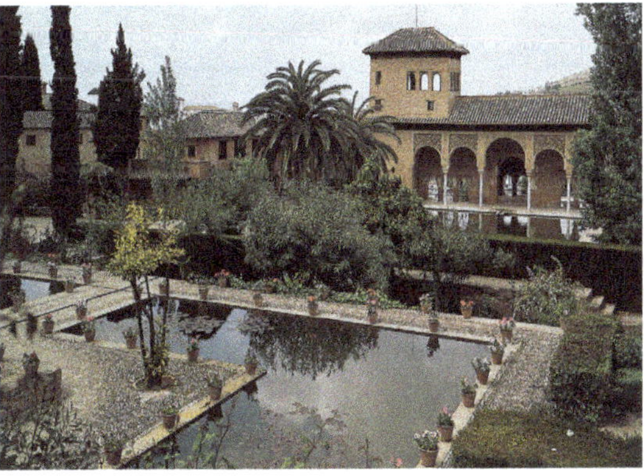

Upon the dissolution of the Almohad Empire, the Nasrid Dynasty (629/1232-897/1492) installed itself in Granada and was to experience a period of splendour in the $8^{th}/14^{th}$ century. The civilisation of Granada would become a cultural

Mertola, general view, Portugal.

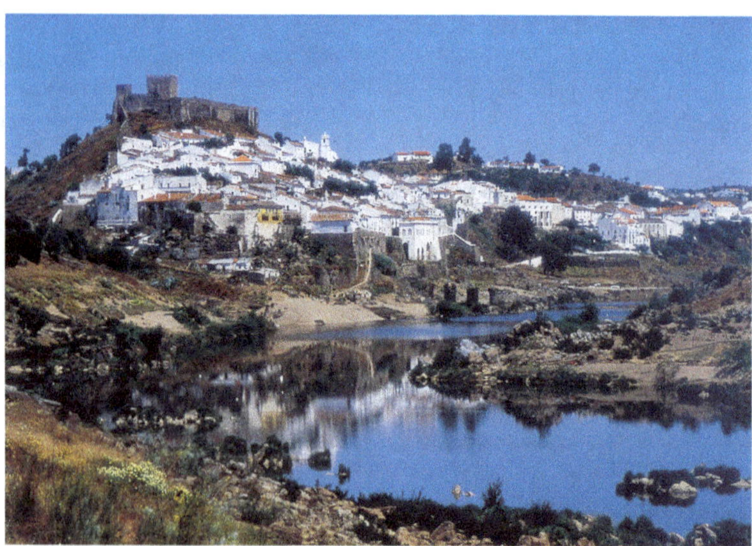

model in future centuries in Spain (Mudejar Art) and particularly in Morocco, where this artistic tradition enjoyed great popularity and would be preserved until the present day in the areas of architecture and decoration, music and cuisine. The famous palace and fort of *al-Hamra'* (the Alhambra) in Granada marks the crowning achievement of al-Andalus art, with all features of its artistic repertoire.

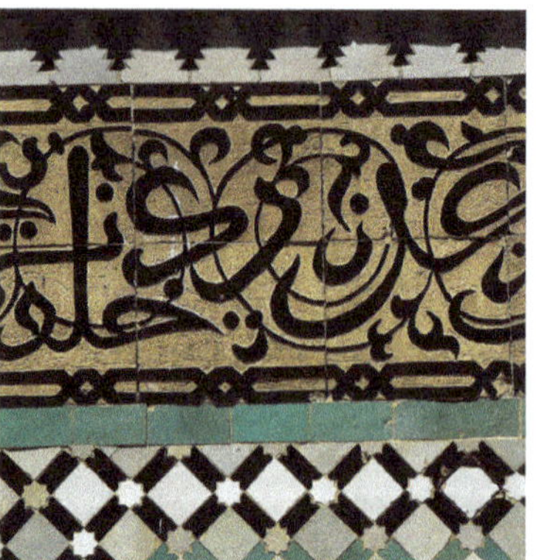

Decoration detail, Abu Inan Madrasa, Meknes, Morocco.

At the same time in Morocco, the Merinids (641/1243-876/1471) replaced the Almohads, while in Algeria the 'Abd al-Wadid's reigned (633/1235-922/1516), as did the Hafsids (625/1228-941/1534) in Tunisia. The Merinids perpetuated al-Andalus art, enriching it with new features. They embellished their capital Fez with an abundance of mosques, palaces and *madrasas*, with their clay mosaic and *zellij* panelling in the wall decorations, considered

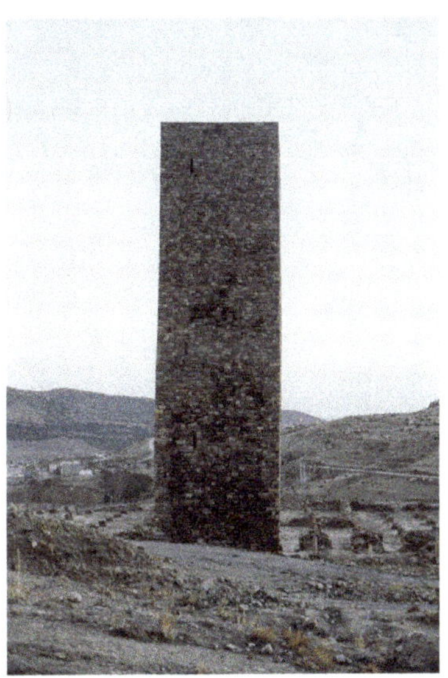

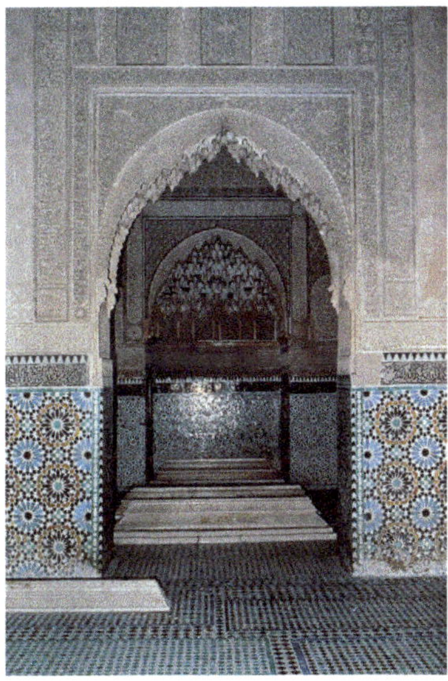

Qal'a of the Bani Hammad, minaret, Algeria.

Sa'adian Tomb Marrakesh, Morocco.

to be the most perfect works of Islamic art. The later Moroccan dynasties, the Sa'adians (933/1527-1070/1659) and the 'Alawite (1077/1659 – until the present day), carried on the artistic tradition of al-Andalus that was exiled from its native soil in 897/1492. They continued to build and decorate their monuments using the same formulas and the same decorative themes as had the preceding dynasties, adding innovative touches characteristic of their creative genius. In the early 11th/17th century, emigrants from al-Andalus (the *Moriscos*), who took up residence in the northern cities of Morocco, introduced numerous features of al-Andalus art. Today, Morocco is one of the few countries that has kept traditions of al-Andalus alive in its architecture and furniture, at the same time modernising them as they incorporated the architectural techniques and styles of the 15th/20th century.

ARCHITECTURAL SUMMARY

In general terms, Islamic architecture can be classified into two categories: religious, such as mosques, *madrasas*, mausoleums, and secular, such as palaces, *caravanserais*, fortifications, etc.

Religious Architecture

Mosques

The mosque for obvious reasons lies at the very heart of Islamic architecture. It is an apt symbol of the faith that it serves. That symbolic role was understood by Muslims at a very early stage, and played an important part in the creation of suitable visual markers for the building: minaret, dome, *mihrab*, *minbar*, etc.

The first mosque in Islam was the courtyard of the Prophet's house in Medina, with no architectural refinements. Early mosques built by the Muslims as their empire was expanding were simple. From these buildings developed the congregational or Friday mosque (*jami'*), essential features of which remain today unchanged for nearly 1400 years. The general plan consists of a large courtyard surrounded by arched porticoes, with more aisles or arcades on the side facing Mecca (*qibla*) than the other sides. The Great Umayyad Mosque in Damascus, which followed the plan of the Prophet's Mosque, became the prototype for many mosques built in various parts of the Islamic world.

Umayyad Mosque of Damascus, Syria.

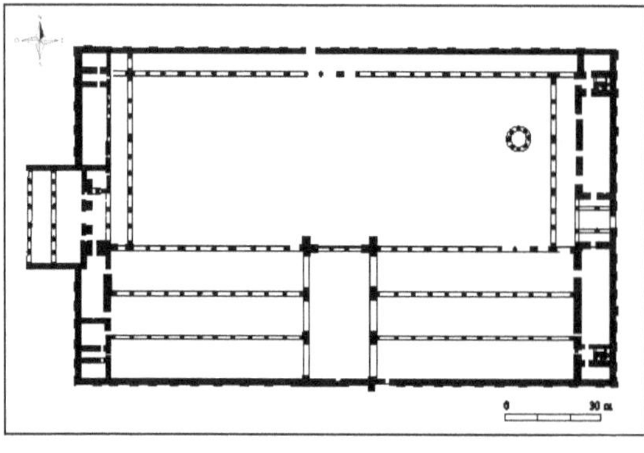

Two other types of mosques developed in Anatolia and afterwards in the Ottoman domains: the basilical and the dome types. The first type is a simple pillared hall or basilica that follows late Roman and Byzantine Syrian traditions, introduced with some modifications in the 5th/11th century. The second type, which developed during the Ottoman period, has its organisation of interior space under a single dome. The Ottoman architects in great imperial mosques created a new style of domed construction by merging the Islamic mosque tradition with that of dome building in Anatolia. The main dome rests on a hexagonal support system, while lateral bays are covered by smaller domes. This emphasis on an interior space dominated by a single dome became the starting point of a style that was to be introduced in the 10th/16th century. During this period, mosques became multipurpose social complexes consisting of a *zawiya*, a *madrasa*, a public kitchen, a bath, a *caravanserai* and a mausoleum of the founder. The supreme monument of this style is the Sülaymeniye Mosque in Istanbul built in 965/1557 by the great architect Sinan.

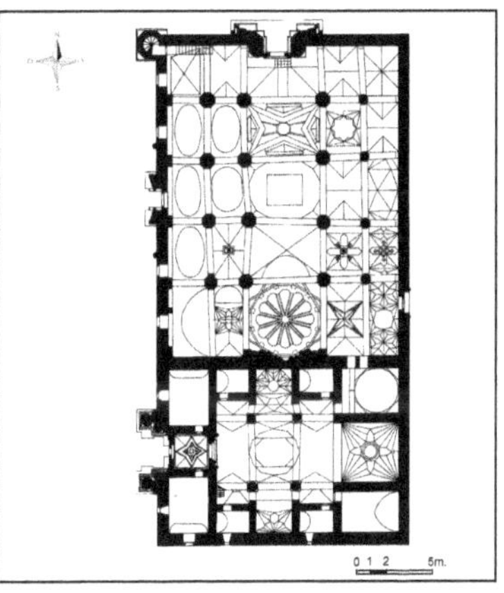

Great Mosque, Divriği, Turkey.

The minaret from the top of which the *muezzin* calls Muslims to prayer, is the most prominent marker of the mosque. In Syria the traditional minaret consists of a square-plan tower built of stone. In Mamluk Egypt minarets are each divided into three distinct zones: a square section at the bottom, an octagonal middle section and a circular section with a small dome on the top. Its shaft is richly decorated and the transition between each section is covered with a band of *muqarnas* decoration. Minarets in North Africa and Spain, that share the square-tower form with Syria, are decorated with panels of motifs around paired sets of windows. During the Ottoman period the octagonal or cylindrical minarets replaced the square tower. Often these are tall pointed minarets and although mosques generally have only one minaret, in major cities there are two, four or even six minarets.

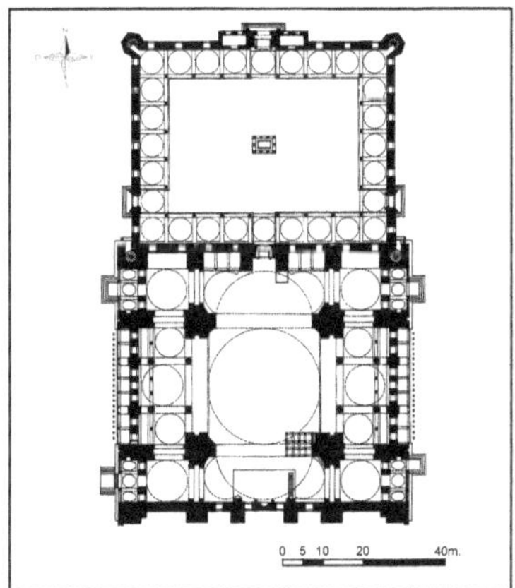

Sülaymeniye Mosque, Istanbul, Turkey.

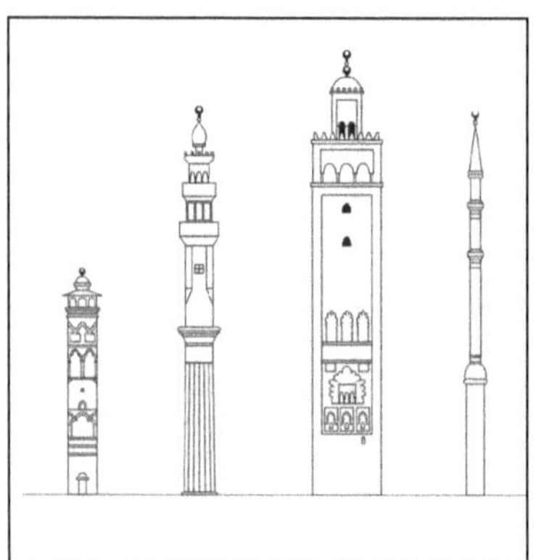

Typology of minarets.

Madrasas

It seems likely that the Seljuqs built the first *madrasas* in Persia in the early 5th/11th century when they were small structures with a domed courtyard and two lateral *iwans*. A later type developed that has an open courtyard with a central *iwan* and which is surrounded by arcades. During the 6th/12th century in Anatolia, the *madrasa* became multifunctional and was intended to serve as a medical school, mental hospital, a hospice with a public kitchen (*imaret*) and a mausoleum. The promotion of *Sunni* (Orthodox) Islam reached a new zenith in Syria and Egypt under the Zengids and the Ayyubids (6th/12th–early 7th/13th centuries). This era witnessed the introduction of the *madrasa* established by a civic or political leader for the advancement of Islamic jurisprudence. The foundation was funded by an endowment in perpetuity (*waqf*), usually the revenues of land or property in the form of an orchard, shops in a market (*suq*), or a bathhouse (*hammam*). The *madrasa* traditionally followed a cruciform plan with a central court surrounded by four *iwans*. Soon the *madrasa* became a dominant architectural form with mosques adopting a four-*iwan* plan. The *madrasa* gradually lost its sole religious and political function as a propaganda tool and tended to have a broader civic function, serving as a congregational mosque and a mausoleum for the benefactor.

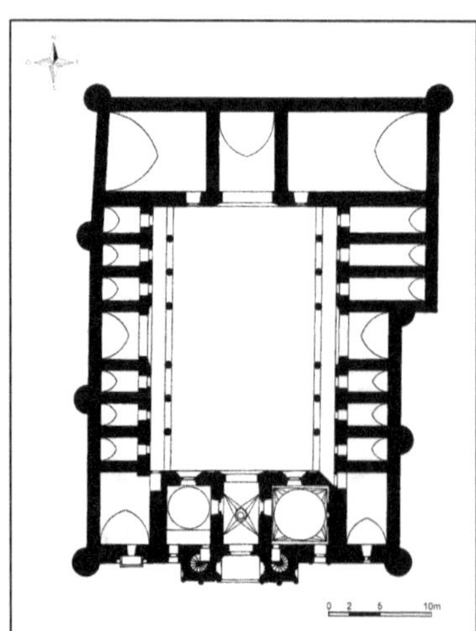

Sivas Gök Madrasa, Turkey.

The construction of m*adrasas* in Egypt, and particularly in Cairo, gathered new momentum with the arrival of the Mamluks. The typical

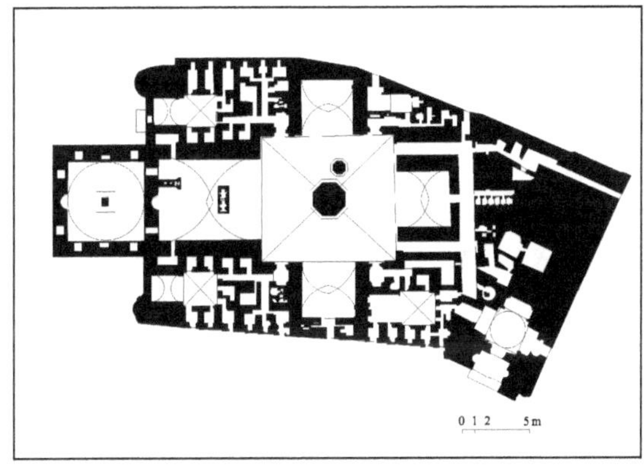

Mosque and Madrasa Sultan Hassan, Cairo, Egypt.

Cairene *madrasa* of this era was a multifunctional gigantic four-*iwan* structure with a stalactite (*muqarnas*) portal and splendid façades. With the advent of the Ottomans in the 10th/16th century, the joint foundation, typically a mosque-*madrasa*, became a widespread, large complex that enjoyed imperial patronage. The *iwan* disappeared gradually and was replaced by a dominant dome chamber. A substantial increase in the number of domed cells used by students is a characteristic of Ottoman *madrasas*.

One of the various building types that by virtue of their function and of their form can be related to the *madrasa* is the *khanqa*. The term indicates an institution, rather than a particular kind of building, that houses members of a Muslim mystical (*sufi*) order. Several other words used by Muslim historians as synonyms for *khanqa* include: in the Maghrib, *zawiya*; in Ottoman domain, *tekke*; and in general, *ribat*. *Sufism* permanently dominated the *khanqa*, which originated in eastern Persia during the 4th/10th century. In its simplest form the *khanqa* was a house where a group of pupils gathered around a master (*shaykh*), and it had the facilities for assembly, prayer and communal living. The establishment of *khanqas* flourished under the Seljuqs during the 5th/11th and the 6th/12th centuries and benefited from the close association between *Sufism* and the *Shafi'i madhhab* (doctrine) favoured by the ruling elite.

Mausoleums

The terminology of the building type of the mausoleum used in Islamic sources is varied. The standard descriptive term *turbe* refers to the function of the building as for burial. Another term is *qubba* that refers to the most identifiable, the dome, and often marks a structure commemorating Biblical prophets, companions of the Prophet Muhammad and religious or military notables. The function of mausoleums is not limited simply to a place of burial

Qasr al-Khayr al-Sharqi, Syria.

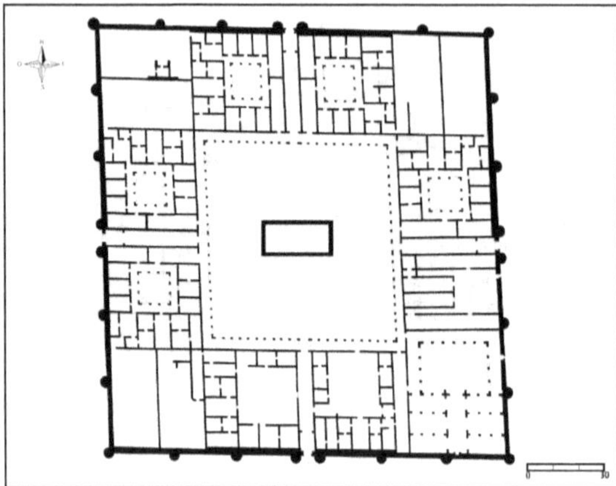

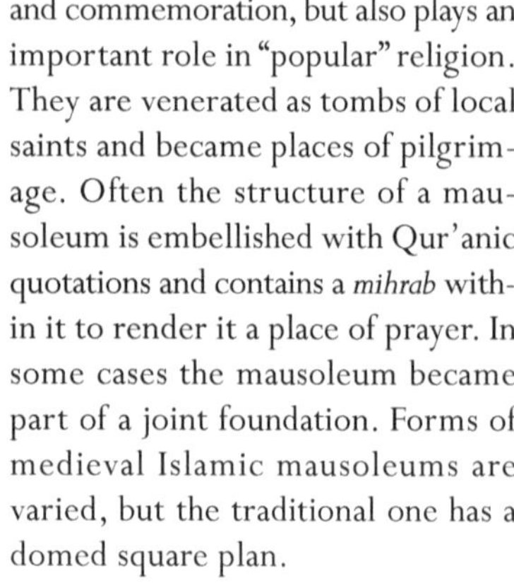

and commemoration, but also plays an important role in "popular" religion. They are venerated as tombs of local saints and became places of pilgrimage. Often the structure of a mausoleum is embellished with Qur'anic quotations and contains a *mihrab* within it to render it a place of prayer. In some cases the mausoleum became part of a joint foundation. Forms of medieval Islamic mausoleums are varied, but the traditional one has a domed square plan.

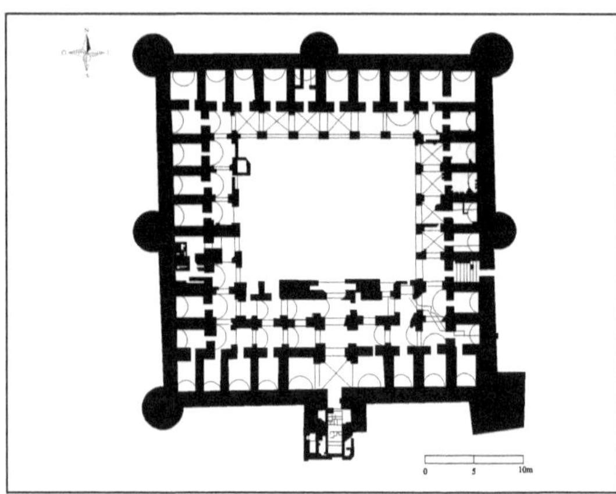

Ribat of Sousse, Tunisia.

Secular Architecture

Palaces

The Umayyad period is characterised by sumptuous palaces and bathhouses in remote desert regions. Their basic plan is largely derived from Roman military models. Although the decoration of these structures is eclectic, they constitute the best examples of the budding Islamic decorative style. Mosaics, mural paintings, stone or stucco sculpture were used for a remarkable variety of decorations and themes. Abbasid palaces in Iraq, such as those at Samarra and Ukhaidir, follow the same plan as their Umayyad forerunners, but are marked by an increase in size, the use of the great *iwan*, dome and courtyard, and the extensive use of stucco decorations. Palaces in the later Islamic period developed a distinctive style that was more decorative and less monumental. The most remarkable example of royal or princely palaces is the Alhambra. The vast area of the palace is broken up into a series of separate units: gardens, pavilions and courts. The most striking feature of Alhambra, however, is the decoration that provides an extraordinary effect in the interior of the building.

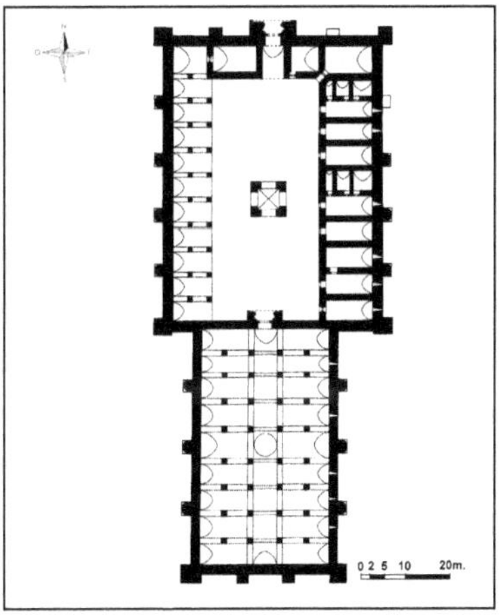

Aksaray Sultan Khan, Turkey.

Caravanserais

A *caravanserai* generally refers to a large structure that provides a lodging place for travellers and merchants. Normally, it has a square or rectangular floor plan, with a single projecting monumental entrance and towers in the exterior walls. A central courtyard is surrounded by porticoes and rooms for lodging travellers, storing merchandise and for the stabling of animals.
The characteristic type of building has a wide range of functions since it has been described as *khan*, *han*, *funduq*, *ribat*. These terms may imply no more than differences in regional vocabularies rather than being distinctive functions or types. The architectural sources of the various types of *caravanserais* are difficult to identify. Some are perhaps derived from the Roman *castrum* or military camp to which the Umayyad desert palaces are related. Other types, in Mesopotamia and Persia, are associated with domestic architecture.

Urban Organisation

From about the 3rd / 10th century every town of any significance acquired fortified walls and towers, elaborate gates and a mighty citadel (*qal'a* or *qasba*) as the seat of power. These are massive constructions built in materials characteristic of the region in which they are found; stone in Syria, Palestine and Egypt, or brick, stone and rammed earth in the Iberian Peninsula and North Africa.
A unique example of military architecture is the *ribat*. Technically, this is a fortified palace designated for the temporary or permanent warriors of Islam who committed themselves to the defence of frontiers. The *ribat* of Sousse in

Tunisia bears a resemblance to early Islamic palaces, but with a different interior arrangement of large halls, mosque and a minaret.

The division of the majority of Islamic cities into neighbourhoods is based on ethnic and religious affinity and it is also a system of urban organisation that facilitates the administration of the population. In the neighbourhood there is always a mosque. A bathhouse, a fountain, an oven and a group of stores are located either within or nearby. Its structure is formed by a network of streets, alleys and a collection of houses. Depending on the region and era, the home takes on diverse features governed by the historical and cultural traditions, climate and construction materials available.

The market (*suq*), which functions as the nerve-centre for local businesses, would be the most relevant characteristic of Islamic cities. Its distance from the mosque determines the spatial organisation of the markets by specialised guilds. For instance, the professions considered clean and honourable (bookmakers, perfume makers, tailors) are located in the mosque's immediate environs, and the noisy and foul-smelling crafts (blacksmiths, tanning, cloth dying) are situated progressively further from it. This geographic distribution responds to imperatives that rank on strictly technical grounds.

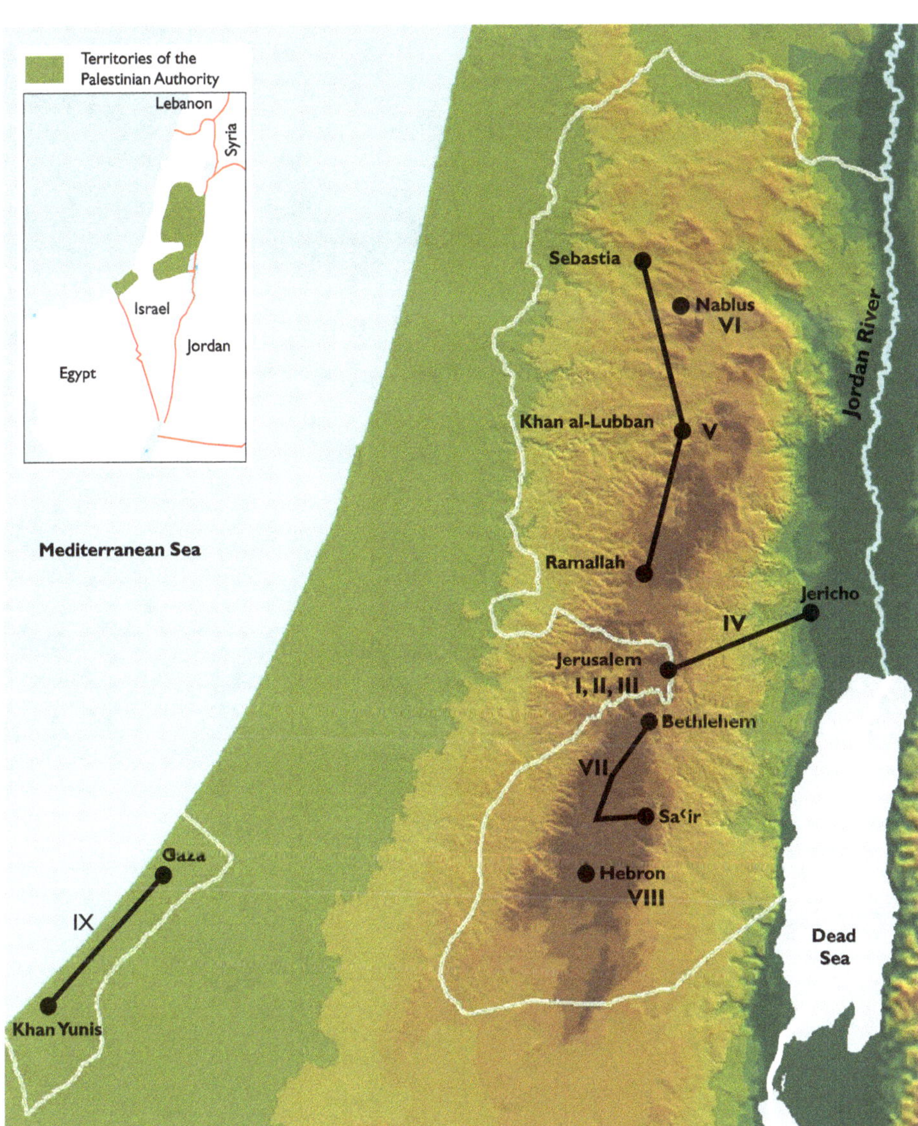

Territories of the Palestinian Authority
Lebanon
Syria
Israel
Jordan
Egypt
Mediterranean Sea
Sebastia
Nablus
VI
Khan al-Lubban
V
Ramallah
Jericho
IV
Jerusalem
I, II, III
Bethlehem
VII
Sa'ir
Hebron
VIII
Jordan River
Dead Sea
Gaza
IX
Khan Yunis

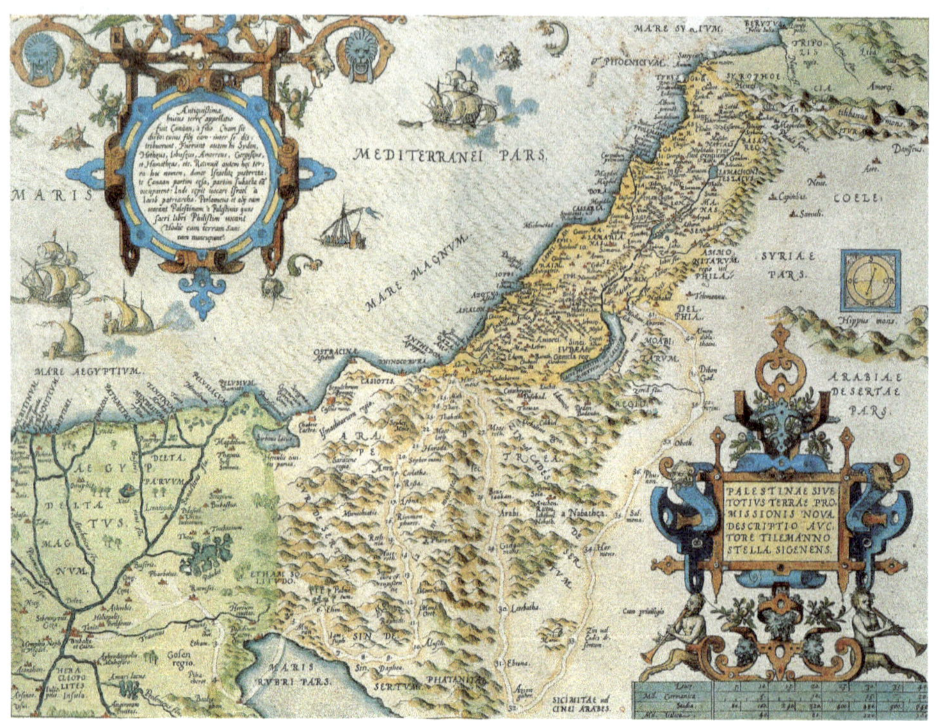

Palestine, from the "Theatrum Orbis Terrarum" by Abraham Ortelius, Antwerp, 1570 (© The Art Archive / Naval Museum, Genoa / Dagli Orti [A]).

ISLAMIC PALESTINE: HISTORY, POLITICS AND RELIGION

Nazmi al-Ju'beh, Yusuf Natsheh

Throughout history Palestine has witnessed different eras and civilisations. Squeezed between two great civilisations, Mesopotamia and Syria on the one hand, and the Nile Valley on the other, it was a passageway through which these civilisations left behind destruction and ruin in addition to a rich cultural heritage. It is no coincidence therefore that Palestine was the first region the Islamic Arab army set foot on in its colossal conquest.

After weathering a short-lived invasion by the Persians in 7/628, which lasted for 14 years, the Byzantines were bundled out of Palestine by the onslaught of Islam. 'Amr Ibn al-'As crossed Aqaba, the Negev Desert and Gaza in 13/635 and proceeded north. Within two years of the Muslim conquest of Palestine the decisive Battle of Yarmuk took place in 15/637. It was the last decisive battle with the Byzantines after which the Muslims conquered the heart of Palestine and Syria. Jerusalem and Caesarea were added to their empire at a later stage.

After an extended period of political and sectarian unrest during the Byzantine rule and its conflict with the Persian Sasanids, a new era of relative stability began in Palestine. The newly established Islamic power did not seek to drastically alter the country. However, it divided Palestine into two administrative *junds* (military provinces): the first, the *Jund al-Urdun* (Jordan), lay in the north and stretched from southern Lebanon and northern Palestine up to Marj Ibn 'Amir and north-eastern Jordan with Tiberias as its capital; the second, the *Jund Filastin* (Palestine), stretched from Marj Ibn Amir to the Negeb and south-eastern Jordan and its capital was Ramla.

All we know about the Orthodox Caliphs' period in Palestine is that 'Umar Ibn al-Khattab built the Aqsa Mosque and that 'Uthman Ibn 'Affan established the first Islamic navy in Acre, fortified its coastlines and supplied it with armed forces. No new cities were built. The greater majority of the inhabitants were Arabs, a few of which had already become Muslims before the conquest.

As a result of the increase in Palestine's political and religious importance, a new building campaign began during the Umayyad period 41/661–132/750. The inhabitants supported the Umayyads and became, with their neighbours in Syria, the backbone of the Umayyad army and rule. Hence it is hardly surprising that the pledge of allegiance to Mu'awiya and the Umayyad caliphs took place in Jerusalem. During the rule of 'Abd al-Malik Ibn Marwan and his son al-Walid Ibn 'Abd al-Malik, the city saw the greatest and most splendid architectural project undertaken by the Umayyads, and possibly in the history of Islamic civilisation; namely the construction of the Haram al-Sharif (the Noble Sanctuary). It immortalised the Umayyads within the Islamic world and beyond. In addition to this, many palaces were built during that period:

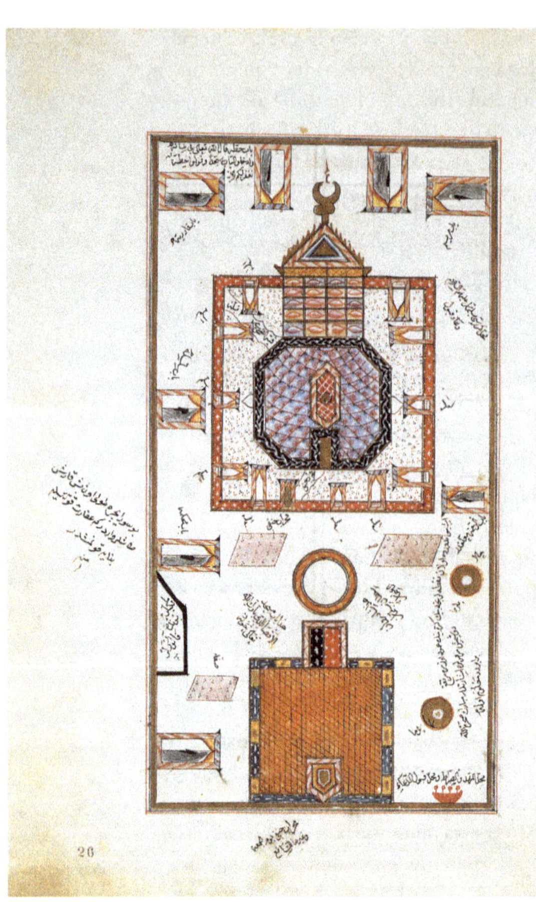

The Haram al-Sharif, with the Dome of the Rock and the al-Aqsa Mosque, Jerusalem, "Nur-I vahhaj li tahsil al-'Ilaj" (Ms. Vat. Ruco 125, f.26r), decorated by the copyist Mustafa Kashif (müzehhib) in 1243/1857 (© Vatican Library).

Dar al-Idarah in Jerusalem, Khirbat al-Mafjar (Hisham's Palace) in Jericho, al-Minya on the north-western coast of the Sea of Galilee, the Sabagheen (Dyers) Palace in Ramla (which no longer exists), and the Baths of al-Hamma to the south-east of the Sea of Galilee. The roads were improved, especially those linking Palestine to Damascus, the capital of the Caliphate. Ramla, the only city to be built in Syria during the Umayyad period, was constructed by Sulayman Ibn 'Abd al-Malik and completed during 'Umar Ibn 'Abd al-'Aziz's reign.

Having witnessed the coming of the Umayyads to power, Palestine also saw the massacre of more than 80 Umayyad princes by 'Abd Allah Ibn 'Ali al-'Abbas at the Abu Futrus River. Upon the death of the last Caliph Marwan Ibn Muhammad in 132/750, the Umayyad period ended and the reign of the Abbasid Dynasty began.

The inhabitants of Palestine were passive witnesses to the take-over of their country by the Abbasids as they had suffered from Umayyad misadministration toward the end of its reign. However, they soon realised the gravity of their loss and rose in opposition to the Abbasid Dynasty. Various resurrections took place in the name of the Umayyads. The Abbasid rule in Palestine was divided into two periods: the first (132/750–264/878) saw Palestine decline and become marginalised as a result of its critical relationship to the central government in Baghdad and the transfer of Islamic rule to Iraq. The second period (264/878–358/969) was one in which Palestine had some political, economic and territorial independence and was connected to Egypt. Small states appeared that were relatively independent from Baghdad, which was going through political unrest at the time.

Qasr Khirbat al-Mafjar, general view, Jericho.

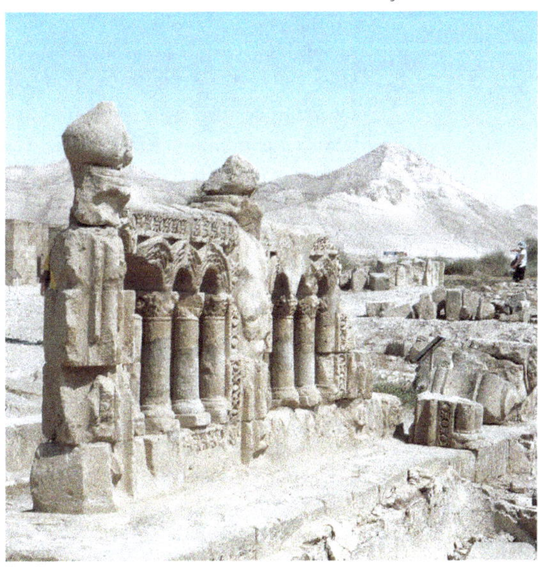

During these two periods, Palestine witnessed several building projects that would match those of the Umayyads'. However, the Abbasids did not spare any effort in maintaining and restoring the religious sites that the Umayyads had built. Abu Ja'far al-Mansur ordered the restoration of the Aqsa Mosque in 154/770–771, following its destruction by an earthquake in the same year. Four years later al-Mahdi did the same, while al-Ma'mun restored the Dome of the Rock in 215/831. A number of the colonnades that surround the platform of the Dome of the Rock were also built at this time. Special attention was paid to the Haram al-Ibrahimi in Hebron and to the water system in Ramla. Historical references also disclose the fact that the Abbasids built a great mosque in Asqalan.

In 254/877, as power of the central government in Baghdad declined, Ahmad Ibn Tulun succeeded in establishing his rule in Egypt and in stretching his authority over Syria and Palestine in 264/877. During this period the country experienced a number of military actions. This fact is reflected in the nature of Tulunid architecture in Palestine, the most famous of which is the construction and fortification of the Port of Acre.

The Qarmatians, who first appeared in Palestine at the end of Tulunid rule in 289/901, caused chaos. This troubled the Abbasid rulers of Baghdad, who were planning to restore their control over Palestine and Syria, and to prevent the establishment of a Qarmatian Isma'ili-Shi'ite State they launched a quick attack in 292/905 and succeeded in crushing Qarmatian rule in both Syria and Egypt.

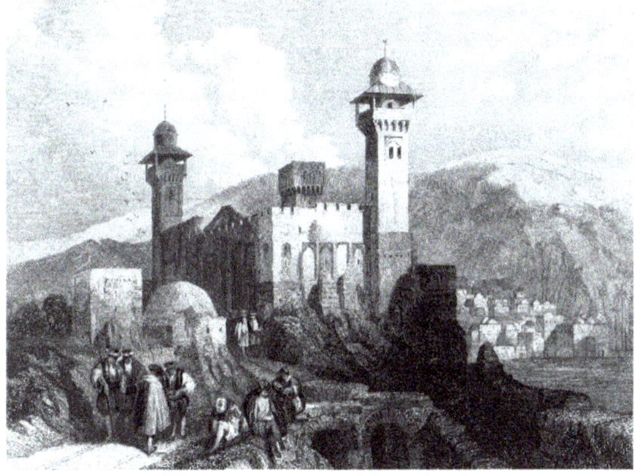

Haram al-Ibrahimi Mosque and Hebron, engraving on steel, Hildburghausen (Bibliographic Institute), c.1850 (© AKG, London).

All the same, Abbasid rule over Palestine did not last for long; the Ikhshidid State (323/934–358/969) emerged, asserting control over Syria first and later expanding over Egypt. The Abbasids tried to restore their power many times in Syria but all their efforts were in vain. During this period, Sayf al-Din al-Hamadani attempted to gain control over Palestine but was hindered by the Ikhshidids. The Qarmatians, however, continued their sporadic attacks on Palestine, which resulted in a period of instability. It is worth mentioning that the Ikhshid and all his successors, including Kafur al-Ikhshidi, were buried near the Aqsa Mosque (in Jerusalem).

At the end of the Ikhshidid rule, Fatimid attacks on Egypt heralded the advent of a new power that redesigned the political and sectarian arena of the region. They succeeded in conquering Egypt in 358/968, when Jawhar al-Siqilli entered al-Fustat and put an end to the Ikhshidid rule, to the Abbasid Dynasty and above all to *Sunni* Islam, which was restored only two centuries later under the Ayyubid Sultan, Salah al-Din (Saladin).

Although the Fatimid Dynasty brought stability to Egypt, as reflected in its magnificent constructions that embellished Cairo, it failed to do so in Palestine. The inhabitants of Syria resisted the Shi'ite Fatimid rule and refused its doctrine. Local Palestinian powers emerged, such as *Banu al-Jarrah Min Tai'*, the rulers of Ramla, who repeatedly sought independence and threatened Fatimid control over Syria. In addition, the Qarmatians continued their successive attacks and posed a real threat to the very existence of the Fatimids. Managing on several occasions to gain independence in Palestine, they minted coins that carried their emblems. Later on the Seljuks launched their attacks against the Fatimids carrying the *Sunni* banner.

Like all previous Islamic dynasties, the Fatimids looked after the holy sites in Palestine. Under the reign of the Fatimid Caliph al-Dahir, the Aqsa Mosque was renovated and a dome was added (which still stands today), after an earthquake hit it in 426/1035. The remarkable wooden pulpit (*minbar*) in the Ibrahimi Mosque in Hebron was built under the reign of Badr al-Jamali, the *amir* of the Fatimid army. It is also reported that the Fatimid al-Hakim bi-Amr Allah ordered the destruction of the Church of the Holy Sepulchre in 400/1009–1010 as a result of his strained relationship with the Byzantines, although he ordered its reconstruction five years later.

In 465/1073, the Ghaznawid ruler Atsiz succeeded in taking over Jerusalem from the Fatimids and submitted it to the Abbasid Caliph al-Qa'im bi-Amr Allah and to the famous Seljuk Sultan Malik Shah. He occupied Acre and restored its commercial role in the region. However, seven years later the kingdom fell under the double attacks of the Fatimids and the Seljuks,

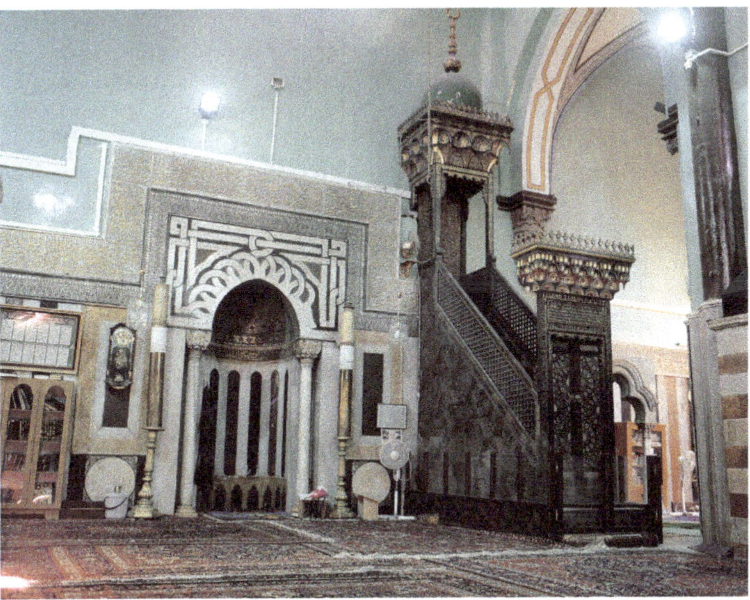

The Haram al-Ibrahimi Mosque, mihrab and minbar, Hebron.

passing into the hands of Tutush (a Seljuk, and Malik Shah's brother), who succeeded in entering Jerusalem in 472/1080. The coastline to the south of Acre and in southern Palestine stayed under Fatimid control. The balance of power between the Fatimids and the Seljuks prevented them confronting each other until the Sultan Malik Shah's death, when Tutush's attempt to replace him weakened the kingdom and exposed it to renewed attacks from the Fatimids. In 491/1098, al-Afdal Ibn Badr al-Jamali succeeded in occupying Jerusalem at the time the Crusaders besieged Antioch. Hardly eight months went by before the Fatimid rule in Jerusalem had to confront a new power, the Crusaders, who succeeded in changing the course of history in the Levant for two centuries.

The Crusaders' campaigns to Palestine followed a famous speech by Pope Urban II at the plains of Clermont in France in 488/1095. The first campaign arrived at the walls of Jerusalem in 492/1099. In the onslaught over the city a terrible massacre took place in which approximately 70,000 people died. One city after another fell into their hands, while the southern coastal plain of Palestine remained under the control of the Fatimids. Despite its colonial nature, the Crusaders' occupation of Palestine was not a social one; they failed to attract a large number of

Europeans to the area and consequently the countryside remained Palestinian. While some of the urban inhabitants mixed, the Crusader's presence in the countryside was confined to the castles. Under these circumstances, Palestine became a symbol of the conflict between the Islamic East and the Christian West. In the eyes of the West, Palestine's fall into the Crusaders' hands symbolised the collapse of the Islamic world; conversely, the Islamic East saw the Arab uprising against the Crusaders as a symbol of their resistance to the West.

Palestine's cultural loss was grave at the time. The Crusaders destroyed hundreds of buildings all over the country and few remained outside the Haram al-Sharif that were built prior to their arrival. The Crusaders' architecture dominated Jerusalem and the main cities in Palestine. On the other hand, they introduced a new style of architecture to the region, namely the Gothic and Romanesque styles. Their different military buildings influenced the later Ayyubid architectural style, while on the administrative side Western concepts of feudal management were introduced. For the first time since Palestine became part of the World Empire, an independent political entity was formed: the Latin Kingdom of Jerusalem.

Having followed the Zangid's plan (which unified the Syrian triangle between Damascus, Aleppo and Mosul and Egypt) Salah al-Din al-Ayyubi succeeded in defeating the Crusaders in Jerusalem. The Battle of Hittin (583/1187) was a decisive victory over the Crusaders and led to the recapture of Jerusalem and most of Palestine.

During the Ayyubid period (583/1187–648/1250), many efforts were made to completely regain Palestine, restore its cultural and demographic aspects and reconnect it to the Arab world, Egypt and Syria in particular. As a result, Palestine was divided into four territories. The Crusaders controlled the coastline between Tyre and Jaffa, while the Ayyubids controlled the other three. The south belonged to Egypt, the north (stretching from Jerusalem through Tiberias and Galilee) to Damascus, while the rest belonged the ruler of Karak in Trans Jordan.

Following Sultan Salah al-Din's death in 589/1193 and internal fights over his succession, the Crusaders' ineffectual attacks managed to shake the Ayyubid Dynasty. Although the Ayyubid period has been characterised by wars and battles, its achievements on the cultural front were enormous. The Ayyubid Sultans and *amirs* made their mark throughout Palestine: in addition to fortifications used to ward off the attacks of Crusaders, they constructed mosques and *madrasas* and bestowed *waqfs* on them.

The Ayyubids forced the Crusaders out of the Levant and gave birth to a unique political system that relied on white slaves to carry out their plans. These slaves later gained power after the death of their masters. Hulago (the Mongol ruler) succeeded in destroying Baghdad in 656/1258 and moved on to Syria. However, the Mamluks managed to defeat him in the Battle of 'Ayn Jalut (658/1259) and gain legitimacy. Moreover, the battle gave them the opportunity to control Syria after the Mongols had crushed the Ayyubid Dynasty. The Mamluks' next task was to eliminate the Crusaders' presence in Syria and Palestine. They finally succeeded in doing so during the reign of King al-Ashraf Khalil al-Malik when Acre, the last of the Crusaders' fortresses, fell into their hands. The wars that had lasted for almost two centuries – in which most of the European nations had participated – finally ended.

The Mamluks divided Palestine into three districts (*niyabas*): Safad, Gaza and Jerusalem. Being the Holy Land and the bridge that connects the two parts of their kingdom, Palestine was given special attention. Aimed at consolidating the relationship between Egypt and Syria through Palestine, the Mamluks invested generously in building a network of *caravanserais* along the main trade and pilgrimage routes. They also built a chain of postal stations between Cairo and Damascus. During the Mamluks' relatively peaceful period, Palestine enjoyed a cultural renaissance. As the Crusaders' threat declined, it became possible for the first time to invest in areas other than the military sector. Hence *madrasas*, *zawiyas*, *takiyyas*, *ribats*, *sabils*, as well as mosques, were built.

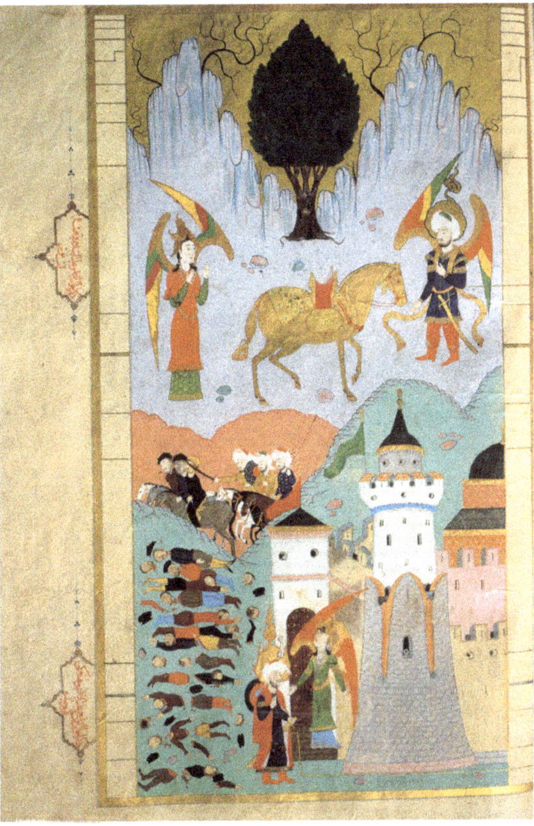

Fight at the gates of Jerusalem. The Muslims push back the infidels and chase them from the town, from "The Fine Flower of Histories", by Loqman, 1583 (© The Art Archive/ Dagli Orti).

Jerusalem received the lion's share of Mamluk attention. Most sultans and *amirs* visited and honoured the place by erecting educational and charitable buildings, which still define the cultural aspects of the city today. Thus the city became the centre to which scholars and the learned came. Many distinguished scientists of the Mamluk period, including the leaders of Sufism, studied in its mosques. To ensure the continuation of its institutions, different *waqfs* were bestowed upon the city, with Hebron, Safad, Acre and Gaza having no lesser share of attention. The Mamluk touch could be seen in shrines all over the country; either newly built, re-constructed or renovated under each of the Mamluk rulers.

The Mamluks were defeated in the Battle of Marj Dabiq, in north Syria, in 922/1517. However, the gradual collapse of the Mamluk State was due to the development of international trade, the disintegration of the Mamluk system and the rise of the Ottoman Empire. Consequently, for four centuries, Palestine became an integral part of a wide-reaching multicultural, multinational and multilingual empire. It had to live under the wings of the Ottoman Empire, whose rule in Palestine can be divided into four periods. The first witnessed the emergence of local disorganised forces (of feudal and Bedouin origins) on whom the Ottomans relied to rule the country. The second started with the turn of power toward foreign forces such as Fakhr al-Din al-Ma'ni, the *amir* of Mount Lebanon. However, the central Ottoman government eliminated him in 1045/1636 and placed the area under their direct control, with Ottoman governors appointed in Damascus and Sidon. The third period saw the emergence of the first Arab semi-independent principality under the leadership of the Zidanis and tens of rural leaders. Ahmad al-Jazar, the *wali* of Acre, also appeared during that period. He was a national hero for having resisted Napoleon's campaign in 1214/1799 after European greed had re-awakened. The fourth period was in the 13th/19th century when the central government tried to improve its administration through the *Tanzimat* system. It also saw Muhammad Ali's conquest of Palestine in 1246/1830–1831 when it was placed under Egyptian rule. In the second half of this century the doors were wide open for Western intervention, missionary activity and, finally, the Zionist movement that prompted an increase in Jewish emigration to Palestine. After four centuries, Ottoman rule ended with the First World War and the British Mandate of Palestine (1917-1948).

Ottoman Palestine was administratively part of the *wilaya* (province) of Syria, which was divided into the five *sanjaks* (districts) of Jerusalem, Gaza, Safad, Nablus and Lajjun. This gave Palestine great importance, bearing in mind that the rest of Syria was divided into only four districts. The Ottomans built and restored many fortresses and *caravanserais* to secure the roads; among these were al-Minya, 'Uyun al-Tujjar, Jenin, Qaqun, Ra's al-'Ayn, Khan Yunis, al-'Arish and Bayt Jibrin. During their first period of rule the Ottomans carried out ambitious building projects, among the greatest of which were the Walls of Jerusalem, the restoration of the Haram al-Sharif, water-supply projects and mosques. In addition to building the citadel of al-Dahir in Hebron, the walls of Tiberias and the citadel and fortifications of Acre, many large projects were carried out in Hebron, Gaza and Acre. The Ottoman influence can still be seen all over Palestine, although their interest declined in the latter period of their rule as a result of wars with Europe.

The *Sufis* and Islam

The successive political and administrative changes hardly altered Palestine's position within the Islamic world. Muslims continued to flow into Palestine throughout the periods detailed above because of Jerusalem's status as the first *qibla*, the third most important of the Holiest Islamic sites and the primary destination of pilgrims, visitors, *sufis* and scholars. From here the Prophet Muhammad made his nocturnal journey to heaven. The Prophet urged Muslims in his *hadith* (prophetic tradition) to visit Jerusalem, and the third most venerated site after Mecca and Medina, lies here. Jerusalem is also close to the Haram al-Ibrahimi (where Abraham the patriarch of the prophets and the first Muslim is buried) and to Christ's place of nativity.

None of the other Islamic territories has as many holy sites. Palestine is the home and cradle of all monotheist religions. Muslims made it a custom to visit Jerusalem after their pilgrimage to Mecca to complete their rituals. They also visited many other holy sites in both cities and villages, placing Hebron at the top of their list. Hence *caravanserais* spread all over the country, the most celebrated of which were the Hebron Guest House (known since the dawn of Islam) and the Hospice of Jerusalem (established during the Ottoman period). Many *sufi* hospices were constructed in order to accommodate the floods of *sufis* travelling into the country. Their visits would often be timed to coincide with significant events such as the Festival of Nabi

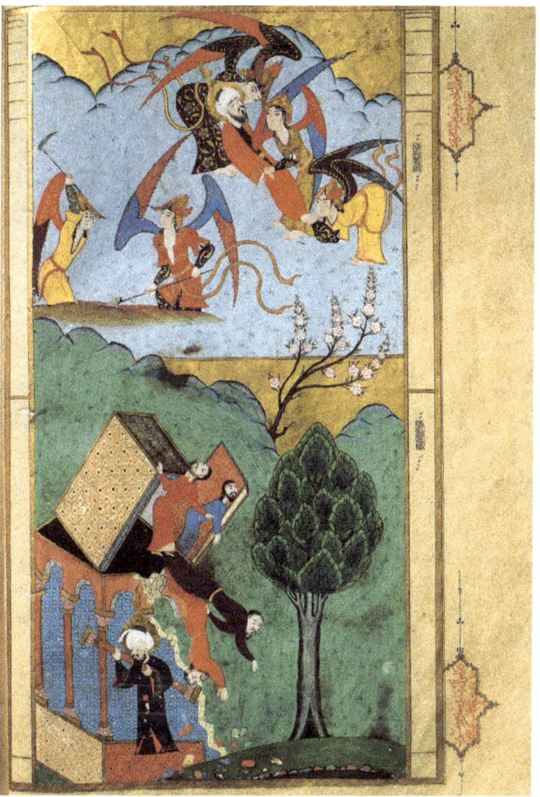

The Prophet Mohamma carried by Angels. Below, The Destruction of the Temple in Jerusalem, from "The Fine Flower of Histories", by Loqman, 1583 (© The Art Archive / Turkish and Islamic Art Museum, Istanbul / Dagli Orti [A]).

Jerusalem, from a 6th-century (Byzantine) mosaic (the oldest representation of the Holy City), Saint George's Church, Madaba, Jordan.

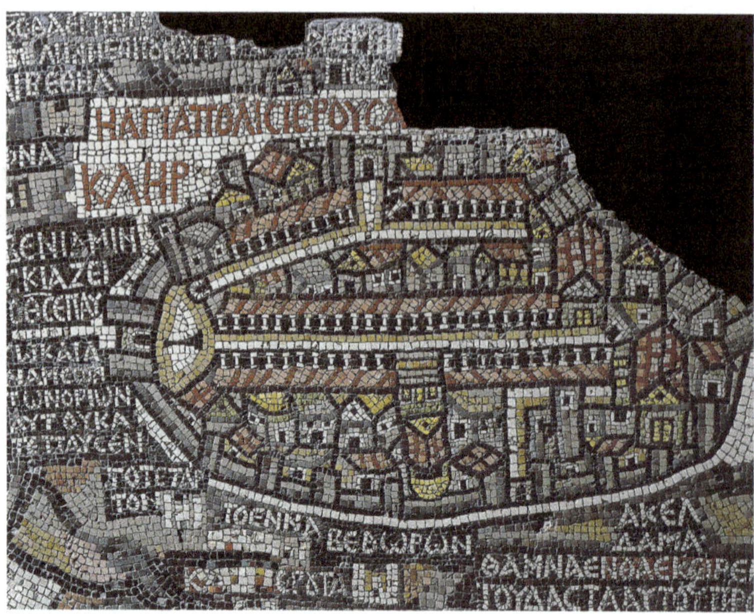

Musa or that of Nabi Salih, when they came to fulfil a vow or settle an overdue debt.

All Caliphs, sultans and *amirs*, without exception, have contributed to this great heritage. Most would have visited Jerusalem, prayed in the *mihrab* of the Aqsa Mosque, distributed alms to the poor, placed a *waqf* (an endowment in perpetuity) on its holy sites and built mosques, *madrasa*s, domes and *zawiya*s in Palestine. In return, they hoped for reward and forgiveness in the afterlife. Many books were written in early Islamic times that praised the virtues of the country and provided a detailed description of the land. Travel books abounded with references and maps leading there, and by the 4th/10th century the "Merits of Jerusalem" literature appeared featuring Jerusalem and describing in detail the merits of every city and holy site in Palestine. They listed the names of the caliphs, the companions of the Prophet and scholars who had visited there, those who had resided or were buried there and those who had helped in conquering it. They also described all the great Islamic events in Palestine. These books became the guides of pilgrims throughout the different Islamic ages, especially during the Mamluk and Ottoman periods.

Various study centres were established in the Aqsa Mosque and its premises. As a result, Jerusalem became an attraction to all the great Islamic scholars. It reached a peak in the Mamluk period when the number of *madrasas* and study centres exceeded 100. Having attracted the greatest scholars of the time, their followers and various students, Jerusalem became an essential stop in the quest for knowledge.

As is the case with many holy sites, the ascetics come to rediscover the self and completely devote themselves to worship. The famous *sufi* scholar, the Imam al-Ghazali spent many years on the premises of the Aqsa Mosque during the darkest period of his life, his journey of penitence and self-discovery, and Abu Bakr al-Ishbili al-Andalusi stayed there despite his initial intention to only seek knowledge and visit the holy sites. The ideal environment for *sufi* people was provided there, which encouraged them to stay for a longer period.

Linguistically speaking, Sufism is derived from the word *suf* (wool) and was ascribed to whoever wore it for modesty. However, idiomatically

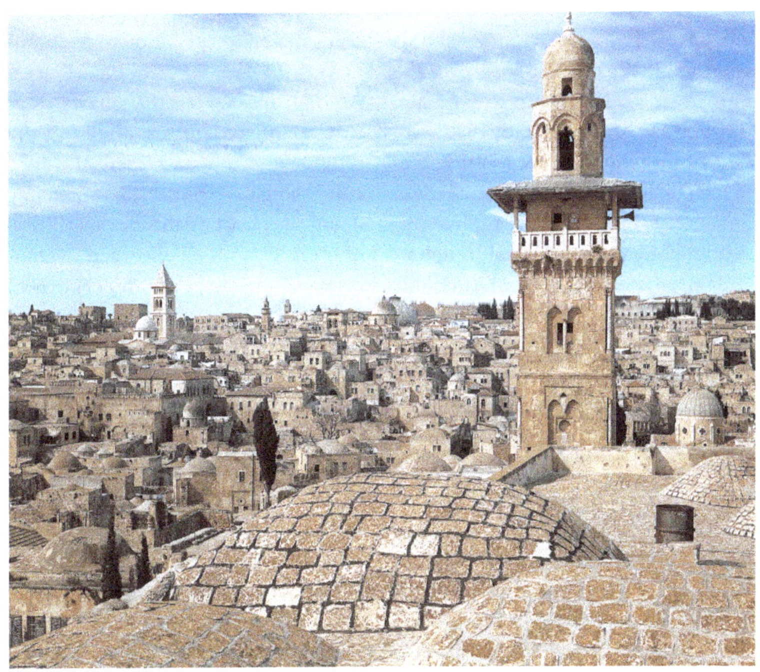

Jerusalem, domes and minarets of the old city (© A. F. Kersting).

speaking, it came to mean devoting oneself to the worship of God and abstaining from all forms of vanity, pleasure, wealth and fame. This quintessence of *sufi* doctrine started early in Islam, as exemplified by the Prophet's life and the lives of many of his companions. Jerusalem's religious importance played a significant role in attracting many ascetics, worshippers and *sufi*s since the Islamic conquest. This is documented by Mujir al-Din al-Hanbali (901/1496), the renowned historian of Jerusalem.

In the following centuries Sufism lost much of its simplicity and purity. Its doctrines and practices developed and became more complex during different stages. Philosophical *sufi* schools emerged that sought to interpret the individual's relationship to God and the universe, delved into the nature of God and the ontology of being, and investigated the tools of knowledge. Sufism was influenced by the various contemporary philosophical, religious and intellectual trends of thought. Rabi'a al-'Adawiyya (d. 185/801) believed that obedience to God stemmed not from fear of hell or desire for paradise but from the pure desire to please Him. Abu Yazid al-Bustami (d. 260/874), on the other hand, discussed the theory of extinction and union, where extinction does not mean annihilation (as in Hinduism) but rather the extinction of individual limitation in the state of union with God. Al-Hallaj (d. 309/922) called for *hulul*, a form of unification between human nature and the Divine. Ibn al-'Arabi (d. 638/1240) believed in universal unity (*wihdat al-wujud*).

This line of Sufism found its way to Jerusalem either by word of mouth or through some of its leaders who resided there. Among them was Ibn Kiram al-Sujari (d. 255/869) the founder of the *khanqa* al-Karamiyya in Jerusalem. He discussed the nature of the Divine and argued that faith starts with the tongue, even if it seems to contradict the heart and mind. This school of thought did not survive for long and another form of Sufism replaced it, supported by the institutions that were founded by different rulers and *amirs*.

Many factors contributed to the elimination of the *sufi* leading figures. Among these were the jurists' fear that the purity and simplicity of the religion would be tarnished, the difficulty the public had in understanding it and, not least of all, the corruption of the politicians who worked to eliminate opponents under the pretext of safeguarding religion and Shari'a. Another *Sufi* Order developed and its most distinguished leader was the Imam al-Ghazali (d. 505/1111) who resided in Jerusalem for a period of time. His theory started a new stream of *sufi* thought, arguing that though the human mind is the most sophisticated tool of understanding and thinking, it is nonetheless unable to interpret the Divine and the metaphysical. The only safe way to reach certainty is through Sufism, which relies on the heart, intuition and taste (not the mind) to reach truth. This can only be achieved through purification and inspiration.

Purifying the self is a luxury that not many can afford; it requires labour, endurance and abstinence from pleasure. Hence the truth-seeker has to pass through the three *sufi* stages: acolyte, oblate and adept. To reach the Divine reality, he should experience eight phases. First comes awakening (coming out of inadvertence), then follows repentance, turning to God, purity (forsaking the desecrated), will, renunciation (privation of sensory satisfaction), integrity (where the internal/external, hunger/satiety and sleep/sleeplessness become one and the same), and finally satisfaction (where affliction becomes a source of pleasure). Liberation leads him to extinction.

As human abilities differ from one person to another, a *sufi shaykh* who has experienced revelation and clarity should supervise this process. Even though the aim is the same, different *sufi* orders followed different paths. Among the 70 Orders that reached Jerusalem were the Qadiriyya, established by the famous 'Abd al-Qadir al-Jilani (d. 561/1166), and the Mawlawiyya Order founded by Jalal al-Din al-Rumi (d. 672/1273), al-Naqshabandiyya, al-Khalwatiyya, al-Bastamiyya and al-Shadhiliyya.

A warm relationship developed between the *sufi shaykhs*, their followers, the rulers, *amirs* and sultans. Hence the state-sponsored *sufi* institutions such as *zawiyas*, *khanqas* and *ribats*. In return, Sufism publicly supported the rulers and their system. As a result tens of *sufi* buildings, some of which have survived, were built in Jerusalem during the Mamluk and Ottoman periods. At a later stage, Sufism fell into rigidity and its backward leaders controlled the minds of the naïve through charms. Devotion to self-renunciation and worship declined, and bitter conflicts developed between them and the jurists.

The Holy Sites and Knowledge

Providing a fertile soil for Sufism to develop was not the only thing that the holy sites offered. Scholars gathered there from different parts of the Islamic world, as Islam highly values knowledge. The first Qur'anic verses emphasise the importance of learning. God spoke to His prophets saying: *"Read in the name of your God, the Creator, who created man from earth. Read in the name of God the bountiful, who taught man what he did not know with the pen"*. The Qur'an also differentiated between the position of scholars and the public, saying: *"Ask yourself whether those who know and those who don't are equal"*. The Prophet himself encouraged Muslims to spare no effort in seeking knowledge from the furthest corners of the universe, *"Even if it was as far as China"* (the furthest corner according to the age).

To acquire profound knowledge, travelling to the sources became a prerequisite for any scholar. The best compliment one would get was *"He travelled much and was educated by distinguished scholars from different parts of the world"*. This travelling phenomenon started in the 1st/7th–8th century when the Prophet's companions went to Iraq, Syria and Egypt, although very few stayed in Hijaz (western Arabia). Among the most famous travellers were the scholars who studied and investigated the prophetic traditions. Travel was further encouraged by pilgrimage to Mecca and Medina, which is one of the essential tenets of Islam. Some scholars ended up settling in one holy city or a metropolis and were called *mujawir*. As science and Islamic tradition were unified, scholars were given every opportunity to assemble and exchange their thoughts and knowledge.

Jerusalem attracted the greatest scholars from all over the Islamic world, who came to visit or even settle there. As mentioned above, this was due to many factors: it is one of the three holy Islamic cities; it is the first *qibla* and the place from which the Prophet Mohammad made his nocturnal ascension to heaven, the ultimate goal of all travellers and the place where resurrection will occur; the site to which Mecca and Medina will hasten on Judgement Day, and where many of the Prophets' companions and followers settled. Jerusalem became one of the six major cities in which scholars and jurists would stop in their quest for knowledge and Islamic education, the others being Cairo, Damascus, Baghdad, Mecca and Medina. Despite all the misfortunes and calamities that beset them, these cities continued to be seen as the centres for education and learning, even though some of them were occupied and destroyed (Baghdad by the Mongols, and Jerusalem by the Crusaders). Even political disintegration in the Islamic world failed to diminish their importance both to scholars and in the development of science in the 4th/10th and 5th/11th centuries.

In addition to being the main place of worship, the mosque was (and still is) one of the most eminent educational centres in Islam since the Prophet's time. The main mosques in Islamic capitals played a leading role in spreading knowledge, and many historical references list the names of the major scholars in Islam. Among them was 'Ibada Ibn al-Samat (d. 34/654), who was the first judge in Jerusalem and Palestine and to whom Caliph 'Umar allocated the task of teaching in Jerusalem. Shadad Ibn 'Aws (d. 58/677–678), the jurists Imam al-Awza'i, Sufyan al-Thawri, al-Imam al-Layth Ibn Sa'd and al-Imam al-Shafi'i were other renowned scholars.

In the 4th/10th and 5th/11th centuries the Aqsa Mosque became a rich scientific centre where the most elite local scholars met with their counterparts from the rest of the Islamic world. Among these were Muhammad Ibn Ahmad al-Maqdisi (d. 380/990) the renowned author of the leading geographic encyclopaedia: *Kitab ahsan al-taqasim fi-ma'rifat al-aqalim* ("The Best Guide to the Regions"), Abu al-Fadl 'Ali Ibn Tahir al-Maqdisi (d. 507/1112), the famous Islamic scholar Nasr al-Maqdisi (d. 490/1096) and 'Ata' al-Maqdisi. Among the leading figures who visited Jerusalem were the Imam Muhammad Ibn al-Walid al-Tartushi al-Andalusi (d. 520/1126), Abu Ghana'im Muhammad Ibn Maymun al-Hafiz al-Kufi, the Ottoman Abu 'Abd Allah al-Dibaji, the Imam Abu Faraj al-Shirazi and Abu Hamid al-Ghazali who retired to the Aqsa Mosque and lived in the Nasiriyya Madrasa where he wrote a number of his works. Debate and discussion were the basis of education and learning during that period, especially as Jerusalem boasted the most celebrated scholars. Al-Ghazali bemoaned the fact that only 360 tutors were available in the Aqsa Mosque. The debates were not limited to Islamic scholars but were extended to all scholars of the monotheist religions. Ibn al-'Arabi (d. 543/1148) described these debates saying: *"We debated with the Karamiyya, the Mu'tazila, the Mushabbaha and the Jews and disputed with the Christians"*.

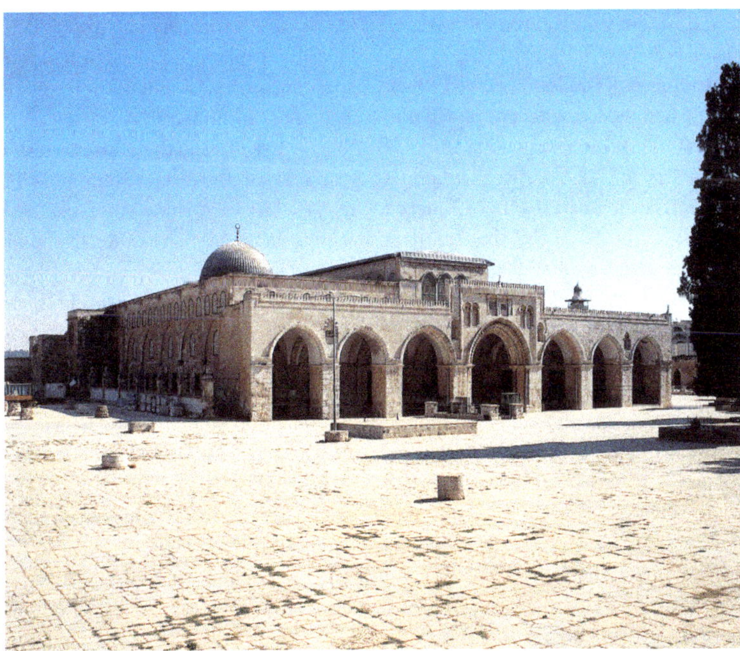

Al-Aqsa Mosque, general view and the main façade. Haram al-Sharif, Jerusalem.

While the subjects of debate were mostly related to theology, jurisprudence and controversial issues, those of education were related to the science of the Qur'an, *hadith* and their different branches. Arabic grammar, morphology, literature, rhetoric and poetry were also discussed and some subjects overlapped. Most of the scholars offered their tuition free of charge and, as was the custom, delivered their tutorials in the Aqsa Mosque while their students gathered around them in a circle. Some used to sit close to a certain column, which was later named after the famous tutor. Whenever the weather allowed it, classes were conducted on the terraces. The tutor followed no specific requirements or curriculum.

Education in Jerusalem received a fatal blow when the Crusaders occupied it in 492/1099. Tuition stopped as many of the jurists and scholars were killed. It was only after Salah al-Din conquered Jerusalem in 583/1187 that scholars were brought together again and given preferential treatment. He built special institutions to help them carry out their work – such as *madrasas*, Qur'anic and oratory centres and *zawiyas* – and the Aqsa Mosque continued to be the place of preaching, guidance and enlightenment. Even though there is evidence that *madrasas* existed in Jerusalem before the Crusaders' occupation, they spread during the Ayyubid period and reached their zenith in the Mamluk period.

Most *madrasas* were named after their founders or after one of their tutors. The four Islamic laws (*madhabs*) were the major subjects taught and it was often the case that each school specialised in one of them. The *waqf* system gave diligent but poor pupils the opportunity to acquire an education and ensured that the *madrasa*'s expenses and the tutors' wages were covered. There were two kinds of position in a *madrasa*: the scientific posts such as those of the *madrasa*'s *shaykh* and those of the main tutors who were entrusted with teaching. Renowned jurists and scholars were appointed by contract. The tutor would confer a degree on his pupils, called a license, which entitled them to teach his books. A tutor had an assistant to help him explain complicated issues to students who needed help. The *madrasa*'s administrative posts were those of the head, the administrative manager of the establishment (who managed its *waqf*, paid out the student's scholarships and looked after the building and its maintenance), and the librarian, registrar, servant and torchbearer. Although the subjects of education remained the same in the 5th/11th and the following centuries, the teaching and scientific methodology deteriorated. Debate and discussion circles disappeared while *ijtihad*, innovation and originality decreased. Monotony, repetition and memorisation became the new methodology in both the Ayyubid and Mamluk periods, while inflexibility and narrow-mindedness characterised the Ottoman period, especially in its latter stages. Despite this, Muhyi al-Din interpreted the works of many leading Ayyubid and Mamluk jurists, scholars, orators, judges and tutors thus preserving Shari'a science and the Arabic language. Finally, one has to mention that these *madrasas* were mostly private ventures that depended on their *waqfs* for survival and they were open to all sectors of society without distinction. Even so, this stage could be considered as lying between progress and backwardness.

THE ARCHITECTURE AND DECORATIVE ARTS OF ISLAMIC PALESTINE

Yusuf Natsheh

Palestine witnessed a phenomenal development in Islamic art, namely in terms of architecture and the complementary minor arts. However, despite the fact that it is a relatively a small country, its arts have flourished remarkably and demonstrated diversity and individuality. It possesses the oldest and most important Islamic monument that exists until today: the Dome of the Rock in Jerusalem. No building has received as much attention or has undergone as much artistic study; considered an independent school of art in itself, it has attracted the attention of architects and scholars for decades.

This can be attributed to many factors, including the abundance of raw materials, the most famous of which is the stone that is used for both building and decoration. Palestine was renowned for its various types of stone, which were easy to carve for decoration and had beautiful colouration (red, black, white and yellow), which led to the development of the *ablaq* style seen in its architecture. The artistic traditions that began in Palestine thousands of years ago have made a significant contribution to the flourishing of the arts, and was further developed when the Hellenistic, Roman and Byzantine influences were amalgamated with local traditions. Situated between Egypt and Syria, the heart and the centre of the Islamic world, Palestine had been exposed to deep architectural and artistic influences originating in Cairo, Damascus and Aleppo, which can be seen clearly during the Ayyubid and Mamluk periods.

Zoomorphic vessel from the Umayyad palace of Khirbat al-Mafjar in Jericho, Rockerfeller Museum in Jerusalem (47-4925) (© Sonia Halliday Photographs, photograph: D. Silverman, courtesy of the Israeli Antiquities Authority).

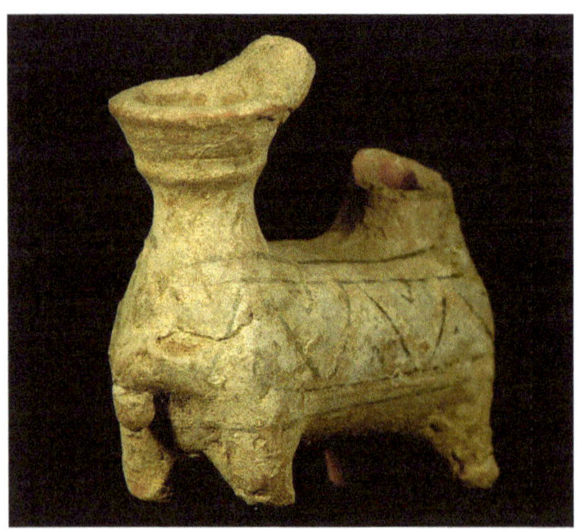

Styles of Architecture through the Ages

The religious status of Palestine played an important role in the development of Islamic art. It is the focal point for the believers of the three monotheistic religions, the place in which various prophets, saints and holy people are buried, and it consists of sacred cities such as Jerusalem and Hebron. Hence the believers were attracted by it, either to visit or to settle in, and many rulers and *amirs*, prompted by good will and the desire to win public support, constructed numerous religious buildings during their reign and supported them through *waqfs*.

The large cities of Palestine reveal the great diversity of Islamic architecture and ornaments with the most important and greatest structures found in Jerusalem, the centre of the earliest Islamic monumental buildings, and the city with the most comprehensive remains charting the evolution of Islamic architecture, particularly the Umayyad style, with Hebron and then Gaza following behind. In Gaza the Mamluk style predominates, as it was the capital of a Mamluk district (*niyaba*) of Syria. In Nablus, on the other hand, the Ottoman style presides especially in the palaces built by its influential families, a phenomenon that Jerusalem never witnessed.

During the Ottoman period, a more localised style of architecture was widely spread in the Palestinian villages that held local government centres, which were called, idiomatically, the "Seat Villages". From here the clan leaders of these villages ruled the neighbouring areas. The palaces that formed independent units resembled small fortresses and the villages' houses and public utilities spread around them.

The types of Islamic buildings that were constructed in Palestine were numerous and served various functions. These included: religious buildings such as oratory and Qur'anic centres, mosques, *madrasas*, *sufi zawiyas*, shrines and mausoleums; social buildings such as *takiyyas*, *sabils*, *ribats*, palaces, houses and *hammams*; commercial centres such as *suqs*, *caravanserais*, *khans*, oil presses and soap factories; and military buildings such as walls, towers, citadels and other fortifications. These structures were built both inside and outside the cities and on the public roads that connected cities and villages.

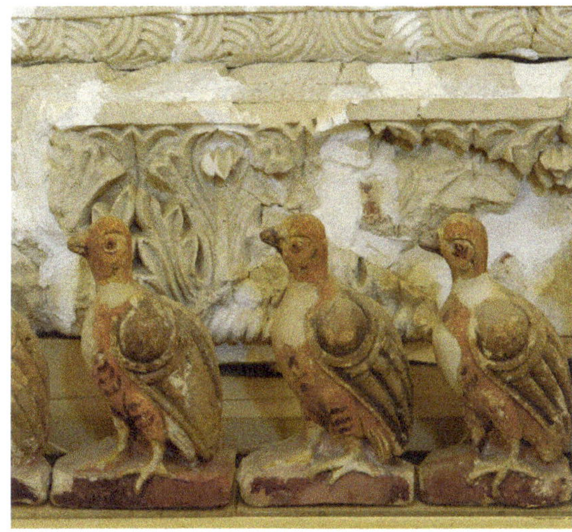

Partridges in stucco, decorative detail of a window, Umayyad Palace of Khirbat al-Mafjar in Jericho, Rockefeller Museum in Jerusalem (© Sonia Halliday Photographs, photograph: D. Silverman, courtesy of the Israeli Antiquities Authority).

The diversity of the artistic and architectural styles to which Islamic Palestine testifies, is on account of the various dynasties that developed and encouraged them, and to which they generally identified themselves; the "Mamluk style" of architecture is a good example of this process. Four important periods can be distinguished:

1. *The Early Islamic Period* (15/637–492/1099) straddles the period of the Islamic conquest of Palestine, to its fall at the hands of the Crusaders. It includes the reigns of the Orthodox Caliphs and the Umayyad, Abbassid and Fatimid dynasties. Although few build-

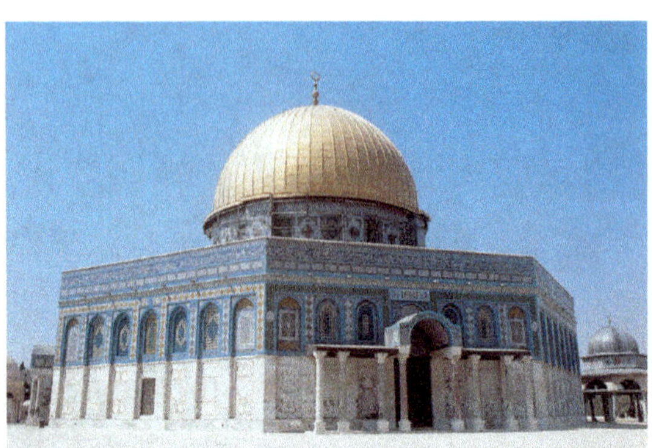

Dome of the Rock, general view, Haram al-Sharif, Jerusalem.

ings of these periods still survive, they are extremely significant from an artistic point of view. Most extant buildings were either ruined by time or destroyed through wars and disasters. This period also constitutes a transitional stage during which power in Palestine moved from the Byzantines to the Arabs.

Many mosques that are dated to this period are called al-'Umari Mosques, after the Orthodox Caliph 'Umar Ibn al-Khattab, the conqueror of Palestine. Nothing of the original structures survives apart from their names, as most have been rebuilt or renovated in the succeeding ages. The name *Umari* here does not necessarily imply that Caliph 'Umar was the founder of these institutions, but rather that they were ancient buildings dating back to his period. The most famous surviving monuments of this period belong to the Umayyad style of architecture, these are mainly found in the Haram al-Sharif in Jerusalem.

'Abd al-Malik rebuilt the walls of the Haram and numerous gates in it. Among these gates are: Bab al-Rahma (Gate of Mercy), Bab al-Tawba (Gate of Repentance), Bab al-Asbat (Gate of the Lions), Bab al-'Atm (Gate of Darkness), including the Double Gate and the Triple Gate in the southern wall. He laid the foundations for the Dome of the Rock, Qubbat al-Silsila (Dome of the Chain) and many other commemorative domes such as the Qubbat al-Nabi (Dome of the Prophet), Qubbat al-Mahshar (Dome of the Resurrection), and started the building of the Aqsa Mosque. The latter was completed by al-Walid, who also built Dar al-Imara (the Umayyad palaces that were uncovered in the southern part of the Haram).

Among the many Umayyad projects in Palestine were the Palace of Khirbat al-Mafjar (Hisham's Palace) in Jericho, and Khirbat al-Minya near Tiberias, a factory in Acre and Ramla, the placing of milestones on the roads and constructing roads. After the Umayyads, most works were focussed on renovation and maintenance, notably in the case of the Aqsa Mosque, the Dome of the Rock and the Haram area. In addition to this, some vital municipal projects were carried out, such as building a cistern in Ramla, extending the Port of Acre and the building of new mosques.

2. *The Ayyubid Period* (583/1187–648/1250) saw abundant architectural activity, particularly in the construction of fortresses, citadels and walls. Following the conquest of Palestine from

the Crusaders, the task of re-Islamisation and restoring the country's Arabic character fell onto the shoulders of the Ayyubids, especially in Jerusalem, Hebron and Nablus. Many of the mosques that had been converted to churches by the Crusaders were rehabilitated, for example the Dome of the Rock, the Aqsa Mosque and many other mosques in various places such as Gaza and Sebastia.

The Ayyubid and Crusader styles of architecture overlapped as a result of the re-use of artistic and architectural elements and the utilisation of similar construction techniques. It became almost impossible to distinguish between the two in some buildings in Jerusalem and the fortresses in Palestine. Many *madrasas*, *sufi zawiyas*, Qur'anic centres, water projects and fountains were built during this period under the auspices of Sultan Salah al-Din and his successors such as al-Mu'addam 'Issa and al-Salih Najm al-Din Ayyub. Various restoration projects, particularly the rehabilitation of the Haram al-Sharif and the Ibrahimi Mosque, were given special attention by the Ayyubid Dynasty. Many Crusader buildings were renovated and re-used to accommodate new functions.

3. *The Mamluk Period* (648/1250–922/1517) is considered the Golden Age of Islamic architecture in Palestine. Many mosques, *madrasas*, *zawiyas*, mausoleums, bridges and commercial utilities, such as *caravanserais* and markets, were built throughout the country. A chain of *caravanserais* and utilities were built along the roads that linked cities in order to facilitate travelling, communication and transportation, such as Khan Yunis near Gaza, Khan al-Lubban on the road to Nablus, Khan of al-Dahir near Jerusalem and Khan of Asdud. Most of these structures were built in Jerusalem, Gaza, Hebron and Safad, and were supported by generous *waqfs* that provided money for their upkeep.

4. *The Ottoman Period* (922/1517–1336/1917) is characterised by different styles of architecture. During the 10th/16th century, the Ottomans concentrated their building activities in Jerusalem, seeking to restore it to its past glory in the Umayyad and early Mamluk periods. The wall of Jerusalem (which still stands today) was built, in addition to various water projects and fountains, the Dome of the Rock and

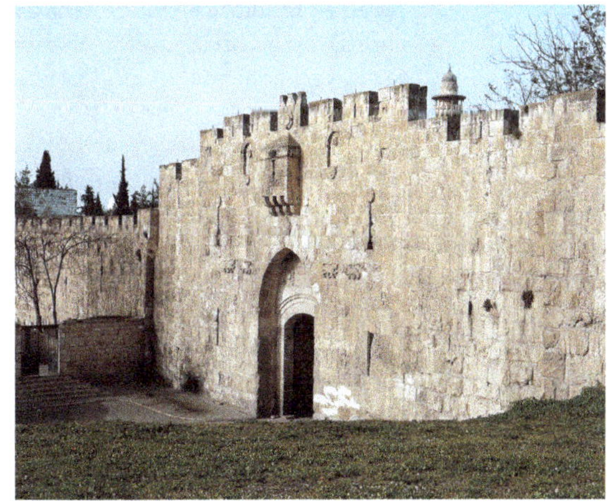

Bab al-'Asbat (Gate of the Lions), situated in the eastern wall, Jerusalem (© Sonia Halliday Photographs).

the Haram al-Sharif were restored, and building of the Khassaki Sultan Complex was undertaken. Gaza was among the cities that were given special attention, as it was the capital of a *sanjak* and the place where the Radwan family lived (who had ruled Palestine and overseen the management of the pilgrimage caravans coming from Syria).
During the 11th/17th century, under the auspices of al-Dahir ʻUmar, Ottoman architectural activity reached cities such as Tiberias that had been obscure during the Mamluk period. A wall was built around this city, many mosques were founded and a network of roads was established that connected it to other cities in Palestine. His activities also extended to neighbouring cities such as Shafaʻ Amr, Acre and Hifa. In the early 12th/18th century Ahmad Pasha al-Jazzar fortified the walls of Acre, which prevented Napoleon's invasion, and he built a mosque named al-Jazzar, an Ottoman architectural masterpiece in the city centre, in addition to many other mosques, *suqs*, *hammams* and *caravanserais*.
Other cities such as Jafa and Haifa received their share of attention too, even if on a lesser scale than Hebron and Nablus. In fact, Ottoman architectural activity in many cities of Palestine was related to the efforts of local ruling families who governed Palestine on behalf of the Ottomans and enjoyed a certain degree of autonomy. Once they tried to achieve complete independence from the Ottoman Empire they were annihilated, but their architectural heritage remained.
The conventional Ottoman-style architecture – based on arches, columns, cross- and barrel-vaults and the use of plaster and mortar – came to an end in the last decades of the Empire, when rectilinear ceilings supported by iron beams became the norm. The style of architecture was diverse and varied during this period (1256/1840–1336/1917) due to different influences, especially from Europe, when in the 19th century European powers became increasingly interested in Palestine. Although traditional techniques of construction have survived along with new ones, stone still remained the essential building material.

To single out the artistic forms and architectural styles of each era would be difficult. This is due to the fact that the architecture and arts of every period have been inspired by similar sources. The fall of a certain political system or dynasty did not necessarily result in the change or abandonment of the prevalent architectural style. Many styles continued and developed throughout different periods as a natural response to the needs of the society. However, few of the characteristics that distinguish one period from another can be delineated even though some could be found as a different form or style in other periods.
The general characteristics of Islamic art in Palestine are identical to those that developed in Egypt and Syria dur-

ing the Umayyad, Fatimid, Ayyubid and Mamluk periods. They had all been under one political rule and one administrative unity. Palestine functioned as a geographical bridge that connected the two countries that had exchanged seats of government at different times. As a result, the characteristics of art and architecture in Palestine are similar to those in Egypt and Syria. The characteristics of the Umayyad style of architecture are numerous. The architectural forms include: inner courtyards and spaces, stone façades, circular and semicircular towers, thick walls, semicircular arches and marble columns and capitals. Different variations of *kufic* script were widespread. Stucco and mosaic decorations were used on walls and floors employing rich geometrical and vegetal ornaments. Figurative art was excluded from religious buildings.

In Ayyubid architecture mosaic and stucco ornamentation disappears, and *kufic* script replaced by the distinguished Ayyubid *naskhi* script. Stone remained as the main material for construction. In the designs of domes, architects introduced solutions to the transition from a square-plan to a circular shape, by using an octagon supporting pendentives or corner squinches.

During the Mamluk period, special emphasis was dedicated to façade portals that were decorated with *muqarnas*, and *mastabas* (outdoor stone benches) that flanked the entrances. Diverse colourful stones were used in the courses, creating the famous *ablaq* ornament. Long strips of Mamluk inscriptions written in both the *thuluth* and *naskhi* scripts, and containing official titles and carved blazons appeared. Special attention was paid to the semi-domes above the entrance portals and there was extensive use of vegetal and geometrical ornaments on the façades, including the arabesque decorations on the *voussoirs* of arches, corbel brackets and volutes, the alternating of joggles, and the geometrical star-shaped and multiangled medallions. Other characteristics included moulded plaster, crenulated balconies, the fan-shaped and cross vaults supported by different arches, holes sustained by pillars, and beautifully decorated columns, walls and stone cantilevers (to carry balconies). In addition there are characteristic elements in the planning that are common to Mamluk buildings, such as the *madrasa*, *ribat* or *turbe*. The function of architecture in Palestine was similar to that in Egypt and Syria, with many civil, religious and military buildings constructed. The *waqf* system ensured revenue was available for the upkeep of pious foundations.

With the advent of the Ottoman Empire both Mamluk and local architectural traditions continued to exist. A local school emerged in Jerusalem whose features became clearer by the end of the 10th/16th century. It did not last for long, however, as Ottoman architectural features gradually started to appear in the architecture of Jerusalem and Palestine at large.

Cylinder minarets replaced the rectangular Mamluk ones, the Ottoman *naskhi* and *nasta'liq* scripts appeared on buildings while the façades or sidewalls were dressed in ceramic tiles, especially in the *mihrab* area. New ornaments and designs appeared, such as circular stone studs of geometric and vegetal motifs on the buildings' façades. The Ottomans also built shallow domes instead of the lofty Mamluk ones and front porches with colonnades and arches. New structural forms appeared such as Sultan Sulayman the Magnificent's wall fountains and *khalwa*s that were built on the platform of the Dome of the Rock.

And yet there are some characteristics that distinguish Palestinian architecture from that in Egypt and Syria. Most of the buildings are smaller and less ornamented than those in Cairo, Aleppo and other Egyptian and Syrian cities (except for during the Umayyad period). In addition, some lack any of the contemporary Islamic architectural characteristics that can be seen in other cities. Being a small territory, situated between civilisations and large countries that played a role in shaping history, Palestine preserved its local character while at the same time it submitted to the artistic influences of neighbouring countries. This explains why many architectural characteristics and ornaments in Palestine find their origin in Cairo, Damascus and Aleppo.

Another phenomenon seen in Islamic architecture in Palestine is the recycling of building materials and artistic ornaments, which can be seen clearly in the re-use of masonry, marble inlays, columns and their capitals and other *spolia*; sometimes a whole structure would be reconstructed and re-used.

Palestine's religious importance within Islam, along with the significanct cultural influence of cities such as Jerusalem and Hebron, has contributed to giving the architecture of Palestine a special character. The edifices in Jerusalem and Hebron are different from those in Cairo, Damascus, Aleppo and even Nablus and Gaza. Both the Haram al-Sharif in Jerusalem, and the Haram al-Ibrahimi in Hebron, have influenced the development of architecture in these cities and contributed to the increase in the construction of religious and charitable institutions.

This resulted in a concentration of buildings in one part of the city and in sacrificing the basic Mamluk architectural plan, especially in Jerusalem, in order to be as close as possible to the Haram al-Sharif. The architect had to adapt the building to the specified area, resulting in the appearance of multistorey buildings and annexes. Unlike in Cairo and other Egyptian and Syrian cities, a four-façade building is rarely seen in Jerusalem. Its mild climate and religious importance attracted a large number of Mamluk princes and idles to it. The city bloomed with construction projects, which had a *sufi* and pious character. The number of visitors continuously increased, hence many hos-

Ceramic bowl from the Umayyad palace of Khirbat al-Mafjar in Jericho, Rockefeller Museum in Jerusalem (47-4920) (© Sonia Halliday Photographs, photograph: D. Silverman, courtesy of the Israeli Antiquities Authority).

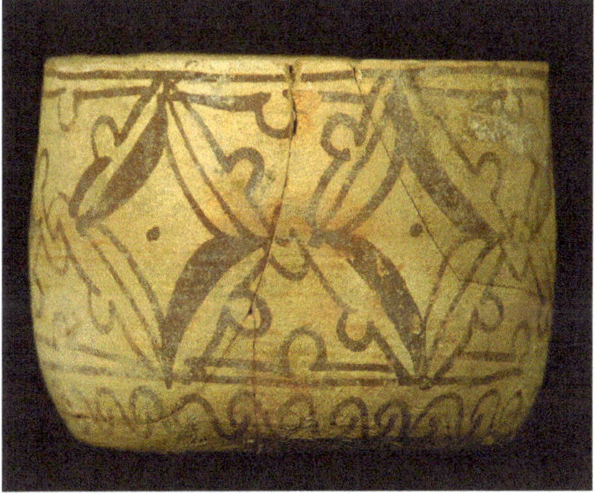

pices and *caravanserais* were built. Islamic architecture in Palestine finally blended with local traditions that had prevailed in the country prior to Islam, with the different schools that had developed in Egypt and Syria.

The Applied Arts

Minor (or applied) arts also prospered in Palestine through support of various ruling families. Among them were metal, wood, pottery, mosaic and glassware, decorative work on the Holy Qur'an and ornamental manuscripts. They all reflected the artistic currents that prevailed there, and in neighbouring countries such as Egypt, Syria and Turkey. The earliest Islamic ornamentatal style is found in the Dome of the Rock. Dating back to the Umayyad period, it made a huge impact on the development of Islamic art and is the first example to reflect its coherence.

Mosaics

No other Umayyad mosaic equals those found in Palestine. The Dome of the Rock, the Aqsa Mosque and Hisham's Palace in Jericho has the greatest share of them. The Great Umayyad Mosque in Damascus, some of Syria's Umayyad mosques and the "desert palaces" in Jordan complement them. This tradition continued in Palestine until the Fatimid period. Spiritual purity characterises these mosaics, which reflect the Syrian-Arab style that was influenced by the Byzantine style. However, mosaic art in Palestine and Syria took a different direction from the Byzantine school. It depended on decorative elements taken from nature and on geometric motifs such as palm trees, acanthus and grape leaves, scrolls, pine cones, circles, squares, triangles, pointed stars, straight, diagonal and undulating lines, straps of undotted *kufic* calligraphy, flowers, petals and grains. These deco-

Ceramic oil lamps from the Umayyad palace of Khirbat al-Mafjar in Jericho, Rockerfeller Museum in Jerusalem (39-402, 40-1402, 43-208) (© Sonia Halliday Photographs, photograph: D. Silverman, courtesy of the Israeli Antiquities Authority).

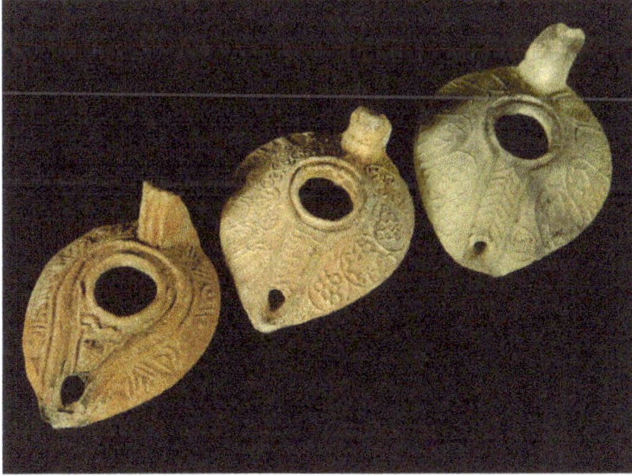

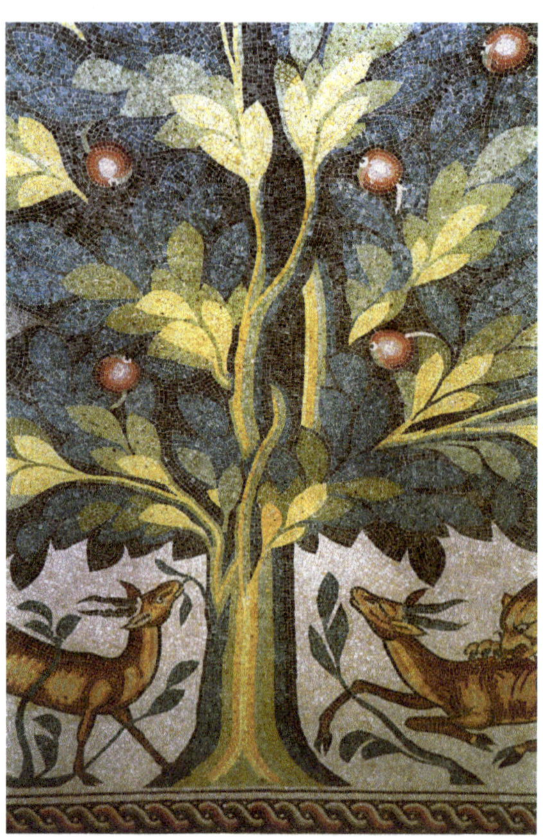

Khirbat al-Mafjar, mosaic floor near the baths of the palace, detail, Jericho (© Sonia Halliday Photographs, photograph: D. Silverman).

rative elements depended on symmetry and opposition. Dark green was used as the background, while gold was used to harmonise the colours and the decorative elements, and to highlight their differences. Many studies have been carried out on them. Some saw in them a representation of paradise as described in the Qur'an, others saw in them abstract decorative motifs, while others read into them political symbolism.

Wood Carving

Wood carving developed in Palestine during the Umayyad period and continued until the Ottoman period. The woodwork seen in the Aqsa Mosque, the Islamic Museum in the Haram al-Sharif and the Palestine (Rockefeller) Archaeological Museum in Jerusalem shows its importance from both functional and decorative aspects. Wood was (and still is) a basic building material in Palestine. It was initially used to support ceilings and make doors, windows and *mashrabiyya*s, an important characteristic in Islamic architecture.

The world's oldest surviving wooden frame is the inner dome of the Dome of the Rock, which dates back to the Fatimid period. The Dome of the Rock consists of two domes with a gap of approximately 1.5 m. separating the inner dome from the outer. Both were built of wood, but the outer one was removed during the renovations of the1960s. Even the fence that surrounds the Rock is made of wood and dates back to the Ayyubid period.

Many of the doors of the Aqsa Mosque, the Dome of the Rock and the gates to the Haram al-Sharif are made of wood and date back to either the Mamluk or the Ottoman periods. Some remarkable Mamluk models can be seen in the Islamic Museum. Many of the wooden beams have calligraphic inscriptions on them that date back to the Mamluk period. The most outstanding pieces of art, however, are the lavishly carved and contoured wooden panels that are made of cypress wood and fixed to the two lower parts of the Aqsa Mosque's pillars. The *mihrab*'s upper part consists of radiant conches. Its arch rests on two columns decorated in linear, spiral or diagonal indentation, laurel and acanthus leaves, vegetal fruits such as palm, grape and pomegranate leaves, baskets and vases. These elements find their origin in Hellenistic woodcrafts, though they were modified in the Umayyad period.

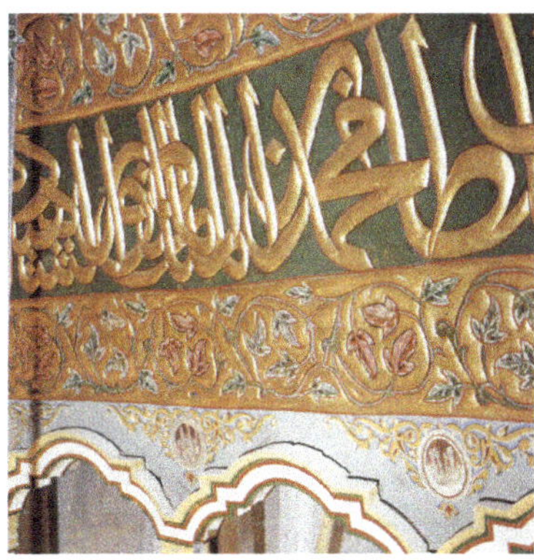

The Dome of the Rock, base of the cupola and detail of the decoration: Arabic inscription of a passage from the Qur'an, Haram al-Sharif, Jerusalem (© A. F. Kersting).

Calligraphy and Inscriptions

The art of calligraphy and engraving inscriptions on stone, marble, wood and metal rate amongst the other famous Islamic arts in Palestine. There is hardly a city in Palestine that does not have such a heritage, reflecting the different periods under which it developed. The most remarkable ones are found in Jerusalem and Hebron. A century ago, the Swiss epigraphy scholar Max van Bershem dedicated six volumes to record the bulk of Arabic inscriptions found in Jerusalem.

In addition to their aesthetic and artistic value and the information they provide on Arabic calligraphy and epigraphy in Palestine and the Islamic world at large, the inscriptions reveal important historical information about the building and the objects they decorate. The inscriptions on the Dome of the Rock are of special importance as they represent the earliest prototype of Islamic epigraphy and scripts. These include a variety of styles, such as *kufic*, *naskhi*, *thuluth*, *nasta'liq* and *diwani* examples. The styles of script also varied between prose and rhymed poetry. They included lines from prayers, names of rulers and information on the work of art and its theme. The characters of the *kufic* script were initially without dots. However, later on the text began to be dotted, vocalised and even decorated. At times the letters were deeply set and raised at others. Even though most have been studied, occasionally new discoveries shed further light on the architectural and artistic history of Palestine.

The writing of the various versions of the Qur'an on paper or deer scrolls represented another outstanding artistic achievement. Due to its sacred and prestigious position in Islam, devout Muslim artists made their own versions of the Qur'an. They would first cut the paper to the required size, which could fall anywhere between a few centimetres and more than a metre. For example the size of Barsbay's Qur'an in the Islamic Museum, which was dedicated to the Aqsa Mosque in 221/835-836, is 110 cm. × 190 cm. Then came the turn of the calligrapher, followed by the checker who proofread every letter, word, pause and vowel. Then the decorator paid special attention to the beginnings of every *Sura* and the divisions between the chapters.

The most important parts were the *Fatiha,* the opening chapter of the Qur'an and the beginning of a manuscript. Here the artist would demonstrate his talent to the full through his use of geometric and vegetal ornaments. After the decorator, the gilder painted specific parts of the Qur'an in gold. Finally came the turn of the binder, who secured the Qur'an between two strong, impressively decorated leather covers. Furthermore, the best quality black ink was used for writing, with red and white ink occasionally being used for punctuation. Different scripts were applied, such as *kufic*, *naskhi*, *ta'liq*, *nasta'liq*, *maghribi-andalousi*, *farsi*, *thuluth* and *ruq'a.*

Until recently, the copies were endowed for mosques, charitable and *sufi* institutions, and the scholastic buildings to which they were dedicated. However, with the advent of printing, these religious masterpieces were moved to museums. The Islamic Museum has a valuable collection of Qur'ans, and on some of them the Persian translation is found alongside the Arabic text. Some of their pages also have some valuable historical information on the calligrapher, the owner of the Qur'an, its readers and the date on which it was completed, in addition to some prayer lines such as *"God forgives all who have read in it"*. The rulers or sultans of the time would commission copies of the Qur'an, which they would dedicate to mosques and scientific centres.

Ornamental Tiles

Another prominent art form in Palestine was the production of ornamental tiles, especially ceramic *qashani* tiles. These were named after the Iranian city of Qashan, from which this art spread to other parts of the Islamic world such as Bursa, Iznik and Kütahya in Turkey. Many skilled craftsmen from these cities came to Jerusalem during the Ottoman period and succeeded in establishing the craft in Palestine, in particular to cater for the needs of the Dome of the Rock. Examples of this art can still be seen today in the markets of Jerusalem, Hebron and Jericho, where tiles, plates, pitchers and glasses have become a key attraction for tourists in Palestine. Their themes extend beyond the old Islamic ones to Christian concepts such as the miracle of the multiplication of the loaves and fishes at Tiberias and pictures of the Church of the Nativity.

Ceramic art first appeared in Palestine in the $10^{th}/16^{th}$ century through Sultan Sulayman the Magnificent who commissioned the renovation of the Dome of the Rock. Its external mosaics had been largely damaged, so Sultan Sulayman ordered their replacement with a beautiful coating of *qashani* tiles. This later extended to most mosques, where entrances and *mihrabs* were covered with decorated tiles. Most of the tiles exhibited in the Islamic Museum and the Dome of the Rock date back seven periods, the oldest of which belong to the 9th/15th–10th/16th centuries, while the most recent ones date back to 1964.

While the colours varied between dark blue, turquoise, yellow, green, black, red and white, the decorations were geometric, vegetal or calligraphic. The most famous calligraphy is that found on the top of the Dome's external octagon upon which Muhammad Shafiq inscribed the Qur'anic Sura of *Ya Sin* in 1292/1874.

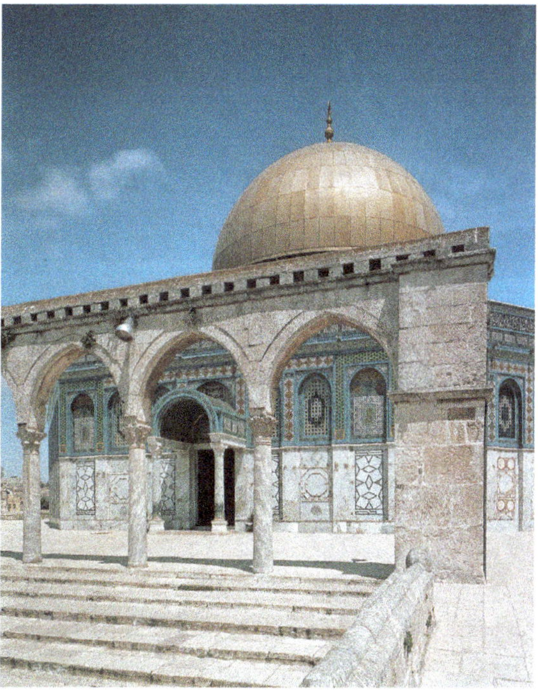

The Dome of the Rock, main entrance, Haram al-Sharif (© A. F. Kersting).

Window Construction and Stucco Work

Stucco window construction and decoration were exemplary in Palestine and dated back to the early Islamic period, the most famous of which is the Abbasid "Samarra" style. It is believed that this type of work first appeared in Palestine's Umayyad period during the building of the Dome of the Rock and the Aqsa Mosque. The co-ordination of the windows was an important part of the planning process ensuring natural light and ventilation were provided. The shapes of the windows were square, rectangular, linear and circular. If the window was close to street level, it had beautifully decorated grills for protection. If, on the other hand, the window was high above ground level it was heavily adorned with plaster decorations. This style continued in Jerusalem until the Mamluk period and is still followed today by skilful local craftsmen in the workshop of the Aqsa mosque.

The structure of these windows is breathtaking – especially when looked at while the sun is shining through them and its beams take on the colour of the minute glass pieces that decorate the background. Examples can be seen in

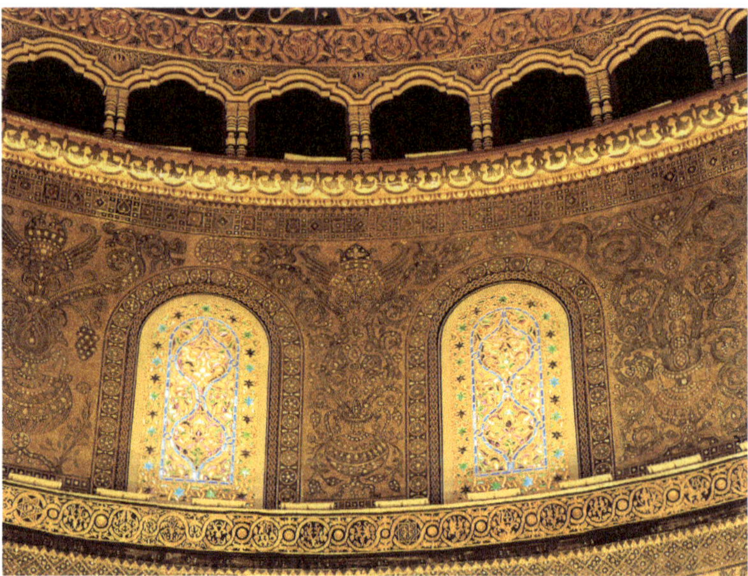

The Dome of the Rock, cupola, detail of the tambour, windows decorated with stucco encrusted with coloured glass, Haram al-Sharif, Jerusalem.

the drum of the Dome of the Rock, the upper part of the Aqsa Mosque's southern walls, the Islamic Museum and in many buildings scattered throughout Palestine.

Manufacturing the windows requires patience, talent and a number of other skills. The first phase starts with laying out the window frame, making a strong wooden cast of it, and then placing it on a flat secure surface. The plaster is then mixed and poured into the cast (which is usually circular or rectangular and ends in a semicircular arch) and this is left to set.

The second stage begins by drawing the ornaments that will decorate the window; usually this consists of delicate vegetal ornaments and geometrical forms. These in turn will often be accompanied by calligraphy of beautiful interlaced characters that quote Qur'anic verses or prayer phrases. The date on which the window was completed or renovated will also be inscribed.

The next stage is the most delicate as the plaster is carved and sculpted into the required form. As the window will be few metres above ground and eye level, the carving has to be tilted, otherwise the ornament cannot be seen and the penetration of light into the centre of the building will be obstructed. Very delicate and minute tools are used for this process. Any slight mistake would mean that a new mould has to be made.

Then comes the last phase when small pieces of glass are fitted as a background behind the plaster decorations. The artist's skill appears when he gives each decorative unit a specific colour to help the onlooker easily follow the overlapping and intertwining units. Making a window of 1.40 m. × 3.50 m. would usually take four to six months.

Coinage

Minting and circulating coins were among the artistic manifestations that had political, cultural and economic implications. This started in the early Umayyad period in Palestine, and more than 15 mints have been found in Jerusalem, Ramla, Tiberias, Bisan, Safuriyya, Asqalan, Gaza and Lydda. These centres provided the local markets and those in Syria with a large number of copper and bronze coins. Minting continued in Palestine in the Abbasid period and during al-Ma'mun's reign (198/813–218/833) Jerusalem became an important coin-minting centre. In the Tulunid period, golden *dinars* were produced, while in the Ikhshidid, Qarmatian and Fatimid periods both silver and golden *dinars* were minted. Qur'anic verses and religious quotations were engraved on them such as *"There is no God but Allah, Muhammad is His messenger"*. Also the name of the ruler in whose reign the coin was struck would be inscribed.

Despite their small size, the coins had what is now very important historical information inscribed on them. The minting technique and the writings on the coins reflected an advanced level of carving, inscription and artistic work and highlighted the sophistication of Islamic art in Palestine. This can be seen in the many coins of these eras that are exhibited in various international and local museums.

A large number of priceless manuscripts, metalwork and glassware, magnificent carpets and textiles, locally embroidered garments and local folk art – such as Hebron glassware, Gaza pottery work, conches and olivewood work – are also found in Palestine. Visitors will find many samples of them while wandering in the markets and shops of Jerusalem and Bethlehem, Hebron, Gaza and Nablus. They all testify to the rich architectural and artistic history of Palestine.

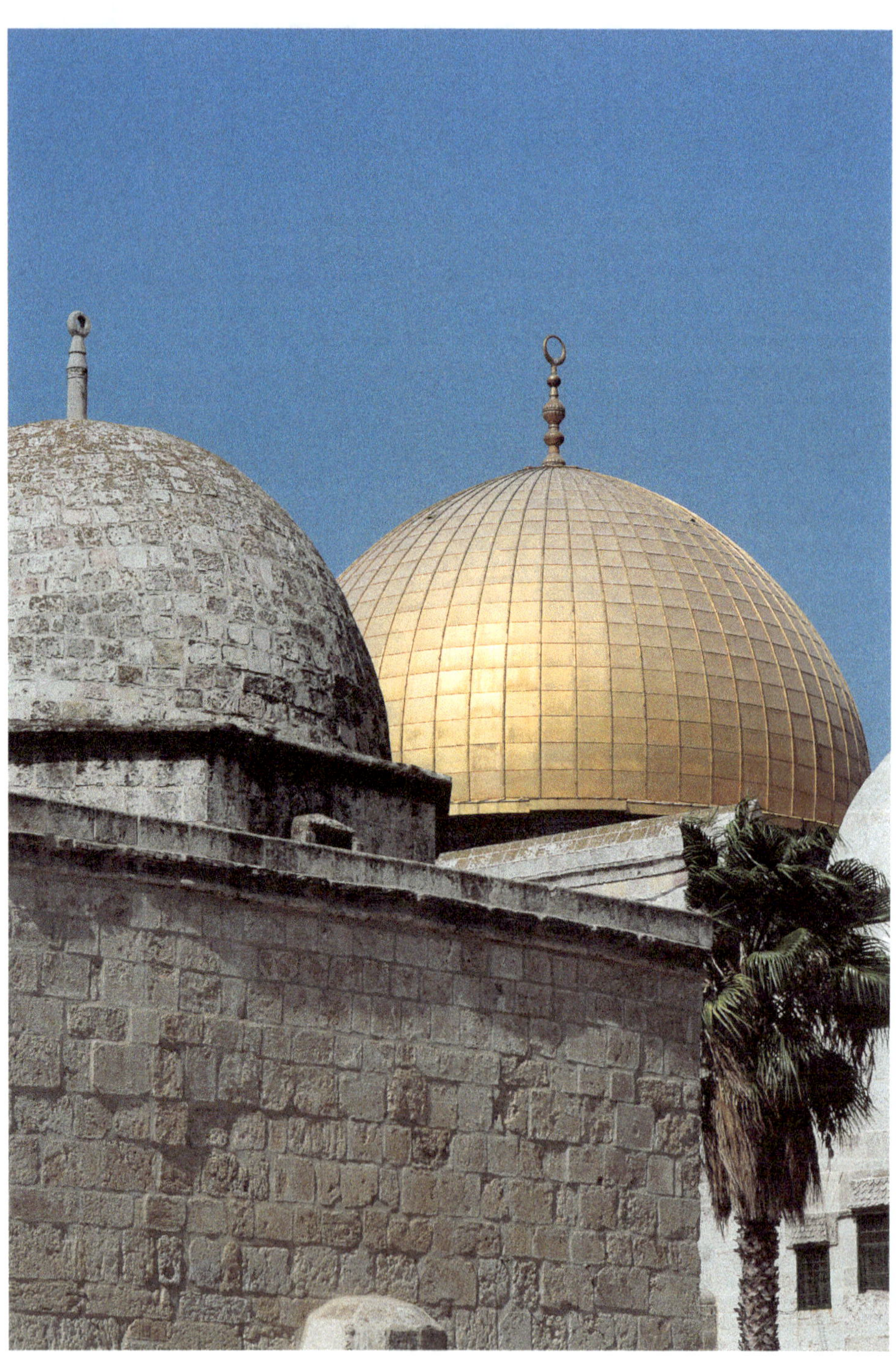

Jerusalem and the Haram al-Sharif: the *Qibla* of Palestine

Yusuf Natsheh, Mahmoud Hawari

I.1 THE HARAM AL-SHARIF

I.1.a The Islamic Museum
I.1.b The Aqsa Mosque
I.1.c The Dome of the Rock
I.1.d Golden Gate (Bab al-Rahma and Bab al-Tawba)
I.1.e North-Western Khalwa of Ahmad Pasha
I.1.f Mihrab of the Mastaba of 'Ali Pasha
I.1.g Sabil Qaytbay
I.1.h Qubba al-Nahawiyya
I.1.i Madrasa al-Ashrafiyya
I.1.j The Citadel (option)

The Manuscripts of the Aqsa Mosque Library
Water Systems of the Haram al-Sharif

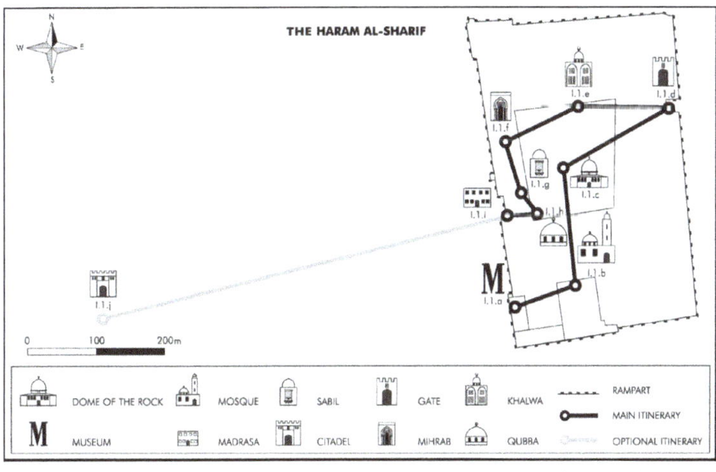

The Dome of the Rock, view from the south-west between Qubba al-Nahawiyya and the Qur'anic school, Haram al-Sharif, Jerusalem.

Jerusalem is one of the holiest cities of all, a religious hearth for Jews, Christians and Muslims alike. The city is loved, venerated and cherished by millions all over the world and throughout its history it has witnessed prosperity, acclaim, devastation and destruction.
Archaeological remains indicate that settlement in this area dates back to the Chalcolithic and the early Stone Age (around 5th and 4th millennium BC). The nucleus of the current city, lying in the village of Silwan to the south of the Haram al-Sharif, was originally founded by the Canaanites (about 2000 BC) who chose its location close to the only spring in the area.
The city grew and developed through various periods. Lying between the Nile and Euphrates Valleys, between great conflicting empires, and having been prone to the wavering loyalty of its local rulers, it was subjected to many foreign invasions. This explains the diversity of its social, racial and religious fabric.
Jerusalem was subjected to one foreign power after another. First came Nebukhadnezzar, the leader of the new Babylonian Empire, who sacked the city in 587 BC. Then after conquering Babylon, Cyrus the Great of Persia ordered in 538 BC the reconstruction of the Temple of Jerusalem and authorised the Jews to return to the Land of Judaea. Alexander the Great then conquered it in 332 BC, followed by his successors the Ptolemaics and Seleucids and, finally the Romans in 63 BC. During the Greek and Roman periods, Hellenistic culture dominated all aspects of life in Jerusalem. A conflict resulted between the symbols and supporters of the pagan civilisation and the local Jewish inhabitants and rulers.
As a consequence of the two Jewish revolts against Rome (66-70 and 132-135), the Jews were not allowed back into Jerusalem. Christians having pagan – but not-Jewish – origin did, however, live in Jerusalem as of the 2nd Century. With the Edict of Tolerance of Milan in 313, and then the Council of Nicée in 325, Jerusalem became increasingly established as a centre of Christianity, and remained so during the entire Byzantine period. The Christian period saw the construction of a number of churches and regular pilgrimages began to the Holy Land and Jerusalem.
The Arab Muslims prided themselves on the fact that Jerusalem was conquered peacefully by 'Umar Ibn al-Khattab in 15/638. He signed a treaty that guaranteed peace and protection to all its Christian inhabitants and their possessions. The Muslim supremacy continued for almost 14 centuries and was only interrupted by the Crusader rule between 492/1099 and 583/1187. The task of developing the city – and the Haram al-Sharif in particular – fell upon the shoulders of the different Islamic dynasties that ruled it, namely the Umayyads, Fatimids, Ayyubids, Mamluks and Ottomans. Tolerance was the dominant spirit during their rule and so most Christian communities continued to live there. In addition the Jews were allowed to return and live in it, as they had previously been expelled from the city.
Being the third holiest city to Islam after Mecca and Medina, the Muslims spared no effort or money in developing and

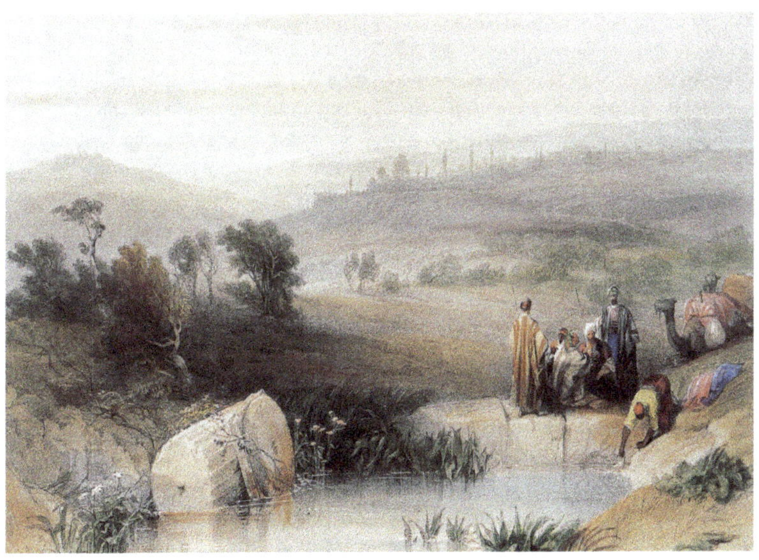

Jerusalem, general view from the north, lithograph by D. Roberts (© Victoria & Albert Museum, London).

embellishing the city, especially the Haram al-Sharif. Mosques, *madrasas*, *zawiyas*, *khanqas*, *caravanserais*, commemorative domes, mausoleums, fountains, baths and markets were built. Hence, Jerusalem was turned into one of the most beautiful medieval cities, rich in its religious, cultural, social and artistic foundations. The Dome of the Rock, which was built during the Umayyad period, is considered a masterpiece in art and is one of the most important Islamic monuments. The Old City of Jerusalem is one of the few Islamic cities to have preserved its medieval character. It is, metaphorically, an unique architectural museum full of splendid Islamic and non-Islamic buildings.

Apart from the Dome of the Rock, the Aqsa Mosque and other buildings that date back to the Umayyad period, most buildings in Jerusalem belong to the post-Crusader period, especially the Mamluk era (658/1260-992/1517). The Mamluk sultans and *amirs* paid particular attention to the city and built tens of religious, scientific and commercial edifices. They endowed generous *waqfs* to guarantee the upkeep of these foundations. The building activity of the period definitely reflected the city's religious significance, whether as a centre of pilgrimage or as a centre of Islamic thought – particularly when it came to Sufism.

Y.N.

I.1 THE HARAM AL-SHARIF

Lies south-east of the Old City of Jerusalem and occupies almost one-sixth of its area; its south-

ern and eastern walls are part of the city's wall. Non-Muslims can enter it through the Bab Maghariba only. Some security measures precede entrance to the Haram and might occasionally take some time. The visitor can exit through any of the gates. Entering the Haram al-Sharif is free, but an entrance fee is charged for visiting the Dome of the Rock, the Aqsa Mosque and the Islamic Museum. Tickets can be purchased with local currency from the kiosk outside the Islamic Museum, and are valid only on the day of purchase. Photography is allowed in the Haram*'s courtyards, but not inside the Museum, the Aqsa Mosque or the Dome of the Rock (unless permission is granted by the Department of Islamic Affairs/al-Awqaf. Prior to entering the Aqsa Mosque and the Dome of the Rock, visitors are expected to remove their shoes and leave bags and cameras outside at their own risk.*

The Haram's layout is rectangular. Ten gates in its western and northern walls lead into it in the following order: Bab al-Maghariba (Gate of the Maghribi), Bab al-Silsila (Gate of the Chain), Bab al-Mathara (Gate of Ablution), Bab Suq al-Qattanin (Gate of the Cotton Merchants), Bab al-Hadid (Gate of Iron), Bab al-Nadir (Gate of the Inspector) and Bab al-Ghawanima (Gate of the Ghawanima tribe) on the north-western corner of the Haram, from the north, Bab al-'Atm (Gate of Darkness), Bab al-Hitta (Gate of Forgiveness) and Bab al-Asbat (Gate of the Lions). All the gates on the eastern and western walls are blocked up and not in use. Most of these gates date to the Mamluk period and were probably built above the foundations of earlier Umayyad and Roman gates.

The Haram al-Sharif is of great significance to Islam. It is mentioned in the Qur'an as the site from which the Prophet Muhammad made his nocturnal ascension to heaven. The first *qibla* in Islam, it is the location from where the resurrection will take place, and, not least, it is the city that the Prophet Muhammad put on an equal footing with Mecca and Medina. In addition to this, it is the jewel in the crown of Jerusalem's architectural and artistic accomplishments. Being the most important site in the Old City, the Haram al-Sharif has also given Jerusalem its sacredness and place in history.

The historical development of Jerusalem has been closely linked to that of the Haram al-Sharif. Its current structure, appearance and divinity are the result of a long historical and architectural development that took place during the reigns of several different dynasties.

After the destruction of Jerusalem in AD 70, and the second Jewish revolt (132–135), the Romans reconstructed the city like a pagan city – named *Colonia Aelia Capitolina* – and erected a temple dedicated to Jupiter Capitolinus. Then, in the Islamic period 'Umar Ibn al-Khattab, and later the Caliph 'Abd al-Malik Ibn Marwan, rebuilt the city and the Haram al-Sharif.

The construction boom continued throughout the period of Islamic rule, especially during the Ayyubid Dynasty (583/1187–648/1250) when the city underwent complete rehabilitation after nine decades of Crusader rule. Islam was reintroduced, the Haram al-Sharif was developed and the Aqsa Mosque and the

Dome of the Rock were renovated. The Mamluks (648/1250–922/1517) developed the area adjacent to the north and west borders of the Haram by building *madrasas* and *zawiyas* in addition to vital projects such as the water supply. They dug cisterns and built fountains. The Ottomans (922/1517–1336/1917) further developed the Haram, particularly the area surrounding the platform of the Dome of the Rock.

The Haram al-Sharif contains many architectural monuments that represent all Islamic dynasties and visiting them all would require a lot of time. Therefore special attention has been paid to ensure that the selected sights in this itinerary will present the most distinguished Islamic edifices and dynasties and reflect the various functions and styles of the buildings themselves.

Y.N.

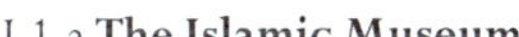

I.1.a The Islamic Museum

Lies in the south-west corner of the esplanade. Opening hours: mornings 08.00–11.00 and 13.00–14.00 except Fridays and public holidays. During the month of Ramadan, it is open during the morning only. The esplanade is closed during prayer times, which vary slightly according to the season, but usually between 11.00–12.30 and 14.00–15.00.

The Islamic Museum was established in 1341/1923 and is considered to be one of the first museums in Jerusalem. It displays treasures that have been either donated or moved there from the buildings of the Haram al-Sharif after it was renovated, in order that the maximum number of visitors could see them. Most of the artefacts represent the heritage of the Haram, Jerusalem and Palestine at large.

The museum consists of two main halls. The first, running vertically from north

Al-Rub'a al-Maghribiyya, double frontispiece, Islamic Museum, Haram al-Sharif, Jerusalem.

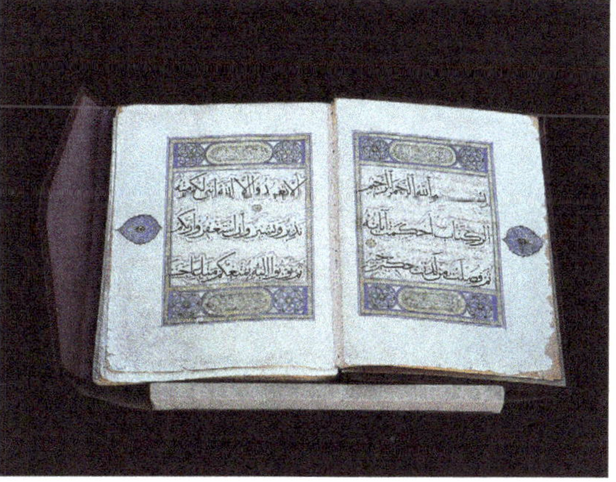

Al-Rub'a al-Maghribiyya, beginning of each chapter of the Qur'an, Islamic Museum, Haram al-Sharif, Jerusalem.

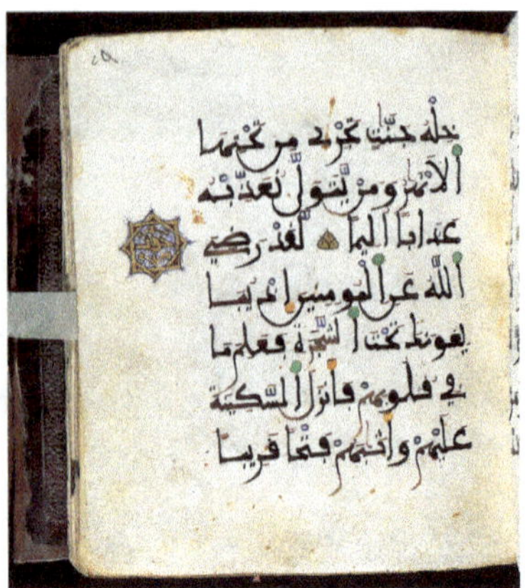

Al-Rub'a al-Maghribiyya, folio in which different colours are used sharing the vocalic and punctuation signs, Islamic Museum, Haram al-Sharif, Jerusalem.

to south, was an Ayyubid mosque. The second, stretching from west to east, dates back to the Crusader times. It holds a rare collection of Umayyad woodwork, the remains of Nur al-Din's *minbar* (al-Aqsa *minbar*), which was damaged by fire in 1969, a unique collection of Mamluk manuscripts and Qur'ans, an assortment of marble, metalwork and decorated tiles. We will pay special attention to the Moroccan Qur'an also known as al-Rub'a al-Maghribiya.

Y.N.

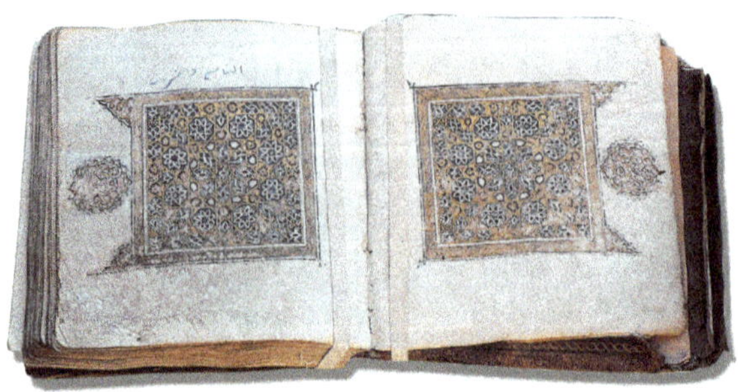

Al-Rub'a al-Maghribiyya, double frontispiece, Islamic Museum, Haram al-Sharif, Jerusalem.

The Moroccan Qur'an

The Islamic Museum holds a priceless collection of Qur'ans, the most important of which is the hand-written Moroccan Qur'an. It consists of 30 volumes written in the *Maghribi* script, which is similar to the *kufic* script in that the latter has acute angles while the former has softer letters. As certified in the last two pages of every volume, 'Abd Allah 'Ali Ibn 'Abd al-Haqq, the King of Morocco, wrote the volumes in Fez (745/1345) and endowed them in a *waqf* to the Aqsa Mosque. This Holy Qur'an is the most splendid among all those that were endowed to the Aqsa Mosque in the 8th/14th century. All its volumes were written on deer scrolls and bound in thick leather, also made of deer scrolls.

Geometric and calligraphic ornaments adorn both sides of the cover. Each side is enveloped in a band made of gold and silver threads that intertwine with another pair of silver threads, inside of which the name of the volume's writer is inscribed. In the middle are two silver circles that share the same centre. On the cover of this volume is a roundel within which is the following Qur'anic quote: *"This is a message and warning from God that there is only one God, and let their minds guide them to Him"*. The roundel on the reverse contains the following quote: *"Whoever replaces God's word with other words has sinned. God knows and hears all"*.

The first two pages of every volume contain intertwined geometric ornaments placed within a square frame. These are in turn filled with vegetal decorations in gold, dark red, blue, white and black. A vegetal ornament is found on the two external angles of every square on each page. In the middle, a tree and golden leaves are seen demarcated in black and shaded in dark red with its borders outlined in blue. On the next page lies a decorated rectangle, inside of which (on a white background) are written the name of the *Sura* and the number of its verses in a golden *kufic* script, punctuated in dark red.

The writing is dark brown and punctuated in different colours: green refers to *hamzat al-wasl*; orange to *hamzat al-qat'*, the *shadda* and the *sukun* are in blue, and the red is used for vowel points. The dot on the letter *fa* is placed in brown under the letter, while the dots on the letters *qaf* are placed above the word in brown. Pause marks are indicated by fir-cones divided into three parts, and punctuated with red points. The name of the *Sura* and the numbers of its verses are written in a gold *kufic* font that ends in a vegetal decoration similar to the one described previously. At the end of the verses of every volume a golden rectangle is found, within which gold *kufic* calligraphy is set on a white background and decorated with different ornaments.

The end of each volume is announced, on the last two pages, by two gilded squares that surround the gilded Maghribi calligraphy: this is where the name of the king appears who transcribed it and who bequeathed it, and also the date on which the copy was finished.

M.H.

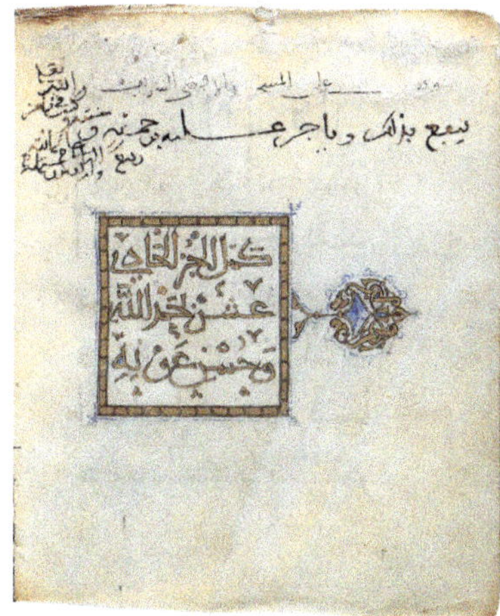

Al-Rub'a al-Maghribiyya, last folio of volume 11, Islamic Museum, Haram al-Sharif, Jerusalem.

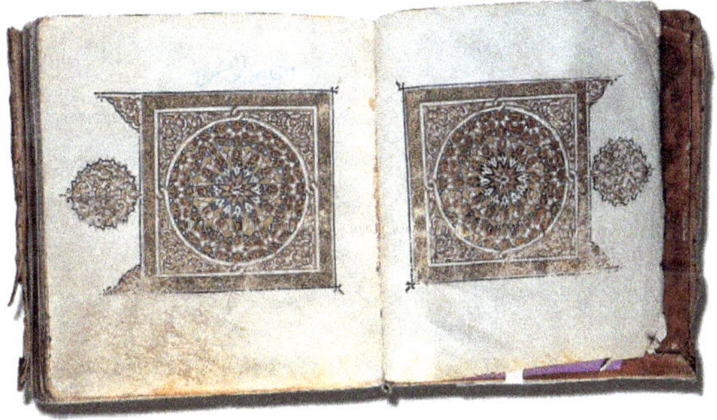

Al-Rub'a al-Maghribiyya, double frontispiece, Islamic Museum, Haram al-Sharif, Jerusalem.

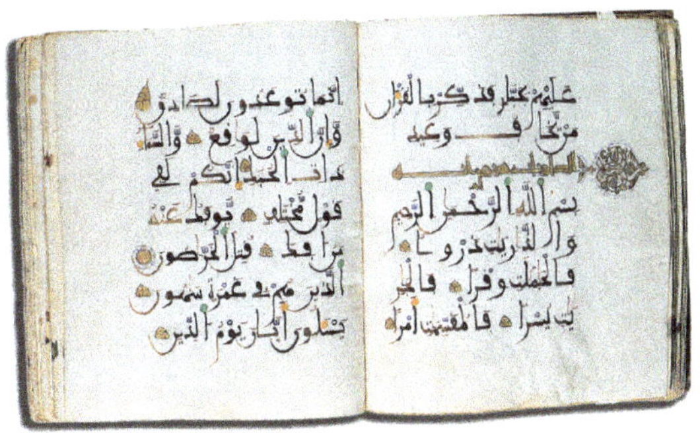

Al-Rub'a al-Maghribiyya, folio in which different colours are used sharing the vocalic and punctuation signs, Islamic Museum, Haram al-Sharif, Jerusalem.

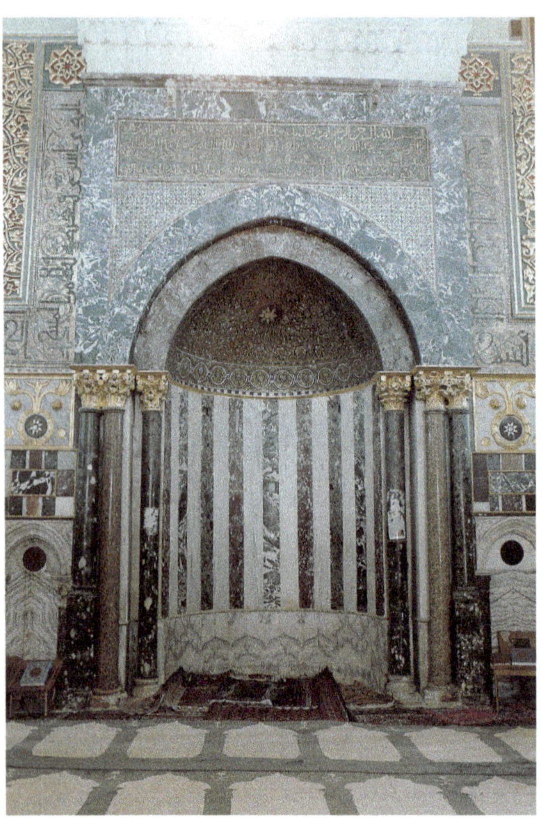

Al-Aqsa Mosque, mihrab, Haram al-Sharif, Jerusalem.

I.1.b The Aqsa Mosque

Situated in the centre of the southern part of the esplanade.
For opening hours, please refer to The Islamic Museum (I.1.a)

Contrary to opinion, the Aqsa Mosque does not cover the whole area of the Haram al-Sharif. Rather, it is the covered building parallel to the southern wall of the Haram. The current building is a result of many architectural developments, which began during Caliph 'Umar Ibn al-Khattab's reign. He had a humble mosque built on the site immediately after he conquered Jerusalem in 15/638 and visited the Haram, accompanied by the Patriarch, Safronius.

Nothing has survived of this mosque. However, huge efforts were made during the Umayyad period (65/685–96/715) to build the second Aqsa Mosque. Experts differ on who commissioned it, although some maintain that Caliph 'Abd al-Malik Ibn Marwan (65/685–86/705) – the patron of the Dome of the Rock, Qubbat al-Silsila Dome and many of the Haram's gates and walls – built it. Others attribute it to his son al-Walid (86/705–96/715), the builder of the Umayyad palaces that have recently been uncovered south of the Aqsa Mosque. Still others believe that the project started during 'Abd al-Malik's reign and was finished in al-Walid's.

The southern wall of the mosque is the only surviving Umayyad part. Here the topography of the mosque descends sharply towards the south, which required levelling the ground through columns and arches, thus creating a platform. Today, these underground structures are called the old Aqsa, and the Marwanid prayer place. Due to the fact that many earthquakes hit Jerusalem and Palestine after the Umayyad period, the mosque was rebuilt several times. The present mosque is a compendium of many restorations and reconstructions that were carried out during the Abassid and Fatimid periods. During the Crusader period, part of it was converted into a

church and a large recess was added that can still be seen today in the last aisle to the east, and part of the western division was used to house the knights.
The restoration of the mosque to Islamic use fell on the shoulders of the Ayyubid and Mamluk Dynasties. Saladin ordered the renovation of the *mihrab* and the addition of the *minbar* in 583/1187, while al-Nasir Muhammad Ibn Qalawun ordered the restoration of its dome in 728/1327–1328, as indicated by the commemorative inscription inscribed in it.
Attempts to obliterate the Islamic character of the mosque did not stop with the Crusaders. On 21 August 1969 a fanatical Australian tourist set light to the mosque causing considerable damage to its southern part. Even though his act was clearly prompted by racist ideology, the Israeli judiciary dismissed the charges of arson by diagnosing him a psychopath. As a result of all these changes, the mosque today is very different from its original layout, which was twice its current size.
The mosque is usually entered through its middle entrance portal, which is one of seven. Each of the portals leads to one of the mosque's seven aisles. These are preceded by seven openings each topped by a pointed arch, the largest of which is the central one. The building is rectangular in plan (80 m. × 55 m.) and consists of seven aisles or porticos that stretch from north to south, the widest of which is in the middle. This ends in a semicircular dome that lies in front of the *mihrab* and stands on four large pointed arches. Hollow semicircular recesses are found in the corners of the arches, which provide a

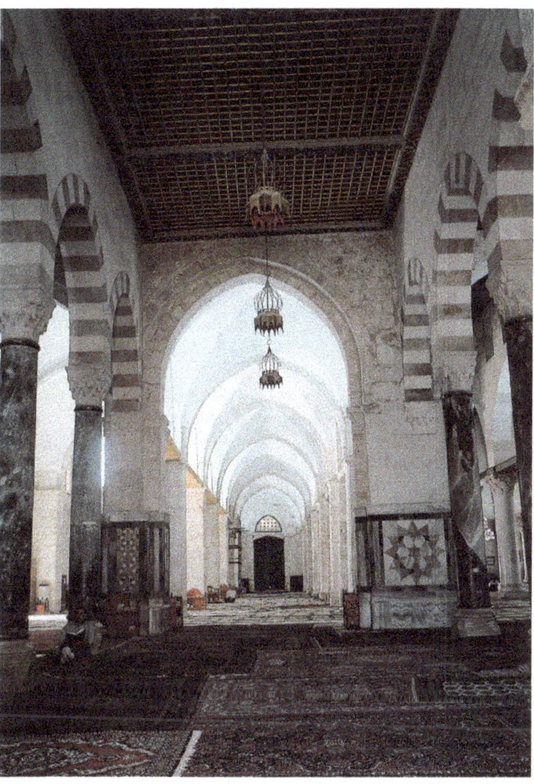

Al-Aqsa Mosque, nave, view towards the north, Haram al-Sharif, Jerusalem.

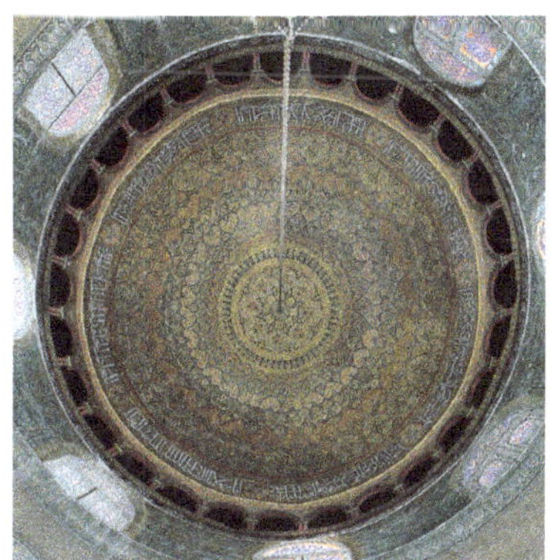

Al-Aqsa Mosque, cupola, Haram al-Sharif, Jerusalem.

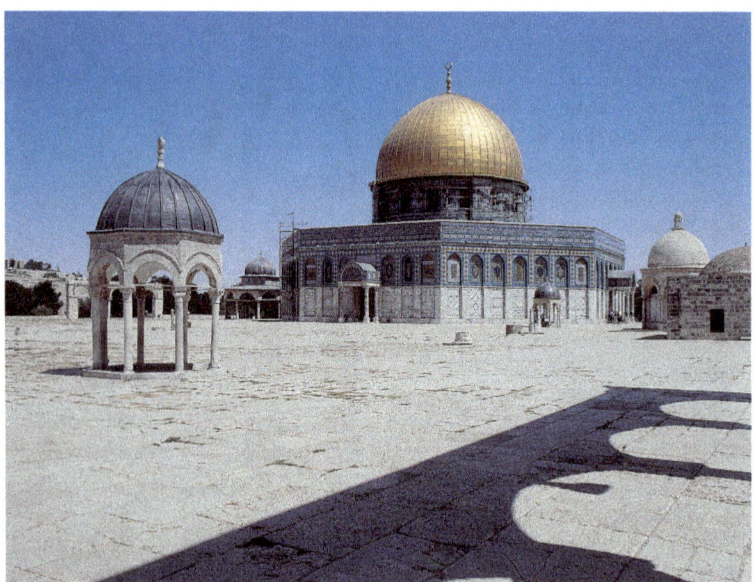

The Dome of the Rock, general view, Haram al-Sharif, Jerusalem.

transition from a square-plan to an octagon and then to a circular dome. The dome is decorated with vegetal, geometric and calligraphic ornaments.

Y.N.

I.1.c **The Dome of the Rock**

Lies in the centre of the Haram al-Sharif and is the jewel in the crown of both Jerusalem and Palestine.
For opening hours, please refer to the Islamic Museum (I.1.a).

The Dome of the Rock is one of the oldest and most unique Islamic buildings. Its symmetry and originality, distinguished ornaments and architecture, constitute a school of art in themselves that has received the attention of many scholars and experts throughout the ages. Many Muslim rulers maintained the structure of the Dome of the Rock throughout the Islamic periods. Restoration work has been carried out without tampering with its original plan or ornaments.

It was built on the rock from which Prophet Muhammad began his nocturnal journey to heaven, under the patronage of the Umayyad caliph 'Abd al-Malik Ibn Marwan in 72/691–692. The site, which was venerated and visited by the Muslims since the conquest of Jerusalem, prompted 'Abd al-Malik Ibn Marwan to build the dome we have today.

The structure of the Dome of the Rock is octagonal in plan and is covered by a semi-

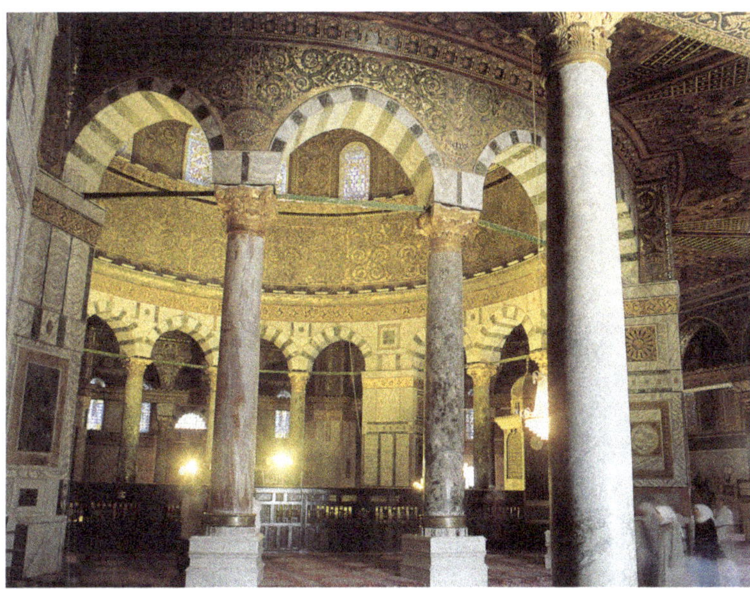
The Dome of the Rock, general view of the interior, Haram al-Sharif, Jerusalem.

circular dome supported by a circular drum. It has four doors, one facing each of the cardinal directions. The lower parts of the external walls are dressed in marble, while the upper parts are covered in ceramic tiles. The latter dates to the reign of Sultan Sulayman the Magnificent who ordered the replacement of the damaged mosaic ornaments between 952/1545 and 959/1552. Similar tiles cover the drum of the Dome. The external cement dome – which, until recently, was wooden (1385/1965) – is covered with brass and painted in gold. The space between the Dome and the external and middle octagon is covered by a wooden ceiling, which in turn is covered in lead from the outside, and decorated in colourful wooden ornaments from the inside.

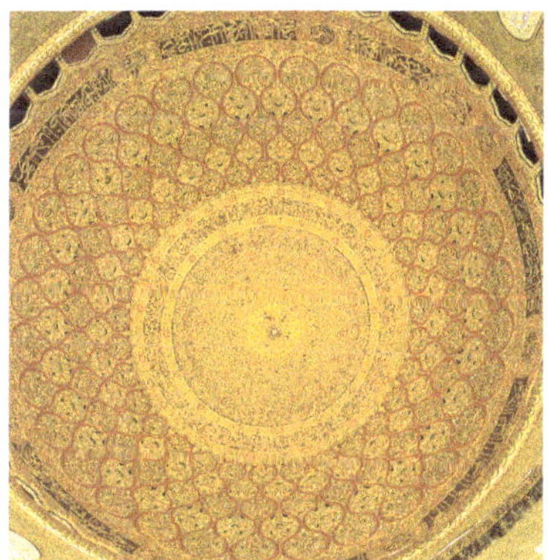
The Dome of the Rock, interior decoration of the cupola, Haram al-Sharif, Jerusalem.

The internal layout of the Dome consists of two octagons, interior and exterior, and both surround the rock on which the Dome is built. While eight pillars and 16 columns form the external octagon, four

The Dome of the Rock, detail of the arches holding up the cupola, Haram al-Sharif, Jerusalem.

The Golden Gate at sunrise, Haram al-Sharif, Jerusalem (© Sonia Halliday Photographs).

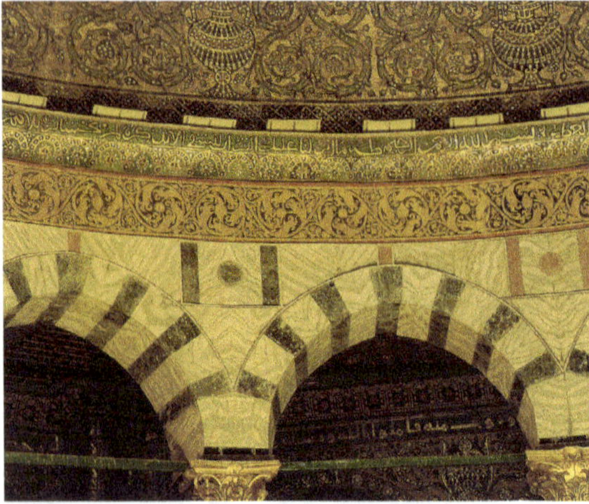

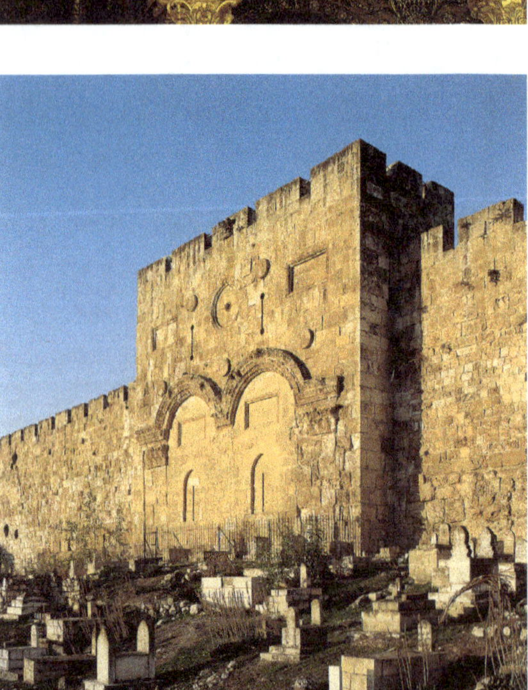

pillars and 12 columns form the internal one. The semicircular arches that connect them are decorated in a bright confection of mosaics and calligraphy. The internal wooden dome (20.44 m. in diameter) is considered to be the world's oldest surviving wooden frame and consists of decorated wooden plates laid on plaster. A space of approximately 1.5 m. separates the two domes and protects them from the effects of the weather. The Dome's circular drum has 16 windows and is decorated by a rich variety of mosaics with scroll motifs and Qur'anic verses.
The Rock lies at the bottom of the Dome and is a natural structure of irregular shape (18 × 13 × 1.5 m.). Below it is a square cave (4.5 × 4.5 m.) that has two *mihrabs*, one recessed and another flat. Many Muslims pray here in the belief that their prayers will be answered.

Y.N.

I.1.d. Golden Gate (Bab al-Rahma and Bab al-Tawba)

Lies in the centre of the Haram's eastern esplanade.
For opening hours, please refer to The Islamic Museum (I.1.a).
Visiting the site requires prior permission from the Islamic Waqf, Department of Islamic Affairs (tel: 02-628 1222).

The date of the gate is unknown. However, both its architecture and decoration indicates it was built during the reign of the fifth Umayyad Caliph, 'Abd al-Malik Ibn Marwan, who ordered a comprehen-

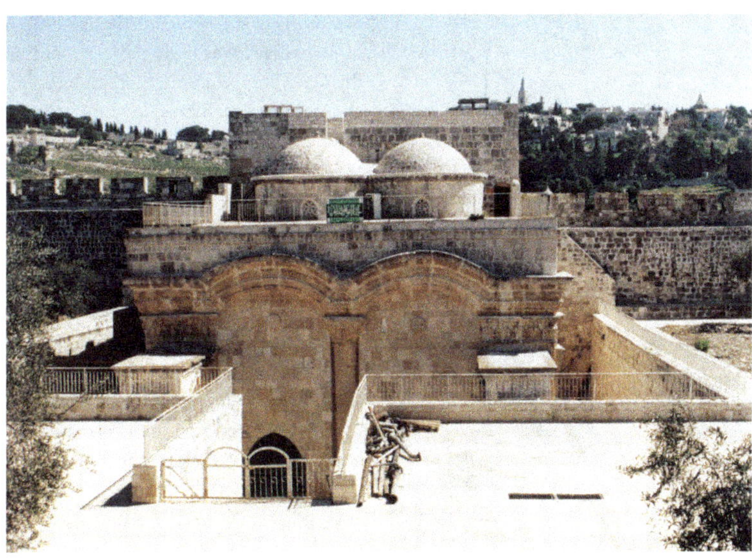

The Golden Gate, view from the west, Haram al-Sharif, Jerusalem.

sive plan to develop the Haram area. Among his projects was the Dome of the Rock, Qubbat al-Silsila (Dome of the Chain) and a number of the Haram's gates and walls.

Many legends surround the Golden Gate, a double gate formed from Bab al-Rahma (Gate of Mercy) and the Bab al-Tawba (Gate of Repentance). One says that when Emperor Heraclius reached the gate in 631, its stones fell in front of him and blocked his entrance. Only when he stood humble before did it open again. Even though this legend first appeared in 215/830, it continued throughout the medieval period. The Crusaders used to open the gate twice a year on Palm Sunday and at Easter, even though Christ entered the city on Palm Sunday from the Gate of Benjamin (known today as Bab al-Asbat). It is also widely believed that Emperor Heraclius entered the city through a gate over which the current gate is built, for recent excavations have uncovered the remains of the old gate below the current one. The gate is referred to in the West as the Golden Gate, a name derived from the Greek word *horaia* (beautiful) and the Latin word *aurea* (golden).

In Arab Islamic literary sources it is referred to as Bab al-Rahma (Gate of Mercy) and Bab al-Tawba (Gate of Repentance). The name is based on the interpretation of a Qur'anic verse (the 13th verse in the *Sura* of al-Hadid), which refers to a gate that leads into mercy (in other words, the Aqsa Mosque) while agony (the Henom Valley) stands outside to the east. No wonder then that the gate

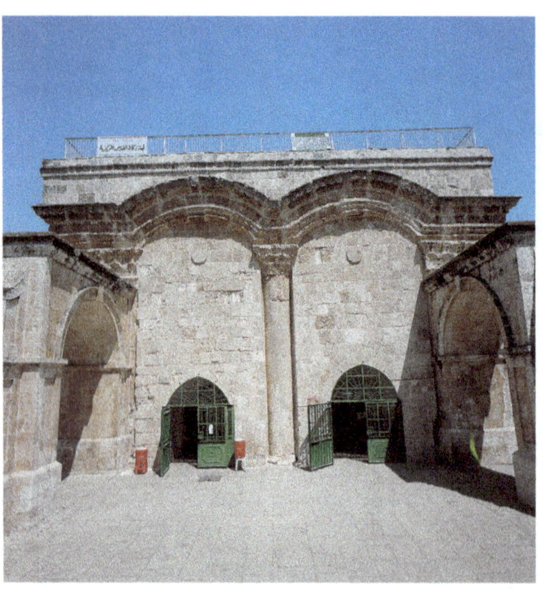

The Golden Gate, view from the west with the central column, Haram al-Sharif, Jerusalem.

has attained an important position in Islam, and became one of the most significant religious and archaeological sites in the Haram area. Its whole adjacent eastern area has been turned into a Muslim cemetery, the oldest and most famous in Jerusalem, which has preserved its name: Cemetery of Bab al-Rahma. Several companions of the Prophet Muhammad are buried here and it is still the place where many Muslims would like finally to rest.

During the Fatimid, Ayyubid and Mamluk periods, the structure of the gate served as a mosque. In the Ottoman period it became the residence of *sufi* followers, especially the Mawlawiyya. In pre-Crusader times, the Madrasa al-Nasiriya, attributed to *shaykh* Nasir al-Maqdisi, and one of the first and most famous *madrasas* in Jerusalem, was built above it. Within the Gate, the prominent *sufi* philosopher al-Ghazali experienced his most crucial intellectual developments during the journey from doubt to certainty. He also wrote there his most famous book, *The Revival of the Religious Sciences of Islam*.

The structure of the gate has four beautiful two-storey façades that complement one another, covered by panels of vegetal and geometric ornaments in relief. The eastern façade forms part of the same city and Haram wall. Access to the building is from the Haram through monumental stairs into the interior, which consists of two porticos stretching from east to west. Each portico consists of three vaults covered by shallow domes and supported by two rows of large columns.

Y.N.

I.1.e North-Western Khalwa of Ahmad Pasha

Lies at the northern wall of the Dome of the Rock's platform and is adjacent to the western border of the Northern Colonnade.
For opening hours, please refer to the Islamic Museum (I.1.a).

A *khalwa* (or cell) usually covers a small, secluded area in a *zawiya*, where a *sufi* finds the ideal atmosphere for meditation, concentration and worship. However, in the Haram it is an independent two-storey structure comprising more than one unit. This style of building was developed here during the Ottoman period and almost 20 cells survive, the most beautiful of which is Ahmad Pasha's.

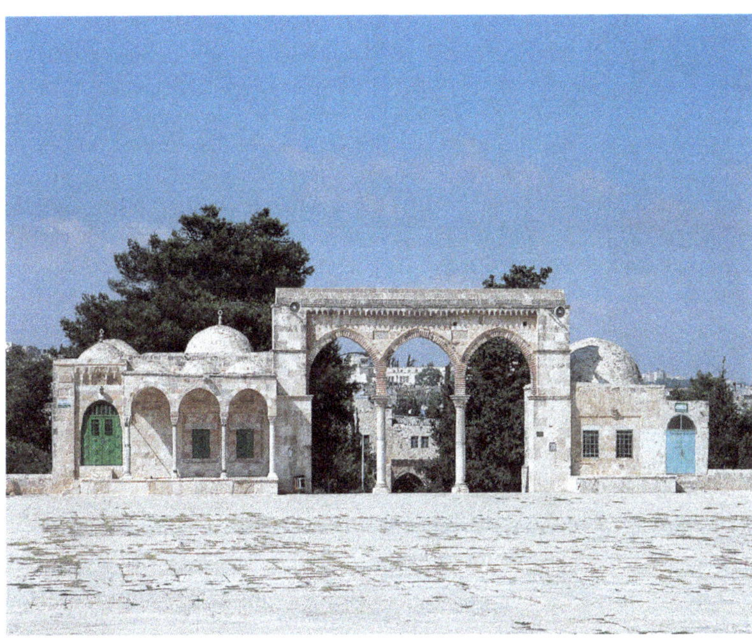

North-western Khalwa of Ahmad Pasha, general view, Haram al-Sharif, Jerusalem.

It is known as the "Mamluk Khalwa" as it carries many of the features of Mamluk architecture in Jerusalem. It is currently being used as the Aqsa Mosque manager's office.

When Ahmad Pasha founded it in 1009/1600–1601, he dedicated it to the *sufi*s and the study of Islamic jurisdiction. He appointed the *shaykh* al-Ghazi Abu al-Su'ud, one of the most eminent *sufi* scholars in Jerusalem, as its Inspector. Ahmad Pasha bestowed upon him a lifetime's annual salary of 600 silver dirhams, which was paid from the revenue of the building's *waqf*. He also stipulated detailed conditions to ensure the good management of the place, its regular maintenance and the continuance of its scholastic activities.

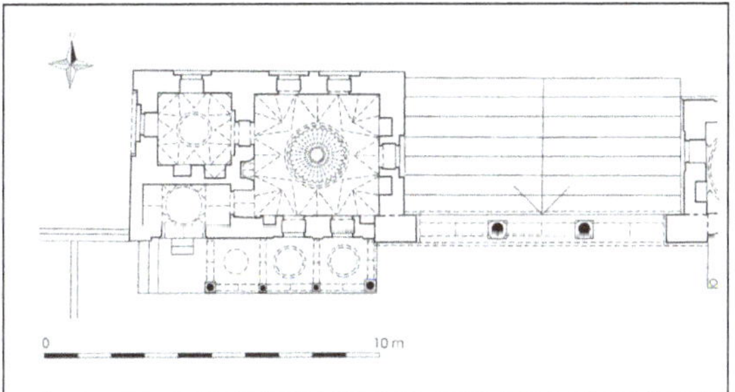

Plan of north-western Khalwa of Ahmad Pasha, ground floor, Haram al-Sharif, Jerusalem.

Ahmad Pasha, the ruler of Gaza at the time, was the descendent of a distinguished family that held important posts within the Ottoman Empire and in Jerusalem in particular. His grandfather, Mustafa Pasha, led missions as far as Yemen during the reign of Sultan Sulay-

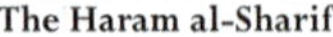

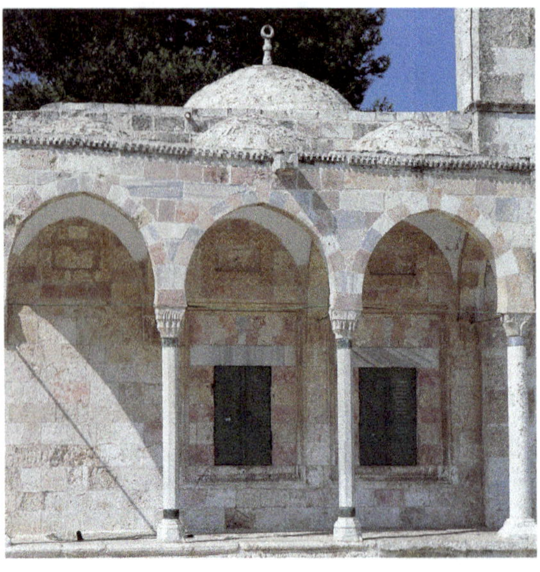

North-western Khalwa of Ahmad Pasha, portico, Haram al-Sharif, Jerusalem.

man the Magnificent. His father was Radwan Pasha, whose relatives were the Radwan family who had ruled the Gaza province during the 10th/16th and 11th/17th centuries. The family's Golden Age was during the reign of Ahmad Pasha. He was considered to be the most famous patron of architecture in Jerusalem at the end of the 10th/16th century and the city had a special place in his heart. He visited Jerusalem many times and the renowned architect, 'Abd al-Muhsen Ibn Namr worked on many of his projects there.

The building consists of two-storeys, the ground floor of which has two parts: the eastern section is a square chamber, whilst the western part has two chambers, which currently house the Haram's emergency electricity generators. The upper storey has a large central chamber, and two further smaller chambers, one of which has a *mihrab* in its southern wall. Rich in architectural detail and ornamentation, the building faces each of the cardinal directions. Their symmetry of components has been co-ordinated in such a way as to reflect the spirit of Jerusalem's architecture and yet remain unique. This singularity is best reflected in the door and window lintels and in the ornamental elements above them.

Y.N.

I.1.f **Mihrab of the Mastaba of 'Ali Pasha**

Lies in the western part of the esplanade and to the east of Bab al-Qattanin.
For opening hours, please refer to the Islamic Museum (I.1.a)

The *mihrab* dates back to 1047/1637–1638, as indicated in the foundation inscription

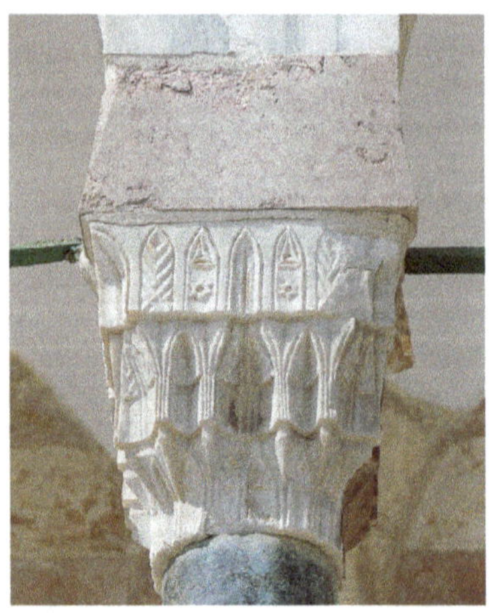

North-western Khalwa of Ahmad Pasha, capital, Haram al-Sharif, Jerusalem.

written on a rectangular marble plaque above its semi-dome. The text consists of two lines of poetry written in the Ottoman *naskhi* script.

'Ali Pasha was the Ottoman ruler of Jerusalem in 1047/1637-1638. His aim was to not only build something that would commemorate his name, but also provide visitors to the Haram with open spaces to pray in. It is believed that many students gathered around his *mastaba* to receive lectures in the open air from their *shaykh*.

The *mihrab*, in the centre of the *mastaba's* southern wall, is a recess surmounted by a pointed arch built in the *ablaq* style. Although the *mihrab* is usually an integral component of mosques – whether the mosque was part of a complex or an independent building – here it is an independent architectural unit.

It was very common in the Haram to find a *mastaba* that had a *mihrab* built on it, however this does not mean that every *mastaba* had a *mihrab*. The *mastabas* of the Haram have been tiled with rows of simple white stones that the weather has turned grey. Close to every *mastaba* was a tree to provide shade from the summer heat, and one or two steps were built into its sides for access.

Y.N.

I.1.g **Sabil Qaytbay**

Lies in the courtyard of the Haram between the western flight of stairs leading to the Dome of the Rock and Bab al-Qattanin.

For opening hours, please refer to The Islamic Museum (I.1.a)

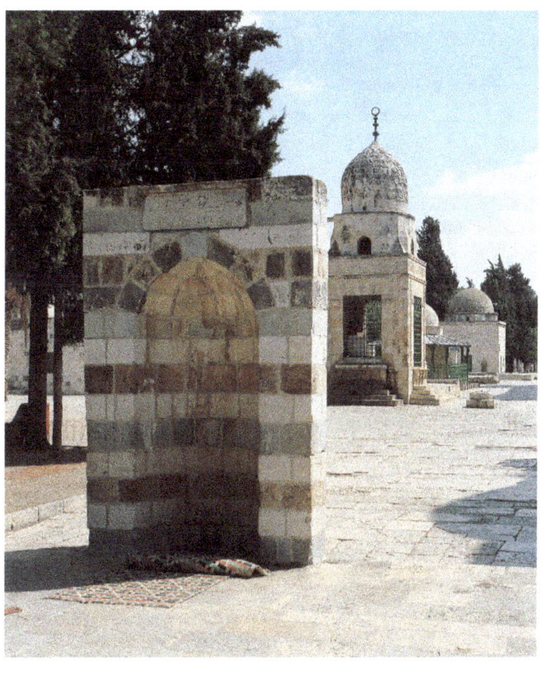

Mihrab of the Mastaba of 'Ali Pasha, Haram al-Sharif, Jerusalem.

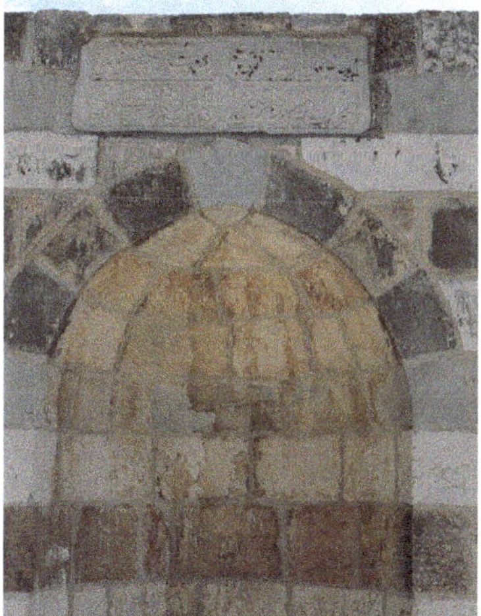

Mihrab of the Mastaba of 'Ali Pasha, foundation inscription, Haram al-Sharif, Jerusalem.

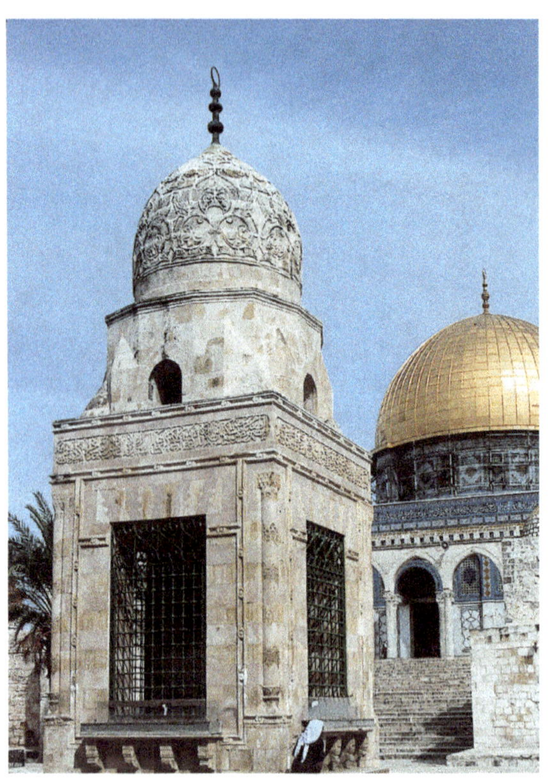

Sabil Qaytbay, sculptured cupola, Haram al-Sharif, Jerusalem (© Sonia Halliday Photographs, photograph: J. Taylor).

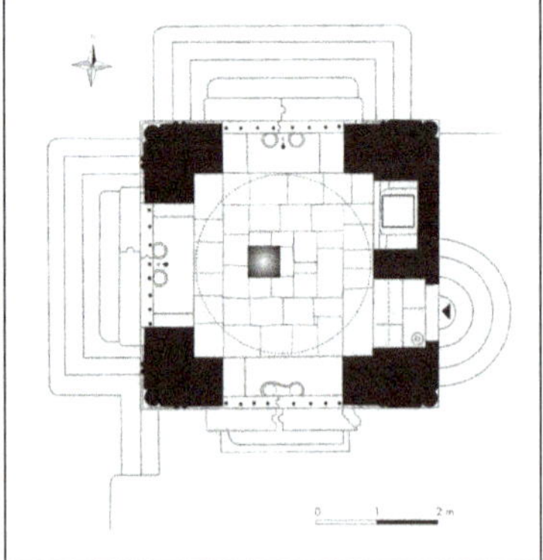

Plan of Sabil Qaytbay, Haram al-Sharif, Jerusalem.

Sabil Qaytbay is one of the most beautiful fountains in Jerusalem and among the most attractive domed buildings in the Haram. It is also a classic example of late Mamluk architecture in general, and the Cairene architectural tradition in particular. One simply has to walk out of the western door of the Dome of the Rock and descend the stepped colonnade opposite in order to reach the quadrangular building that is erected on a *mastaba* and which is covered by a uniquely decorated stone dome.

The *sabil* was first built by Sultan Sayf al-Din Inal (865/1465) and was later rebuilt by Sultan Qaytbay in 887/1482 as an extension of the neighbouring Madrasa al-Ashrafiyya. Nothing is left of the earlier structure built by Sultan Inal except for the well on which it was built. It was renovated by the Ottoman Sultan 'Abd al-Hamid II in 1300/1882-1883, as is indicated in the inscription that appears on it. Recently, the Committee for the Restoration of the Aqsa Mosque undertook the repair of the fountain and its renovation.

The fountain stands on the northern part of a *mastaba* that has a *mihrab* in its southern quarter. It rises to a height of 13 m. and has three parts. The first consists of a quadrangular base or chamber that has high windows on three sides and decorative grills that date to the Ottoman period. The windowsills are supported by carved stone corbels; its lintels are made of delicately joggled stone. The door of the *sabil* is on the east side and can be reached through a circular staircase that stands on the floor of the *mastaba*. Four steps from the north and west lead to its bed. At the corners of the building are columns with capitals decorated in the *muqarnas* style. The stonework of the building is in the *ablaq* style, where red and cream-colour stone is banded together. On the top part of the building is a band of commemorative inscription that includes Qur'anic verses and details concerning the founder, all in Mamluk *naskhi* script.

The middle part of the building comprises the drum of the dome, which acts as the transition zone between the quadrangular base and the circular dome. A small window pierces the centre of each of the four sides for ventilation. Small pyramid-like pillars are found on the sides of the drum, transforming the square into an octagon and then into a 12-sided polygon.

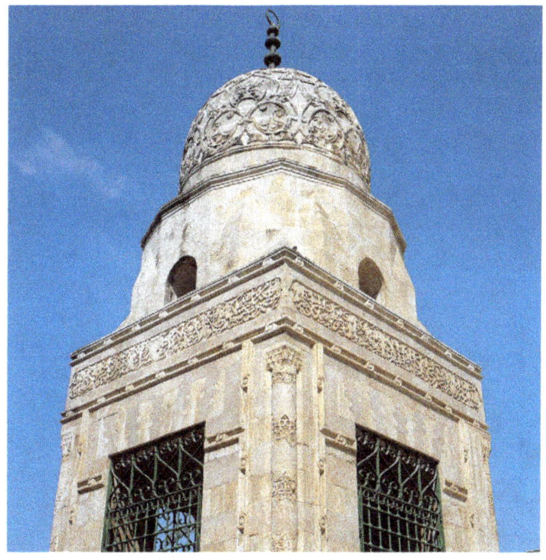

Sabil Qaytbay, sculptured cupola, Haram al-Sharif, Jerusalem (© A. Walls).

The upper part consists of a distinguished, high stone dome that is covered in unique carved arabesque decorations. It is the only dome outside Cairo in the Mamluk-Egyptian style. Even so, it is unparalleled even in Cairo, as similar carved domes usually surmount mausoleums. Fountains in Egypt were usually built within a complex and did not have domes.

This style of architecture and decoration was mainly inspired by Egyptian building traditions. It is not surprising that the stonemasons and craftsmen were Egyptians who brought with them the construction techniques of stone-relief domes that adorn the mausoleums and tombs in Cairo. It seems likely that the builders

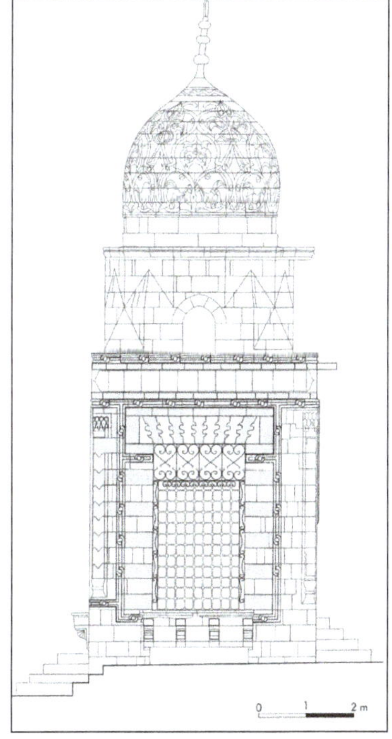

Sabil Qaytbay, south elevation, Haram al-Sharif, Jerusalem.

Sabil Qaytbay, interior view of the cupola, Haram al-Sharif, Jerusalem (© A. Walls).

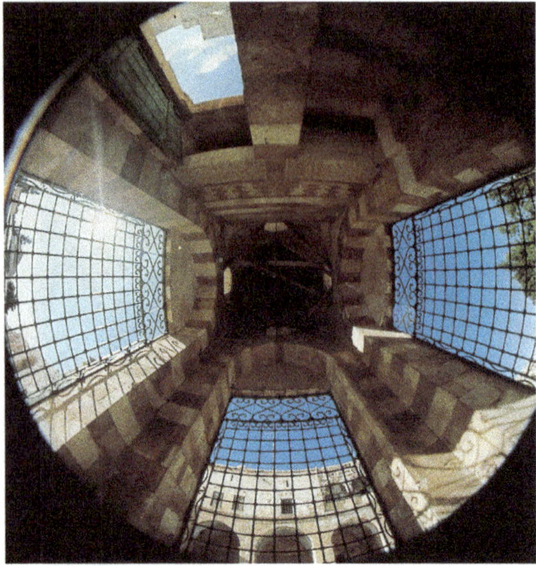

Qubba al-Nahawiyya, entrance, Haram al-Sharif, Jerusalem.

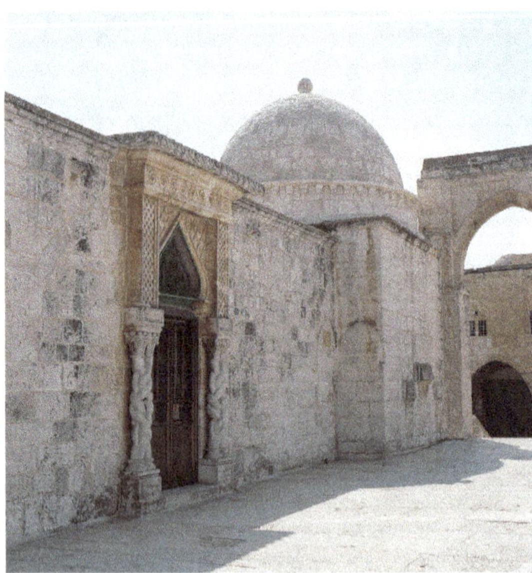

who erected the *sabil* are the same as those who later built the Madrasa al-Ashrafiyya.

M.H.

I.1.h Qubba al-Nahawiyya

Lies in the south-west corner of the Dome of the Rock, above the stairs leading to its platform from Bab al-Silsila Gate.
For opening hours, please refer to the Islamic Museum (I.1.a).

The domed structure was built in 604/1227–1228 by the *amir* Hussam al-Din Abu Sa'd Qaymaz al-Mu'addami, the *wali* of Jerusalem, by order of al-Mu'addam 'Isa, the Governor of southern Syria and Palestine during the Ayyubid period. The inscription on the northern wall of the western room certifies this, as does the writing of two renowned historians of Jerusalem: Ibn Fadl Allah al-'Umari (746/1345) and Mujir al-Din al-Hanbali (900/1495). The main purpose of the building was a school where Arabic grammar was taught. Al-Mu'addam 'Issa was known to be greatly interested in Arabic grammar and to have written books on the subject. Describing the building, al-'Umari mentioned that al-Mu'addam had appointed an *imam* to lead the daily prayers there, a *shaykh* from his Madrasa al-Mu'addamiyya to teach 25 pupils who were followers of the Hanafi School. He endowed the village of Bayt Laqya as a *waqf* for the upkeep of the school.
The edifice is an architectural masterpiece and is built on two separate levels due to the nature of its topographic location.

The lower floor, built at the same level as the Haram's courtyard, has cross-vaulted rooms and a small entrance in the western wall of the building leads to them. They were used mainly to store oil used for the lamps of the Aqsa Mosque and the Dome of the Rock. Today, these serve as offices of the Jerusalem Tribunal Courts. The upper storey is on the same level as the platform of the Dome of the Rock and consists of two rooms covered by stone domes and separated by a connecting middle hall. The western dome, distinguished by its height and elegance, dates back to the original construction stage in the Ayyubid period. The dome above the eastern room is shallow and Ottoman in style, which indicates that it was probably added at a later stage when the original twin dome was ruined.

The building's façade consists of varying architectural elements (such as arches and marble columns) that have been added during different periods. The main portal, thought to have been built in the second half of the 14th/20th century, is distinguished by its ornamental richness, in particular the marble columns with carved capitals dating from the Crusader period. An inscription written in the Ottoman *naskhi* script is found on the western side of the façade, referring to a fountain built in 1137/1724–1725 by the benefactor Hassan al-Hussayni, but while the inscription survived, the fountain has now disappeared. The western dome kept its original shape on the inside. The transition zone between the square room and the circular dome is richly decorated in ornamental shell-like and arabesque motifs. A commemorative inscription is

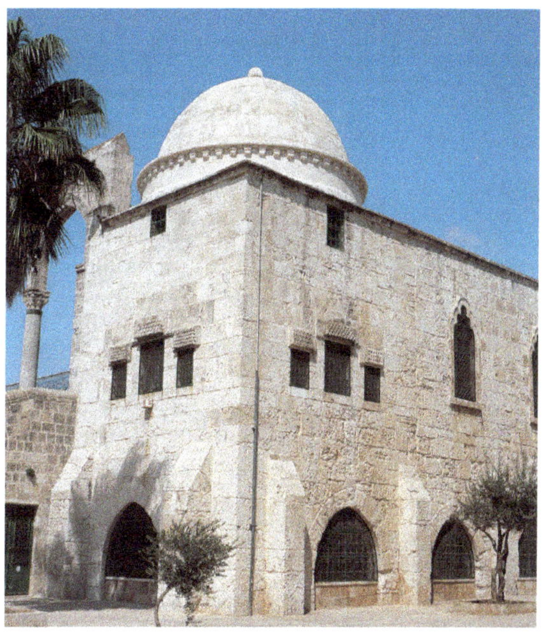

Qubba al-Nahawiyya, general view, Haram al-Sharif, Jerusalem.

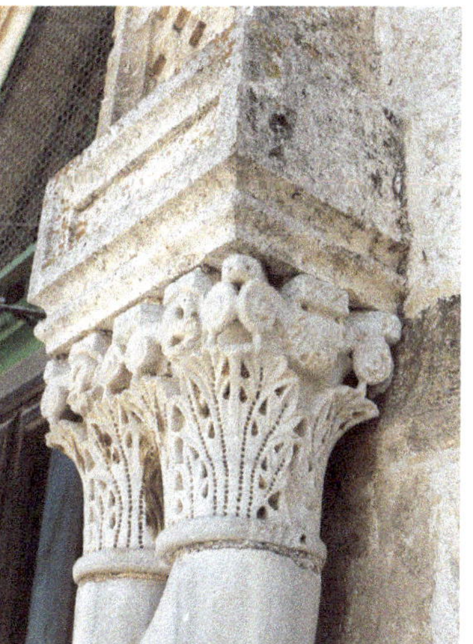

Qubba al-Nahawiyya, entrance capitals, Haram al-Sharif, Jerusalem.

Madrasa al-Ashrafiyya, ground floor plan, Haram al-Sharif, Jerusalem.

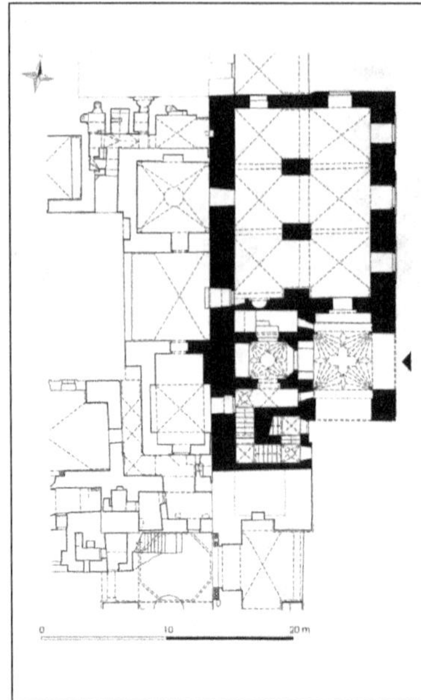

Madrasa al-Ashrafiyya, elevation of the main façade (east), Haram al-Sharif, Jerusalem.

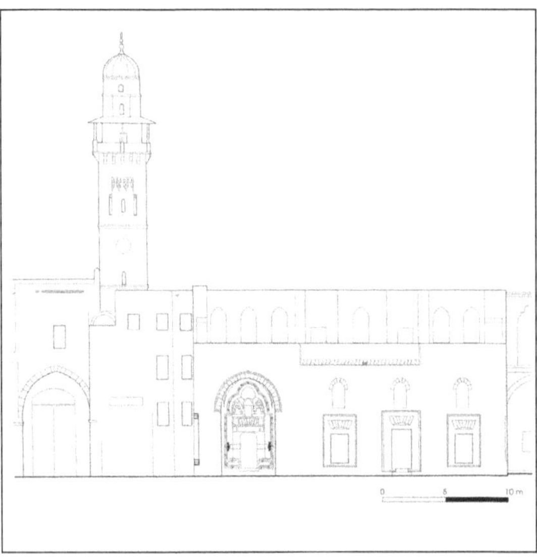

found on an interior wall written in the Ayyubid *naskhi* script. The rooms of the upper level are currently being used to house the offices of the Mufti of Jerusalem.

M.H.

I.1.i **Madrasa al-Ashrafiyya**

Situated on the western border of the esplanade between Bab al-Silsila and Bab al-Mathara, opposite Sabil Qaytbay.
For opening hours, please refer to the Islamic Museum (I.1.a).

The Madrasa al-Ashrafiyya is renowned as the most splendid in Jerusalem, not only for its architecture and artistic design, but also as being the most important educational institution. The historian Mujir al-Din al-Hanbali 901/1496 described it as the third jewel in Jerusalem's crown after the Aqsa Mosque and the Dome of the Rock. It is named after the Mamluk Sultan al-Ashraf Qaytbay, who rebuilt it between 885/1480–887/1482 – hence it is also called the al-Sultaniyya Madrasa.
Demolished and rebuilt, the *madrasa* was initially constructed during the reign of Sultan al-Dahir Khushqadam by the Amir Hassan al-Dahiri, who was the Inspector of the two Haram sites between 869/1464 and 872/1467. He died before it was completed, so the Amir Hassan al-Dahiri transferred the building to Sultan Qaytbay. The latter commissioned the Amir Bardabak al-Taji, who had become the new Inspector of the two Harams, to complete the construction.

It was finally finished in 875/1470, as indicated on the inscription plaque that is still on the old wall of the *madrasa* near Bab al-Silsila. The official inauguration date was 877/1472, when the sultan appointed Shihab al-Din al-'Umari, as the *shaykh* of the *madrasa* and employed a number of *sufi* scholars to teach there. He also bestowed a generous *waqf* upon it. Mujir al-Din al-'Umari mentions that he allocated enough funding to cover the salaries of 60 *sufis* (45 dirhams each per month), a *shaykh*, (500 dirhams per month) and many other employees, plus the running costs of the institution. Included in his *waqf* were 28 villages in Gaza, Ramla, Jerusalem and Hebron, and a *caravanserai*, a *hammam*, two presses, a mill, a bakery, a stable, and shops and houses in Gaza.

When Sultan Qaytbay saw the *madrasa* for the first time in 880/1475, he was deeply disappointed as it looked the same as other buildings in the Haram, and he ordered it to be destroyed. He commissioned a group of Egyptian architects and craftsmen to build it under the auspices of a Coptic architect. When it was completed in 887/1482, it was considered to be a masterpiece of Mamluk architecture and no other *madrasa* in Jerusalem could rival it. This was confirmed in the description of the well-known Dominican priest Felix Fabry who visited it in 888/1484. Sadly, a large part of the *madrasa* was demolished in 903/1497–1498 when an earthquake hit the city, although it was rebuilt and renovated according to its original plan.

The *madrasa*'s educational activities continued for three centuries and many trav-

Madrasa al-Ashrafiyya, entrance, Haram al-Sharif, Jerusalem.

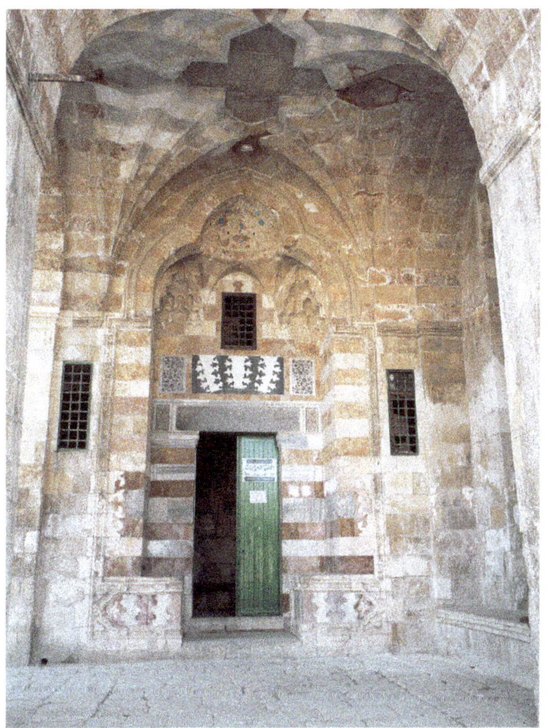

Madrasa al-Ashrafiyya, detail of the entrance, Haram al-Sharif, Jerusalem.

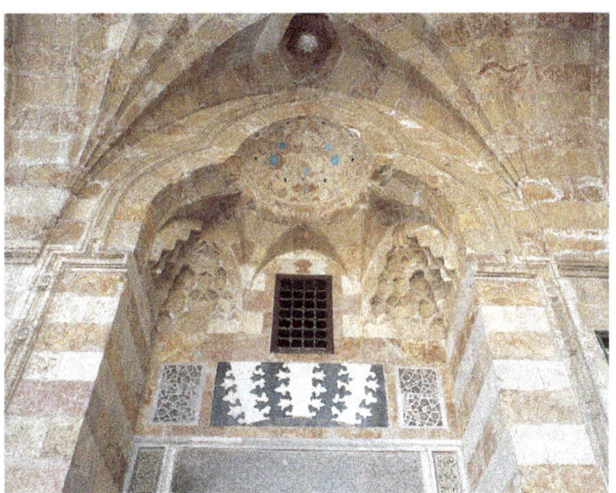

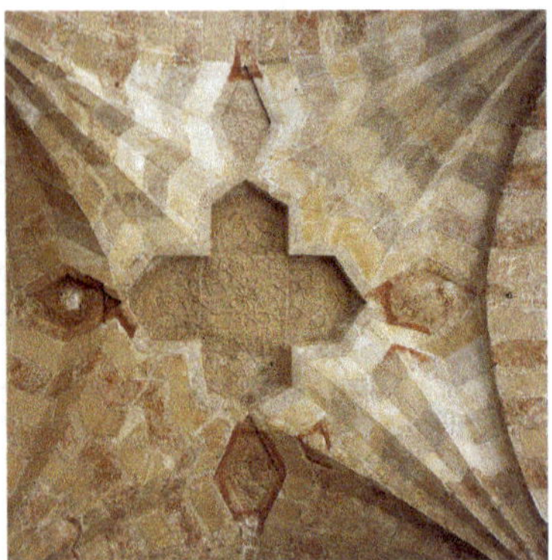

Madrasa al-Ashrafiyya, entrance vault, detail, Haram al-Sharif, Jerusalem.

ellers and historians who had visited it between the 10th/16th and 11th/17th centuries, marvelled at its beauty. The Turkish traveller, Evlia Çelebi described it in 1080/1669–1670: *"The Madrasa al-Sultaniyya is the best madrasa in Jerusalem".* The *sufi* scholar 'Abd al-Ghani al-Nabulsi stayed there in 1102/1690–1691 and described it as a great *madrasa* of immense importance.

The Madrasa al-Ashrafiyya consists of two storeys. The main entrance portal of the building, accessed from the Haram's courtyard, is distinguished by lavish architectural and ornamental details and is the epitome of Mamluk art and architecture. It has a porch open on both its southern and eastern sides, which is supported by two pointed arches that are covered by a fan-shaped vault. The door is set in a deep recess covered by a semi-dome that is carved and lavishly decorated with glazed ceramic tiles. The door leads into a vestibule that ends in a large assembly hall to the north. Two windows and a door on the eastern wall of this hall overlook the Haram's courtyard. Its northern wall also has a window and a door, while the southern wall has a window and a colourful decorated *mihrab*.

Today, the hall serves as a workshop for the conservation of the Haram's manuscripts and documents. To the south of the vestibule lies a stone staircase that leads to the upper floor and to the minaret above Bab al-Silsila. The southern part of this floor is ruined, although its Mamluk layout can still be observed, representative of the Mamluk four-*iwans* cruciform plan. In the centre there is a courtyard surrounded by two main *iwans* in the north and south, and two smaller *iwans* in the east and west. Of these four *iwans*, only the southern one has survived, with its *mihrab*. The south-west part of this storey has a number of rooms that today form part of a school for the religious education of girls.

M.H.

I.1.j **The Citadel** (option)

Located to the west of the city, opposite the wall and immediately south of Bab al-Khalil.
Open: 08.00 to 17.00. Entrance fee.

The Citadel is one of Jerusalem's most important landmarks and constitutes a typical example of Islamic military architecture. It was built on this strategic spot to defend the western entrance to the city. One of the main factors behind the choice of its location was the fact that old fortifications already existed there. The Citadel's current structure dates to the reign of the Mamluk

Sultan al-Nasir Muhammad Ibn Qalawun, who commissioned its reconstruction in 710/1310–1311. This date is on the inscription plaque above the main eastern entrance, as mentioned by the Swiss scholar Max van Berchem in 1894, however the plaque disappeared soon after. The renowned Egyptian historian Ahmad al-Qalqashandi (756/1355–821/1418) states that the Sultan al-Nasir Muhammad Ibn Qalawun ordered the rebuilding of the Citadel in (716/1316–1317); it was designated as a military stronghold housing the city's garrison and the seat of the Mamluk administration in Jerusalem. The British archaeologist, C. N. Johns, who had conducted excavations during the 1930s and 1940s, concluded that the external wall of the Citadel and its towers date to the early Mamluk period. Similar styles are seen in Karak and Shawbak Castles in Jordan. The building does, however, also include some earlier components dating to the Hellenistic, Roman, and early Islamic periods, and also sections that were added later, in the Ottoman period.

The plan of the citadel is an irregular rectangle, comprising formidable walls and five high towers, and is surrounded by external fortification and a moat. The main entrance to the citadel is through the eastern gatehouse that was added by order of Sultan Sulayman the Magnificent in 939/1532–1533. It leads to the main interior gate via two bridges. The first wooden drawbridge stretches over an external moat and leads to the barbican, and then to the second stone bridge that stretches over the interior moat. A stone frame above the interior gate probably had the inscription plaque, mentioned above, on it. Turning right, and then left from the entrance, one reaches an octagonal room covered by a vault that has an opening for ventilation. From here a staircase leads to the top of the north-east tower, called the Tower of David, which probably dates to the time of Herod Antipas (4 BC–AD 39). A stunning panoramic view of the city – especially of the Haram al-Sharif – can be captured from here.

Excavations carried out inside the courtyard of the Citadel have uncovered a section of wall and two square towers that date to the 2nd or 1st century BC, and a circular tower and part of a wall that date to the Umayyad period (41/661–132/750). The hall on the top floor of the south-west tower was converted into a mosque during the reign of the Sultan al-Nasir Muhammad Ibn Qalawun, as confirmed by the commemorative inscription plaque found on the eastern wall of the mosque. Another inscription on the same wall mentions that a tower was built in the Citadel by the Ayyubid *amir* ruler al-Mu'addam 'Issa in 610/1213–1214. Neither of the inscriptions is in its original location. Sultan Sulayman the Magnificent commissioned the renovation of the mosque in 938/1531–1532, and a beautiful *mihrab*, a superb *minbar*, and a minaret were added at the same time. The current cylinder minaret was, however, rebuilt in 1065/1655 during the time when Muhammad Pasha was the Ottoman Governor of Palestine.

M.H.

THE MANUSCRIPTS OF THE AQSA MOSQUE LIBRARY

Yusuf Natsheh

Palestine was at the vanguard of scientific learning and Islamic culture from the beginning of the Islamic Conquest until the Ottoman period. Its religious importance to Muslims, the Aqsa Mosque and the many *madrasas* founded in the Haram al-Sharif, encouraged scholars and scientists to visit and even settle there. Discussion circles were founded and many subjects were studied, among which were Islamic jurisdiction, language, poetry, linguistics, religious studies and the interpretation of the Qur'an and the *Hadith*.

Many local and visiting scholars from different parts of the Islamic world wrote their books in Palestine and encouraged their circulation among the students there. Some even brought manuscripts along with them from Cairo, Damascus, Baghdad, Mecca and Medina. Many libraries were founded in both public institutions and privately, the most distinguished of which were those of the Aqsa Mosque, the Dome of the Rock and Shaykh Muhammad al-Khalili.

Due to the various misfortunes that beset Palestine during different periods, many of these manuscripts were scattered, lost or ruined. This prompted the Islamic Supreme Council in 1340/1923 to establish a modern library to house the remaining collection. The library was moved to different corners of the Aqsa Mosque before it was finally established in Masjid al-Nisa' (the Women's Mosque) to the east of the Islamic Museum's Eastern Hall.

The manuscripts date back to the Mamluk and Ottoman periods, the oldest of which dates to the $7^{th}/13^{th}$ century. They cover different Islamic subjects such as the sciences of the Qur'an, including the art of recitation, interpretation, the science of *hadith* and terminology, the principles of religion, Sufism, ethics and jurisdiction, the four *Sunni* rites, Arabic language and literature, history, philosophy, astronomy and arithmetic.

Despite all efforts made to preserve these manuscripts (fumigating them twice a year, and the chief librarian writing three indexes to them) they suffer from humidity, need regular maintenance and delicate restoration. To redress this shortage, the Welfare Association has planned, in collaboration with the Administration of Waqfs and Islamic Affairs, a modern centre in Jerusalem for the restoration and maintenance of the manuscripts. The plan is to establish it in the Ashrafiyya Madrasa, which housed the Aqsa library until 2000. Both parties are co-operating with the Italian Renovation Institute in Florence to accomplish this project under the auspices of the United Nations Educational, Scientific and Cultural Organisation (UNESCO), and many students have volunteered to come to Jerusalem and help treat and maintain these manuscripts.

WATER SYSTEMS OF THE HARAM AL-SHARIF

Yusuf Natsheh

In the Qur'an God says: "*From water, We brought everything to life*". The scarcity of water in Jerusalem played a vital role in deciding where the first nucleus of the city began. The only spring in the city, 'Ayn Silwan, dictated where the city centre would lie and, as water is vital to carry out ablutions before each of the five daily prayers, water has acquired a religious significance in Islam.

As the Haram al-Sharif is one of the most venerated of Islamic sites and the place from which the Prophet Muhammad made his nocturnal journey to heaven, it has attracted visitors, past and present, from all over the Islamic world. The busiest periods have always been during the month of Ramadan and on other different religious occasions. The Islamic rulers therefore had to secure the water necessary for their nation's survival and for their religious rituals. Hence three projects were undertaken: first, a number of cisterns and reservoirs were built in the Haram al-Sharif; second, aqueducts brought water from nearby water sources and the Haram and, finally, many fountains were built within the Haram and the area surrounding it.

As mentioned in historical references, the number of cisterns in the Haram al-Sharif reached somewhere between 22 and 37. While some are deep, others are fairly shallow; in total, they secure 10 million gallons of water. They can be easily distinguished as most have a protruding stone or marble bore that rises above ground level, while others have stone cisterns beside them or a dome or fountain built on top. Many stories have spread around these cisterns. The name of the Waraqa Cistern (the Leaf Cistern), for example, was given to it after a man descended the cistern to look for his bucket. Reaching the bottom, he found a door that led to a garden. He took one of its leaves and went up again. The source of the cistern's water has always been the rain.

The cisterns not only provided water to the visitors of the Haram al-Sharif, but also to the residents of the city at large. During drought periods, however, it failed to provide enough water so the authorities had to seek additional sources. The solution was found in utilising the springs of the neighbouring village of Irtas, which lies south of Jerusalem and whose water was widely used during Roman times. Water was supplied to the Haram from an aqueduct (*qana*) that poured water into a vessel built by the Ayyubid Sultan al-Malik al-'Adil in the western border of the Haram. Historical sources mention that the aqueduct (named Qanat al-Sabil) was renovated in the Mamluk period by the *amir* Tankiz, and then again by Sultan Qaytbay.

In addition to this aqueduct, many fountains (*sabils*) were built in the Haram during the Ayyubid and Mamluk periods, among which were: the Cistern of al-Mu'addam 'Issa, Sabil Sha'alan and Sabil Ibrahim al-Rumi. However the most beautiful one is Sabil Qaytbay, opposite the Madrasa al-Ashrafiyya. *Sabils* of a different style were built in the reign of the Ottoman Sultan, Sulayman the Magnificent. Six *sabils* were built within the Haram and around its main entrances, all of which are fabulous examples built into the walls. Many others were constructed in the Mamluk style, but the Qanat al-Sabil continued to be maintained.

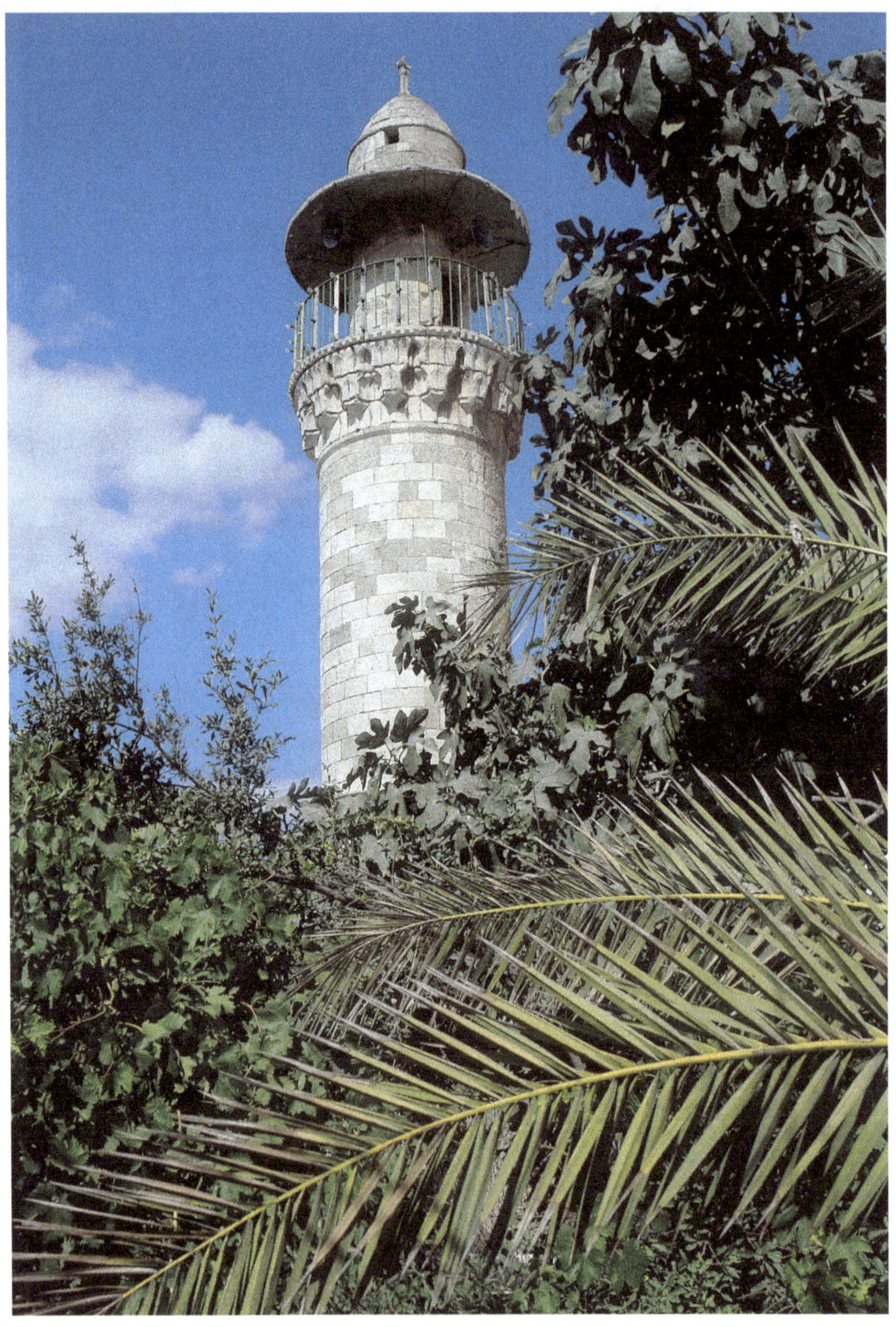

Sufi Institutions in Jerusalem

Yusuf Natsheh

II.1 JERUSALEM

II.1.a Khanqa al-Duwadariyya
II.1.b Zawiya al-Khalwatiyya (al-Hamra')
II.1.c Khanqa al-Mawlawiyya
II.1.d Zawiya al-Qadiriyya (al-Afghaniyya)
II.1.e Ribat Bayram Jawish
II.1.f Ribat al-Mansuri
II.1.g Khassaki Sultan Complex

The Suqs
Fortifications and Gates of the Old City

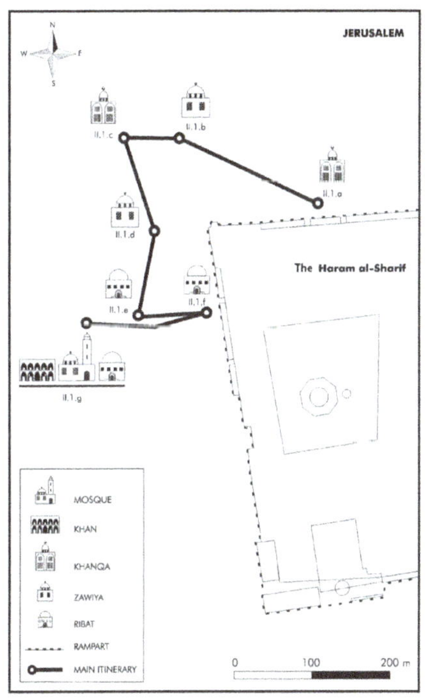

Zawiya al-Khalwatiyya, minaret, Jerusalem.

"*Our Protector and Comforter*" is a prayer and an appeal to God from His good and devout subjects to guard them from misfortune and cure illness. Although a common prayer to all believers in God it is, after the worship of God, the heart and core of *sufi* philosophy and the way to ultimate happiness. This itinerary, as suggested by the title, aims at introducing the forms of *sufi* institutions that were established in Jerusalem.

Sufism in Islam went through many phases. At an early stage its followers met in mosques and private residences. Later on, when it became more public and open, the need for communal institutions arose; in Jerusalem this started in the Ayyubid period and further developed and diversified in the Mamluk and Ottoman periods. *Sufi* edifices were given different names, the most famous of which was the Arabic *zawiya*, although the Persian *khanqa* or *ribat* were also commonly used. The architecture of these institutions and the ways in which they were run financially and administratively were, however, very similar.

This itinerary will include eight monuments of different *Sufi* Orders, most of which date back to the Ottoman period and few to the Mamluk period. While the Ottoman period witnessed expansion and development in the *Sufi* Orders, most of the Mamluk edifices were ruined due to the fact that their *waqfs* ceased and they were short of money. Although history books mention *Sufi* Orders existing prior to the Crusader period, the oldest surviving buildings date back to the Ayyubid period.

The architectural details and ornaments of an edifice usually reflected the wealth and ideology of the era in which it was built. All the same, a *sufi* edifice had more or less the following parts: a number of small rooms that provided solitude and isolation; a large hall for *sufi* meetings and rituals; occasionally a small mosque for prayer, study and preaching; a modest kitchen and utilities; a minaret used to transmit the *zawiya*'s activities to the area (like an advertising tool for Sufism); an open courtyard, in part of which trees and flowers were planted, and a cistern to collect rainwater.

These edifices enjoyed Islamic waqfs, which defined their relationship to the governing and judicial authorities and stipulated clauses and terms that regulazted their revenues, expenditures, wages, duties and the rights of their members.

II.1 JERUSALEM

II.1.a **Khanqa al-Duwadariyya**

Lies south of the Madrasa al-Salamiyya on Tariq Bab al-'Atm; just off Tariq al-Mujahidin. Visitors are not allowed on the site, as it is currently a private school.

Finding the building is easy – walk westwards from Bab al-Asbat (Gate of the Lions), turn left at Tariq Bab al-'Atm and you will see the entrance. It will take a while for the visitor's eyes to adapt to the darkness of the area and behold the beauty and details of its entrance and western façade.

Al-Duwadariyya, named after its founder the Amir 'Alam al-Din Abu Musa al-Duwadar, is known from its commemorative plaque as the House of the Virtuous. Until recently it was called Madrasa al-Bakriyya (after the first Caliph, Abu Bakr al-Siddiq). Establishing *sufi* institutions was a main duty of important *amirs* during the Mamluk period. The Amir 'Alam al-Din carried out many important missions, held vital administrative, military and educational posts and served different Mamluk sultans, such as Baybars (658/1260–676/1277) and al-Nasir Muhammad Ibn Qalawun, whose rule stretched over three periods. He was known to be sympathetic to Sufism and was a great patron of science and scholars. His residence was likened to a mosque.

The inscription above the entrance offers important information on the history and the sponsors of the edifice. It was founded in 695/1295–1296 to house 30 *sufis*, Arabs and non-Arabs – 20 single and ten married – and to host *sufi* visitors for a period of ten days. It stipulated that the holy Qur'an, *hadith* and Shafi'i law be taught there. A generous *waqf* was bestowed to guarantee its perpetuation, which included the village of Bir Nabala to the north of Jerusalem, the village of Hajla and many different buildings in Jerusalem, Nablus and Bisan.

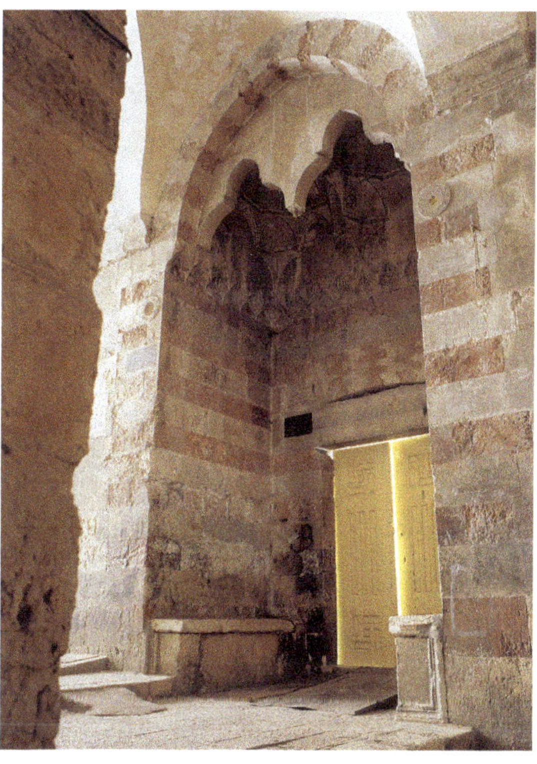

Khanqa al Duwadariyya, entrance, Jerusalem.

What distinguishes al-Duwadariyya is its original architectural design. The entrance on the western façade is a unique masterpiece in the architecture of Jerusalem, even though a similar style can be found in Damascus. Alternating red and white stones in the *ablaq* style extend to the vault that covers its receding entrance. A stone lintel is seen above the entrance and is followed by a relief mosaic arch. Above the arch lies the calligraphic inscription mentioned above, followed by three rows of beautifully

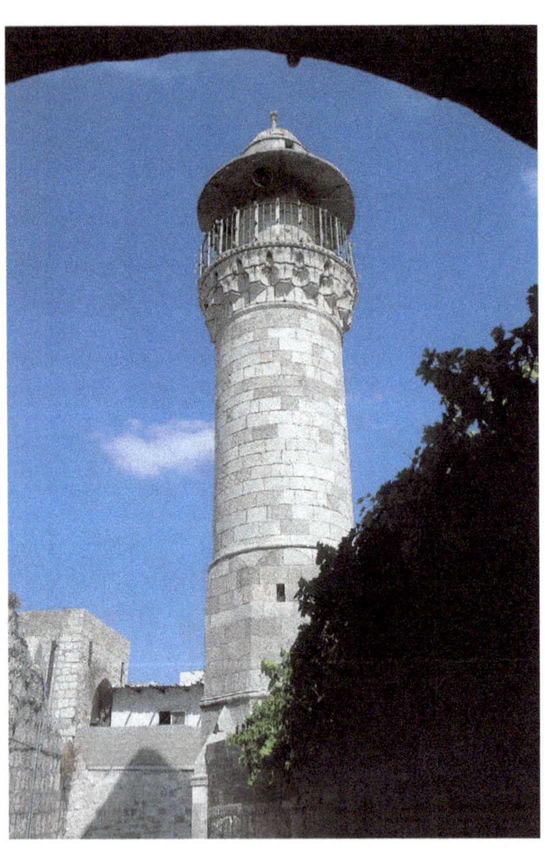

Zawiya al-Khalwatiyya, minaret, Jerusalem.

designed stone stalactite decoration known as *muqarnas*. The *muqarnas* on the entrance cap are preceded by two triangular pointed arches, which in turn are preceded by a colourful, mosaic pointed arch.

The entrance leads into an open rectangular courtyard covered with large stone tiles. The northern and southern parts of the courtyard are surrounded by small chambers, which once housed *sufis*. In its southern section, a rectangular hall is found that consists of three parts with two windows on both its outer sides. A relief mosaic arch and a circular window are found on top of their sills. In the centre is an entrance leading to a hall, in which *sufi* residents held their meetings and Qur'an and *hadith* were taught.

II.1.b **Zawiya al-Khalwatiyya (al-Hamra')**

Situated in the northern part of the Old City, to the west of the road leading to the al-Hamra' (or Red) Minaret and close to Tariq al-Bastami. Permission to visit the site needs to be granted by its overseer. The best time to visit is before noon or afternoon prayers.

Although the Khalwatiyya *Sufi* Order officially appeared in Jerusalem in the Mamluk period, this *zawiya* was built during the early Ottoman period in 939/1532–1533. A *waqf* document in Jerusalem's Tribunal Court reveals that the revenues of different lands in the city were allocated to the *zawiya* and to its employees.

The *zawiya* is attributed to the *shaykh* Ala' al-Din Abu Hassan, a follower of the Khalwatiyya Order. A pioneer of Sufism in Jerusalem in the 10th/16th century, he was called: *"the leading wise man and the cream of the cream among the devoted ascetics"*. The followers of this Order, especially his descendants, played an active role in the social and religious life of Jerusalem. Many of them were bookkeepers in addition to running the *zawiya* and looking after its *waqf*. 'Abd al-Qadir Shalabi was the bookkeeper of Bayram Jawish's *waqf*.

Shaykh 'Ali's pious and ascetic way of life persuaded many influential *amirs* to sponsor him and his *zawiya*. A *waqf* of land and buildings was endowed upon the *zawiya* in the first half of the 10th/16th century by many people, among which were both Haji Bek, the governor of Nablus, and Qasim Bek, the Governor of Safad.

Unfortunately very little of the *zawiya*'s utilities have survived. The *sufi* retreats disappeared completely as did the original mosque, the ceremony hall and many other utilities, including the mill and the weaving shop that were part of its *waqf*. The current area is much smaller than the original one. The properties and utilities of the *zawiya* were expanded south to the end of the road to what, inaccurately, is called today Mosque of Shaykh Rihan.

All the same, the remains of the *zawiya*, namely the open courtyard and beautiful minaret, give a fair idea of the beauty of the original building. Trees and flowers are planted in the courtyard as it stands today, which is rectangular and has a cistern and a toilet unit. The minaret lies to the north-east, standing independently from the mosque, which was built at the end of the 13th/19th century. The minaret is 18 m. high and built of white stone, which has turned grey over time, and red stones are found randomly between some of them. Its base is square, holding an elegant cylindrical shaft, where squinches help the transition from a square into an octagon. The minaret's circular gallery, upon which the *muezzin* stands to call people to prayer, rests on a *muqarnas* ledge and is covered by a small dome. A parasol is erected here to protect the *muezzin* from the heat and the rain. The mosque is usually crowded five times a day when people are called to prayer from its minaret.

II.1.c **Khanqa a-Mawlawiyya**

The Khanqa al-Mawlawiyya lies to the north of the Old City and slightly north of Tariq al-Mawlawiyya, which connects the Red Minaret Road from the east and the main road of al-Sa'diyya neighbourhood. The site can be visited during the day. Out of courtesy, permission should be obtained

Zawiya al-Khalwatiyya, decorative detail of minaret, Jerusalem.

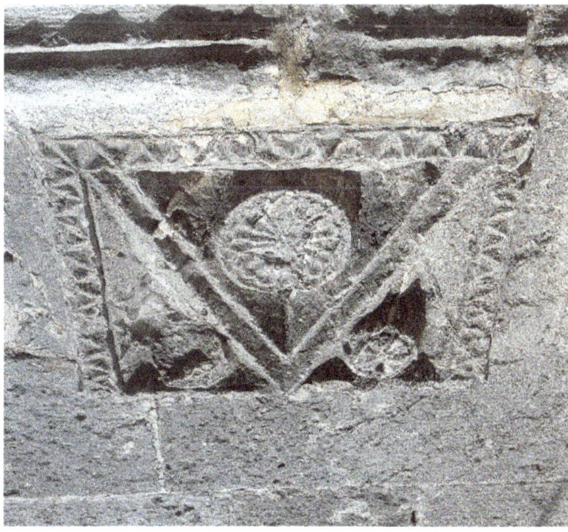

from its residents and the people present in the lower hall.

The various units of the Khanqa al-Mawlawiyya Complex date back several periods. The mosque's hall definitely originates from the time of the Crusaders, while the hall on street level could be of an even earlier date. Many units on the second floor are Mamluk in style. The minaret and the audience hall on the third floor date back to the 10th/16th century.

The complex had a religious function both when it was the Church of St Agnes during the Crusader period, and when it was later turned into a mosque. This function was further emphasised during the Ottoman period when it became the home of the Mawlawiyya Sufi Order in Jerusalem. This Order is attributed to the renowned *sufi* Jalal al-Din al-Rumi who is buried in Konya (Turkey). Throughout the meetings, music and rhythmic dancing accompanied the prayer rituals and a long headcover was worn. The order was active in Jerusalem until the beginning of the 14th/20th century, but went into decline during the second half of the century, when many of its utilities were thus turned into houses. Even so, daily prayers are still conducted in the mosque and calls to prayer are still heard from its minaret every day.

Khanqa al-Mawlawiyya, entrance, Jerusalem.

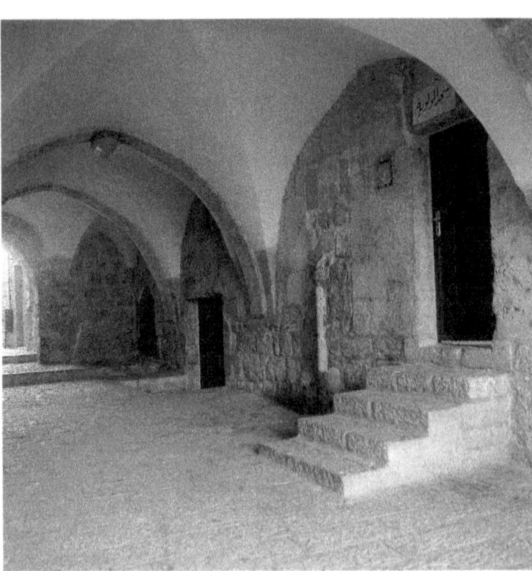

Many *amirs* contributed to the development and sponsorship of the complex, the last of whom was Khadawri Bek, known as Abu Sayfin, the governor of the district of Jerusalem in 990/1586-1587. He added the third floor in which the audience hall is located, and where the Mawlawiyya *sufis* worship and turn to God. Khadawri Beik had a generous *waqf* of 500 gold coins allocated to the *khanqa*. Much money was saved out of the *waqf* in the 11th/17th century after the staff wages and the expenses of running the site had been fully paid. Among its employees were an Inspector, an *imam*, a *shaykh*, a reciter of the Qur'an, two *muezzins*, a servant, a torchbearer and a porter.

The western façade of the edifice is simple. The door on its northern section leads to a large rectangular hall that has been recently renovated and re-opened. In the middle of the façade, a hanging door leads to an irregularly shaped open courtyard via many steps. Around it are the *khanqa*'s different utilities. The rectangular mosque lies to the north of the courtyard and consists of three aisles that are covered by cross vaults supported by two rows of large pillars. When this hall was turned into a mosque, a *mihrab* was added to the centre of the southern wall. The minaret lies in the south-east corner of the mosque and has a large base. Its shaft is cylindrical and similar to the typical Ottoman pencil-like minarets, but is less elegant and has more of a local character. The tomb of Shaykh 'Ali, a follower of the Mawlawiyya Order, is found in the courtyard. To the south there is a room, the floor of which drops below the level of the courtyard and in which the tombs of three leaders of the Order are found. The audience hall – which overlooks the Old City – and the minaret's entrance are accessible by a staircase. An inscription is found on the lintel of the entrance, honouring the name of the founder and giving the date of construction. The *sufi* traveller 'Abd al-Ghani al-Nabulsi visited the site and he wrote a vivid description of it, and of the religious rituals and music that the Mawlawiyya sect performed in his presence.

II.1.d **Zawiya al-Qadiriyya (al-Afghaniyya)**

Situated on Tariq Barquq just off Bab al-Ghawanima, which is one of the esplanade gates. Visiting it requires prior arrangement with the shaykh *of the* zawiya.

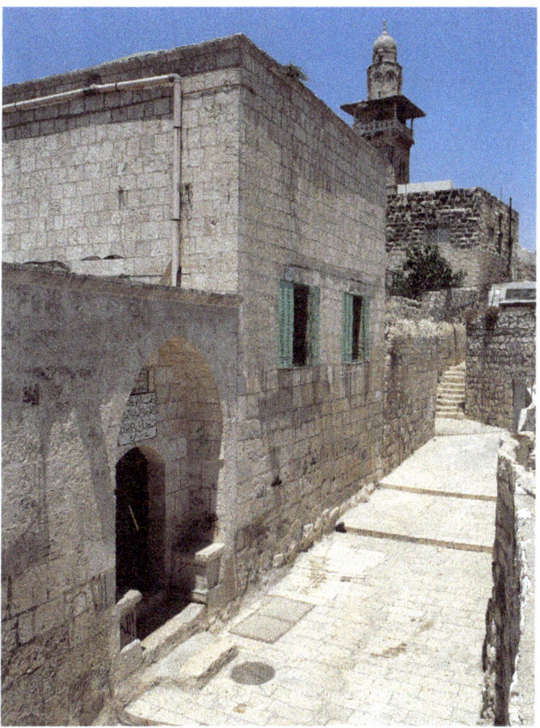

Zawiya al-Qadiriyya, principal façade, Jerusalem.

Finding the Qadiriyya is easy because it is the only public building on the northern side of Tariq Barquq with a distinguished entrance. It was named after Shaykh 'Abd al-Qadir al-Jilani, the founder and leader of the Qadiriyya *Sufi* Order. Today it is called the Zawiya al-Afghaniyya (The Afghani Zawiya), in point of the fact that a group of Jerusalem-based Afghans have been living there and managing it for the last few decades.

The Zawiya al-Qadiriyya has maintained its original architectural structure and still carries out its original functions. Its fol-

Ribat Bayram Jawish, first floor plan, Jerusalem.

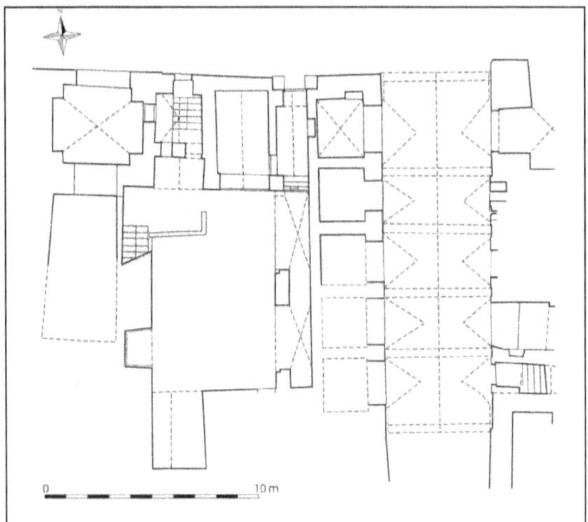

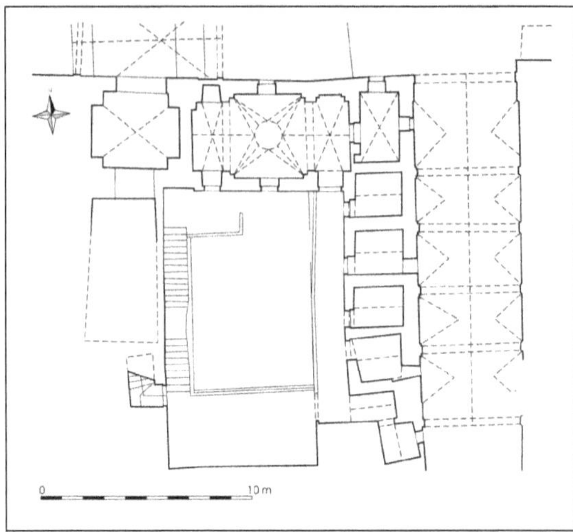

Ribat Bayram Jawish, ground floor plan, Jerusalem.

lowers regularly meet with the current Shaykh ʻAbd al-Karim al-Afghani at least twice a week in addition to Fridays.

Muhammad Pasha, the Governor of Jerusalem, commissioned the building in 1043/1632–1633. He was renowned for sponsoring *sufi* institutions in Jerusalem and was interested in the city's architecture and development, and his love of Jerusalem made him move there after his retirement. He allocated the *zawiya* a huge sum of money in a *waqf* to cover the expenses and guarantee its perpetuity, stipulating that the money should be invested in trade and that the profits should cover the costs of running it.

The Zawiya al-Qadiriyya has two external façades: one to the west that has only few small windows to admit sunlight into the retreats of the *zawiya*, and a second main façade that lies to the south containing the only entrance to the edifice. When compared to the entrance of the Duwadariyya, this entrance is very simple and only a pointed arch can be seen on it. The elevated entrance is three steps above street level and has a *mastaba* on either side of it. A plaque is found above the entrance on which the name of the *zawiya*, its Order, founder and the date of the building are engraved.

A short corridor leads into a rectangular open courtyard, with a large part of it planted with various trees and plants. It has hardly changed from the description found in the *waqf*, which dates back four centuries. Eleven small chambers surround it from the south and west.

The utilities and assembly hall lie to the north and are built on two levels. The ground floor is the original, while the upper floor was added later to accommodate the *shaykh* of the *zawiya*. The building also has a hanging mosque to the east of the entrance that can be accessed by ascending the stairs.

II.1.e **Ribat Bayram Jawish**

Lies in the south-west corner of the junction between Aqabat al-Takiyya, Tariq Bab al-Nadir and Tariq al-Wad. Visitors are not allowed on the site, as it is currently a residence and a school.

The inscription plaque above the entrance shows that the edifice was completed on 20 *rabi' al-awwal* 947/25 July 1540 and that the *amir* Bayram Jawish Ibn Mustafa commissioned it. His aim was to offer lodgings to the poor.
Even though there are no Arabic translations of the historical references pertaining to Bayram Jawish, the documents in the Tribunal Court of Jerusalem provide us with enough useful information about this important 10th/16th-century Ottoman figure. He held many important civil and military posts and his activities covered various aspects of life, society, economics, architecture and administration. Among these, for example, was his running of Khassaki Sultan's complex with a firm and trustworthy hand. He supervised the construction of the Mawardiyya and the completion of the two *hammams* that were part of Khassaki Sultan's *waqf*. He also contracted architects to restore a canal and traded in soap, sugar, fat, and estates and land all over Palestine and Syria. He went to Egypt to ask architects to work on the Wall of Jerusalem, officially commissioned by Muhammad al-Naqqash, the manager of the project. All this in addition to building his home, an orphanage and the *ribat* mentioned above.
Ribat Bayram Jawish has two façades, the main one being that on the northern side where the entrance is, on Aqabat al-Takiyya. The second lies to the east and faces Tariq al-Wad. The current edifice consists of three levels. The first two levels are the originals built during Bayram's time, while the third was added at a later, but unknown date. On the first level – immediately after the entrance – is a small rectangular corridor that leads to an open courtyard. Small chambers surround the courtyard from the north, east and south where *sufi*s and the poor resided. The second level has a small open

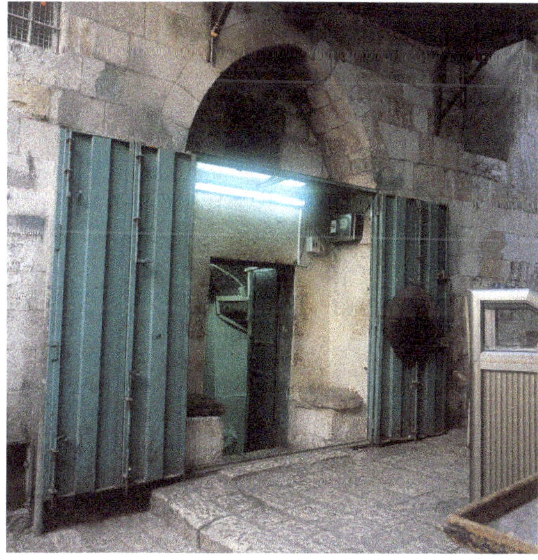

Ribat Bayram Jawish, entrance, Jerusalem (© Sonia Halliday Photographs, photograph: D. Silverman).

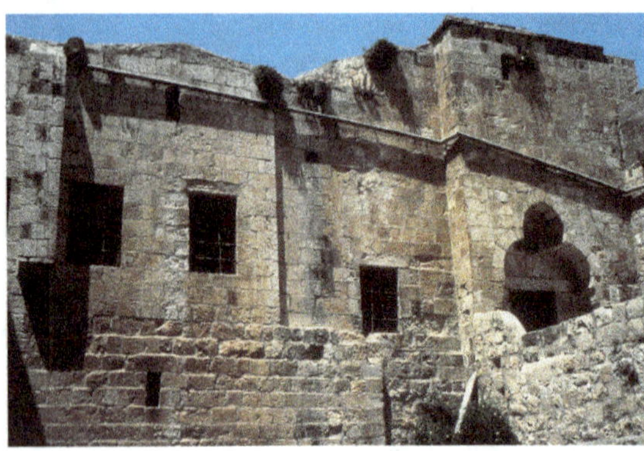

Ribat Bayram Jawish, inner façade, Jerusalem (© M. Hamilton Burgoyne).

courtyard, which is reached by a staircase in the courtyard on the first floor. Its corridor leads to six chambers and then to a hall that consists of three parts.

II.1.f **Ribat al-Mansuri**

Lies to the south of Bab al-Nadir, near to the entrance of the esplanade. Visitors are welcome during the day.

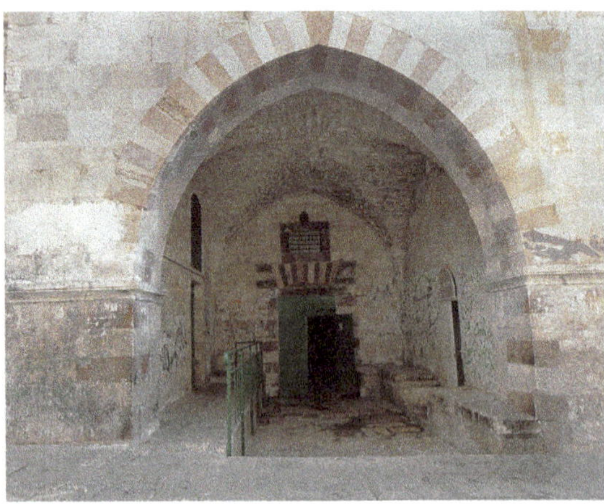

Ribat al-Mansuri, view of the entrance from the exterior, Jerusalem (© Sonia Halliday Photographs, photograph: D. Silverman).

The *ribat* dates back to the Mamluk period, confirmed by the inscription plaque on top of the southern wall of the entrance, which indicates that Sultan al-Mansur Qalawun commissioned it in 681/1282–1283. He wanted to establish a place that would house both pilgrims and the poor. Qalawun was one of the main Mamluk Sultans to have established a number of foundations during the Mamluk dynasty in Egypt and Syria. He ruled between 678/1279 and 689/1290 immediately after Sultan Baibars. Even though his greatest architectural projects were carried out in Cairo, holy cities such as Jerusalem and Hebron had their share of his attention. He built a *ribat* and a hospital in Hebron, but most of these edifices have not survived.

There are no records of the administrative, financial or social activities of the building. Some documents, however, reveal that the revenue from a number of buildings in different parts of Palestine were allocated there, not to mention the fact that it was built by the head of the Mamluk state. This *waqf* allowed the *ribat* to resume its activities throughout Mamluk times until the end of the Ottoman period, when a group of Sudanese Muslims came to Jerusalem and settled there. They still live there and one has a good chance of finding them seated in front of the *ribat's* entrance. They are usually very friendly, so greeting them would be courteous before asking their permission to visit some of the *ribat's* utilities. The *ribat* was also used as a prison, hence its alternative name The Ribat Prison.

Ribat al-Mansuri, interior, Jerusalem (© Sonia Halliday Photographs, photograph: D. Silverman).

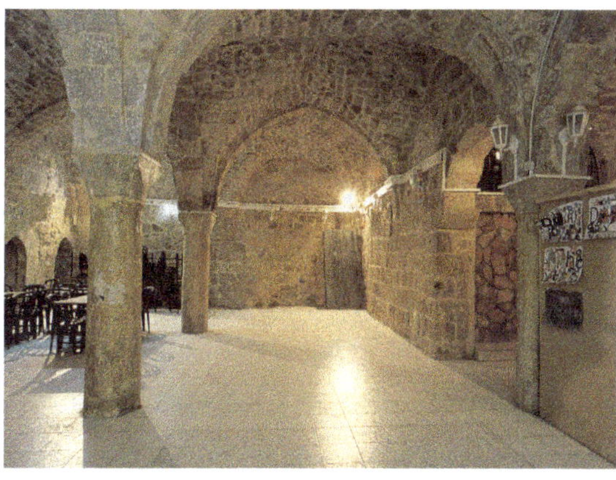

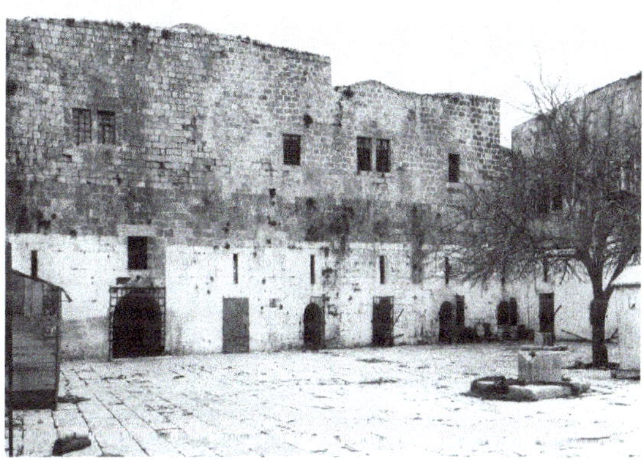

Ribat al-Mansuri, interior façade, Jerusalem (© The Creswell Archive, Department of Eastern Art, Ashmolean Museum, Oxford).

The *ribat*'s façade faces Tariq Bab al-Nadir and consists of two storeys: the lower dates to the Mamluk period, while the upper is of the Ottoman period. Its beauty can still be traced in the co-ordination of its windows, its colourful stones, the pointed arch of its entrance portal, the ornamental frame that separates its two parts, and the upper arch that is decorated with chevron fluting.

Its interior layout reflects its original function and has three architectural units, the first of which is a rectangular entrance. The tiled floor drops slightly below street level and on both the eastern and western sides a large stone *mastaba* with a cross vault is found. The inscription plaque mentioned above is found on its southern wall. The second architectural unit consists of a large rectangular hall that lies to the east of the entrance and is reached through a corridor. A row of four columns, which carry pointed arches, divides the hall into two rooms. The hall once hosted many pilgrims who came to Jerusalem from all over the Islamic world; today it has been turned into a place that serves several different functions, in addition to cultural activities. The third architectural unit is a large open courtyard that lies to the west of the entrance. Many rooms of different sizes (one containing a tomb) surround it. These rooms were home to a large number of *sufi*s and also to the poor from Jerusalem and all over the Islamic world, and today they still house many descendants of the different sects that chose to move to this holy city. As a result of the difficult economic and social circumstances facing the inhabitants of the city, the courtyard has had modern parts added that distort its beauty.

II.1.g **Khassaki Sultan Complex**

Located in the heart of the Old City, in the centre of the southern part of Aqabat al-

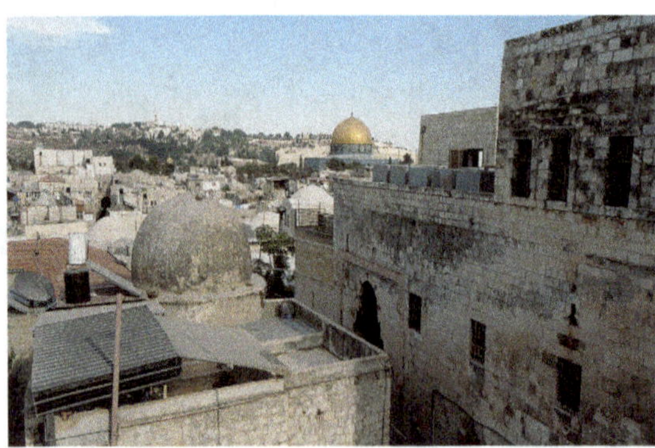

Khassaki Sultan Complex, tomb and palace in the foreground, the Dome of the Rock with the Mount of Olives in the background, Jerusalem (© Sonia Halliday Photographs, photograph: D. Silverman).

Takiyya, which connects Tariq Khan al-Zayt to the west and Tariq Bab al-Nadir to the east. Visiting the external part is possible during the day, but visiting the interior requires prior arrangement with the officers at the southern entrance.

It took four years to complete the complex (959/1552–963/1556), making it the largest charitable institution in the whole city.

Khassaki Sultan Complex, north entrance (side view with road), Jerusalem (© Sonia Halliday Photographs, photograph: D. Silverman).

The complex is vast and has two entrances. The northern one lies on Aqabat al-Takiyya, while the southern one lies on Aqabat al-Saraya. In the local language, *al-Takiyya* means "*the place where food is served free of charge*". *Al-Saraya*, on the other hand, means the seat of the governor or the *wali* and is named after the Ottoman mayor's residence prior to the British Mandate.

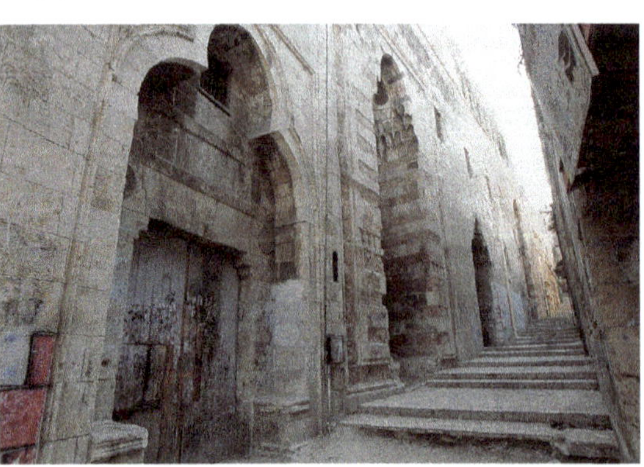

The complex is attributed to Roxelane, the wife of the Ottoman Sultan Sulayman the Magnificent (926/1520–974/1566), known as Haseki Hürrem (the cheerful, good-humoured one). Ottoman sources refer to her as Khassaki Sultan, in other words the Sultan's favourite and beloved. Khassaki Sultan endowed generous *waqfs* on her social and charitable project to guarantee the perpetuation of its activities. The revenues of 30 towns and villages in Palestine and other places went into its budget. She added to them a *waqf* of four more villages donated by Sultan Sulayman to support her *waqf* after her death. These villages were located in different regions in Gaza, Nablus, Jerusalem, Sidon and Tripoli.

The complex consisted of four different sections, some of which have survived:

A large *caravanserai* to accommodate travellers and traders. It consists of a large entrance that leads to a corridor with rooms on both sides. The corridor ends in an open courtyard, which is surrounded by more corridors that form the *caravanserais*. These parts can be seen today from the southern entrance, though some of their functions have changed.

A mosque for prayer, reciting the Qur'an and praying for the benefactor. It has many domes and arches. However, its exact location is unknown and it is presumed that part of it was demolished and that the current student refectory was built over it.

A *ribat* of 55 rooms to house *sufis*, the poor and visitors. Like the mosque, its location is also unknown today. It seems that most of the rooms have been demolished and changed into other utilities, although it was probably east of the southern entrance where the printing shop currently stands.

A large kitchen, a bakery, a mill, many storage rooms and a fountain to provide water to the residence have all survived and can be seen after entering the courtyard from the northern gate and turning east via some stairs. The kitchen continues to provide delicious soups every morning plus meat and rice during Ramadan and every Tuesday, even though the *ribat*'s *waqf* ceased long ago.

This active institution was administered by a number of senior Ottoman employees. The Inspector was posted from Istanbul and was helped by approximately 50 members of staff, each having a detailed job description allocated to him in the *waqf*. Among the employees were a person who washed the cups, another who picked the rice, two chefs and their three assistants, a renovator, and a maintenance person who would look after the building. In addition to the running costs, the total annual wage bill was approximately 795.5 silver dirhams.

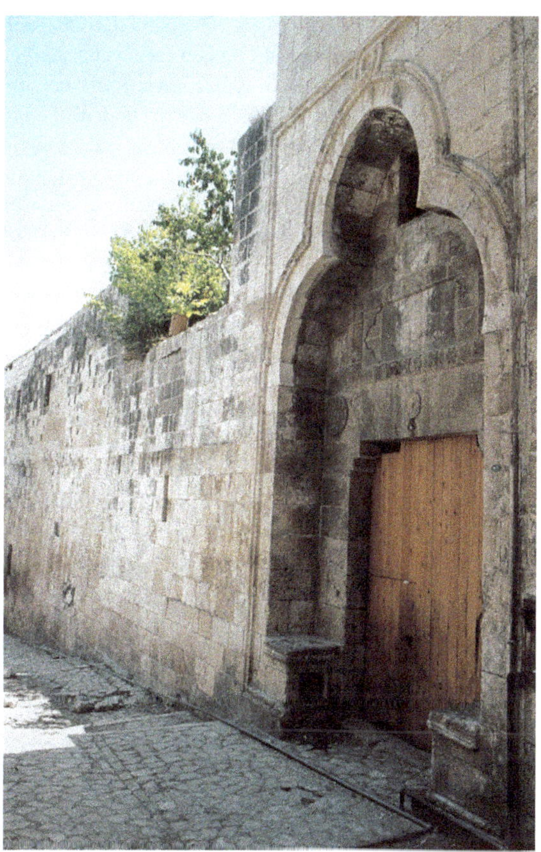

Khassaki Sultan Complex, north entrance portal, Jerusalem (© M. Hamilton, Burgoyne).

THE *SUQS*

Yusuf Natsheh

Islamic cities in medieval times were renowned for their important markets (*suqs*), such as the Khan al-Khalili in Cairo, Suq al-Hamidiyya in Damascus, Suq al-Safafir (copper craftsmen) in Bagdad, and the Egyptian Bazaar in Istanbul. In Jerusalem there were many markets mentioned in the diaries of travellers, the most famous of which was Suq al-Qattanin (Market of the Cotton Merchants). Other markets include: Suq Khan al-Zayt (Olive Oil Market), Suq al-'Attarin (Spices Market), Suq al-Lahhamin (Butchers' Market) and Suq al-Khawajat (Textile Market). Suq Khan al-Zayt, oriented north to south, starts from the junction a few metres south of Bab al-'Amud and continues to Suq al-'Attarin. It was famous for its abundant olive presses and soap factories until the early 19th century, with each press having a huge storage room for olive oil. The market is long and has shops on both sides. Part of it is covered to protect visitors from the heat and rain.

Suq al-'Attarin, which extends southwards from Suq Khan al-Zayt, is one of three joint markets, which date back to the Mamluk and Ottoman periods. Parts of its foundations are thought to date back to the Crusader period. Excavations have revealed that it was built on the ruins of an earlier market dating back to the Roman/Byzantine period. The *suq* is covered by cross vaults, each with an open skylight in the centre, and it is a wonderful experience to see the sunbeams reflected on the colourful goods – everything turns vivid and pleasant. Until recently this market specialised in Arab and Oriental perfumery and spices, but today the development and modernisation of the city has reduced the number of these shops to only three.

Parallel to Suq al-'Attarin are the two other markets with the same design and architectural components. The western one is the Suq al-Lahhamin, which has an array of shops that sell all kinds of meat. Half a century ago a large proportion of these shops used to be centres of traditional Arab smiths, where hammers, forging and blowing were used on copper and other metals. The Armenian community is renowned for this craft. The eastern market, of which only the southern part can be seen because its northern section still needs to be uncovered, is known as Suq al-Khawajat.

The roofs of these three markets provide good panoramic views over the Old City, its mosques, churches and other buildings. They can be reached by ascending the stairs at the end of Suq al-'Attarin, found by turning left, passing through Suq al-Lahhamin and then turning south at Suq al-Husur (Mat Market).

FORTIFICATIONS AND GATES OF THE OLD CITY

Mahmoud Hawari

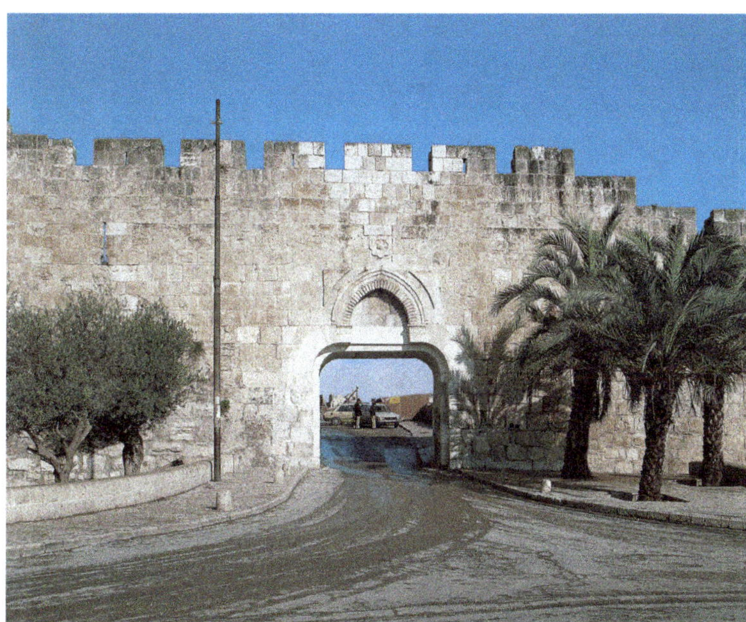

Bab al-Maghariba (Gate of the Maghribi), placed in the western wall, Jerusalem (© Sonia Halliday Photographs).

The walls of the Old City of Jerusalem are among its most important landmarks and have maintained their original form for hundreds of years. The city's fortifications have been exposed to partial ruin, rebuilding and renovations many times throughout their history. They were last severely damaged during the wars between the Ayyubids and Crusaders in the early 7th/13th century. When the Mamluks came to power (long after the Crusaders had been defeated) they did not fortify the walls of the city, preferring instead to rebuild and fortify the citadel, turning it into an administrative and military centre. The gates of the city, on the other hand, were kept in their original form and were used throughout the Mamluk period to gain entrance and exit from the city. Mujir al-Din al-Hanbali, the renowned Jerusalem-based historian, mentioned in 901/1496 that nine gates were used during his time: Bab al-Maghariba (Gate of the Maghribi), Bab Sahyoun (Gate of Zion) also named Bab al-Nabi Dawud (Gate of David), Bab al-Sir, Bab al-Mihrab, Bab al-Rahba, Bab Deir al-Sarb, Bab al-'Amud "Gate of the Column" (Gate of Damascus), Bab al-Da'iya and Bab al-Asbat.

For the most part, the walls and city gates were restored, with parts being rebuilt between 944/1537 and 947/1541, during Ottoman Sultan Sulayman's time.

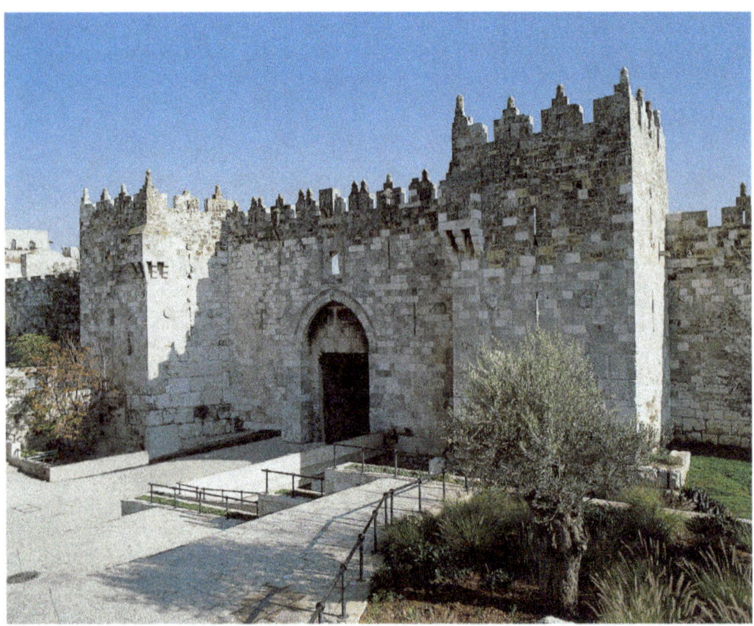

Bab al-'Amud, "Gate of the Column" (Gate of Damascus), situated in the northern wall, Jerusalem (© Sonia Halliday Photographs).

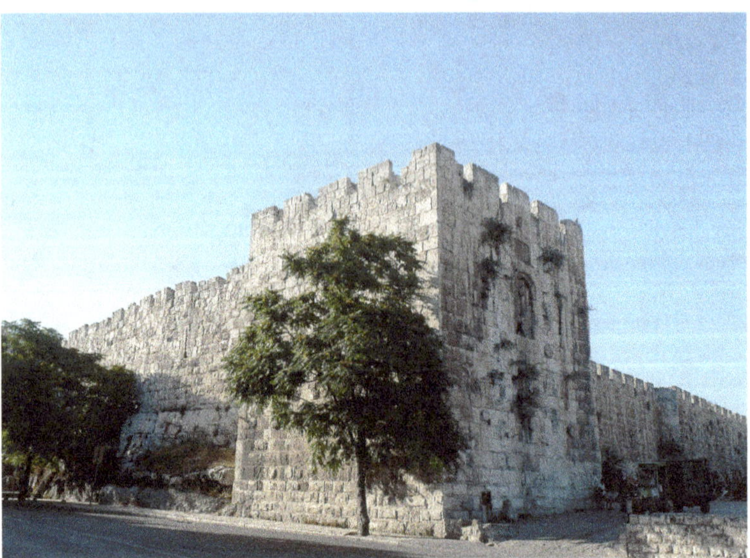

Al-Qalaq Tower, general view, Jerusalem.

These walls follow approximately the line of the walls that surrounded the city during the Ayyubid period (7th/13th century) and are 4,018 m. long and 11.6–12.2 m. high. They carry 35 towers, 17 machicolations, 344 arrow slits, 16 inscriptions and a large number of decorative medallions.
Seven of the city's gates are open today: Bab al-Khalil (Gate of Jaffa) on the western wall; Bab al-Jadid (New Gate), Bab al-'Amud (Gate of Damascus) and Bab al-Sahira (Gate of Herod) on the northern wall; Bab al-Asbat (Gate of the Lions) on the eastern wall, and Bab al-Maghariba (Gate of the Maghribi) and Bab al-Nabi Dawud (Gate of Zion) on the southern wall.
Visitors have access to the whole wall-walk apart from the section that lies between Bab al-Asbat and Bab al-Rahma (Golden Gate) Cemetery. A special permit from the Islamic Endowment Department or the cemetery's watchman is needed. A ticket must be purchased from Bab al-Khalil or Bab al-'Amud to climb on top of the walls and enjoy the view. Visitors are advised to wear suitable shoes to avoid slipping and during the summer a bottle of drinking water and a hat are recommended.

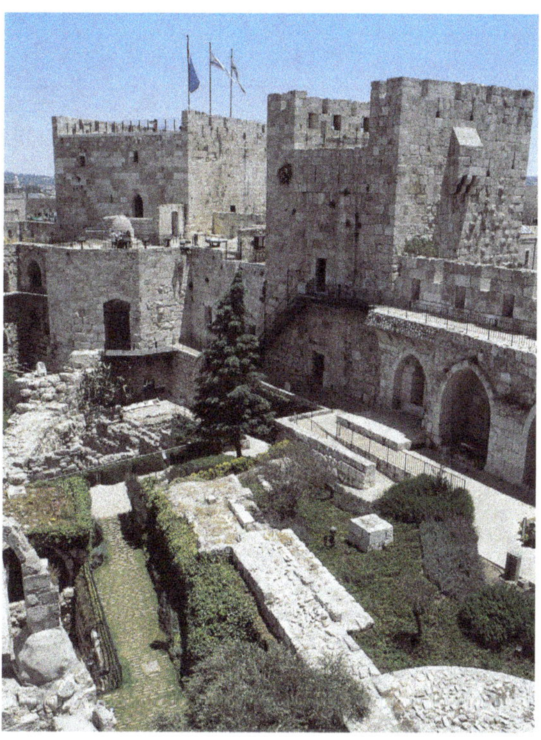

Citadel, general view of the interior, Jerusalem.

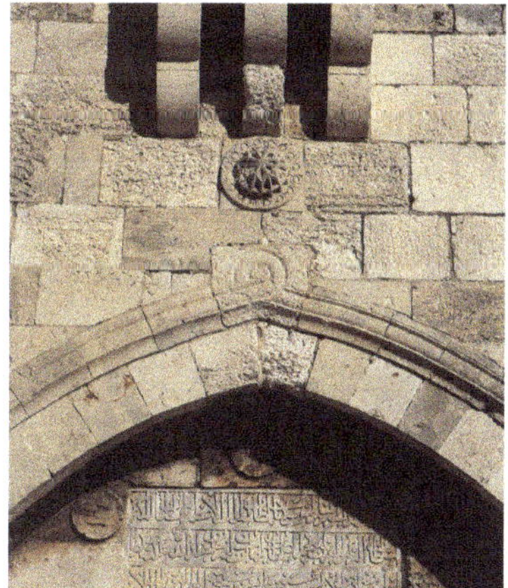

Bab al-Khalil, detail, Jerusalem.

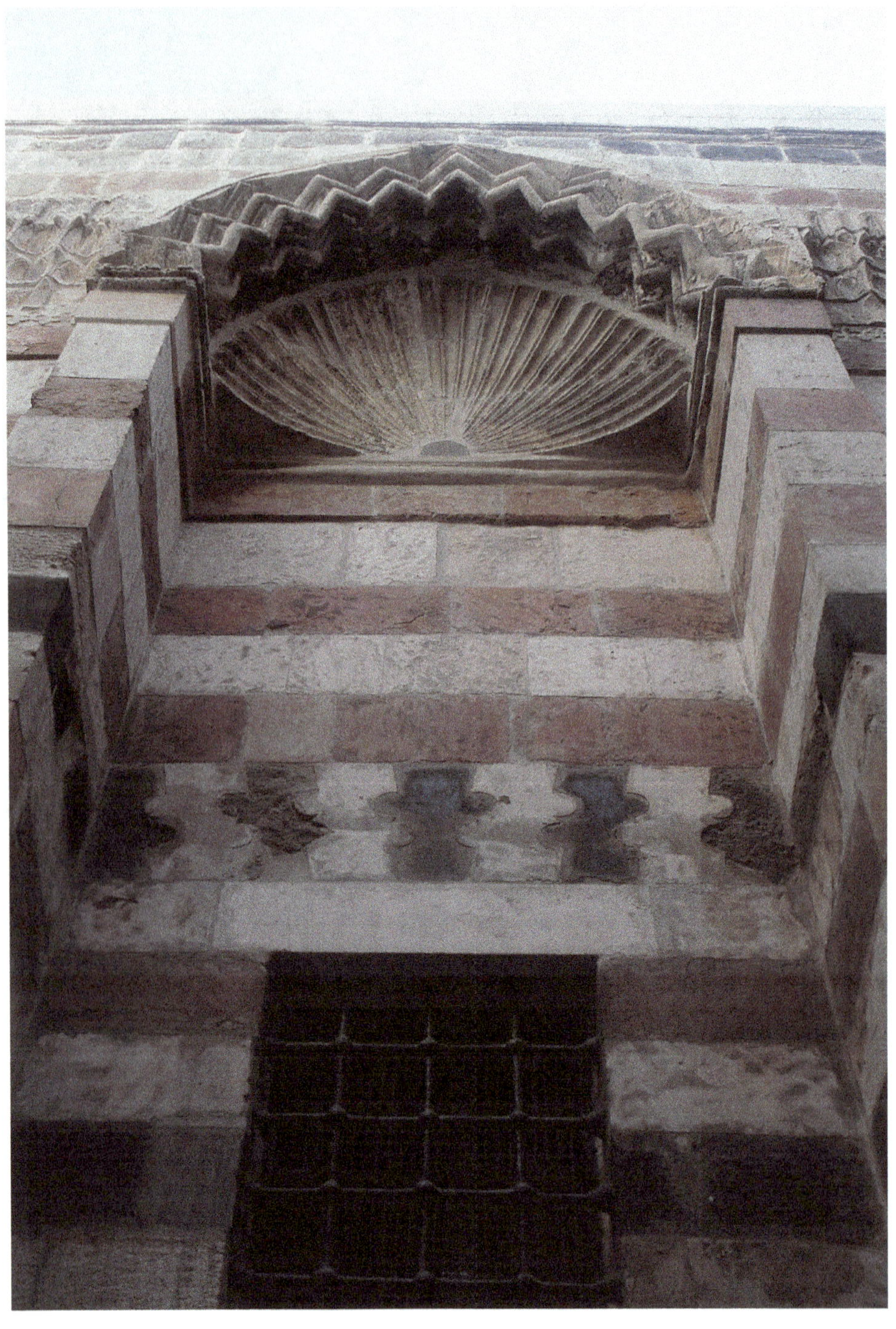

Jerusalem: the Centre of Religious Study and Knowledge

Yusuf Natsheh

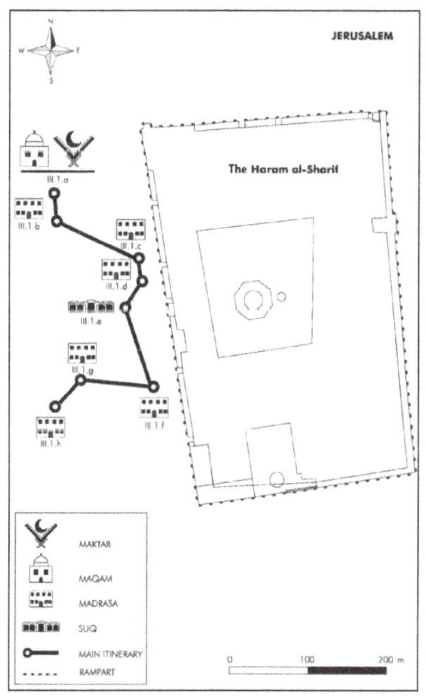

Madrasa al-Mawardiyya, entrance, detail, Jerusalem.

Pilgrimage, Sufism and science were the three elements that distinguished Palestine and Jerusalem. Following Itinerary II, which explored Sufism in Jerusalem, this itinerary will deal with the scientific institutions that developed in the proximity of the Haram al-Sharif.

Discussing the scientific institutions in a separate chapter is only a matter of methodology. Many themes of the itineraries in this book overlap, especially when it comes to the scientific centres and the *sufi zawiyas* – after all, Jerusalem's important position within Islam encouraged the development of both. The terms and the regulations governing their different *waqfs* were the same and their cultural activities were rather similar, specifically those related to the Qur'an and the *Hadith*.

As the *madrasas* and *zawiyas* lie close to each other, one cannot avoid returning to some places in order to see different edifices, especially when it comes to the junction between Tariq al-Wad, Tariq Bab al-Nadir and Aqabat al-Takiyya, which are visited in both Itinerary II and in Itinerary III.

This itinerary covers eight sites and has two "windows"; the first of which discusses the *waqf* system in Islam and Palestine, while the second goes over the diary and activities of a student in a *madrasa*. Special attention has been paid to the unity of the subject. Apart from it being built in the same period and sharing some architectural and artistic features, Suq al-Qattanin is the only site that does not fit directly into this itinerary (even though a large part of its revenue was dedicated to the Madrasa al-Tankiziyya). Suq al-Qattanin also connects the two centres of this itinerary – Tariq Bab al-Hadid and Tariq Bab al-Silsila.

Our journey here starts where Itinerary II ends. The visitor is advised to start the itinerary from Bab al-'Amud, although, equally, it could be started from the end of the itinerary (al-Taziyya) and continued in reverse order. The best time to visit these sites is from early morning until noon because some are used as offices and are, therefore, closed in the afternoon.

Focusing on the areas adjacent to the Haram – on Tariq Bab al-Hadid and Tariq Bab al-Silsila – this itinerary covers an important sector of Mamluk Jerusalem. Visitors will also experience the city's topography, the diversity of its main and side roads, plus the pressing problems of the Old City.

III.1 JERUSALEM

III.1.a Maktab and Maqam of Bayram Jawish

Lies in the north-west corner of the junction where Tariq Bab al-Nadir and Aqabat al-Takiyya meet with Tariq al-Wad. Visitors are welcome during al-Sadaqat Library opening hours.

According to the inscription above the entrance, Maktab Bayram Jawish was restored in 947/1541. This suggests the building had another function before Bayram Jawish renovated the site to make it his family's final resting place and a *maktab* for the education of boys (see Ribat Bayram Jawish, II.1.e). The architectural design of the original section served this dual function, but today it is no longer used for education and is known instead as the burial ground of Bayram. His tomb has been covered in cloth and its surface is currently used to exhibit the religious publications and books of the Sadaqat Committee, with any profits used for charity work.

In 948/1543, Bayram Jawish endowed in a *waqf* the revenue of grape and fig plantations in the village of Bayt Sahur to this *maktab*. At a later stage he joined it to the *waqf* of his *ribat*, making his *waqf* the second largest in Ottoman Jerusalem after that of Khassaki Sultan. It came to a total of 15,000 silver dirhams, which he allocated to the purchase of lands and property in different parts of Palestine. He stipulated that their revenue should go to his *maktab* and *ribat*. He allocated to the children's tutor three silver dirhams per day and provided him with free accommodation. He also stipulated that the orphans be taught the Qur'an, *Hadith* and the basics of reading.

The *maktab* has two façades that overlook the road. The main façade faces east to Tariq al-Wad and has the only entrance to the building, above which lies a stone plaque honouring the founder and giving the date of construction. Stones in many colours decorate it. An arcade added to the building at a later stage blocks the upper part. The second southern façade overlooks Aqabat al-Takiyya. The building consists of two storeys. The ground floor is the original one that was renovated by Bayram; it has a T-shaped hall divided into two parts by a large arch.

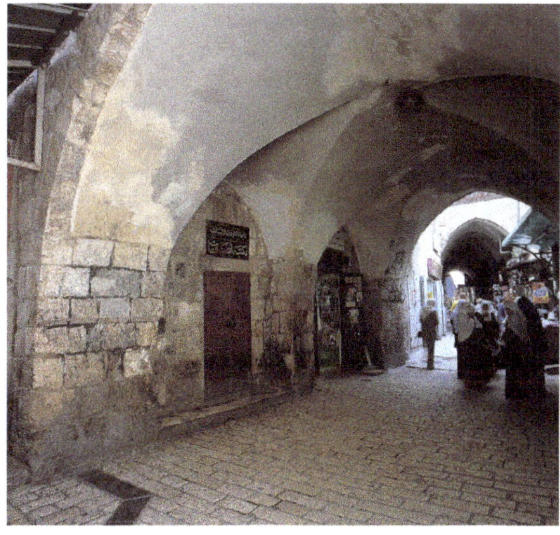

Maktab and Maqam of Bayram Jawish, entrance, Jerusalem.

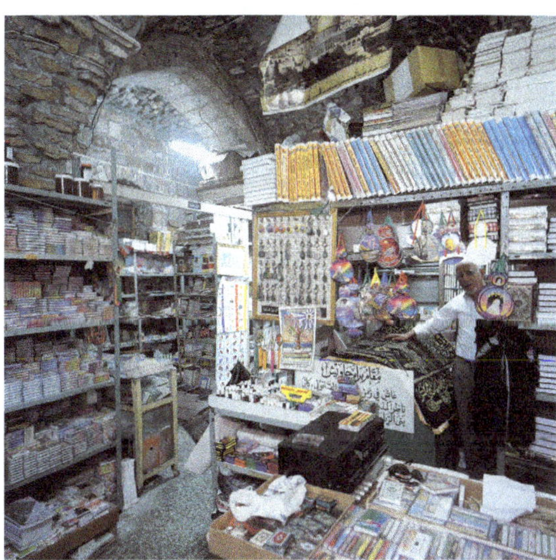

Maktab and Maqam of Bayram Jawish, eastern interior area sheltering the tomb of Bayram Jawish, Jerusalem.

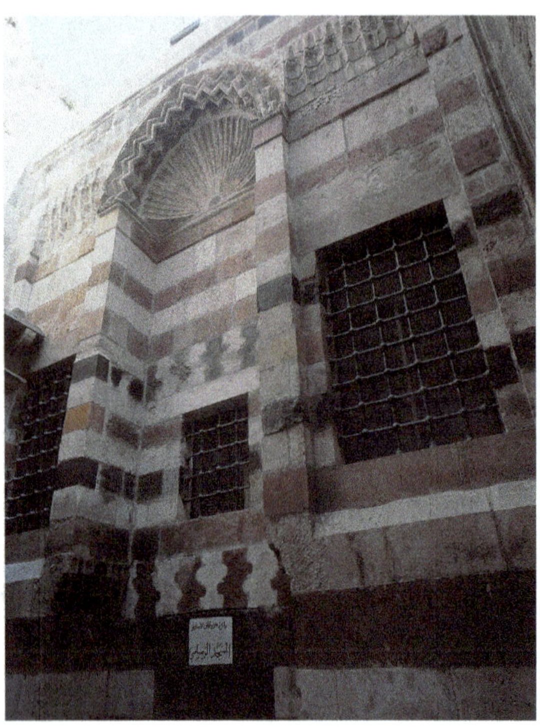

Madrasa al-Mawardiyya, entrance, Jerusalem (© Sonia Halliday Photographs, Photograph: D. Silverman).

The first storey and the eastern part contains the Tomb of Bayram Jawish, while the second upper part (added at a later stage) consists of a relatively small open courtyard that is surrounded by several rooms to the east and west.

III.1.b **Madrasa al-Mawardiyya (al-Rasasiyya)**

Lies to the south of Aqabat al-Takiyya, between Ribat Bayram Jawish to the east and an unidentified building to the west. Access to the interior of the building is not possible at present.

The date of this edifice is unknown, with no *waqf* document or foundation inscription to shed light on it. Thought to be part of Ribat Bayram Jawish, and thus identified as an Ottoman building, the structure contains both Mamluk and Ottoman elements. However, it may well be dated to a period between the late 9th/15th century and the early 10th/16th century.

No information is available on the patron of the edifice or the nature of its *waqf*. Named after one of its famous *shaykhs*, until recently it was known, incorrectly, as Madrasa al-Rassasiyya (Arabic for "lead") as lead was the material used to bind its lower stones together.

Documents in the Tribunal Court of Jerusalem reveal that al-Mawardiyya had many *waqfs*, but these were insufficient to cover its expenses. To renovate its utilities, money was borrowed in the hope that future revenues would repay the debt. Failing to do so, the Mawardiyya was turned into a private residence; the tenant was expected to carry out renovations in return for living there for a limited number of years, but a jurist first had to approve the tenancy. As a result, in the first half of the 10th/16th century, Bayram Jawish allocated to it 3,600 silver Ottoman coins in return for living there while his house was being built to the east of his *ribat*. A certain Hajj Sinan al-Sughanji also lived there for a time and renovated parts of it. An Islamic orphanage to teach preparatory and secondary level pupils currently uses most of the building, except for the mosque.

Another document outlines the *madrasa*'s units and the borders that separate Khassaki Sultan's complex from Ribat Bayram Jawish. The Mawardiyya consisted of three rooms: a grand *iwan* facing the largest room, a mosque and two open courtyards. In one of these rooms, 'Arif al-'Arif – the famous historian and author of a volume on the History of Jerusalem – received his primary and secondary education in the early 20th century. The northern façade of the *madrasa* is breathtaking. It was built in the *ablaq* style with alternating black, red and white stones. A slightly receding entrance portal is found in the centre and a small *mastaba* is found on either side. A red stone lintel above the entrance portal is surmounted with an *ablaq* stringcourse of black and white joggling. The entrance portal is topped by a scalloped shell within which is enclosed a semicircular arch of chevron moulding. A staircase to the west of the entrance leads to the mosque of the *madrasa* and the rest of the units listed above, which are on a slightly higher level than is the ground floor.

III.1.c **Madrasa and Khanqa al-Jawhariyya**

Lies to the north of Tariq Bab al-Hadid, adjacent to the ribat *al-Kurd, which is close to the western wall of the esplanade.*
Some of its internal units can be visited from morning until early afternoon, especially the parts housing the Department of Islamic Archaeology. However, permission should be sought from the staff in the building.

The inscription plaque above the entrance reveals that the building was constructed in 844/1440. It was originally built to accommodate *sufis* and to encourage the recitation of the Qur'an. The Department of Islamic Archaeology uses today part of the building, while the other part has been turned into a residence.

The founder of this edifice is Jawhar al-Qunquba'i, who was originally an Abyssinian eunuch given as a gift to the Mamluk Sultan Barquq (784/1382-801/1399). Freed later on, he served many *amirs* and held many high positions. He became the treasurer of Sultan al-Ashraf Barsbay (825/1422-842/1438) and played an important role in the financial decisions of the Mamluk Dynasty. In 843/1439, he was allocated the management of the *harem* in the Sultan's palace. Sultan Jaqmaq conferred on him

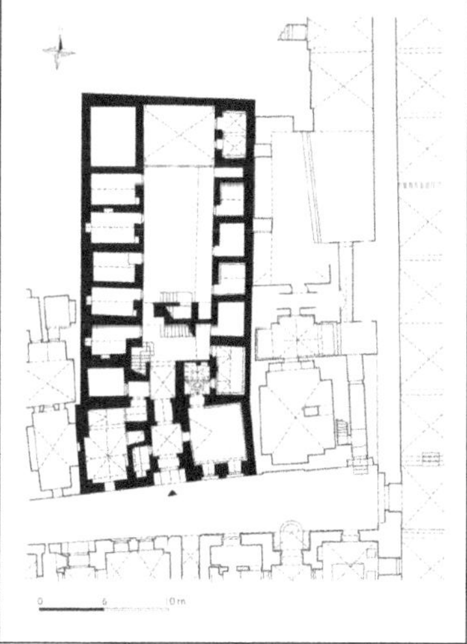

Madrasa and Khanqa al-Jawhariyya, ground floor plan, Jerusalem.

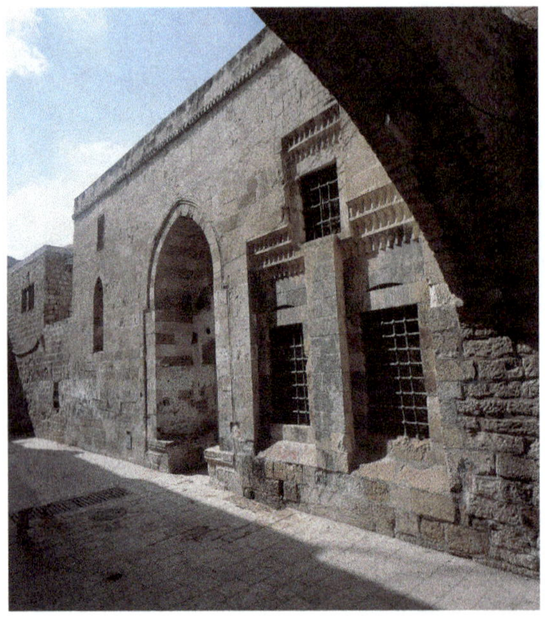

Madrasa and Khanqa al-Jawhariyya, southern façade, general view, Jerusalem.

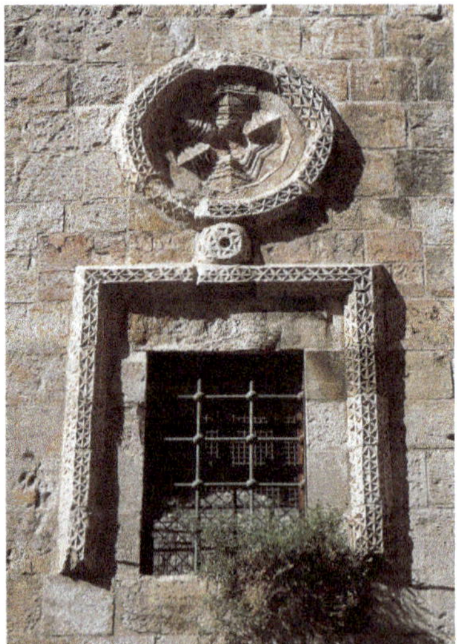

Madrasa and Khanqa al-Jawhariyya, decorative rose window, Jerusalem.

the title of the "*shaykh* of *shaykh*s" and the servant of the Haram al-Nabawi in Medina. Jawhar died in 844/1440 in his seventies, hardly a month after his *madrasa* in Jerusalem was completed. He was, however, buried in the *madrasa* he had built in Cairo close to the Azhar Mosque.

Jawhar allocated a generous *waqf* to his *madrasa*, which befitted his wealth and the ambitious staff employed at his institution. It included land in the villages of Taqwa, Tulkarem, Bayt al-Zaytun and Kufiya. Among the staff were an inspector, schoolmaster, a *sufi shaykh*, 25 *sufi*s, a prayer reader, a teacher for the reciting of the Qur'an, 10 orphans, a servant, a returns extractor, two workers and the registrar. Jawhar also stipulated in his *waqf* that widows were to be given bread on a daily basis and he allocated a specific budget for the oil lamps. The annual expenditure of his *madrasa* reached 9,600 silver coins and 11,376 lbs. of bread.

The Jawhariyya played a leading cultural and social role in the Mamluk and Ottoman periods. Elite jurists and scholars taught there, including Shaykh Kamal al-Din Ibn Abi Sharif al-Qudsi, one of the most renowned *shaykh*s of the Madrasa al-Salahiyya. Many of Jerusalem's distinguished guests stayed there; among them were judge Sharaf al-Din Musa al-Ansari, the Sultan's deputy in 845/1471, and judge Shihab al-Din Ibn Jubaylat who had come to Jerusalem to investigate the building of a synagogue by the Jews of the city after it had been destroyed. He listened to their testimony in the Jawhariyya.

Eventually the edifice suffered from similar problems to all the other institutions and was turned into a residence at the end of the 13th/19th century. Moreover, recent digging of a tunnel carried out by the Israeli authorities along the west wall of the Haram badly damaged the building and as a result the building required some renovation work.

The Jawhariyya has one façade orientated to the south. An entrance portal with a pointed arch leads through a corridor to an open courtyard – flanked by several rooms and halls that lie to the east and west of the corridor. On both the west and south sides are chambers, which surround the courtyard, while an *iwan* is situated in the northern zone. The stairs to the south-west of the courtyard lead up to the first floor, which also has many rooms, among which are offices occupied by the Department of Islamic Archaeology. A second group of stairs is found to the east of the corridor that follows the entrance, leading to the rest of the first floor. The chambers lie exactly above those on the ground floor. The Khatib family resides in the other large halls. The second floor, dating to the Ottoman period, is reached from the first floor.

III.1.d **Madrasa al-Arghuniyya**

It is built against the west wall of the Haram at the end of Tariq Bab al-Hadid, which connects Tariq al-Wad and the esplanade.

Visitors are not allowed inside. However, the northern façade of the building can be closely examined from the street at any time of the day.

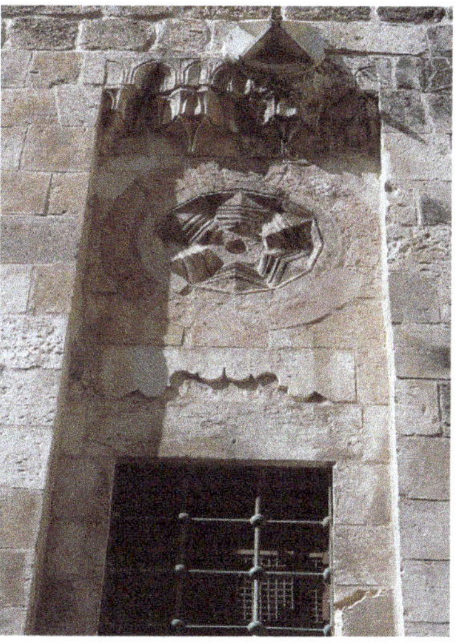

Madrasa and Khanqa al-Jawhariyya, decorative rose window and muqarnas, Jerusalem.

As the foundation plaque of the building reveals, the edifice was designed to be a *madrasa* and a *turbe* (mausoleum). It was completed in 759/1358 during the reign of Rukn al-Din Baybars al-Sayfi and only a few months after the death of its founder, the Amir Arghun in 758/1357. Arghun was a bright, ambitious Mamluk *amir*. He reached the military rank of *amir arba'in* (commanding forty soldiers) at only seventeen years of age, when he was known as Arghun al-Saghir (Young Arghun). A prince would have to attain an advanced rank in the Mamluk army before he became *amir al-mi'a* (hundred), then *muqaddam arif* and to be allocated high princely posts. Arghun attained this rank during the reign of Sultan Sha'ban. A decree was issued to replace his title of al-Saghir, with that of al-Kamili, in reference to al-Kamil Sha'ban. Severe penalties awaited anyone who continued to

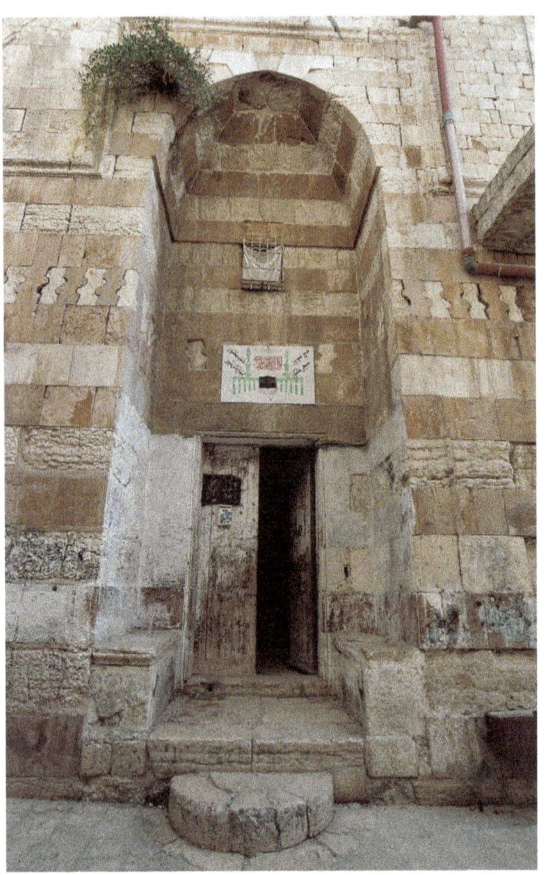

Madrasa al-Arghuniyya, entrance, Jerusalem (© Sonia Harding Photographs, Photograph: D. Silverman).

The Madrasa al-Arghuniyya attracted many distinguished personalities. Judge Sa'd al-Din Sa'd al-Dayri (d. 867/1462–1463) received his education in jurisprudence there and judge Ghars al-Din Khalil al-Kinani, previously a teacher at the Madrasa al-Salahiyya, lived there in 879/1474. Later before 897/1491–1492 it became the residence of Khadr Bek, the Governor of Jerusalem. Many Ottoman documents reveal the names of distinguished scholars and tutors who were employed at the *madrasa* and who contributed to its remarkable fame. Various members of the al-'Afifi family have held the post of the *madrasa*'s *shaykh*; this helps to explain why the institution was lately called the Madrasa al-'Afifi.

In 1931, the Hashemite King Hussein I – the leader of the Arab revolt against the Turks during the First World War – was buried in the *madrasa*'s eastern *iwan*. Today, most of this building has been turned into a residence.

call him al-Saghir. Arghun ruled the provinces of Aleppo and Damascus and led an army to the Kingdom of Zulghadar; he was then called to Cairo, the centre of the Mamluk government, in 755/1355. Mysterious circumstances surround his arrest and imprisonment in Alexandria, and he was later exiled to Jerusalem where he settled and established his *madrasa*.

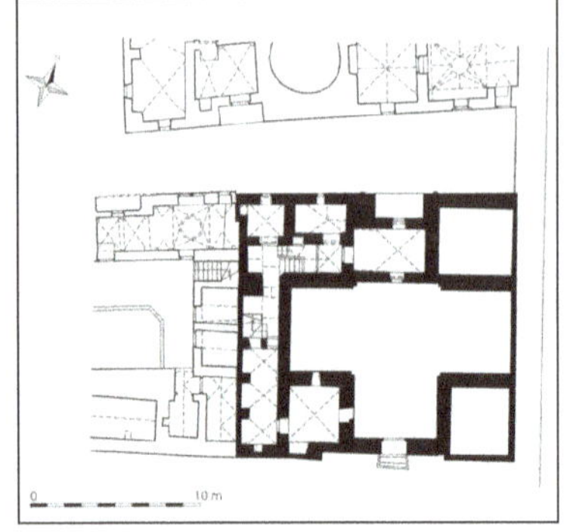

Madrasa al-Arghuniyya, ground floor plan, Jerusalem.

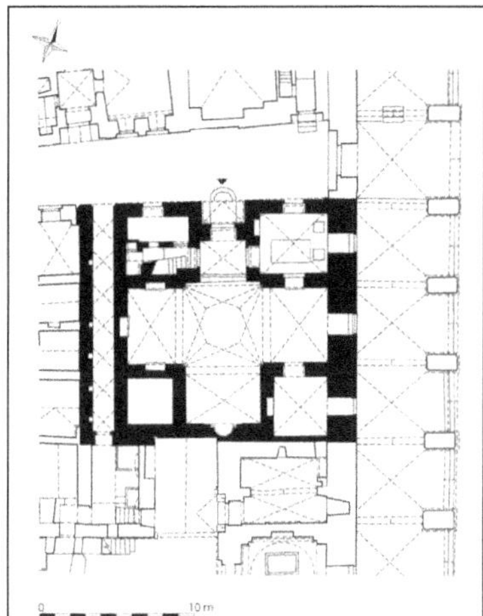

Madrasa al-Arghuniyya, upper floor plan, Jerusalem.

The Arghuniyya has a splendid northern façade of mosaic stones arranged in a colourful *ablaq* style. Its commemorative entrance recedes slightly to accommodate two *mastabas* on each of its sides, preceding the rectangular portal that leads to the interior. The inscription plaque above the entrance holds the Jamdariyya coat of arms (the person in charge of the Sultan's attire), which was Arghun's coat of arms when he held this position. To the east of the entrance there is a rectangular window with beautiful grills dating to the Mamluk period. These grills draw attention to the exquisite stringcourse joggling on the projecting edge of the window. The building has a balanced architectural design that consists of a square central hall covered by a cross vault, and surrounded by four horizontal *iwans*, the largest of which is in the south.

III.1.e **Suq al-Qattanin**

Lies in the middle of the Haram's western border. The site is open to visitors at all times.

The complex is known today as Suq al-Qattanin (Market of the Cotton Merchants). This name, which dates back to the $10^{th}/16^{th}$ century, is not the original one. The locals occasionally call it Suq al-'Atm (the Dark Market), because of its darkness when compared to the uncovered parts of the Haram.
The *suq* is considered to be one of the most perfectly preserved and beautiful markets in Palestine. Creswell, the famous scholar of Islamic architecture, listed it as the finest in Syria. Mujir al-Din, the renowned historian on Jerusalem and Hebron, commented on it in the early $10^{th}/16^{th}$ century, saying: *"Among the distinguished places in Jerusalem is Suq al-Qattanin, which is adjacent to the Gate of the* [Aqsa] *Mosque from the west. It is a unique and perfect suq of high altitude".*
The *suq*, which is really more a commercial centre, was commissioned by Sultan al-Malik al-Nasir Muhammad Ibn

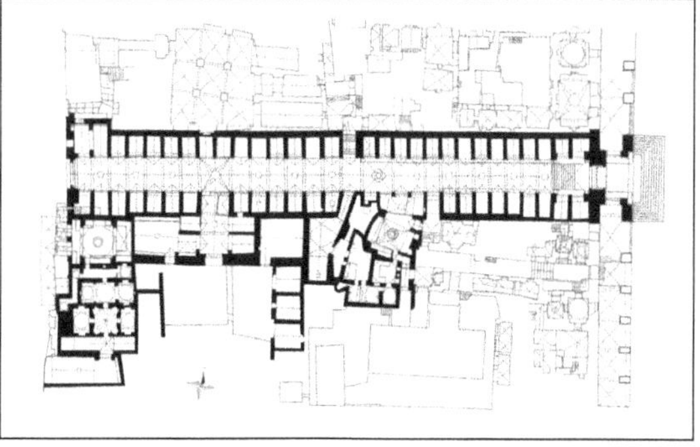

Suq al-Qattanin, ground floor plan, Jerusalem.

Suq al-Qattanin, eastern entrance, Jerusalem.

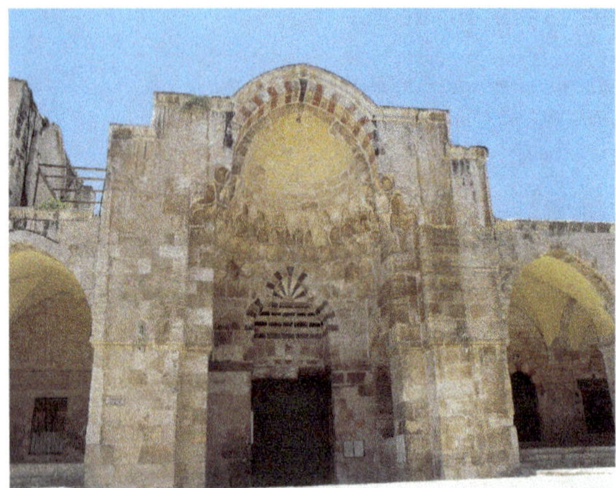

Suq al-Qattanin, western entrance, Jerusalem.

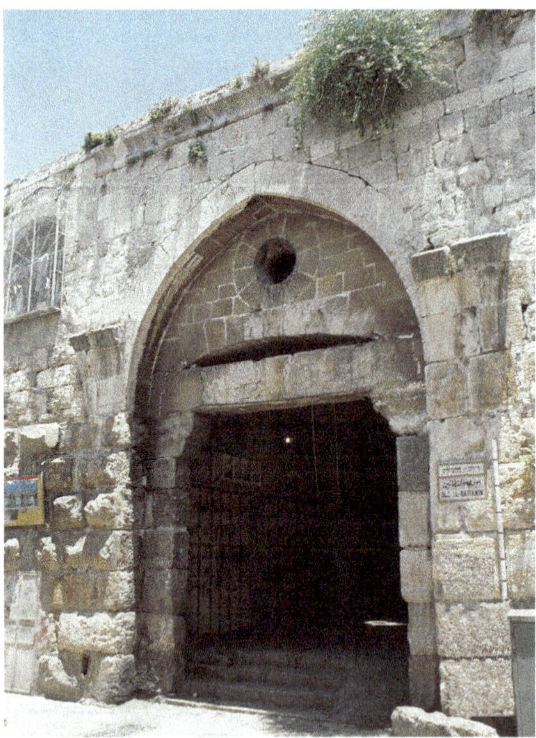

Qalawun whose rule extended from the end of the 7th/13th century to the beginning of the 8th/14th century. His architectural contributions in Jerusalem exceeded all those of other Mamluk sultans and even those of Amir Tankiz al-Nasiri, who was the Vice-Sultan of Syria between 712/1312 and 740/1340. The revenue from the shops in Suq al-Qatanin was divided equally between the *waqf* of the Haram and that of the Madrasa al-Tankiziyya. Now, however, as the *madrasa* no longer operates, the Administration of Waqfs collects the revenue. The *suq* was initially renovated in 1974, and there are plans to renovate it again in the future and revive it both economically and culturally.

The complex contains a *caravanserai*, two *hammams* and a long *suq*. The *suq* is approximately 95 m. long if measured from the east to the west. Two rows of shops (with 30 shops in each row) are found on the southern and northern parts. The *suq* has a barrel-vault consisting of a series of arches, which divides the roof into 30 sections. Each section has a skylight to allow light and air into the *suq*. The *suq* has two entrances, one to the east and the other to the west. The eastern entrance is one of the Haram's most important gates: built with special attention to detail, it is a unique architectural masterpiece. It is a recess that has a trefoil arch, encircled by another large semicircular recess that is carried on five rows of stone stalactites (known as *muqarnas*). The red, black and white stones of the entrance have been arranged in a co-ordinated *ablaq* style, which was very common in the Islamic architecture of Jerusalem, especially during the Mamluk period. The western entrance, on the other hand, is much simpler in its design and consists of a rectangular opening, above which is a flat arch consisting of seven interlaced joggled stones. On top of it lies a relieving arch and a circular window; they, in turn, are found inside a recess with a pointed arch.

III.1.f **Madrasa al-Tankiziyya**

Lies in the eastern part of Tariq Bab al-Silsila. Occupied by the Israeli forces, this beautiful building cannot be visited. Visitors, however, can have a close look at its façade.

Before the gate to the Sancutary is a small open courtyard, with the Ribat Tankiz allocated for women, found to its north. To the north-west lies the *sabil* of Sultan Sulayman I (943/1536) and behind it lies the Turbe al-Sa'diyya (711/1311). The façade of Madrasa al-Tankiziyya occupies the southern part of the courtyard.

The Tankiziyya has been called several different names throughout its history. In its *waqf* document it is described as a *khanqa* while many other references refer to it as a *madrasa*. The foundation plaque above the entrance refers to it as "a place". This indicates it was built as a huge complex for various functions; in fact the three-storey edifice is enormous.

According to its inscription, the Amir Sayf al-Din Tankiz al-Nasiri commissioned the building in 728–729/1329 in the hope

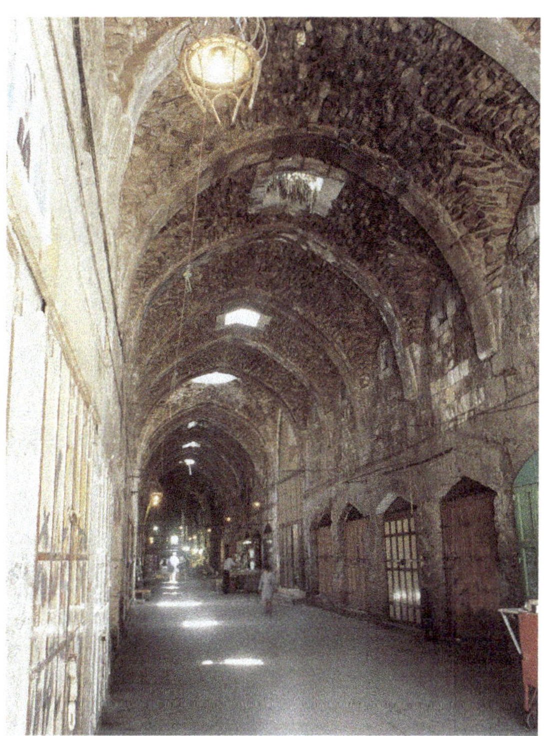

Suq al-Qattanin, general view, Jerusalem.

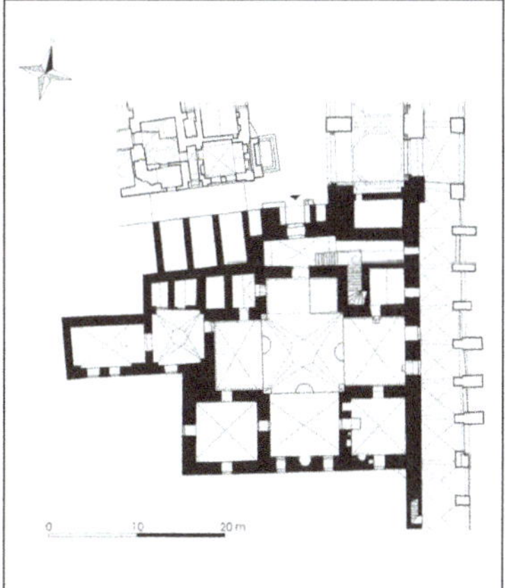

Madrasa al-Tankiziyya, ground floor plan, Jerusalem.

Madrasa al-Tankiziyya, section, Jerusalem.

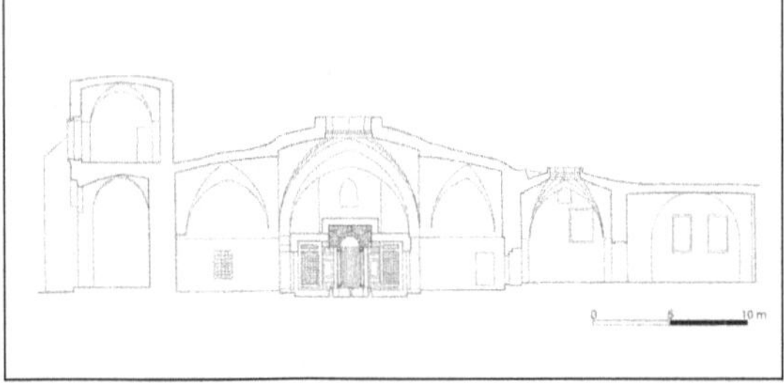

that he would "receive God's mercy". Like many Mamluk *amirs*, he started his life as a slave and gradually attained different Mamluk positions until he became the highest military and administrative figure in Syria during the reign of Sultan al-Nasir Muhammad Ibn Qalawun. He married his sons to the Sultan's daughters and remained a central figure, until his fortune changed when he was discharged in 740/1340.

Madrasa al-Tankiziyya, entrance, Jerusalem.

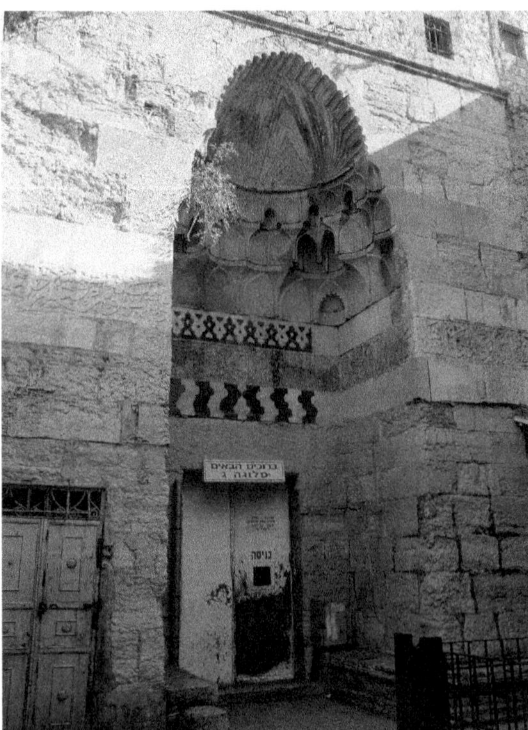

Tankiz was renowned for his patronage of various architectural projects in Damascus, Jerusalem and Palestine, among other places. These included religious buildings, *caravanserais*, *hammams*, and water-supply systems. His enormous fortune enabled him to undertake these vast projects, which can still be seen today, especially in Jerusalem. In addition to the complex discussed here, he built Suq al-Qattanin in Jerusalem, which included two *hammams*, one *caravanserai* and a *ribat* for women. It is thanks to him that the renovations on the Noble Sanctuary were carried out during this era.

The Madrasa al-Tankiziyya's *waqf* included the village of 'Ayn Qinya, which lies west of Ramallah, and all the surrounding land, in addition to the revenue from two *hammams*. The number of employees listed in the *waqf* reflects the wealth the institution enjoyed, and the role it played both culturally and educationally. The salaries of the administrative and educational staff were as follows: a tutor received 60 dirhams and an assistant 30 dirhams; of the 15 students, the advanced received 20 dirhams, the intermediate 15 dirhams and the novice 10 dirhams; the *shaykh* of *Hadith* received 40 dirhams, the *Hadith* reader received 20 dirhams and each of the *Hadith* students 7.5 dirhams; the Qur'an reader received 15 dirhams; the two *charge d'affairs* received 20 dirhams each; the porter received 20 dirhams; the *sufi shaykh* received 60 dirhams; each of the 15 *sufis* received 10 dirhams; the cook received five dirhams, and the servant received three dirhams. In addition, each was given a portion of bread and olive oil. Every visiting *sufi* could lodge here for 10 days, during which time he was given 1.5 dirhams and a 1.5 lb. of bread on a daily basis.

The Tankiziyya is also rich in architectural detail. Its northern façade has a Majestic, commemorative entrance portal that consists of a recess covered by a dome on which incisions that form a colonne-fluted frieze that reflects the light in all directions.

Three tiers of *muqarnas* support the semi-dome. Above the entrance is a massive lintel on which a row of joggled *ablaq*-inlay tiers rests. The foundation plaque lies above it and Tankiz's coat of arms is engraved in the centre (a large chalice inside a circle). This emblem refers to the post of butler, which was one of the most important posts held by Tankiz during his distinguished career. The portal of the structure resembles the portal of a mosque built by Tankiz in Damascus, indicating the influence of various architectural and artistic schools on the architecture of Jerusalem. The entrance opens into a vestibule that has a door in its southern wall, which leads into the interior of the *madrasa*. Here a vaulted courtyard is surrounded by four *iwans*. The structure consists of numerous rooms and halls.

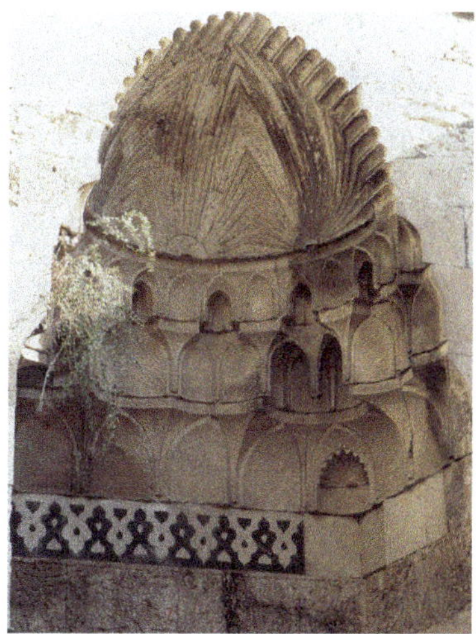

Madrasa al-Tankiziyya, detail of the entrance, Jerusalem.

III.1.g **Madrasa al-Taziyya**

Lies to the north of Tariq Bab al-Silsila, adjacent to Aqabat Abu Madyan (Zawiyat al-Maghariba) that leads to the west wall. Being a private residence, the interior is not open to visitors.

Although the inscription on the southern façade above the main window commemorates the death of the *amir* Taz in 763/1362, it does not refer to the date of the construction of the building or the founding of its *waqf*. However, by relying on architectural evidence, the mausoleum that has been used in the past as a *madrasa*, was probably built in 762/1361.

Its founder was the Amir Taz who was a Mamluk slave of Sultan al-Nasir Muhammad Ibn Qalawun. He held various significant posts during the Mamluk Dynasty such as that of the sultan's butler

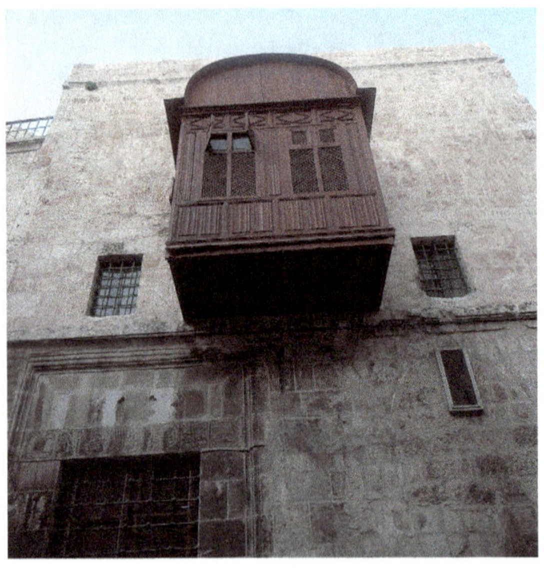

Madrasa al-Taziyya, western façade, mashrabiyya, Jerusalem.

(*saqi*), which was a very delicate post during this period. The emblem of the butler was a chalice, which explains the existence of one amidst the above-mentioned inscription plaque. After he had attained the post of Governor of Aleppo, his luck declined; he was arrested and later exiled to Jerusalem where he resided and established Madrasa al-Taziyya. Many historical references mention him, his relatives, and others whom he freed from bondage in Jerusalem.

Despite the fact that the foundation inscription refers to the edifice as a mausoleum, reality and documents reveal it had various functions. Salaries were paid to its jurists, readers and tutors; these were covered by its *waqf*, which comprised the village of al-Miniya, which lay northwest of Lake Tiberias.

The Taziyya has one western façade that is divided into two parts, lower and upper. The lower part has a simple door that leads into the interior. To the west of the entrance is a rectangular window that is surrounded by a deep-set frame and covered by Mamluk-style metal grills. On top of it is a lintel upon which a foundation inscription was engraved. Above it is another lintel of beautiful joggled inlay. The stones of this part have been constructed in the *ablaq* style. The upper part of the façade, on the other hand, has well-arranged courses and a wooden *mashrabiyya* dating back to the 13th/19th century, and three windows above it.

The building consists of two floors. The first floor has two parts; the southern part has an entrance, stairs and two halls, each of which is covered by a cross vault. The northern part of the first floor also has two large halls that are reached through a corridor that lies to the east of the halls

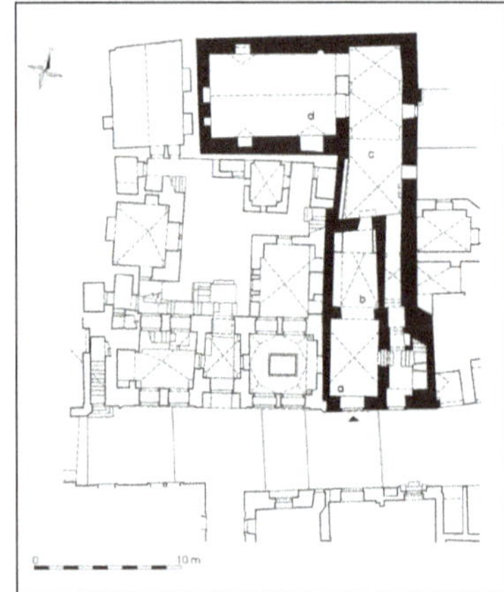

Madrasa al-Taziyya, ground floor plan, Jerusalem.

in the southern part. There is also an *iwan* that leads to a large, cross-vaulted hall and which overlooks the main road from the south. Some residential quarters are found to the north, most of which were rebuilt during the Ottoman period, and some of which have been covered by a small, shallow vault.

III.1.h **Madrasa al-Tashtamuriyya**

Lies south of Tariq Bab al-Silsila between Aqabat Abu Madyan and Tariq Harat al-Sharaf. The Madrasa is open to visitors in the morning, but permission to visit must be obtained from the staff.

The Tashtamuriyya's distance from the Haram has been compensated for by its excellent location, on crossways, and the freedom its architect enjoyed in designing it (it varies greatly from other firmly established architectural designs).

According to the inscription plaque on its northern façade, the Amir Tashtamur al-'Ala'i commissioned the building in 782/1380–1381. He was famous for keeping the company of scholars and debating with the religious authorities, and he also had a passion for poetry and music. During his administrative and military career in the Mamluk period, he held a variety of high-profile posts. Among these were the post of *dawadar kabir* (Secretary of State) to the Sultan al-Ashraf Sha'ban and that of the Governor of the Safad province. He was also the leader of the Egyptian military. He eventually chose to retire to Jerusalem after he had some disagreements with other *amirs*. He lived there until his death in 786/1384 and was buried in his *turbe* or mausoleum that is located in his complex, the subject of this stop.

The Tashtamuriyya was called a *turbe* by Mujir al-Din (the famous historian of Jerusalem), while the documents of the Tribunal Court of Jerusalem called it a *madrasa*. However, in the inscription plaque above the northern facade it is called "a place". The latter name seems

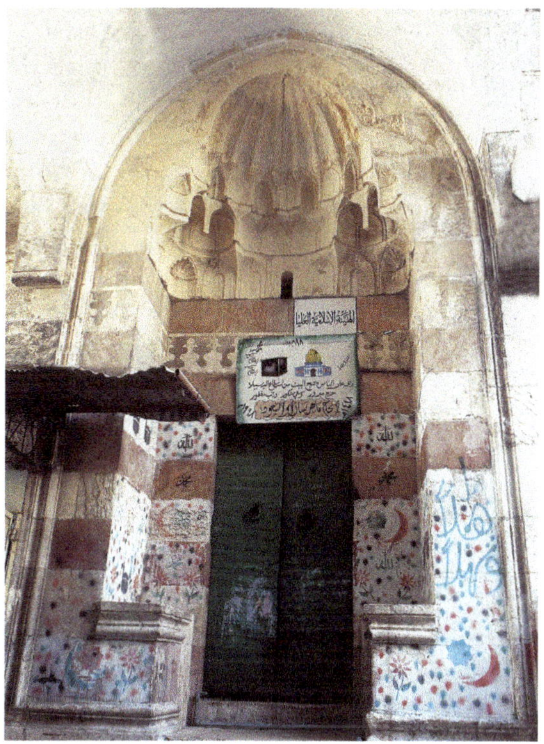

Madrasa al-Tashtamuriyya, entrance, Jerusalem.

Madrasa al-Tachtamuriyya, tomb of Tachtamur al-'Ala'i, Jerusalem.

Madrasa al-Tachtamuriyya, ground floor plan, Jerusalem.

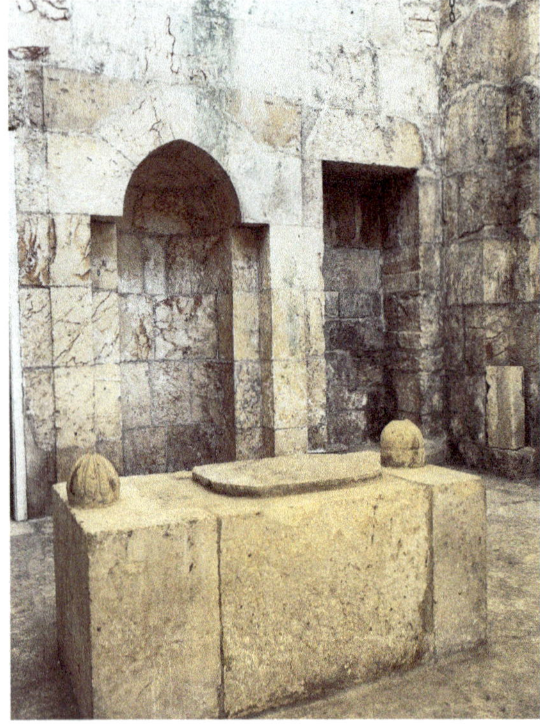

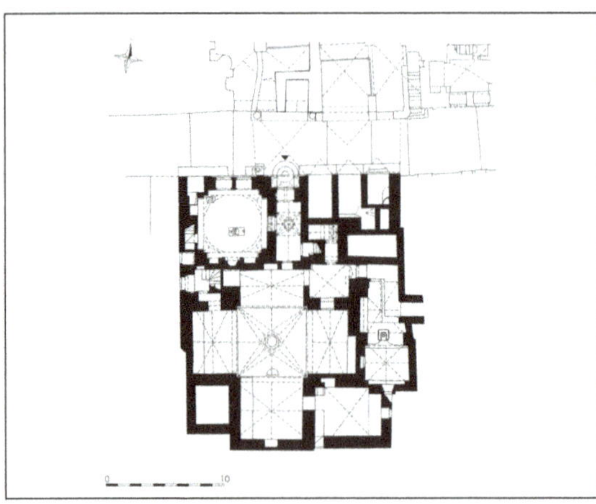

the most appropriate, although the units of the building entitle it to be a multi-functional complex. The edifice has three elaborate façades (southern, western and northern), a commemorative portal, a vestibule, a mausoleum, a *madrasa* of four *iwans*, a *sabil*, shops and various rooms and halls.

Circular stairs built in front of the northern façade lead to the interior. The façade consists of two parts: western and eastern. The first part has two large rectangular windows that have metal grills. On top of each window is a lintel with a row of joggled *ablaq* in red, black and white above it. Above this is the inscription band, which in turn is surmounted by another row of joggled *ablaq* inlay identical to the one below it. All these are placed within a frame of concave and moulded ornaments. The courses of stone continue uninterrupted, except for a window that allows light into the tomb chamber, and which covers the area right up to the shaft of the dome covering the top of the tomb chamber. In front of the two windows lies a small fountain (a concave stone basin) and to the west lies a small shop. Above this is a stone gallery that stands on four corbels, and which has recently been renovated. The eastern part has an elaborate *muqarnas* portal built of coloured stones with *mastabas* on either side; it has a trefoil recess with a *muqarnas* hood.

The entrance portal leads into a dark, rectangular vestibule covered by a wooden roof. A door pierces each of its three walls. The first leads into a square-plan tomb chamber with a coloured marble floor. Two cenotaphs lay to its south, covered by a semicircular dome. The second door leads into a central courtyard that is covered by a cross vault and surrounded by four *iwans*. The southern one is larger and has a concave *mihrab* at the centre of its southern wall. The third eastern door leads through to stairs up to the upper floor of this complex, where a number of residential rooms are found.

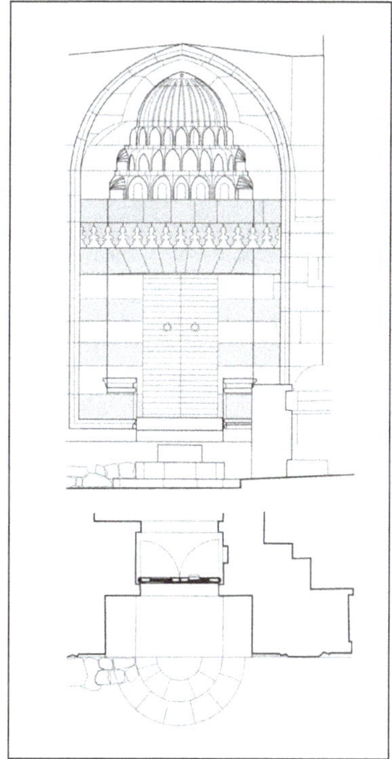

Madrasa al-Tachtamuriyya, main entrance gate, elevation and plan, Jerusalem.

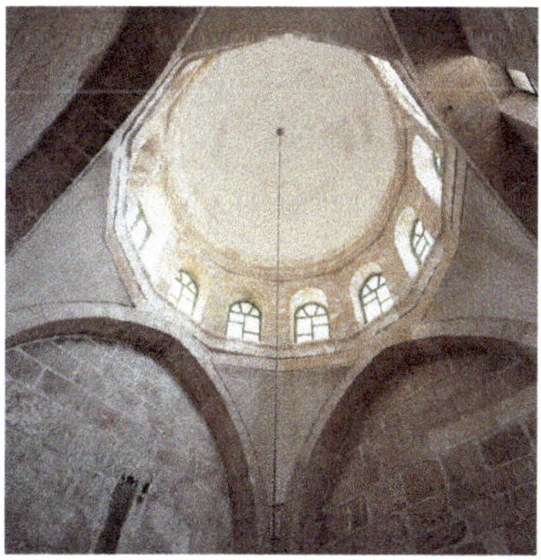

Madrasa al-Tachtamuriyya, cupola of the funeral chamber, Jerusalem.

THE *WAQF* SYSTEM

Yusuf Natsheh

A *waqf* is a monetary or property endowment in perpetuity given to institutions and sometimes to individuals throughout the Islamic history of Jerusalem. The *waqf* system has answered both the religious and worldly demands of Muslims; the revenue was used to build and renovate public places such as mosques, *madrasas* and fountains and to support scholars, students and the poor financially. A *waqf* could consist of land in a town or village, a specific amount of money, or the revenue from an agricultural or industrial venture. Moreover, the property endowed could be inside or outside Palestine.

Due to Jerusalem's venerated position in Islam, the Islamic *waqf* system was adopted in the city early on. The Caliph 'Uthman Ibn 'Affan (23/644–35/656) endowed the Spring of Silwan (south of the Old City) as a *waqf* to take care of the poor. In the successive period, this *waqf* system was used to protect the interests of the Haram al-Sharif. Its range increased and became more general after Saladin's recapture of Jerusalem. Examples are the *waqf* of the Madrasa al-Salahiyya and that of the Maristan al-Salahi in the Ayyubid period, the *waqfs* of the Tankiziyya and the Duwadariyya in the Mamluk period, and the *waqf* of Khassaki Sultan in the Ottoman period. The system is still followed in Palestine, but rather as a *waqf* for one's offspring.

A *waqf* was generally legalised through a document or a decree if the donor was a sultan through a reference in the foundation inscription, as seen in the *waqf* of the of the Khanqa al-Duwadariyya or, again, through a detailed letter that was registered, documented and signed by witnesses in the Tribunal Court. The latter was the most common and many of the Mamluk and Ottoman *waqfs* were carried out in this way. In order for the registration to be legal the donor is obliged to prove that the property is his own. Once the *waqf* is signed it is a legal document and, therefore, there is no way out of it. It cannot be sold, or exchanged, and in only very exceptional circumstances can its stipulations be altered; on these rare occasions it can be changed but only after a judge has approved it and if the change serves the interest of the *waqf*. A *waqf*'s document usually outlines the reason behind building it, its function and the employees it needs to hire, their salaries and duties.

The size of the *waqf* and its revenue depends on many factors, namely the donor, the place upon which it is endowed and its duration. A *waqf* has been made for the preservation of a drinking cup. The *waqfs* of the Haram al-Sharif in Jerusalem, the Ibrahimi Mosque in Hebron and the Maqam of Nabi Musa (the Prophet Moses) are considered the largest and richest *waqfs* of the Mamluk period. Despite all the advantages of the *waqf* system, it fails to consider the inflation that hits local economies. Trusts and long-lease rents have contributed to ruining the *waqf* system, which has suffered decades of monotony and routine.

THE DAILY LIFE OF A STUDENT IN A *MADRASA*

Yusuf Natsheh

The Islamic historical sources about Jerusalem hold very little information on a student's life and activities at the *madrasa*. However, reading fragmentary information in various sources and *waqfs*, could provide some idea about life in these institutions.

Before being admitted into the *madrasa*, a student was expected to have some basic knowledge that was accumulated during childhood and adolescence. If he were lucky he would have been raised in a home where resources and books were abundant, and he would have received an early education from his father or relatives. If he were half-lucky, he would have an affluent father who could afford private tuition by the leading *shaykhs* of his time. If he were unlucky, he would receive his education in a school sponsored by the rich to educate orphans; this amounted to receiving free paper and ink, a piece of bread, and necessary clothes on an annual basis. At this stage he would learn the principles of reading and writing, and memorise parts of the Qur'an and the *Hadith* tradition. Some distinguished students – such as Mujir al-Din al-Hanbali, the famous historian of Jerusalem in the Mamluk period – had memorised the whole of the Qur'an by the time he was 10 years old. After the student was admitted into the *madrasa* he would be given a grant from the *waqf*'s revenue throughout his study period and in accordance with the stipulations of the donor. In return, he had to attend classes, study and pass his exams. He might also be given a dormitory, especially if he had come from another city or was single. He would be placed in one of the following categories: advanced, intermediate or novice. In addition to studying the seven readings of the Qur'an and their interpretations, he would be given the choice of either studying Islamic jurisprudence in accordance with one of the four *suni madhhabs (Hanafi, Shafi'i, Maliki* and *Hanbali)* or studying the *Hadith* tradition and its interpretation. He might also receive education in literature and Arabic linguistics.

Whatever his choice, he had to study hard in order not to be dismissed. His day started at dawn and ended at sunset. He woke for group morning prayers at dawn, and then he read the Qur'an alone or with other students. He had to mention the donor of the *waqf* in his prayers and pray for his soul if he was dead. Then he would have breakfast, after which he would head towards one of the four *iwans* in the *madrasa* to meet with his fellow students and the *shaykh* of the *madrasa* who would give them a lecture in their chosen field. During this session, he would have every opportunity to ask questions and debate points; if he needed further help, he could seek it from the *shaykh*'s assistant after noon prayers and lunch. In the afternoon he headed to the Aqsa Mosque to listen to the preacher and the Islamic legal advice given in public. After sunset and evening prayers, he had time enough left to study and revise his lessons before retiring.

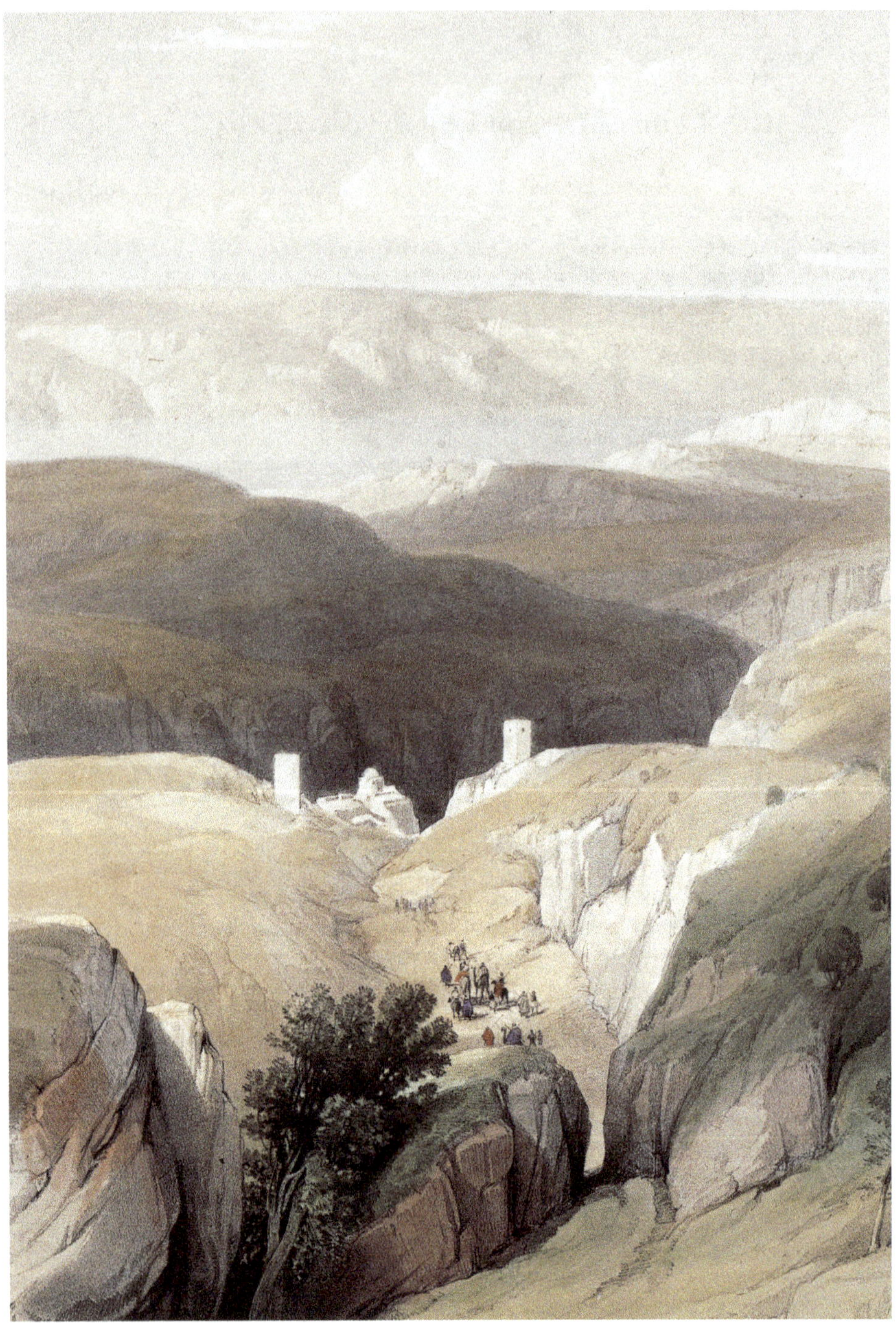

A Journey into the Wilderness

Yusuf Natsheh, Mahmoud Hawari

SCENIC OPTION
Panoramic View of the Old City of Jerusalem

IV.1 MOUNT OF OLIVES
IV.1.a Zawiya al-As'adiyya
IV.1.b Mosque of Qubbat al-Su'ud (Dome of the Ascension)
IV.1.c Maqam of Rabi'a al-'Adawiyya

IV.2 AL-'AYZARIYYA
IV.2.a Mosque of al-'Uzayr

IV.3 MAQAM OF NABI MUSA

IV.4 JERICHO
IV.4.a Qasr Khirbat al-Mafjar (Hisham's Palace) (Option)

Mawsim of Nabi Musa
Desert Monasticism

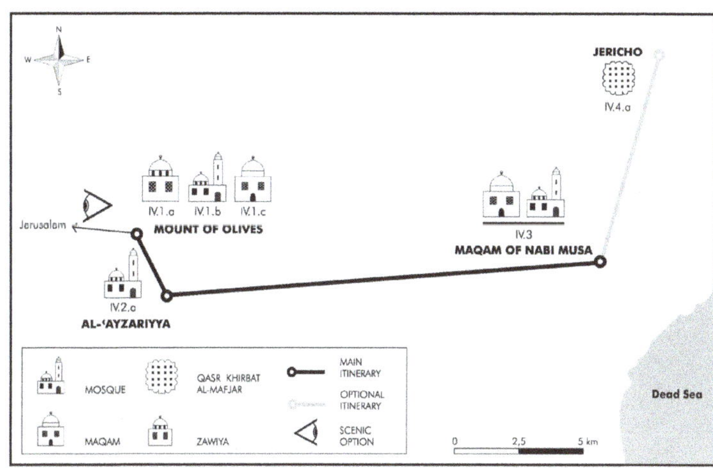

The Dead Sea from the heights of 'Ayn Gedi, near the Monastery of Saint Saba, lithograph by D. Roberts (© Victoria & Albert Museum, London).

The journey from Jerusalem to Jericho is special from both a geographical and historical perspective. Captivating views of mountains and valleys, semi-desert scenery, historic sites, Islamic sanctuaries and Christian monasteries lie along the route. The winding road from the top of Jerusalem's Mountains (800 m. above sea level) descends towards the Jordan Valley and the Dead Sea (the lowest point on earth at 400 m. below sea level) and finally reaches Jericho (the lowest city on earth at 250 m. below sea level).

The visitor will start the journey from the observatory of the Mount of Olives at al-Tur Village. To the west, north and south there unfolds a panoramic view of the Old City of Jerusalem, its surrounding mountains and valleys, and the western slopes of the Mount of Olives that are rich in archaeological sites and historic monuments. To the east is the bewitching sight of vast desert, the Dead Sea and the Jordan Valley; on a clear day, one can see as far as the mountains of Jordan. Heading north for about half a kilometre, one will arrive at a crossroads where the visitor can stop to see the first of three sites in this itinerary: the Zawiya al-As'adiyya, the Mosque of the Dome of Ascension and the Maqam of Rabi'a al-'Adawiyya.

Heading towards the south-eastern slopes of the Mount of Olives, one will arrive at the village of al-'Ayzariyya and visit the Mosque of al-'Uzayr that lies to the east of the Franciscan Church of Saint Lazarus (whom Christ raised form the dead). From here the visitor continues east towards the Jordan Valley on a new tarmac road that has replaced the narrow and winding path between Jerusalem and Jericho. Then the scenery changes, for while covered in green and colourful flowers that are numerous during the spring, the mountains and valleys look barren thoughout the summer. Bedouin encampments scatter the area that has attracted early Christian monks since the Byzantine period (5th and 6th centuries). Some of the monasteries associated with these monks still survive today, including St George's Monastery (Deir al-Qilt), which lies in the Wadi Qilt north of the Jerusalem–Jericho road.

Eighteen kilometres from Jerusalem, the visitor should turn off the main road and continue southwards for about half a kilometre until reaching a huge architectural complex covered by white domes. This is the Maqam of Nabi Musa (the Shrine of the Prophet Moses), which was built in the Mamluk period and is considered to be one of the most important commemorative shrines in the Jerusalem area. Some additions were made to it in the Ottoman period.

Having visited the *maqam*, the visitor should return to the Jerusalem–Jericho road and continue east until s/he reaches the Jordan Valley. This valley is considered part of the Syrian-African rift that stretches from the north of Syria to East Africa. The road continues east towards the Dead Sea and the River Jordan, which flows into it. The Dead Sea is a unique phenomenon; the Romans called it the Asphalt Sea, while Arab historians called it the Sea of Lut or the Sea of Sodomy (after the stories in the Old Testament) and the Stinking Lake, because of the smell of sulphur. It was the Crusaders who named it the Dead Sea because it lacks any signs of life.

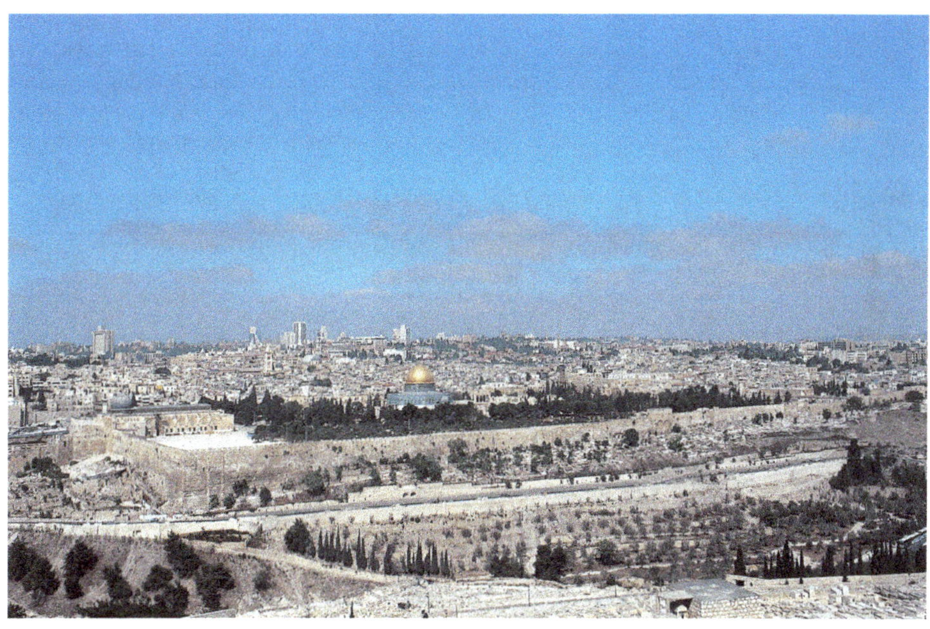

Jerusalem, panoramic view from the Mount of Olives

Another road turns north towards Jericho. This city lies in the middle of an oasis that is rich in water springs, palm and fruit trees, and contains various historic sites that date back to different periods. Among them is the Qasr Khirbat al-Mafjar (Hisham's Palace) that dates back to the Umayyad period.

M.H.

SCENIC OPTION

Panoramic View of the Old City of Jerusalem

Located on the south-west side of the Mount of Olives, in front of the al-Aqwas al-Sab'a (Seven Arches Hotel), where a mirador is found that offers magnificent panoramic views of the Old Town of Jerusalem.

From this point, the visitor can enjoy breathtaking panoramic views of the Old City of Jerusalem. The beauty of its layout and architecture and the solidity of its walls become clearer from this vantage point. The boundaries of the Haram al-Sharif – which were designed by the Umayyad Caliph 'Abd al-Malik Ibn Marwan at the end of the 1st/7th century – with its various edifices, domes and magnificent minarets can be seen clearly. In the centre lies the Dome of the Rock with its golden dome, while to the south is the Aqsa Mosque covered by its grey, lead dome. The historic

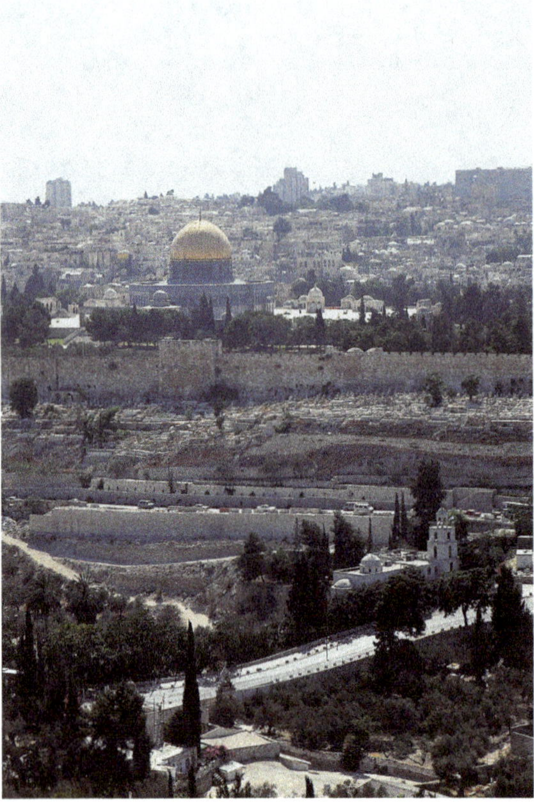

The Dome of the Rock, panoramic view from the Mount of Olives.

buildings are concentrated in the north and west borders of the Haram. The eastern and western walls of the Old City and their gates can also be identified, most notably the double Golden Gate (Bab al-Rahma and Bab al-Tawba), and Bab al-Asbat (Gate of the Lions). The Citadel and its lofty, impenetrable towers can be seen to the west, while the towers and domes of the churches bestow unrivalled glamour and beauty upon the city.

It is no wonder this view bewitched Mujir al-Din al-Hanbali (c.901/1496), the famous historian of Mamluk Jerusalem, who wrote: *"Seeing Jerusalem from afar is a wonder in its luminosity and beauty especially when seen from the east, from the Mount of Olives or from the direction of the* qibla*".*

M.H.

IV.1 MOUNT OF OLIVES

IV.1.a Zawiya al-As'adiyya

Lies on the eastern part of the Mount of Olives adjacent to the Mosque of Qubbat al-Su'ud and many important churches connected with Jesus Christ. The courtyard is open during the day except during prayer times. Permission to visit the site is required from the supervisor.

This *zawiya*, sometimes called *khanqa*, is named after its founder Shaykh Abu Sa'id As'ad Efendi, the Supreme Mufti in Constantinople (Istanbul), who also conferred a *waqf* upon it. Parts of the *zawiya*, the mosque in particular, were built in 1023/1614-1615 as the inscription plaque above the entrance certifies. In 1033/1623, As'ad Efendi bestowed a generous *waqf* on it through his legal deputy Muhammad Pasha, the Governor of Jerusalem at the time. He stipulated that the annual revenue of the *waqf* – which included many buildings, some land and a bakery in the village of al-Tur – should be spent on maintaining the *zawiya* and covering its expenses, including those of its followers, visitors and employees (inspector, *imam*, *muezzin*, porter, servant and money collector). Shaykh Shams al-Din Muhammad al-ʻAlami, one of Jerusalem's *sufi* leaders in the first half of $10^{th}/16^{th}$ century, was appointed as the inspector of the *waqf* and the *shaykh* of the *zawiya*.

The inscriptions on the walls of the central courtyard, together with the architectural features of the building, indicate that it was built over several periods. Two inscription plaques are found in addition to the one mentioned earlier. One is dated 1143/1730–1731 and refers to the crypt leading to the Shaykh al-ʻAlami's tomb, while the second (1323/1905–1906) indicates the date when the vestibule was built.

The building consists of many units that can be accessed via a staircase that starts at street level at the end of which two entrance portals are found. The eastern portal leads to the Mosque Qubbat al-Suʻud (Dome of the Ascension), while the southern portal leads to the courtyard of the *zawiya*. The courtyard is rectangular with a modern stone-tiled floor. To the west of the entrance is a door on the northern wall that leads to stairs down to the crypt where Shaykh ʻAlami and some members of his family are buried. Facing the north door, another door in the centre of the courtyard's southern wall, leads into the mosque of the *zawiya*.

The mosque is rectangular (10 × 6.5 m.) and has several windows on its west wall that allow in plenty of light. A concave *mihrab* lies in its southern wall. A pointed arch divides the ceiling into two sections: the southern part is square and covered by a shallow dome, while the northern one is covered by a cross vault. A third door on the west wall of the courtyard leads to another open courtyard, which is irregular in shape

Zawiya al-Asʻadiyya, general view, Mount of Olives, Jerusalem.

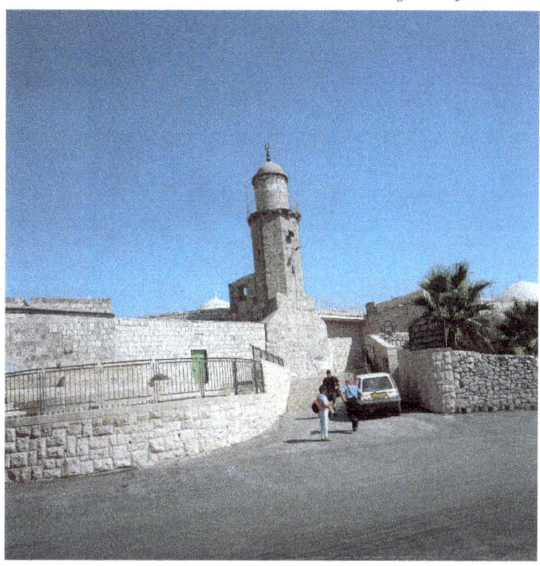

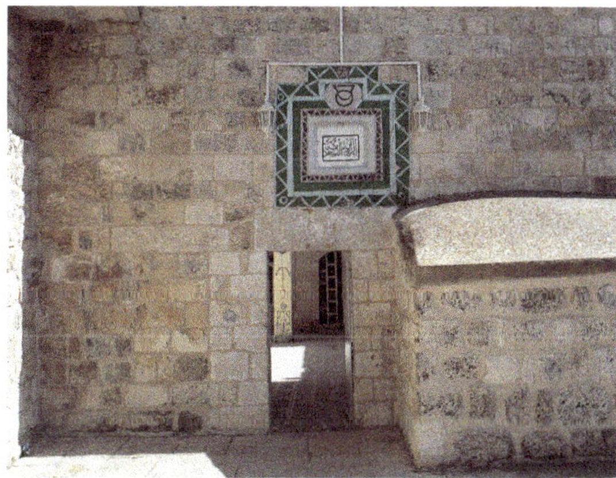

Zawiya al-Asʻadiyya, entrance, Mount of Olives, Jerusalem.

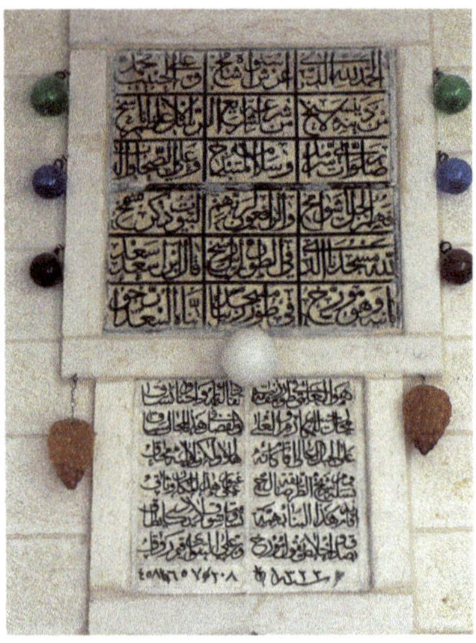

Zawiya al-As'adiyya, foundation inscriptions, Mount of Olives, Jerusalem.

and on a lower level than the indoor courtyard. Toilet facilities have been built in the northern area, while the southern part has many tombs. The eastern area of the *zawiya* is a residential area where 'Alami's descendants live; this can be reached through a fourth door on the south-eastern border of the courtyard.

Y.N.

IV.1.b **Mosque of Qubbat al-Su'ud (Dome of Ascension)**

Open daily 08.00–16.00. The admission fee is nominal.

This site is one of the most distinguished in Jerusalem. It commemorates the Ascension of Jesus to heaven after his Resurrection according to the Christian tradition. It is mentioned in the Book of Luke, and although no precise location is mentioned, it is widely believed that this place is the site of the Ascension.

Before the spread of Christianity, Christians used to celebrate the Ascension secretly inside a cave in the Mount of Olives. The first church to commemorate the Ascension was built during the Byzantine period, before 392, although it has not survived. Many attempts have been made to reconstruct it, relying on descriptions by Byzantine travellers and archaeological research. The earlier circular plan was replaced in the Crusader period by an octagonal structure and was encircled by a fortified monastery. During this period the validity of the Ascension was firmly established.

After Saladin's conquest of Jerusalem the site was converted into a mosque. Since then it has become an Islamic *waqf*. Now the Administration of Waqfs and Islamic Affairs manages it as any other holy place, and access is guaranteed to all Christian communities. Both the mosque and courtyard around it have been recently renovated.

During the renovations carried out at the time of Saladin and his successors, many elements of the Crusader architecture survived, in particular the marble columns and their capitals. A *mihrab* was added to the southern part of the octagon, the spaces between the columns were blocked, and the floor tiles were restored.

The current mosque is octagonal in plan. Marble columns are seen on the corners of the octagon and their capitals are decorated with animal and vegetal ornaments.

The visitor can enter the site from a door on the western side. The floor is covered in small stone tiles. A rectangular stone frame encircles the area where supposedly the footprints of Christ lie. In the circular external courtyard, many altars are found that belong to different sects. On the walls are a number of iron rings, which were used to tie tents or parasols during the annual celebration commemorating the Ascension.

Y.N.

IV.1.c **Maqam of Rabi'a al-'Adawiyya**

The maqam *lies on the Mount of Olives next to the Zawiya al-As'adiyya. Visitors should make contact with the attendant prior to their visit.*

Architectural examinations and excavations carried out in 1995 reveal that the *maqam* is a composite of different periods. The earliest finds date back to the Byzantine period, as the disovery of some ceramic fragments testify. On the west wall, there is a Greek inscription. It reads: "*Courage Dometilla. None is immortal*". Even though some believe the site was built to honour Saint Pilagia, it was probably used as a burial place. A *kufic* inscription has also been found dating to the early Islamic period; although it has never been deciphered it may have religious significance since many stories have circulated since the 6th/12th century that refer to Rabi'a al-'Adawiyya's

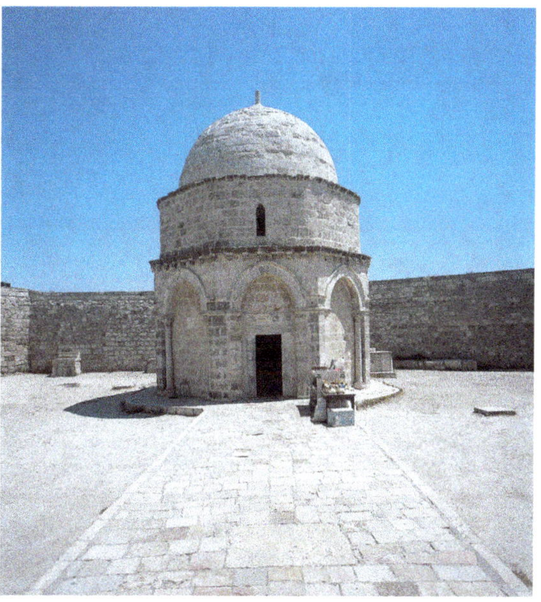

Qubbat al-Su'ud Mosque, general view, Mount of Olives, Jerusalem.

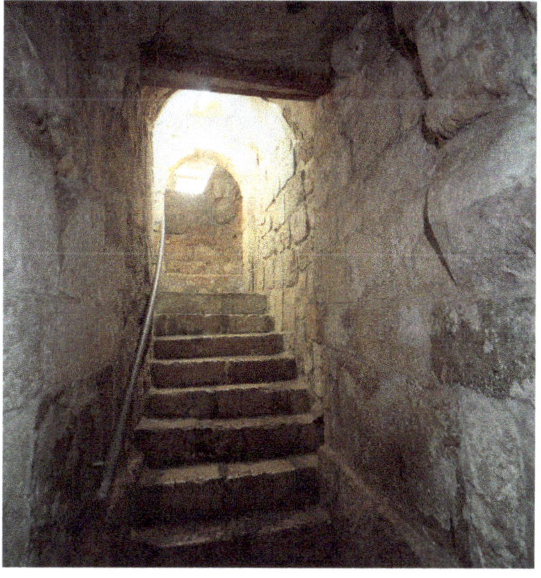

Maqam Rabi'a al-'Adawiyya, staircase, Mount of Olives, Jerusalem.

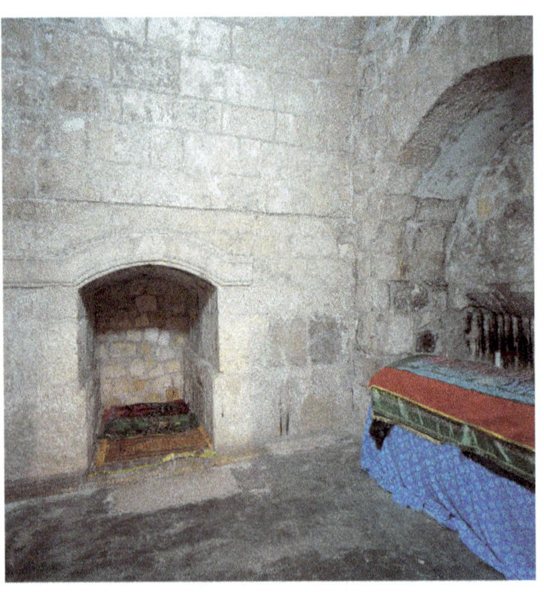

Maqam Rabi'a al-'Adawiyya, interior of the funeral chamber, Mount of Olives, Jerusalem.

place of burial. Furthermore, the ceramic material that has been uncovered here dates to both the Ayyubid and Mamluk periods, not to mention a wall that dates back to the 7th/13th – 8th/14th centuries.

The site is named today after Rabi'a al-'Adawiyya. The Islamic historical sources refer to more than one person with the same name. The most famous was Um al-Khayr Rabi'a al-'Adawiyya al-Basriyya, the famous *sufi*, who died in 185/801 in Basra, Iraq. Another is the wife of Rabi'a, Ahmad Ibn Abu al-Hawari, who is probably buried at this site. 'Abd Allah al-Mukhlis commented on this in the 1930s, saying: *"It might well be that the Rabi'a buried here on the Mount of Olives and below the Zawiya al-As'adiyya is neither al-'Adawiyya nor Ahmad Ibn Abu al-Hawari's wife but another Rabi'a whose history time has erased but whose name it has kept".*

The Shrine has a simple rectangular entrance. On top of it is a stone lintel, and above it a window. The entrance was originally an arch that was blocked up at a later stage. Its interior consists of two parts one of which, to the west, is a square room covered by a barrel vault. On its southern wall is a *mihrab*, which indicates that the area was used for prayer. Stairs, approximately 5 m. in length, separate the western from the eastern part. The floor of the eastern section drops below the level of the western part, which has a cement floor, an indication that it was built in modern times. This room is rectangular (5.6 x 3.4 m.) and is also covered by a barrel-vault. A cenotaph lies in the centre of the room.

Y.N.

IV.2 AL-'AYZARIYYA

IV.2.a Mosque of al-'Uzayr

The Mosque is located in the town of al-'Ayzariyya, which lies on the eastern slopes of the Mount of Olives on the road that links Jerusalem with Jericho. Visiting the exterior courtyard is allowed but only outside prayer times and with the imam's *permission.*

The mosque can be reached from the main Jerusalem–Jericho road by turning left onto a tarmac side-road, which lies a few meters to the north-east of the front square of the Church of St Lazarus.

In Roman and Medieval times, as well as in recent times, al-'Ayzariyya was the final station before entering Jerusalem from the east, as it was for Christ when he came to Jerusalem from Galilee and was welcomed into the house of Mary, Martha and Lazarus in al-'Ayzariyya. According to the New Testament, it is the place where Christ performed the miracle of raising Lazarus from the dead. It is thanks to this event, along with the location of the tomb of Lazarus that a town first began to grow, it was further developed during the Byzantine period, and then continued to flourish in medieval times. Its Arabic name was derived from Greek (*Lazarion*) meaning the place of the Lazarus.

Architectural evidence and a number of historical references indicate that in the Byzantine period two churches and a monastery were built on this site (one church was ruined by an earthquake in 390 and a second was built in the 6th century). Parts of these edifices were probably reused and renovated during the Crusader period. However, when Saladin conquered Jerusalem in 583/1187, the buildings were in a dilapidated condition. Believing that Christ is a messenger from God, and also in his miracle of raising Lazarus from the dead, the Muslims built a mosque on top of the earlier remains and called it the Mosque of al-'Uzayr.

There is no exact date given for when the mosque was built. Its architectural fabric, however, shows that it is a composite of many styles that developed in different periods, the last of which was the Ottoman period. The records of the Tribunal Court of Jerusalem show the mosque was renovated in the 10th/16th century, and then again in the following centuries, the last of which has been documented by a commemorative inscription found above the entrance. The inscription is written in three lines of Ottoman script and is set within an ornamental frame. It states that the mosque was renovated during the reign of Sultan 'Abd al Hamid II (1293/1876–1327/1909).

The simple door of the mosque leads to a stairway that descends into an open courtyard below street level. The courtyard is rectangular and surrounded by

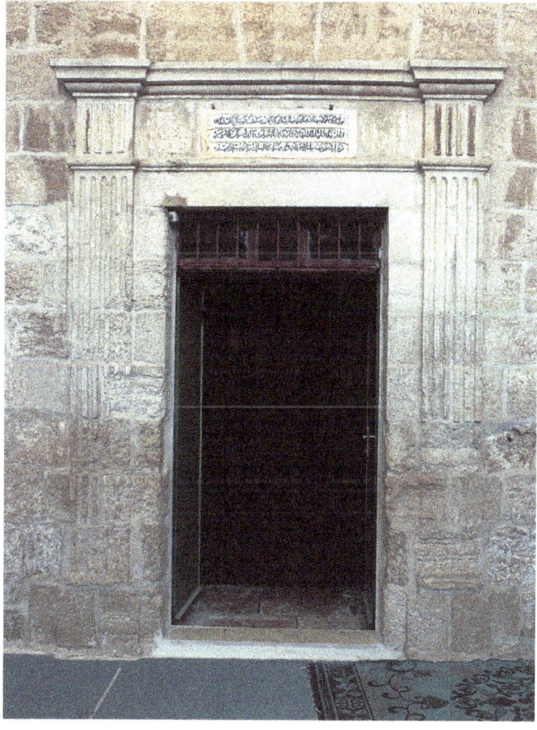

Al-'Uzayr Mosque, entrance with commemorative inscription, al-'Ayzariyya.

walls, the stones of which date to different periods as indicated by their sizes, shapes and styles. A modern, simple and concave stone *mihrab* has been built into the southern wall, and a rectangular door leads into the prayer hall of the Mosque, on top of which lies the Ottoman inscription mentioned previously. The prayer hall is rectangular in shape and the floor is covered in carpets. A huge pillar standing inside the entrance supports the barrel-vault ceiling. To the east, is an Ottoman-like rectangular cenotaph, which is attributed to the Prophet al-'Uzayr (St Lazarus). On the southern wall is a *mihrab* covered in typical Ottoman-style ceramic tiles, while at the far end is a rectangular opening that is currently blocked off, but which previously would have led to the tomb of Lazarus. Today, the tomb can be reached from an entrance to the west of the mosque's entrance.

Y.N.

Al-'Uzayr Mosque, tomb of the prophet al-'Uzayr, al-'Ayzariyya.

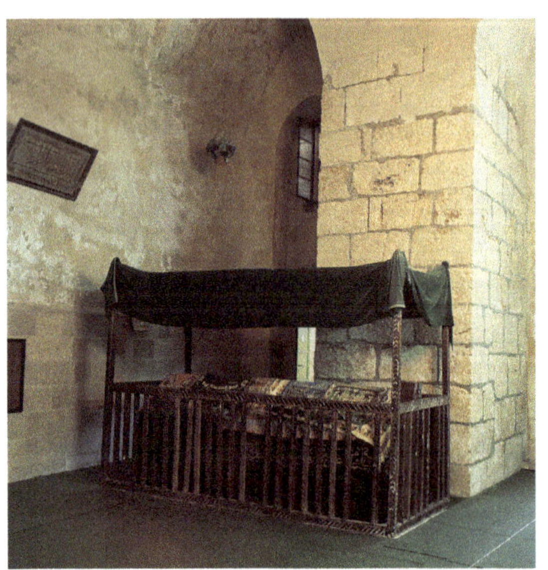

IV.3 MAQAM OF NABI MUSA

Lies 28 km. east of Jerusalem. Look out for the signpost on the main Jerusalem–Jericho road. It is open all day, but visitors to the interior are allowed in only outside prayer times.

The Maqam of Nabi Musa lies in a remote desert area amidst sand dunes, and overlooks the Dead Sea area. Its serene and quiet surroundings encourage meditation and contemplation, and provide a similar environment to that in which the three monotheist religions (Judaism, Christianity and Islam) developed.

The *maqam* was built for many reasons. Firstly, Islam and the Qur'an both acknowledge Moses as one of the prophets of God. Secondly, Muslims consider their creed as an amendment and a conclusion to the other two preceding religions (Judaism and Christianity). The Qur'an says: *"The prophet believes in all that God has asked him to do. The believers are all those who believe in God, His angels, books and prophets without exception. For all have followed God's way."* Thirdly, constructing a vast *maqam* in this area could be seen as stemming from a desire to strike a balance with other monasteries that had been built there since the Byzantine period. Encouraging a large crowd to assemble on specific occasions served many purposes: it diverted the public's attention away from their daily worries, it

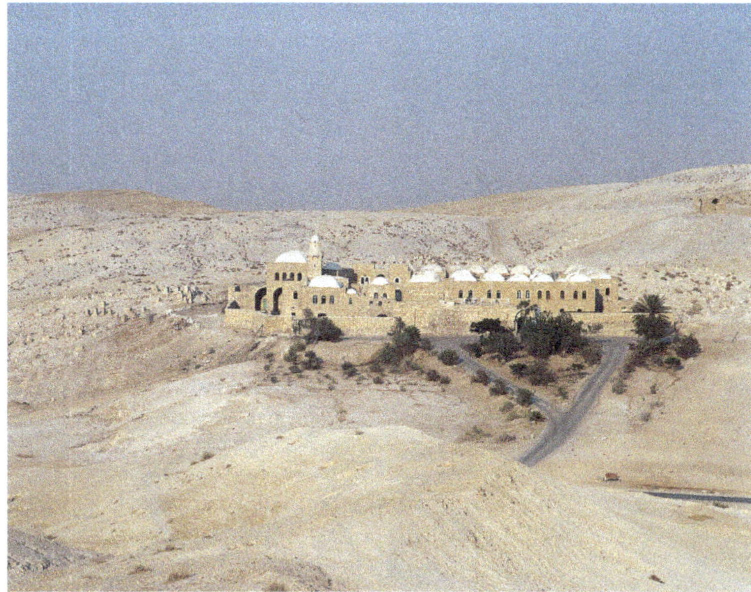

Maqam Nabi Musa, general view.

served as a social occasion where economic transactions were made, and it also sent a message of solidarity to their enemies.

Various historical references mention that the Festival (*Mawsim*) of the Nabi Musa started in the Ayyubid period, but no architectural remains from this period survive. The earliest remains date back to the time of the Mamluk Sultan Baybars, who ordered the building of the *maqam* in 668/1269-1270. Baybars was one of the founders of the Mamluk Dynasty, a firm warrior administrator, who was renowned for his patronage of architectural activities in various parts of the Mamluk Empire; Jerusalem, Palestine, and especially in Cairo. From Baybars' time until the British Mandate (1917-1948), many ren-

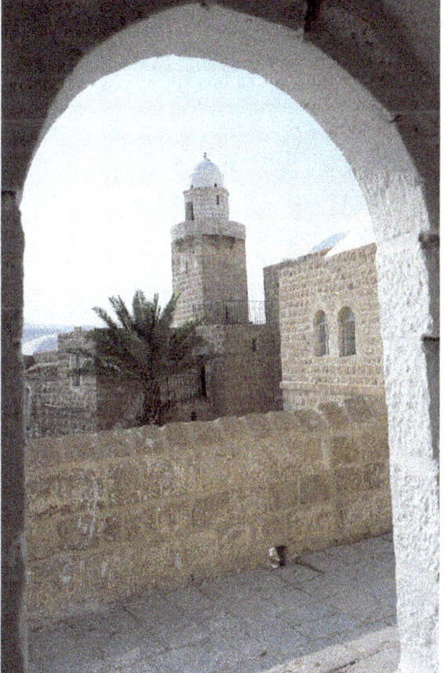

Maqam Nabi Musa, minaret of the mosque.

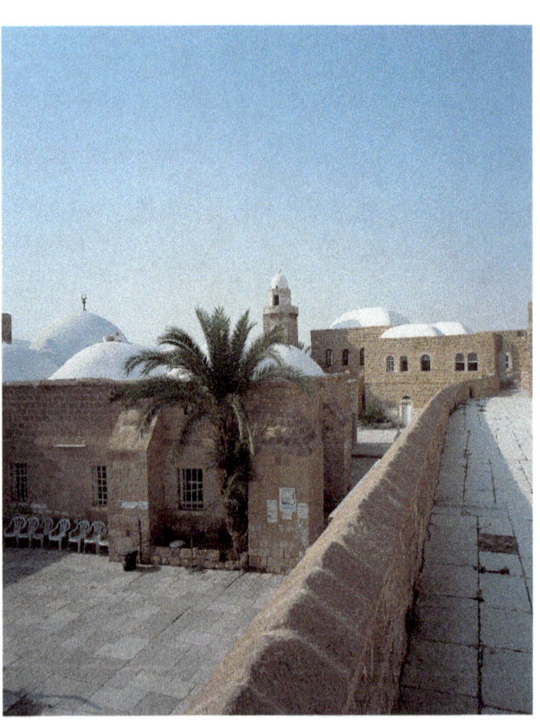

Maqam Nabi Musa, interior view with the minaret of the mosque.

ovations and extensions took place on the site, particularly during the Ottoman period; often undertaken by people who wanted to remain anonymous. Among those who took care of the *maqam* in the Ottoman period was Efendi Husam al-Din (1013/1604–1605), Shaykh Muhammad al-Khalili (1139/1726–1727) and Muhammad Tahir al-Hussayni, the Mufti of Jerusalem (1303/1885–1886).

Architecturally, the Maqam of Nabi Musa is the second largest religious site in Palestine after the Haram al-Sharif. It covers an area of approximately five hectares and is surrounded by walls. It consists of three storeys; on the western façade is a portal that leads into an open, central courtyard via a corridor where there is a mosque of five aisles, a *maqam,* and, at the centre, several water cisterns. More than 100 rooms and halls of different sizes surround the courtyard. The complex has an underground stable, porticoes, and stores, two bakeries and two kitchens on the ground floor. It also has a minaret of medium height and from the *muezzin*'s gallery one has a fantastic view over the mountain range of Jordan. From the west, the complex is preceded by a large square where various shows and activities take place during the festival high season, but which is used as a car park ordinarily. A large cemetery that is still used to bury those who wish to be blessed by the *maqam* lies to the east and the north of the complex. In addition to the festival season that draws huge crowds, the complex attracts many local visitors, but also large groups of Moslems and non-Moslems from India, South-East Asia and Europe throughout the year.

Y.N.

IV.4 JERICHO

IV.4.a **Qasr Khirbat al-Mafjar (Hisham's Palace)** (option)

Situated 2 km. north of Jericho. Open: 08.00–17.00. There is an admission fee.

Excavations carried out in the 1930s and 1940s by Richard Hamilton and Demetris Baramki uncovered a large palace that dates back to the Umayyad period. It has been attributed to the Umayyad Caliph Hisham Ibn 'Abd al-Malik, but now it is thought more likely that his successor, al-Walid Ibn Yazid, built the Palace because of its lavish appearance and splendour, which accords more with the latter's decadent lifestyle. Although it took 20 years to build, it did not survive for long, as an earthquake struck it only four years after it was completed in 129/747.

Hisham's Palace in Jericho is the greatest and most beautiful of the many palaces and settlements built in the southern area of the Syrian Desert, namely the Jordanian Desert, revealed in the stucco wall decorations, some of which are exhibited in the Palestine (Rockefeller) Archaeological Museum in Jerusalem, and mostly by way of the stunning and perfect mosaic floor, which nothing rivals in beauty except for the Dome of the Rock. The area was a favourite winter residence for the Caliph, due probably to the desert topography of Jericho and its climate, but also to the proximity of an abundant water supply from the springs of 'Ayn al-Dyouk, which permitted the construction of an 8 km.-long aqueduct to transport water to the palace, and which transformed the region into a green oasis.

Due to the significance of Hisham's Palace in the history of Islamic art and architecture, and its vitality and importance in attracting tourism to the Jericho area, the palace underwent many renovations. The

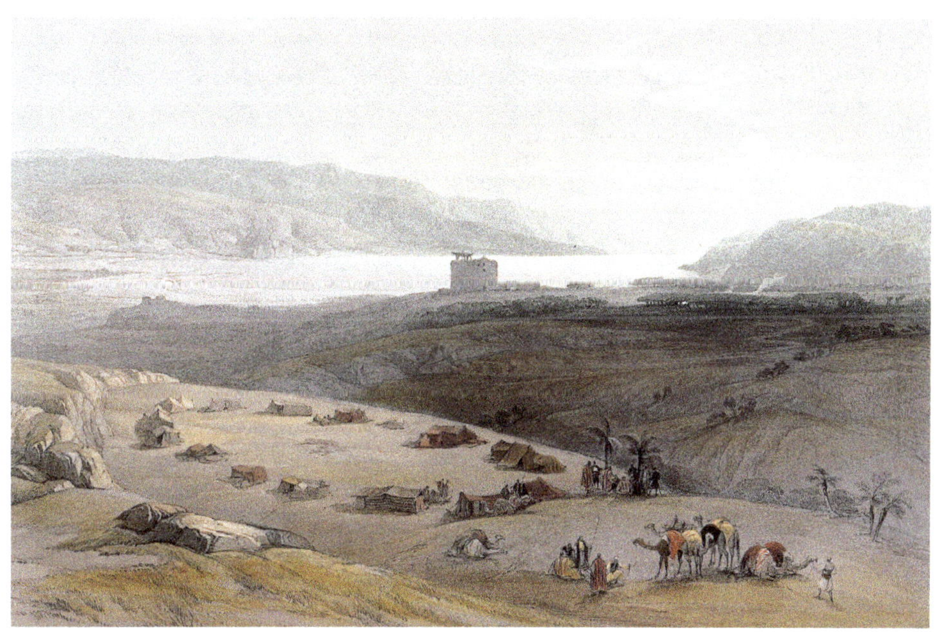

Encampment near Jericho, general view, lithograph by D. Roberts (© Victoria & Albert Museum, London).

latest was carried out in 1994 as a result of a grant from the Italian Government to the Palestinian Department of Antiquities. It was carried out by a joint Palestinian-Italian team and under the supervision of UNESCO.

The archaeological excavation and renovation projects revealed the following parts of the palace: the external entrance, where the ticket office is located, leads into an open courtyard where some surviving architectural remains of the earthquake are exhibited. North of this courtyard is a pool that has a mosaic floor, and to the west lies the entrance to the palace. This leads to a vast courtyard in the centre of which is a decorated window. Rooms and halls on two levels surround it from the south and west. In the centre of the southern corridor is a small mosque. The base of the minaret is next to it. This was the Caliph's private mosque. The public mosque lies to the north of the eastern portico. The niche of the *mihrab*, which points towards Mecca, is seen on the southern wall. A corridor leads to the splendid palace *hammam*. A pool lies in front of it, and many rooms lie to the north of it. One room may have been used as a reception hall; covered as it is by a remarkable mosaic floor considered to be the most beautiful in the country. A hot-room and toilets were also found.

Y.N.

MAWSIM OF NABI MUSA

Yusuf Natsheh

There was rigorous religious, social and economic activity in Palestine particularly during the Ayyubid period when the whole population, including the governors, began to visit different Palestinian religious shrines. This phenomenon, known as *mawasim* (plural of *mawsim*) or festivals, which was firmly established in the Mamluk period, continued throughout the Ottoman period, and still continues today; it was only suspended during times of political unrest. Among the *maqams* that have been associated with annual religious festivals are: the Maqam of ʻAli Ibn ʻAlim Ibn in Arsuf; the Maqam of Nabi Rubin, South of Jaffa; the Maqam of Nabi Salih in Ramla; the Maqam of al-Hussayn in Asqalon; the Maqam of al-Darum near Gaza and the Maqam of Nabi Musa.

The greatest and most famous of these festivals is that of Nabi Musa (the Prophet Moses) which starts on the Friday preceding the Greek Orthodox Good Friday, between 22 March and 25 April. It lasts for one week.

Its procession was documented at the end of the 19th-early 20th century, as follows: "*The inhabitants of Jerusalem and the inspectors of the maqam's waqf gather in the courtyard of the Aqsa Mosque. The procession will head towards Jericho via Tariq al-Mujahidin, Bab al-Asbat and then to Ra's al-ʻAmud. The inhabitants of Nablus, Hebron and other cities follow them in a procession carrying flags and banners decorated by Qur'anic verses and calligraphy, which refer to the Orthodox Caliphs and the leaders of Sufism. Folk dancing and music accompanies the procession. Some people rode on horses to the site. When the crowds arrive at the site, especially different Sufi Orders their zeal is reflected in the fast rhythm of their drums and the beating of their tambourines. Their spectacular dancing, swinging with a stick and their skilful fencing mix with women's joyful shrills and the cheers of the crowds.*"

Prayers took place in the *maqam*, where the Qur'an was also read. The crowds amounted to thousands, so tents were erected around the shrine to accommodate them. The newcomers took the place of those leaving. This festival, like others, was an opportunity for many to honour their vows, to circumcise their boys and have their hair cut for the first time. Free food was offered to a large number of people in the crowds, sponsored by a generous *waqf* allocated for visitors to the site. Many goods were available to satisfy the different needs of visitors. A special kind of sweet was made specifically for the occasion, called the Sweet of Nabi Musa. The celebration lasted for a week, the crowds returning on a Thursday in procession to the Aqsa Mosque. Three flags were carried in the procession, that of the Nabi Musa, the Nabi Dawud (the Prophet David) and the Aqsa Mosque. On arrival, the flags were put in store at the mosque until the following year.

DESERT MONASTICISM

Yusuf Natsheh

During the Byzantine period, a new phenomenon began in Palestine whereby urban monks would retire to the Jerusalem Desert. The phenomenon originated in southern Egypt and then spread to Palestine. An archaeological survey has uncovered more than 80 such monastic sites in the Jerusalem Desert, in an area that stretches 80 km. × 20 km. Among these sites are the Monastery of Mar Saba near the village of al-'Ubaydiyya in the Bethlehem area; the Monastery of St George of Koziba in Wadi al-Qilt on the Jerusalem-Jericho road; the Monastery of Hajla close to the River Jordan and Monastery of the Temptation (Qarantal) in Jericho.

The monastic phenomenon has been associated with three figures, each influencing his successor. The first was the monk Chariton, who established the first monastic community (*laura*) in 330, then Euthymius (376–473) who attracted thousands of followers, and finally Sabas (439–532); the greatest organiser of this movement.

This Mononastic order had two ways of life: the first was called *coenobium* while the second was known as *laura*. According to the *coenobium* way of life, a group of hermits would live together in a monastery and co-operate with each other. Each member would carry out a certain task in addition to worship, meditation, prayer and reading. They would usually have one group prayer and one individual prayer each day. However, they ate together and shared their daily social activities. This kind of Order required a complex surrounded by walls and different utilities such as a church, an assembly hall, a dining hall, a close-by water supply, a garden for planting and some retreats. The *laura* way of life, on the other hand, was characterised by the solitary living of a group of monks in a specific environment. Each would live in a cave or a retreat, eat alone and worship God alone for five days a week, then meet up on a Saturday and Sunday with his colleagues in the public prayer area, take some food and return to his retreat.

Whatever way of life was chosen, shared or solitary, it was characterised by simplicity and abstinence. The monks basically ate bread, and the vegetables and fruits that the harsh surrounding environment provided. Occasionally they would carry out some simple activity such as reclaiming land for agriculture, or weaving baskets and ropes to exchange for other products from the neighbouring villages. Large monasteries usually imported wheat from Jordan. Their seclusion and retreat from the tumults of city life gave many monks the opportunity to polish their poetic, literary and theological talents – hence the cultural life of Christianity was greatly enriched.

The Monastery of St George of Koziba in Wadi al-Qilt provides a good example of this phenomenon. It can be reached either from Jerusalem by turning north at the entrance to Jericho Observatory, or from Jericho by taking the first right after leaving the city. The visitor will enjoy a wonderful view of the desert just before reaching the site. The monastery can be visited between 09.00 and 15.00, but is closed at noon for one hour. Coffee and cold water awaits the visitor following the hardship of descending the valley, and then climbing up to the monastery, by following the course of the Roman aqueduct that, incidentally, has been repeatedly renovated.

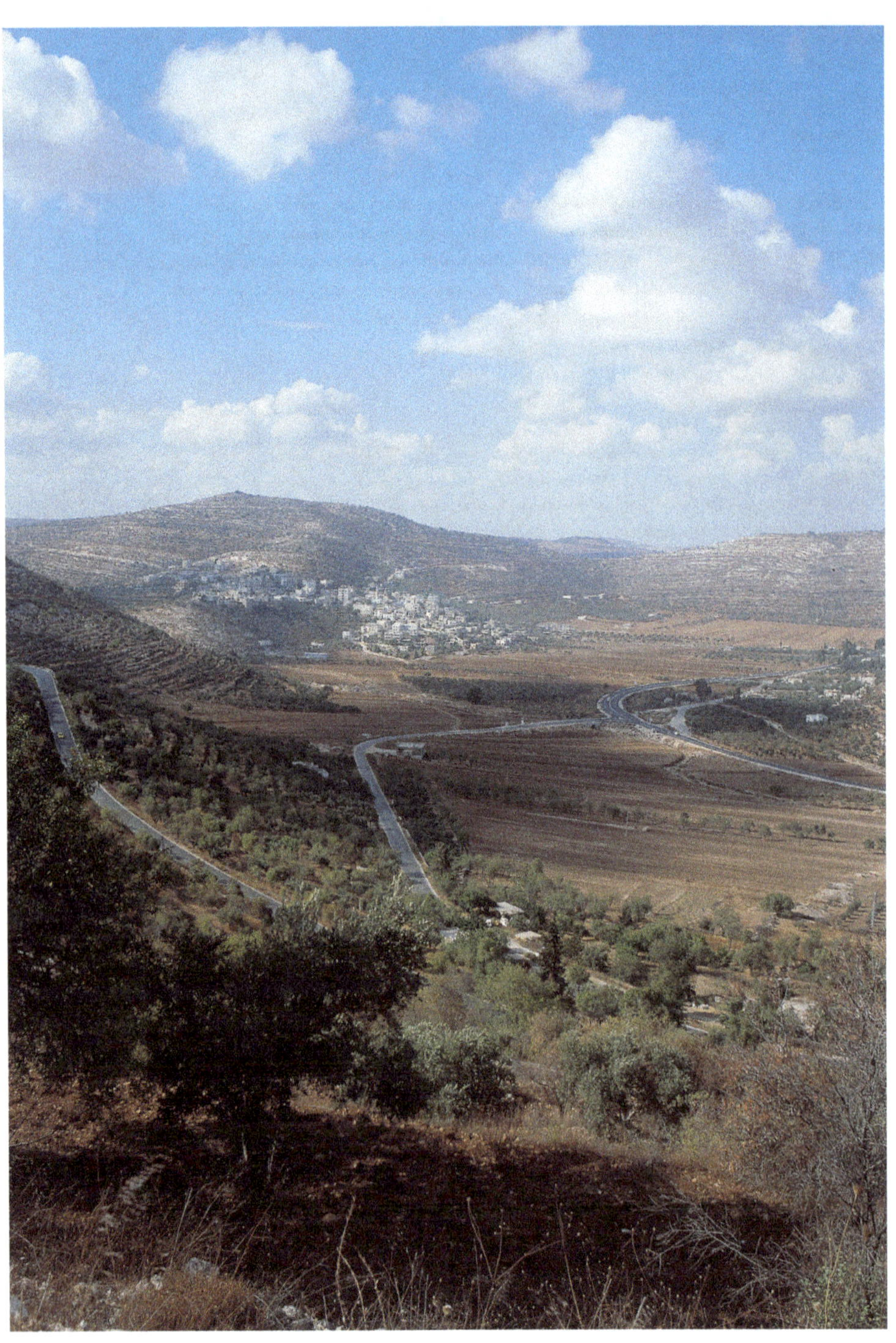

The Course of *Khans* and of Sufism

Marwan Abu Khalaf, Nazmi al-Ju'beh

The Postal Service between Cairo and Damascus

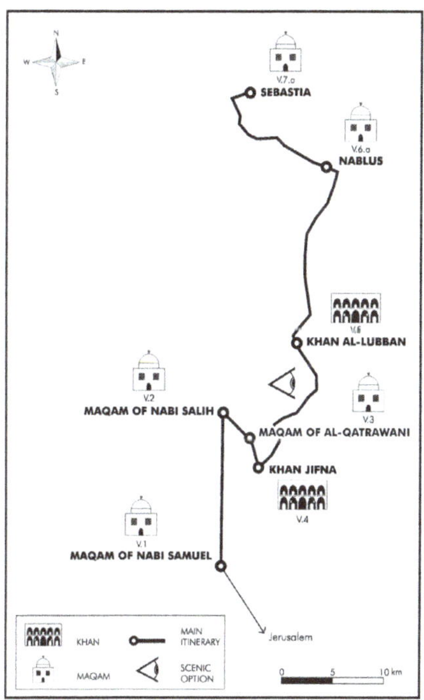

Plain of al-Lubban, general view.

Many factors contributed to the spread of *caravanserais* in Palestine: first and foremost was the country's central geographic location; secondly, was the fact that it was the focal point connecting Egypt to Syria, the Fertile Crescent and the Arabian Peninsula; and, finally, that the coastal road Via Maris ran through it, which was used for various military, commercial and communication purposes.

Historical sources suggest that the Umayyad Caliph 'Umar Ibn 'Abd al-'Aziz (99/717–101/720) was the first to order the building of *caravanserais* to host travellers. They continued to flourish until the middle of the 13th/19th century. The *khan* at the village of Abu Ghosh to the west of Jerusalem presumably dates to the Umayyad and Abbasid periods and was in use during both the Crusader and Mamluk periods; it is the only surviving monument of this period in Palestine.

Caravanserais in Palestine were found either on the main roads connecting major towns, such as Jerusalem, Gaza, Nablus and Ramla, or inside the cities and villages. Among those built on the main roads was the Khan of Jaljuliya, Khan of Jubb Yusuf, Khan al-Minya, Khan Yunis and Khan al-Tujjar. *Caravanserais* reached their zenith in the Mamluk period, which is considered to be the Golden Age of Islamic architecture both in Egypt and Syria. Their number continued to increase until the early Ottoman period.

The purpose behind building *khans* was to protect merchants and pilgrims from robbery and to provide places of rest and accommodation. They also served as postal stations until the Mamluk Sultan Baybars separated the postal roads from those of the *caravanserais*. Postal stations were then built and mail was more efficiently regulated between Cairo and Damascus.

A *caravanserai* consisted of a rectangular or square building that had an open courtyard in the centre. The structure had two storeys: the first consisted of stables for dromedaries and horses and storerooms for the guest's goods; the second was used to accommodate guests. During the Mamluk period in particular, mosques were added to these buildings. It also had a water source to cater for the needs of travellers. Often when a *khan* was located outside the city, its walls were fortified; however when it was built within the city, it was called a *wikala*.

The sanctity of Palestine within Islam has meant that it has always attracted huge crowds of people, explaining the construction of many *khans* all over the country. They provided important services to pilgrims, visitors and *sufis* arriving in Palestine, especially during the various Islamic festivals. In the villages, the residences of *sufis* took a different form, installed within *maqams* along with the shrines and tombs of their devout leaders. Most villages had more than one shrine where villagers would leave offerings, light candles and honour their vows.

Some of these *maqams* had special festivals associated with them, during which various folk celebrations would take place, the drums of the *sufis* and *dervishes* would pound, and many neighbouring villagers would come to ask for mercy and pray for a better future.

In this itinerary we shall explore *khans* and *maqams* on the road between Jerusalem and Sebastia, north-west of Nablus. We shall begin at the Maqam of Nabi Samuel (Shrine of the Prophet Samuel) located north-west of Jerusalem, and end with the Maqam of Nabi Yahya (Shrine of St John the Baptist) in Sebastia. We shall also discuss the postal road that connects the two Mamluk capitals, Cairo and Damascus, through Palestine.

M.A.K

V.1 MAQAM OF NABI SAMUEL (St Samuel)

The site can be reached by car or bus. Following the Jerusalem-Ramallah road, turn left at al-Ram junction. Passing through the villages of Bir Nabala and al-Jeib, turn left towards the south where the Maqam of Nabi Samuel can be seen on the mountain. The site, which is currently run by Orthodox Jews, can be visited at any time.

The Maqam of Nabi Samuel is situated on top of a mountain 6 km. north-west of Jerusalem. At 885 m. above sea level it is the highest mountain in the Jerusalem area, where, from the summit, a panoramic view of Jerusalem can be seen. This acclaimed religious site dates back to the Byzantine period, when Emperor Justinian ordered the construction of a church on the spot where it was thought St Samuel was buried. The Crusaders re-emphasised the religious significance of the location, and even its military importance, by

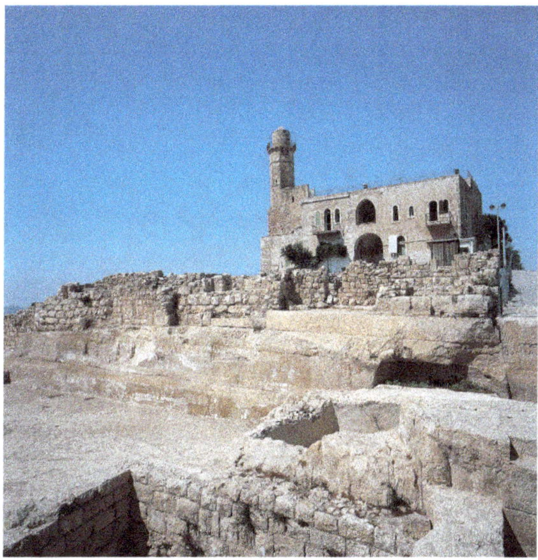

Maqam Nabi Samuel, general view.

building there a church and a monastery. They called it the Mountain of Joy, because it was the site from which they first saw Jerusalem. The site was rehabilitated during Saladin's time, and has since received the attention of many Muslim rulers. Jews have always been allowed to visit the site and place their candles side by side with those of Muslims.

The Crusaders' shrine was converted into a mosque and a *mihrab* was added. Many chambers were also added to the building, which was expanded several times to accommodate the increasing numbers of pilgrims and visitors. Few *sufis* on arriving in Jerusalem would miss the opportunity of visiting this site and spending a night at the Maqam of Nabi Samuel, which was run by the 'Alami family from Jerusalem.

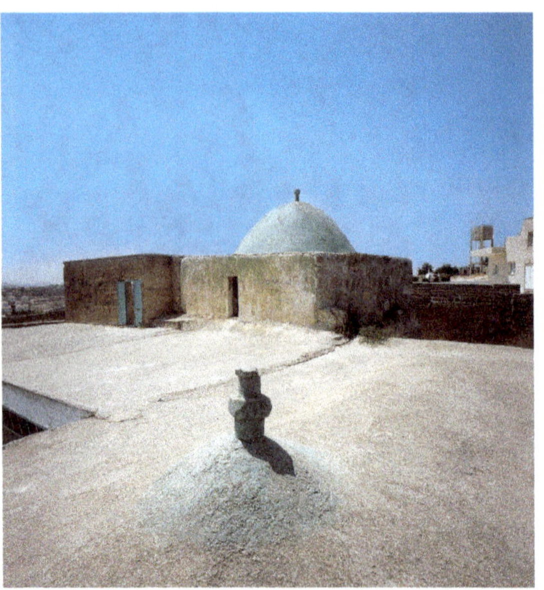

Maqam Nabi Salih, general view.

Today the site can be spotted many kilometres away and from all directions. The Crusaders' influence can still be seen in the remains of the cantilevers and the Gothic pillars, and so can the Mamluk additions to the building. The mosque's cylinder minaret was built by Shaykh Muhammad al-Khalili in the 12th/18th century, and he also built the shrine and the mosque above it. During the First World War, large parts of the structure were damaged. However the Supreme Islamic Council restored the damage in the 1920s, as certified by an inscription above the entrance.

The shrine looks like a citadel. In the centre of the entrance is a large portal that leads into a vast hall. The cenotaph is found in the centre of the hall as is customary in other commemorative Islamic shrines (such as the tombs of the Ibrahimi Mosque in Hebron). In the centre of the southern wall lies a *mihrab*, while at the end of the northern wall a narrow staircase leads to the crypt that looks like a natural cave with candles surrounding the cenotaph. To the side of the main entrance is a high staircase that leads to the roof and the minaret; from the south-eastern corner the visitor can observe the whole of Jerusalem.

If there is time to spare an exploration of the archaeological excavations around the site that have revealed Roman, Byzantine and Crusader remains, especially the water reservoirs and the stables that have been cut into the rocks, is highly recommended

N.J.

V.2 MAQAM OF NABI SALIH

The village of Nabi Salih lays approximately 15 km. north-west of Ramallah. It is reached by following the western slopes from the Maqam of Nabi Samuel to the town of Bitunia, Ramallah and then Bir Zayt. The site is open all day, except during prayer times.

The Qur'an mentions the Prophet Salih nine times; it was he who was sent by God to guide the people of Thamud, and so nine shrines were built to honour him in different places throughout Palestine, the largest and most famous of which is the one in Ramallah. The shrine stands on the ruins of a Byzantine church to the south-east of the village. The church's apse can still be seen close to the shrine's western wall. This indicates the site has been visited since the Byzantine period. Even though the building is not dated, it probably belongs to the either the Mamluk or Ottoman periods. The remains of the old village, and the lodgings of the visitors and hermits, are scattered throughout the peripheral area.

Interestingly, the shrine has remained intact. It consists of a rectangular building; a simple *mihrab* is found in the centre of the southern wall. Close to the prayer room is another large room where the caretaker and visitors to the shrine stayed. A door leading to the cenotaph is situated on the west wall; while to the west of this shrine lays a huge square. Here, the annual folk and religious festival takes place; offerings are made, food is presented to the visitors, candles are lit on the cenotaph and successive prayers are made.

Visitors are cheered and welcomed by the villagers who all belong to the Tamimi family (originating from Hebron) and are descendants of Tamim Ibn 'Aws al-Dari, the famous companion of the Prophet Muhammad. His descendants are also found in Jerusalem, Nablus and the Ramallah area.

N.J.

V.3 MAQAM OF AL-QATRAWANI

Turn east from the Maqam of Nabi Salih towards the town of Bir Zayt. From the centre of Bir Zayt, head north towards the village of 'Atara. On top of a mountain, lying south-west of the village and on the site of the Monastery of al-Iqbal, a solemn shrine composed of two domes can be seen.

In the middle of a vast, stretching expanse of land scattered with oak trees and thorns lies a rectangular building covered by two domes. The shrine has high ceilings carried by cross vaults of white carved stone on which traces of candles and burning can still be seen today. The building is in the Mamluk style, although excavations under the shrine have uncovered the remains of a Byzantine church thought to have been the Church of St Catherine. According to popular belief the name Qatrawani is derived from Catherine.

When water gets scarce, farmers come to the shrine from the surrounding area to pray for rain and make offerings to

Maqam al-Qatrawani, general view.

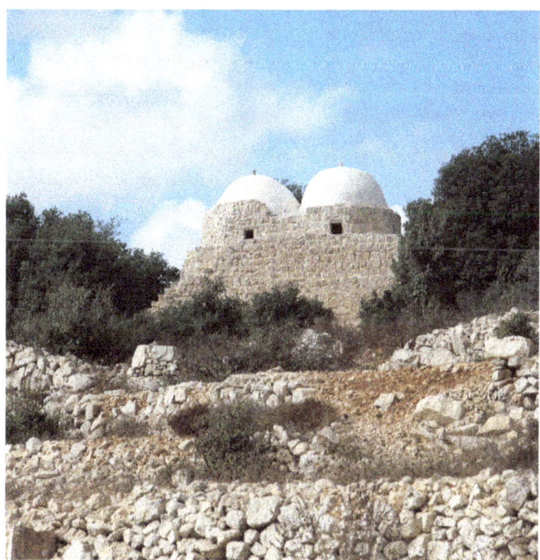

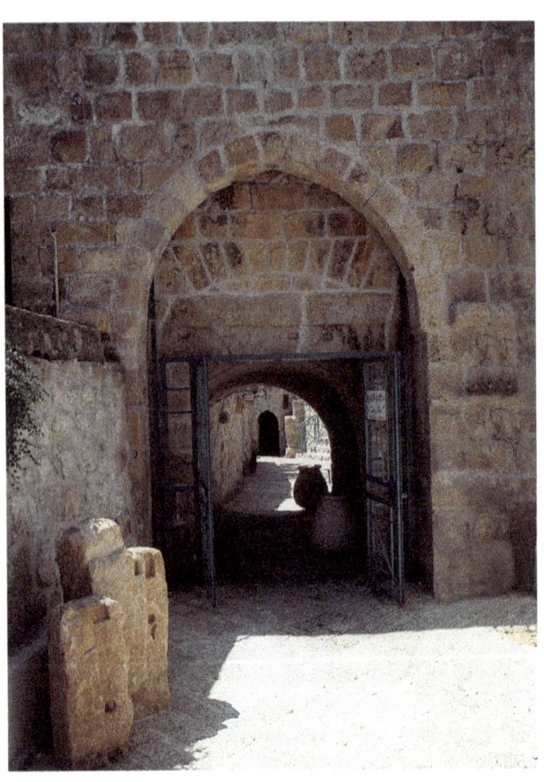

Khan Jifna, entrance.

Maqam al-Qatrawani. Muslims, who come to the shrine, often pray in front of the *maqam*'s *mihrab*.

The inhabitants of the neighbouring villages have appointed a caretaker to look after the shrine, its visitors, and the poor who seek help; they have built a room for him to the west of the shrine. A number of tombs found close to the edifice are those of people who sought to be buried close to the Maqam al-Qatrawani in the hope of being blessed.

N.J.

V.4 KHAN JIFNA

Lies 50 m. from the village's central roundabout, to the north-west. It was fully renovated in 1998–1999 and became part of Jifna's public utilities. Part of it is used today as local council offices and the rest as a restaurant and park.

Visiting the site is possible at all times. Food and drink can be purchased.

To reach the caravanserais, *turn east from the Maqam of Nabi Salih towards Bir Zayt. Continue through the olive and apricot groves until you reach Jifna, which lies 2 km. east of Bir Zayt and 23 km. north of Jerusalem.*

Jifna is situated on a fertile hill that overlooks a valley covered by almond, apricot and olive trees. In Arabic (spoken) *Jifna* means vineyard (written Arabic *jifan*), and it was called so due to the large number of vineries in the area during the Crusader period, and today this small village keeps the same name. Some attribute the name to Jifna, the grandfather of the Ghassanids; the Arab tribe that ruled a large part of Syria under the control of the Byzantine Empire. Remains of the village attest to this, as does the fact that a village by the name of Deir Ghassana lies to the north-west of the village of Nabi Salih.

Jifna's importance is linked to several different factors: According to the Apocryphal Christian tradition, it was the place where the Holy family of Christ and his parents Mary and Joseph, stopped to rest under a fig tree. For this reason it lies on the pilgrimage route from Acre to Jerusalem going through Nazareth, Sebastia, Nablus, and then Jerusalem and Bethlehem. The fact that the small town is surrounded by fertile lands and has abundant water resources drew the attention of the Crusaders. However, archaeological and historical evidence indicates that settlement in Jifna dates back to the Roman period and that the area remains a settlement, uninterrupted, until the end of the Ottoman period: the greater part of the old centre of the village dates to this period.

The Khan Jifna is the town's most distinguished structure. It has an imposing military character and hence it is called the *Burj* (Tower). Its foundations probably date back to either the Roman (63 BC–AD 324), or the Byzantine (324–637) period. Its restoration began during the Crusader period at the end of the 11th century, and continued to the end of that century. During the Mamluk and Ottoman periods many further alterations and additions were made to it.

The building, of rectangular plan (the southernmost wall is 40.6 m. long, and the western wall 50 m.), includes several rooms and halls in the north and southwest; a corridor to the east leads to an inner courtyard where all the doors to all the rooms face the courtyard, and no windows overlook the street from the west side. The building has an oil press, a room thought to have been a prison cell at one time, and corridors that connected certain parts of the building to others, and probably some other areas that have not yet been uncovered.

M.A.K.

Khan Jifna, internal courtyard, view of the stairs to the upper floor.

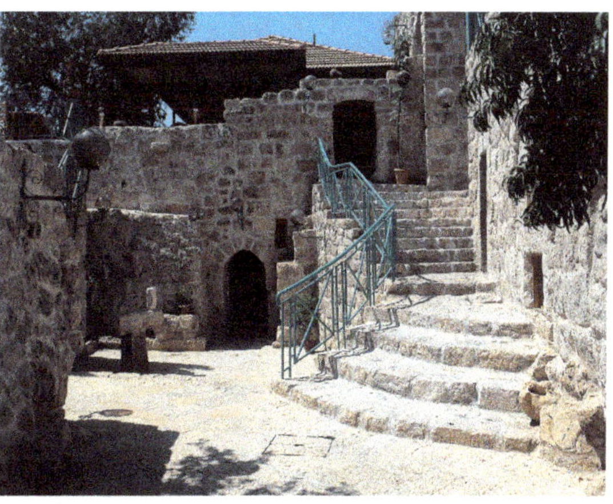

Khan Jifna, internal courtyard, general view.

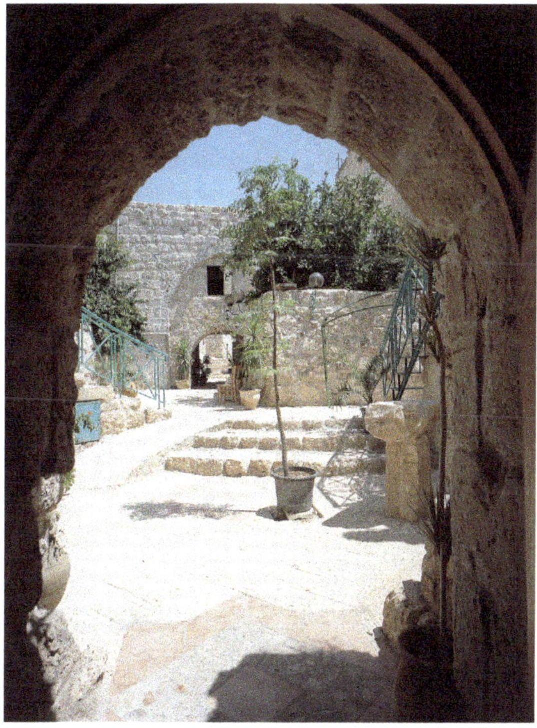

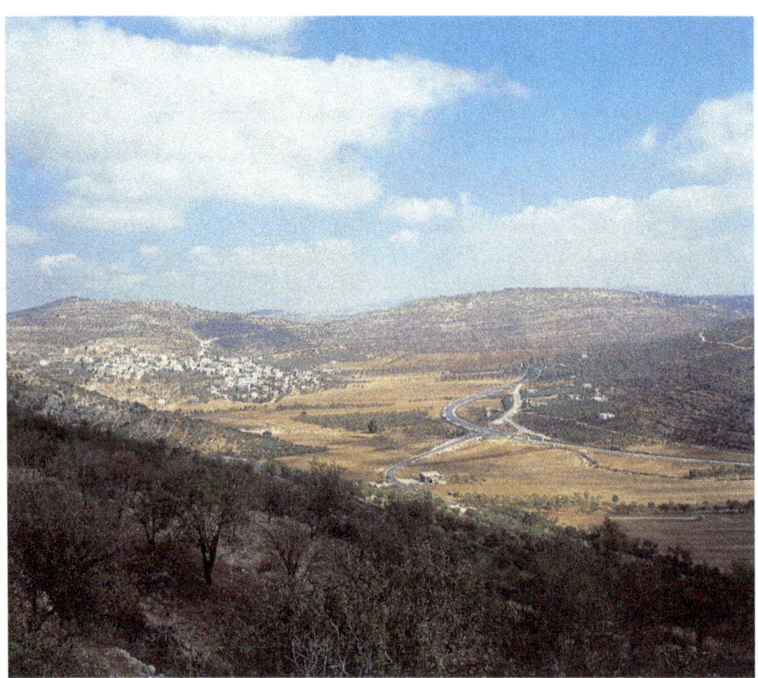

Plain of al-Lubban, general view.

SCENIC OPTION

Plain of al-Lubban

Lies 15 km. north of the town of al-Bireh on the main Jerusalem–Nablus road. The visitor will arrive at a high mountain ridge to the south of the village of al-Lubban, which overlooks a captivating view of the Plain of al-Lubban.

This fertile plain, which has alluvial soil and is surrounded by the slopes of the mountains, is intensively cultivated with vegetables and pulses. The remains of a *caravanserai* lie on its southern edge, which is surrounded by almond, fig, plum and pine trees. Olive, almond and oak trees cover the slopes of the surrounding mountains.

M.A.K.

V.5 KHAN AL-LUBBAN

Lies 41 km. from Jerusalem. Having visited the Khan Jifna, return to the road leading to Nablus. After 1 km. from the crossroads of the village of Sinjil, turn left off the main road. The road will start to wind and descend

Khan al-Lubban, entrance, internal view.

Khan al-Lubban, main hall.

sharply until you reach the Plain of al-Lubban. It is recommended that the visitor stop off and take in the view of the plain from one of the bends. The caravanserai *is at the end of the winding road on the right. The site is open at all times.*

The exact date of the building is unknown although its style indicates it goes back to the late Mamluk or early Ottoman period. A large part of its western side and part of its northern side were renovated and rebuilt during the Ottoman period. This can be clearly inferred from the size and style of the stones. Due to its strategic location, the *caravanserai* was used as a police station during the British Mandate and Jordanian rule.

The building is square-plan; each side is about 23 m. long. Unlike other *caravanserais*, it has only one storey, possibly due to being pretty close to the towns of Nablus and al-Bireh.

A large part of the original structure has survived and its entrance leads to an open courtyard and to a vaulted hall. Stables are found on either side of the entrance. The rooms to the east and west of the courtyard were for administration purposes, while those to the north were used to lodge visitors. The mosque's location, however, has not been identified. Recently further alterations to the building have been carried out to make it more accessible to visitors.

In addition to its vital location, the fact that a fresh-water well already existed nearby was an additional factor behind placing the building here.

M.A.K.

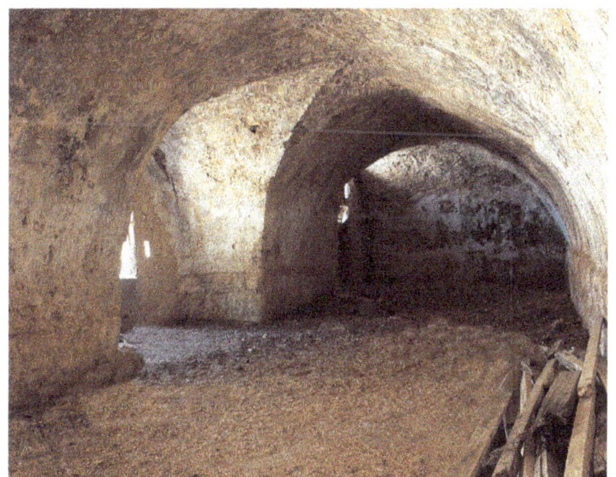

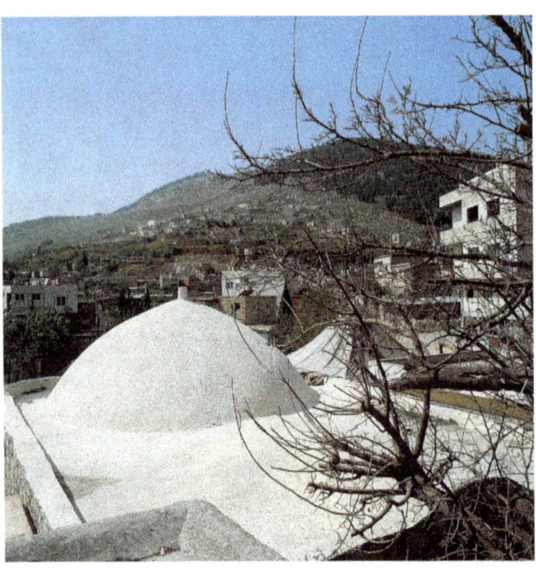
Tomb of Joseph, Nablus.

V.6 NABLUS

V.6.a Tomb of Joseph

Lies in the centre of the village of Balata, which today forms the eastern quarter of Nablus.

Folk tales differ with regard to the location of the Tomb of Joseph, with at least two potential places identified. The first is the Ibrahimi Mosque in Hebron (VIII.1.a), and the second is this location. Some historical sources mention that he was first buried in Nablus, and then moved to the Ibrahimi Mosque where a dome was built above his tomb. The site is venerated by the three monotheist religions due to Joseph's distinct place in each of them.

The shrine stands on top of an old well and consists of a square burial room that has a *mihrab* and which is covered by a dome. Nothing in the building indicates that any special attention was paid to it, possibly because most sultans paid more attention to the tomb in the Ibrahimi Mosque. The room is preceded by an open hall, which overlooks an open courtyard. Another small room is found to the west that was probably used by the attendant of the shrine.

The edifice is in the local style that spread throughout the Ottoman period. The Ministry of the Waqf and Religious Affairs, which owns the site, has assigned the *shaykh* Fayad 'Abd Allah family to look after it. The family has a document signed by the Ottoman Sultan 'Abd al-Hamid that assigns them to serve and look after it.

N.J.

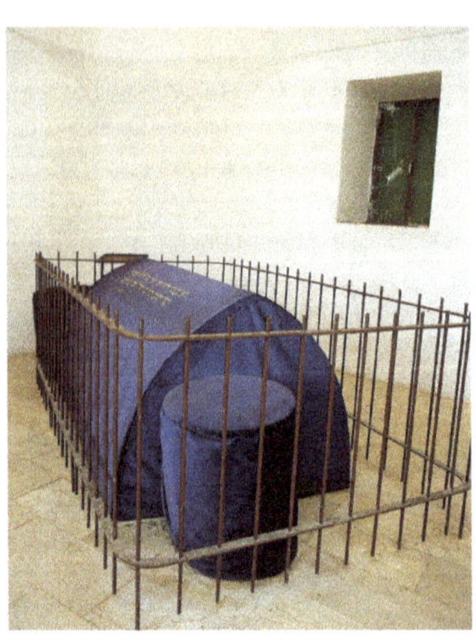
Tomb of Joseph, funeral chamber, Nablus.

V.7 SEBASTIA

V.7.a Maqam of Nabi Yahya (St John the Baptist)

The maqam *is in the mosque's courtyard in the centre of the village of Sebastia. To reach it, go through Nablus, and then turn left to get to a crossroads leading to Tulkarem and Jenin. Continue north towards Jenin for about 2.3 km, to a desert road, which leads to the village of Sebastia. Leaving the village, the visitor can take the road that runs through the famous Roman colonnaded street that lies within the remains of the ancient city. The site is open all day.*

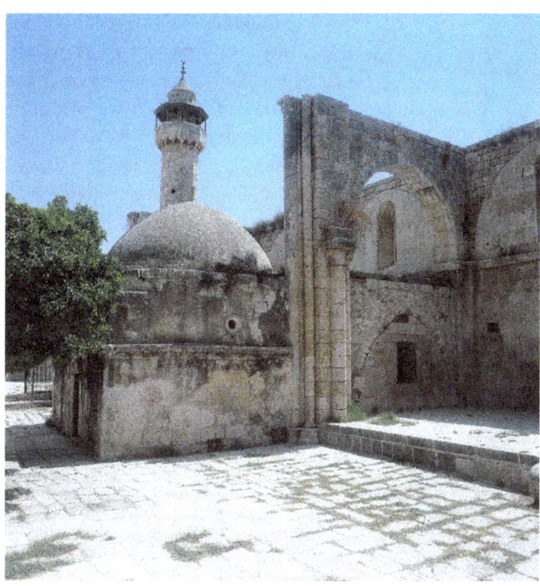

Maqam Nabi Yahya, north façade seen from the interior of the courtyard, Sebastia

The village of Sebastia stands about 15 km. north-west of Nablus on the scenic slopes of the Samarian hills, 463 m. above sea level. Herod built the city of Sebastia in 25 BC, over the ruins of ancient Samaria, the capital of the Kingdom of Israel. The site has been excavated several times, in 1908, 1931 and 1935, and finds from various periods, as early as the Stone Age, have been uncovered.

When Christianity became the official religion in the Byzantine Empire in the early 4th century, the inhabitants of Sebastia were divided between paganism and Christianity. The popular story that St John the Baptist, who was executed by Herod Antipas and subsequently buried in Sebastia, was widespread then and became firmly established.

The presence of three statues inside the *maqam* confirmed this belief. One represents a dancer holding a human head on a plate. The second represents Herod holding his beard in remorse for having killed St John the Baptist, while the third is that of the decapitated head of St John the Baptist. Sadly, the Israeli Antiquities Authority took the statues away in 1987, and no one knows the whereabouts of the statues now.

Popular tradition relates that the parents of St John the Baptist, Prophet Zacharias and his wife, are also buried at the site, which further confirms popular belief that this is the place where St John the Baptist was imprisoned and later buried. Another tale mentions that the Saint is buried in Damascus, and there is even some mention that he lies buried in the Beqa' Valley (actually Beqaa Valley), east of Lebanon.

Two Byzantine churches were built in the village, and its only mosque seems to have been built close to one of the ruins. The mosque was built in the time of Caliph 'Umar Ibn Khattab, and Sebastia was one of the first villages in which an "'Umari Mosque" was built. However, an earthquake destroyed the mosque in the 6th/12th century and the Crusaders built a church on top of it.

In (583/1187), following Saladin's conquest over the Crusaders in the Battle of Hittin, Saladin ordered the construction of a *maqam* to commemorate St John the Baptist. In 1310/1892-1893, the Ottoman Sultan 'Abd al-Hamid II added two rooms to the eastern part of the mosque, where prayers are now held, and where there also sits a minaret.

The site has attracted monks, *sufis* and many visitors. 'Abd al Ghani al-Nabulsi describes the shrine as follows: *"We arrived at this village and entered its mosque which was originally a vast monastery. We saw unusual buildings, which had been largely ruined. We descended the stairs to the grotto. At the bottom was a small window behind which it is said that John the Baptist and his father rest."*

The *maqam* has two rooms. The first is of a square-plan and surmounted by a dome; this room lies above the tomb and can be reached by using the corridor in front of its northern façade. The second room contains a *mihrab*; it is adjacent to the first and can be accessed by a door through the first room.

M.A.K.

THE POSTAL SERVICE BETWEEN CAIRO AND DAMASCUS

Marwan Abu Khalaf

The postal road between Cairo and Damascus was one of the most important routes to pass through Palestine because the coastal road, Via Maris, ran through it. Historical sources reveal that *caravanserais* served as postal stations on most trading routes connecting all parts of the Islamic world but, during the Mamluk period, especially during al-Dahir Baybars' reign (658/1260–676/1277), postal routes were separated from *caravanserai* routes, with many new postal stations built on the roads connecting Cairo to Damascus.

Postal communications played an important role in the Islamic Empire because the service connected the diverse areas of the empire, and ensured the speedy delivery of news and orders. Most sultans paid special attention to these buildings, particularly in the early period when their region was still prone to renewed attack from the Crusaders.

Most postal buildings were rectangular in design and had some units built to accommodate a small number of men that would stop there with their horses. Each of these would consist of small rooms, a simple mosque, a well or a cistern and a stable, as can be seen in Yibna, Qaqun, al-Lujjun and Jisr Banat Ya'qub.

Among the postal roads connecting Cairo to Damascus was the one described by Ibn Fadl Allah al-'Umari in his famous *Al-Ta'rif bi-l-mustalah al-sharif* ("An Introduction to the sacred Terminology"). Starting from Gaza, the postal road in Palestine went two ways: the first led to al-Karak in Jordan, while the second led to Damascus via Bayt Daris, Yasour, Lidda, al-'Awja, al-Tira, Qaqun, al-Fandaqumiya, Jenin, Zar'in, Bisan, al-Majami', al-Zahra' and Irbid.

In the 10th/16th century, the postal road started in al-'Arish, continued via Khan Yunis, Gaza, al-Majdal, Yibna, Ramla, Ra's al-'Ayn, Qaqun, al-Lujjun, 'Uyun al-Tujjar, al-Minya, Jisr Banat Ya'qub, al-Qunaytra, and then reached Damascus.

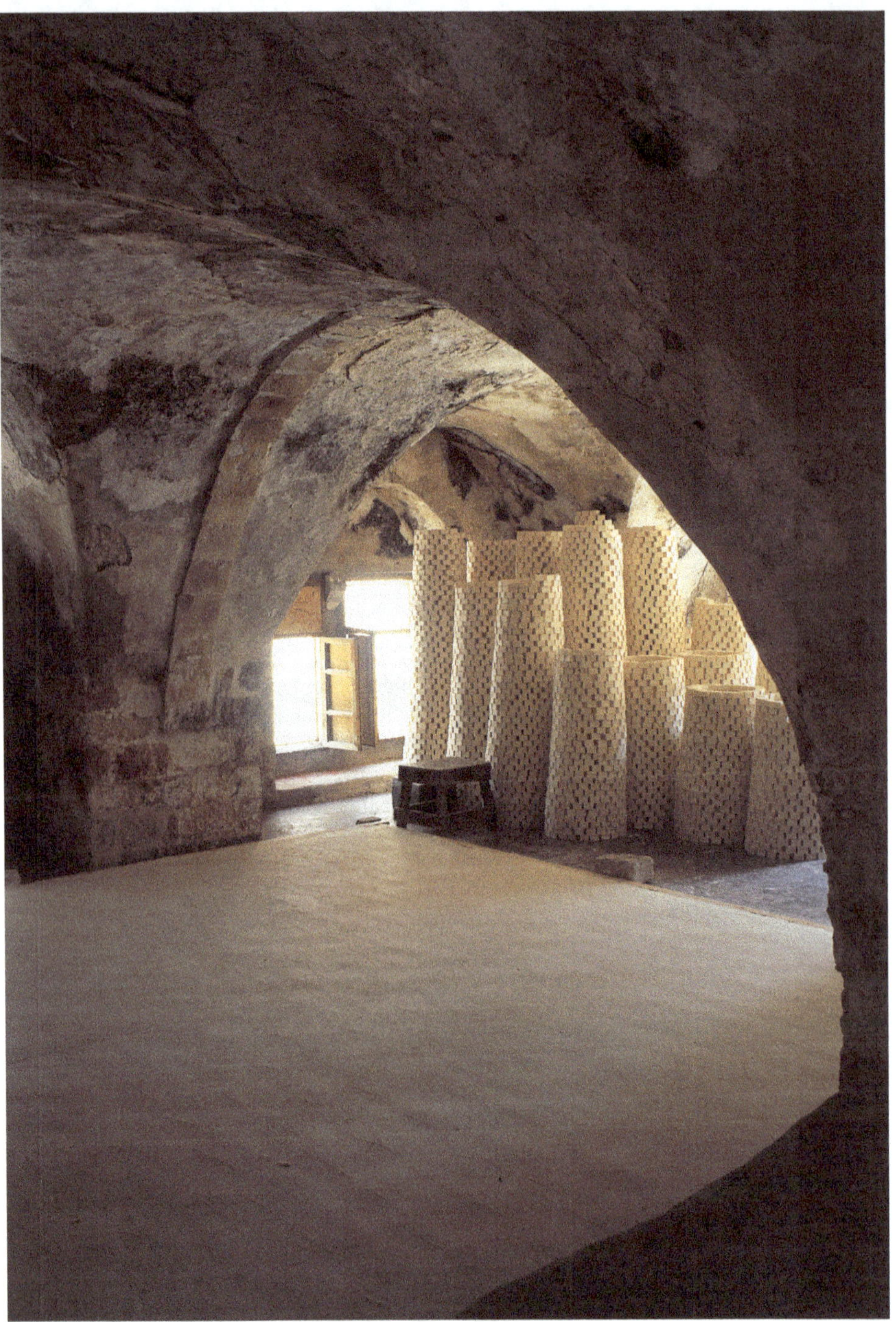

Nablus: the City of *Hammams* and Soap

Marwan Abu Khalaf, Naseer R. Arafat, Nazmi al-Ju'beh

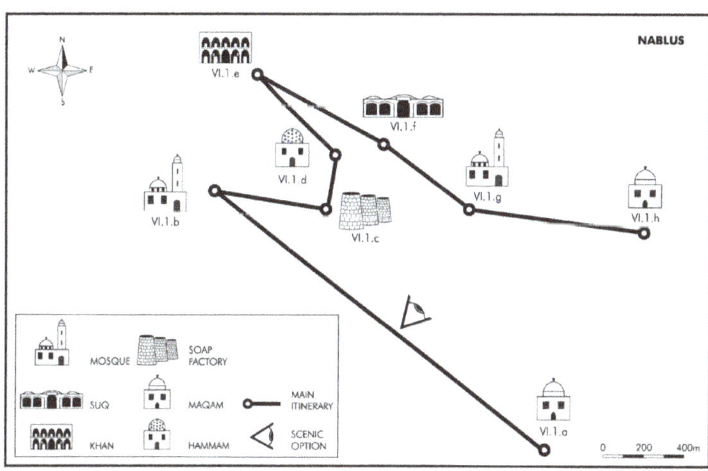

Tuqan Soap Factory, bars of soap being dried.

This itinerary covers Nablus, the largest town in the West Bank. Beautifully situated between the scenic Mounts of Ebal and Garizim, it lies 67 km. north of Jerusalem and lies at an altitude of 570 m. above sea level. Nablus was renowned for the large number of public baths and numerous soap factories it owned, hence the title of this itinerary. It is documented that more than 30 factories were active there at the end of the 13th/19th century. Though first settled in the second millennium, its archaeological and historical remains date back to different periods between the Roman (63 BC–AD 324) and the end of the Ottoman period (1336/1917).

Nablus became an Islamic city in around 15/636–637 and was mentioned in many historical sources of the early Islamic period. The most important reference came from al-Muqaddasi in the 4th/10th century who called it "the little Damascus" as it had much in common with the Syrian capital, such as dense olive trees, stone houses and streams that ran through the city.

The Crusaders occupied Nablus in 492/1099 when Prince Tancred succeeded in adding it to his domain: the Principality of Galilee. During the time of Baldwin I, Nablus was part of the Kingdom of Jerusalem, and many churches and other religious buildings were constructed there during this period.

Following the Battle of 'Ayn Jalut in 658/1260, Nablus surrendered to the rule of the Mamluk Sultan Baybars. Contemporary Mamluk historical sources describe it as a city rich in water and fertile lands; it also witnessed lively scientific and intellectual activity over several centuries, and many of its scholars influenced the climate of thought in the Islamic world. Many remarkable buildings were constructed that carried the general and local character of Islamic architecture; some of which are mentioned in historical sources. Among these were mosques, shrines, *zawiyas*, fountains, mills, *caravanserais* and markets.

This one-day itinerary focuses on the Old City and numerous important historical and archaeological sites that are within easy reach. Diversity has been the basis of the selection, which covers the Great Mosque, the Soap Manufactory of the Tuqan Family, Suq of Khan al-Tujjar, Mosque, Khan al-Wikala al-Gharbiyya and Hammam al-Jadida in addition to two *maqams*. Two "windows" are included, one on palaces and the other on the manufacture of soap. There is also an optional site to visit, namely Mount of Garizim (Jabal al-Samara, or Mount of the Samaritans).

Finally, Nablus is famous for its Middle Eastern sweets, especially *kunafa*, that are worthwhile trying. It is also highly recommended that the visitor buy a piece of the unparalleled Nablus soap.

M.A.K.

VI.1 NABLUS

VI.1.a Maqam of Ghanim

The maqam *is reached via the road south of Nablus, ascending Mount Garizim from its south-western slopes. On the top of the mountain stands the* maqam, *overlooking Nablus. The site is open during the day.*

The shrine lies north-east of the citadel ruins that were built by the Byzantine Emperor Justinian, and rebuilt by the Crusaders; it includes the remains of an octagonal church. It was built to honour the *shaykh* Ghanim al-Burini (b. 563/1167), to whom Saladin had assigned its inspection (al-Ghawanima Quarter in Jerusalem is named after his family). It is widely believed that both he and his sons used the building as a retreat. The shrine's strategic location makes it even more possible to believe that it was used as a watchtower, as it has a similar two-storey square structure to that of other watchtowers in the southern parts of Palestine.

The shrine consists of two adjacent rooms inside of which lies a simple tomb. From the top of the shrine the whole city of Nablus can be seen. It is said that during the periods of Crusader invasions, the shrine was the central lookout point, providing warning of immanent danger (fire was used at night and smoke during the day).

N.J.

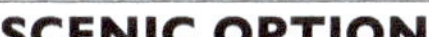

SCENIC OPTION

Garizim Mount (Mount of the Samaritans)

The Mount of Garizim (known locally as *jabal* al-Tur) is 880 m. above sea level.

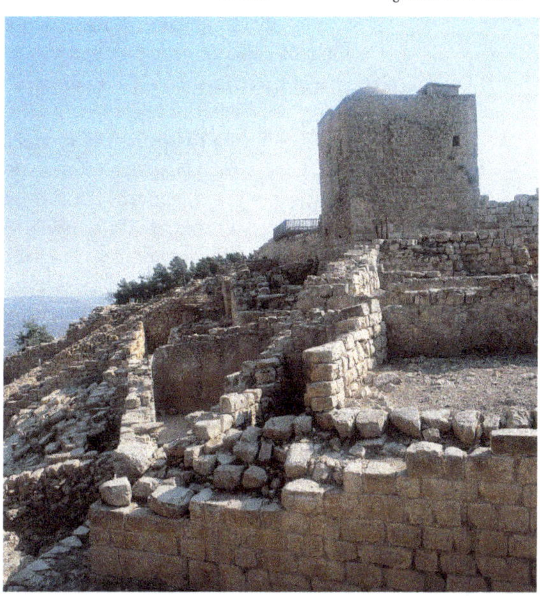

Maqam Ghanim, Nablus.

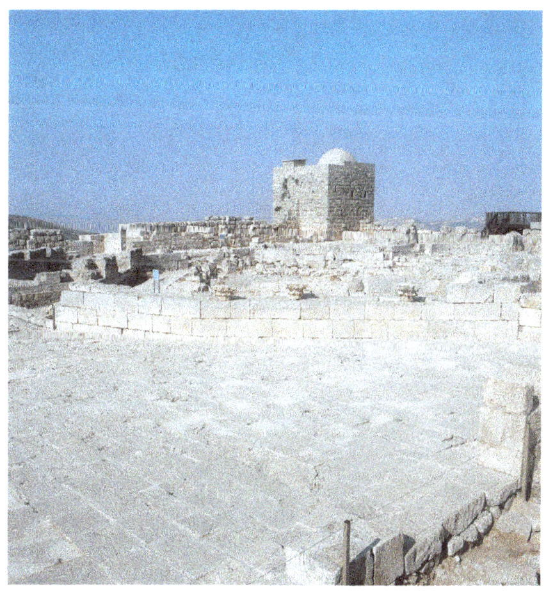

Maqam Ghanim, general view, Nablus.

Scenic Option

Sacred to the Samaritans who believe it is Mount Moriah, the site of Abraham's sacrifice of Isaac, it is the place of their pilgrimage and where they come to offer sacrifices during Passover. The modern Samaritans (*Samarian,* which means conservative, were a splinter sect from Judaism) believe they are descendants of the Israelites who did not leave Palestine for Babylon. They adopt a form of Judaism whereby they only believe in Moses and consider themselves the descendants of Haroun. They remain a conservative, strict and separate society that only follows the five books of Moses in the Old Testament: Genesis, Deuteronomy, Numbers, Exodus and Leviticus. They perform the ablution ritual prior to prayers and the women cleanse themselves of the impurities of menstruation and the post-partum period. During their morning prayers, Samaritans kneel and prostrate themselves facing Mount Garizim, their *qibla.* They refrain from working on the Sabbath and spend Friday night praying and glorifying God. They celebrate Passover, Pentecost and Tabernacles.

The highlight of Passover is the bloody sacrifice of sheep carried out in an open field surrounded by a fence, which has a well in its centre. The sacrifice is performed over the well, while two other wells are used as kilns. Close to the site lies their synagogue in the middle of a new living quarter. They believe the Mes-

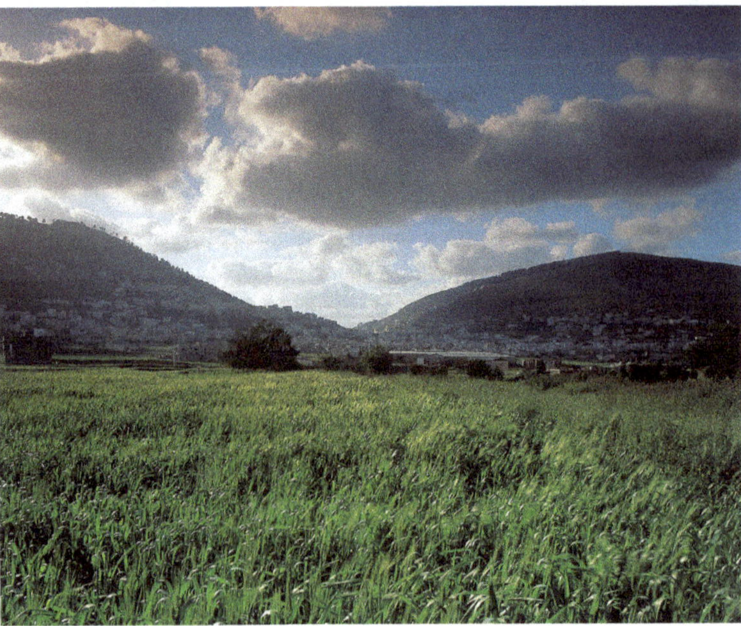

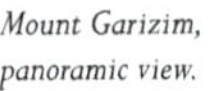

Mount Garizim, panoramic view.

siah will come to Mount Garizim. Although they rely on the lunar calendar they actually have two calendars; one starts with the day of Creation, whilst the other starts with the day of Exodus.
The sect lives in complete isolation and marry only within their own community. Hardly exceeding 450 people in total, they are the smallest sect in the world. Most of them live on Mount Garizim, and a few in Holon near Tel Aviv, using Hebrew for prayer and Arabic in their daily life. During the reign of Alexander the Great the Samaritans built a temple on the mountain, which they considered their spiritual and religious centre. Even though it was completely destroyed by the Hasmonean King, John Hyrcanus in 125 BC, part of its remains can still be seen today on the eastern slopes of the mountain, to which a staircase leads. The Samaritans took part in many rebellions against the Romans, which resulted in a frightful reduction in their number, their self-isolation and seclusion.

N.J.

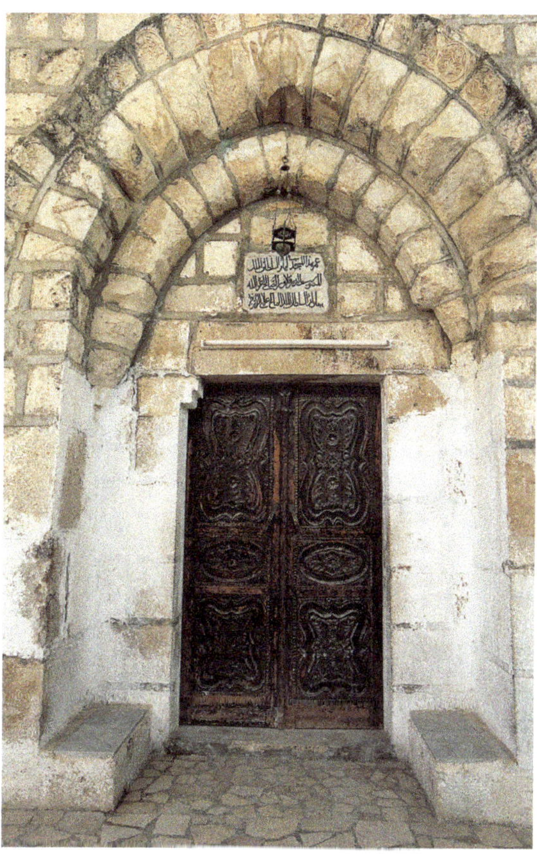

Al-Khadra' Mosque, entrance, Nablus (© Sonia Halliday Photographs, Photograph: D. Silverman).

VI.1.b **Al Khadra' Mosque (Maqam of Sittna al-Khadra')**

Situated in the area of Ra's al-'Ayn, west of Nablus and close to 'Ayn al-'Asal. The Mosque and shrine can be visited during the day except at prayer times.

According to the local heritage of Nablus, Khadra was one of Jacob's daughters who refused to be married to a pagan tribal *shaykh*. When she prayed to God for help her husband-to-be died, and so the shrine was built in commemoration of him. It is also believed to be the location where Jacob mourned the death of his son Joseph; a small dark room, known as Jacob's Grief, is found close to the shrine's western door. It is believed that the room was built on top of a grotto, and a few *dervishes'* tools can still be seen around the shrine.
The mosque's architectural details reveal it was originally a Crusader church built

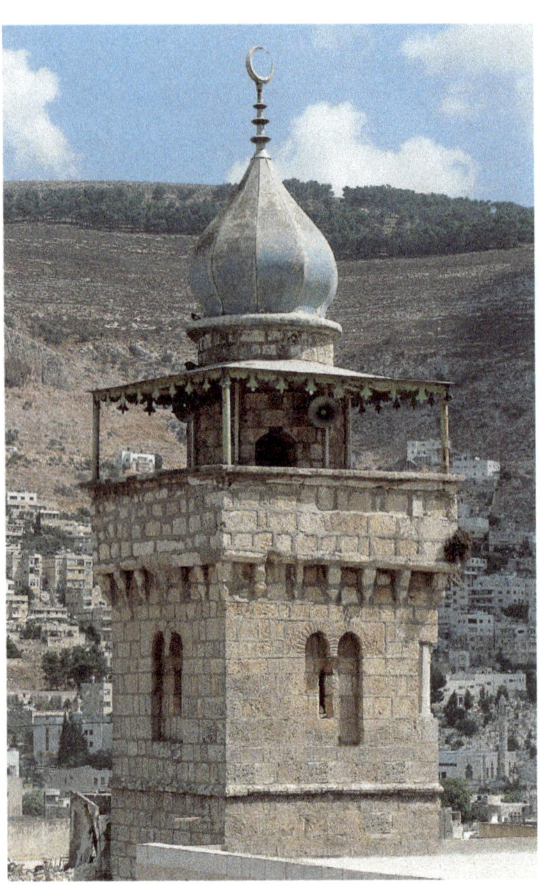

Al-Khadra' Mosque, minaret, detail of the upper section, Nablus (© Sonia Halliday Photographs, Photograph: D. Silverman).

between 492/1099 and 583/1187. The Ayyubids converted it into a mosque after they had conquered the city in 583/1187–1188. The marble inscription plaque above the northern middle entrance, however, states that the mosque was rebuilt during the reign of the Mamluk Sultan al-Mansur Sayf al-Din Qalawun (678/1280–689/1290), under the auspices of his son al-Salih 'Ala' al-Din 'Ali Ibn Qalawun (679/1281–687/1288), the current minaret was added then. In the Ottoman period, the northern, upper parts of the mosque and the ornaments on the *mihrab*'s niche were renovated. It is probable that these renovations were carried out during the 11th/17th century, as the Turkish traveller Evilia Çelebi visited the site in 1082/1671–1672 and did not refer to any demolished parts of the mosque.

The building consists of a northern courtyard, a prayer hall and a minaret. The courtyard is rectangular and has a marble pond and a fountain in the centre. An ablutions unit lies to the north-west, and a number of fairly recent tombs to the south-east.

The prayer hall is rectangular aligned east–west and lies south of the northern courtyard, with three symmetrical entrances on its façade. Each is surmounted with a stone frame that forms

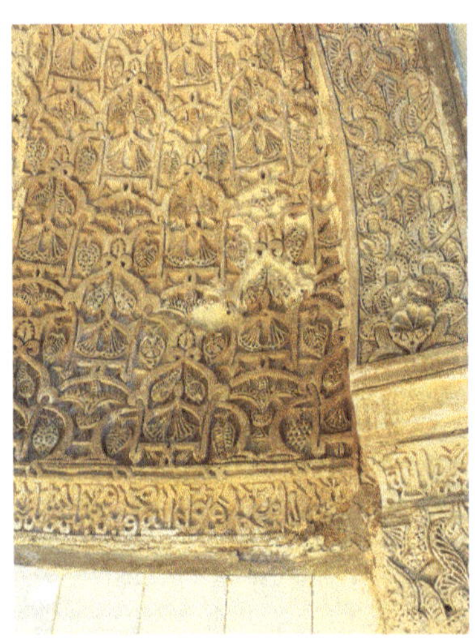

Al-Khadra' Mosque, mihrab, detail of decoration, Nablus.

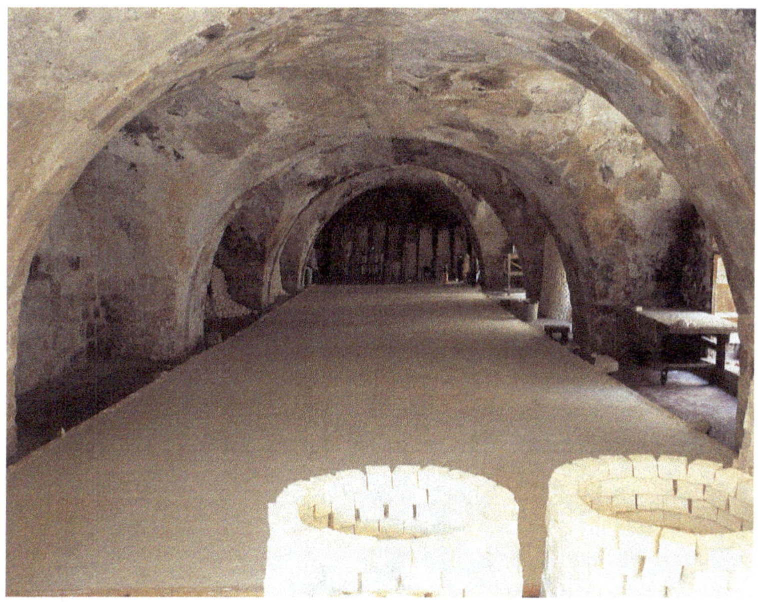

Tuqan Soap Factory, upper floor with soap paste spread out to dry, general view, Nablus.

a pointed arch and is decorated by spiral and circular vegetal ornaments. The ornaments form a circle that covers the surface of every single stone. A large *mihrab* lies in a niche at the centre of the southern wall. Its vault has leaf, vegetal and pinecone ornaments and Qur'anic verses written in the *naskhi* script are found on the bottom. Next to the *mihrab* lies a beautiful, modern, wooden *minbar*.

The minaret stands a few meters away from the north wall of the open courtyard. Its square stone base, which supports the minaret, consists of two parts. These carry the gallery, which in turn stands on corbels that form a small circular dome in the centre.

M.A.K.

VI.1.c The Tuqan Family Soap Factory

Lies south-west of al-Tuta Square in the centre of al-Qaryun Quarter in Nablus.
The site can be visited every day except Fridays, provided a prior arrangement has been made with the owner. It provides an opportunity to buy soap made of natural olive oil.

Established by the Tuqan Family at the end of the 13th/19th century, this soap factory is a large two-storey rectangular building, whose main façade overlooks al-Tuta Square. The façade is quite simple but has a large entrance portal at the centre to facilitate the entry of oil carriers and the exit of boxes of soap. The door is wooden and has a pointed arch above it, flanked by several windows

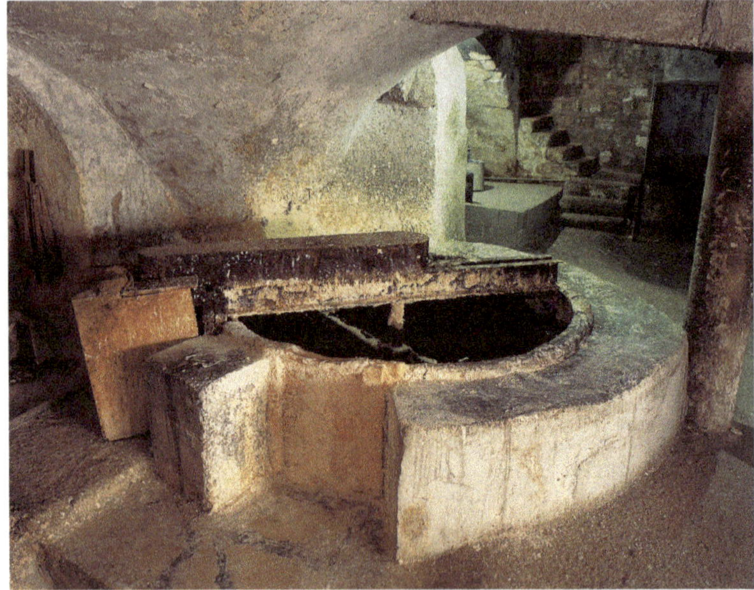

Tuqan Soap Factory, room used for boiling soap, a soap vat, Nablus.

topped by pointed arches, which are usually closed from the inside. Unlike the lower part of the entrance, the upper part is covered by large windows to allow ventilation which helps the soap dry.

The large entrance leads into the ground floor, which is the administrative and production sector, including the finance office and the manager's office. Soap manufacture takes place on this floor, which consists of a large hall with a high cross-vault ceiling, supported by stone pillars in the centre. A large area, called *al-balat* (the pavement), has a huge pot in which the process of cooking the soap takes place. In front of it is a semicircular basin called a *mibzal*, and next to this are several square containers for fermented and pure water. Under the pot is a small room that contains the furnace. The cooking process takes place here, enabling the soap to develop. It can be reached through a staircase opposite the *mibzal*. On top of the furnace is a chimney that extends high above the factory. Also on this floor is a cistern for storing oil when it is in season.

On the south-eastern side of the factory is a staircase that leads to the upper floor, which consists of a large flat space called *mafrash*. Here the sticky soap is spread until it dries. Then it is cut into shapes by sharp metal tools. The pieces are arranged into a cylindrical lighthouse shape to allow the air through until they are completely dry and ready to use. The ceiling of this floor consists of successive shallow domes supported by arches that stand on pillars.

M.A.K.

VI.1.d **Hammam al-Jadida (al-Shifa')**

Situated on al-Nasr Street opposite al-Bek Mosque in the centre of the Old City. Open daily to visitors in order to bathe or just to visit. Tuesdays are allocated to women.

To the inhabitants of Nablus, going to the public baths has always been associated with fun and cleanliness. Women would take fruit to eat, and they would dance, and sing all sorts of songs for every social occasion or celebration held within its walls. Hence public *hammams* were closely linked to the social life of Nablus. They provided the place where many social occasions, including weddings and boys' circumcisions, were celebrated. A *hammam* would be privately hired for the bride and her family and another for the groom, his family and friends. After each had bathed, a procession led by the groom would head towards the bride's house. This would be accompanied by singing, the beating of a tambourine and the sprinkling of rice grains and perfume by shopkeepers.

It is called Hammam al-Jadida because it is the most recently built *hammam* in Nablus. Its second and current name, *al-Shifa* (healing), has been derived from the lines of poetry that are engraved on an inscription above its entrance. The *hammam* is part of a complex that is owned by

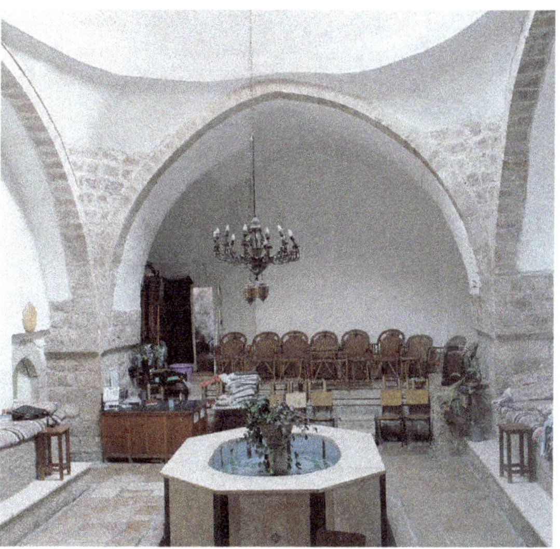

Hammam al-Jadida, reception hall with central fountain, Nablus.

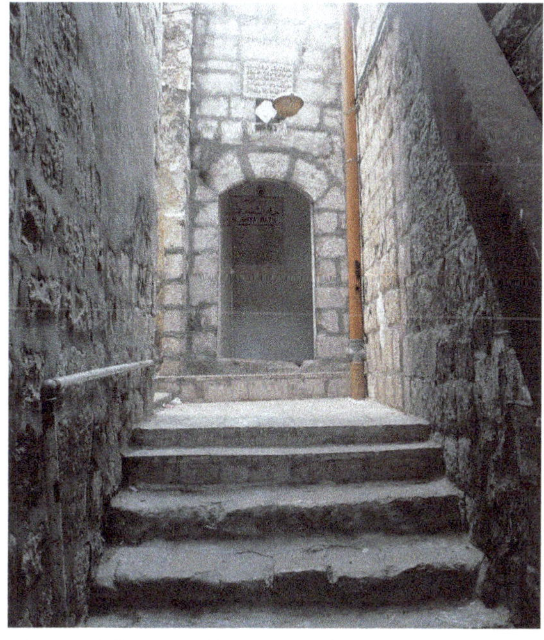

Hammam al-Jadida, access stairs, Nablus.

the Tuqan family and was built by Salih, Ahmad and Mustafa, the sons of Ibrahim Tuqan in 1149/1736–1737, as confirmed by the inscription.
The layout of the building is very simple, although it has many parts. The first part, immediately after the entrance, comprises a large reception hall called "the summer dressing room". There is a fountain in the centre and stone benches distributed along the sides where visitors can recline as they sip drinks and puff on a *narghile*. This hall distinguishes itself by its beautiful wooden columns and its two raised platforms, upon which special furniture sits. The vaulted ceiling has skylights. Next to this hall is another one called "the winter dressing room"; this has the same function as the first except it is used during the winter months. Hence the ceiling is lower and has no skylights, and the fountain is smaller.
Bathing takes place in the warm hall, which is large and surrounded by many small rooms. It is covered by a semi-barrel vault, which is built of clay vessels in order to preserve the interior temperature. Some beautifully shaped, glass-covered, circular skylights have been cut into it. The heating process of both the water and the floor is remarkable: smoke resulting from the burning process passes underneath the stone tiles, thus heating the floor and the *hammam*. Lying on the floor is like having a sauna and has many healthy advantages. Narrow corridors with low ceilings and two doors at each end have been built between the different parts of the *hammam* to prevent the heat from escaping.

N.J.

VI.1.e **Khan al-Wikala al-Gharbiyya**

Lies in the west end of the Old City, at the western entrance to Suq al-Haddadin (market of the blacksmiths). The khan *is open to visitors all day. The municipality has recently bought the place and is planning to renovate and rehabilitate it.*

The location of this *khan* reflects the far-sightedness and practicality of its planners. It separates the industrial from the residential area and is the first place a caravan encounters when entering the city. Once the raw materials were bought from the market, it was immediately dispatched to the artisan centre adjacent to the *khan*, which specialised in smithing and copperbeating. Once the products were manufactured they were exhibited for sale without the need to move them on camels or donkeys to the markets.
The Khan al-Wikala had an impressive and practical design that suits the purpose for which it was built. Its large entrance gate allowed camels and donkeys (the main means of transportation) to pass easily through. The first thing a merchant encountered on entry was the large courtyard with a fountain in the centre. He had rooms to store his goods and a place for his animals in the stables. His own room was on the first floor, accessible via a staircase.
The building consists of two storeys; each is 1,000 sq. m. The entrance is on the ground floor and leads to an open courtyard surrounded by stores and stables where all commercial transactions took place. A portico, with semi-circular arch-

es resting on stone columns, surrounds the courtyard and leads to the upper floor.

The upper rooms are simple in their design. Each has a door and a window that overlooks the inner courtyard and another window that overlooks the road. The western part of the building is largely demolished, but what remains reveals that it consisted of three storeys. The date of the building is unknown; all the same, its architectural style probably indicates a date of the late Mamluk period.

N.J.

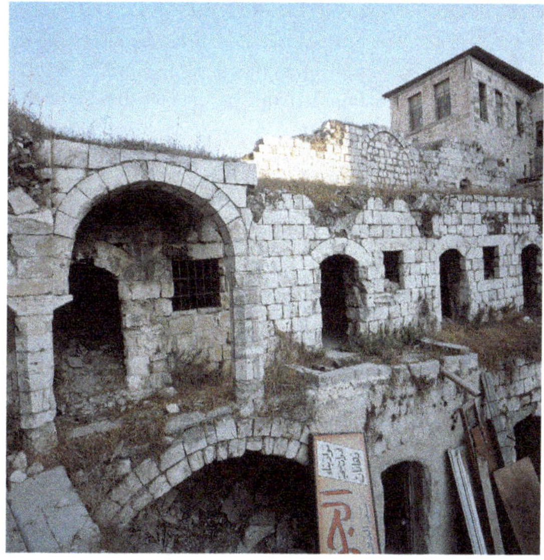

Khan al-Wikala al-Gharbiyya, eastern façade, Nablus.

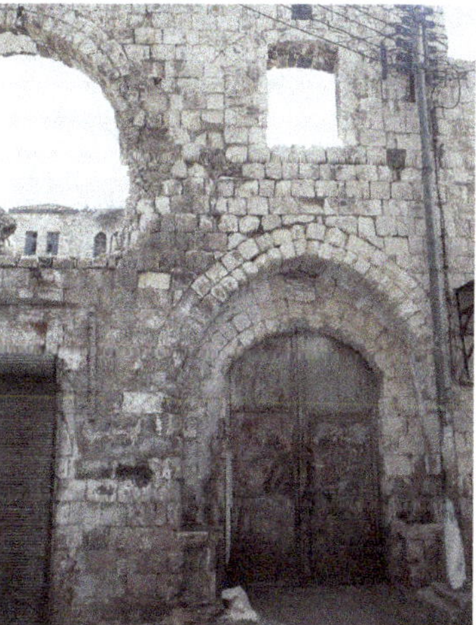

Khan al-Wikala al-Gharbiyya, southern façade, Nablus.

VI.1.f Suq of Khan al-Tujjar and Wikala al-Farrukhiyya

Located in the centre of the Old City of Nablus. The site is open to visitors all day.

The location of the City of Nablus on the historical trade routes in Palestine had an enormous influence on boosting building activity there, which was funded by commercial revenue. A series of *khans* and *wikalas* were built during successive Islamic periods both inside and outside the city. However, all that remains of them today are a few intact examples and some ruins, in addition to some remaining fragments of their written history.

Suq of Khan al-Tujjar

The Suq of Khan al-Tujjar (also called Suq al-Sultani, the Sultan's Market), as its name indicates, was the centre of economic and commercial life in Nablus. It was described in the records (*sijils*) of the Tribunal Court of Nablus and was also mentioned in the writings of Evlia Çelebi, a Turkish traveller who visited the city in 1082/1671–1672. Lala Mustafa Pasha, a Turkish minister and the *wali* of Syria (975/1567–979/1571), founded the *suq* and bestowed a *waqf* upon it.

The *suq* is a large structure measuring 80 m. × 40 m.; two rows of shops are found on either side of a long lane. Its floor is made of beautiful flagstones, and it is covered by a series of high cross vaults, each of which is separated by pointed arches and pierced with skylights for ventilation. In the centre of the *suq* is a high dome that stands on a circular drum and has several openings for ventilation and light. Underneath it, and just in the centre of the shops to the south, lies a staircase that leads outside. Opposite, in the centre of the shops to the north, is an entrance that leads to Khan al-Tujjar, which the Turkish traveller Evlia Çelebi described as a fortress that had 150 adjacent rooms.

Suq of Khan al-Tujjar, western entrance, Nablus.

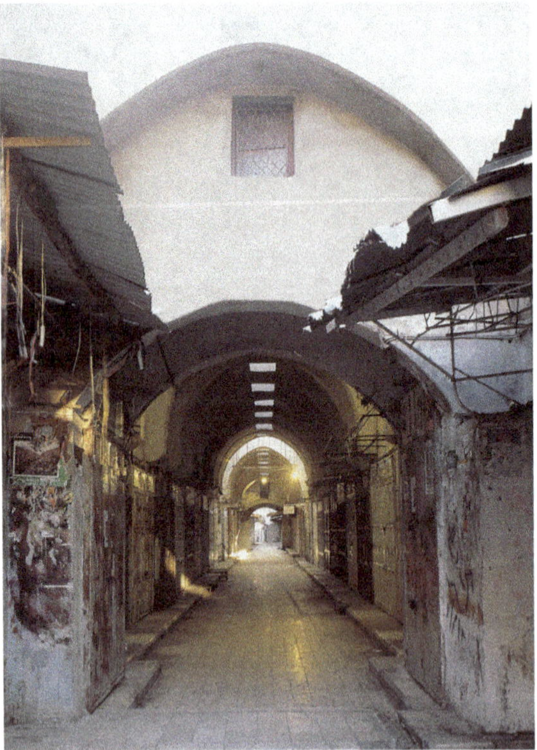

The *khan* consists of two storeys: the first has open spaces that overlook the central courtyard, which was used in the past as stables but has now been turned into shops; the second storey is reached through a stone staircase that lies west of the courtyard. It consists of many rooms of different sizes that were used for guest accommodation. The rooms consist of three rows of domes preceded by three upper rooms from the west, east and south, which all overlook the central courtyard. Today they form the main road, or Suq al-Sagha (the Gold Market). Historical sources mention that there was a spring and a mosque that had a dome made of lead, the only one in Nablus, to the west of the *khan*. However, none of these structures has survived to the present as a result the earthquake that hit Nablus in 1345/1927, which also damaged the *khan*. Ihsan al-Nimr, the historian of modern Nablus, mentions that the second storey of the *khan* had a *madrasa* to teach the four schools of Islam, namely the *Shafi'i, Hanafi, Hanbali* and *Maliki*.

Wikala al-Farrukhiyya

At the northern end of Suq al-Tujjar the remains of the Wikala al-Farrukhiyya can be seen. It was named after its founder the Amir Farrukh Ibn 'Abd Allah al-Sharkasi in 1030/1620, a famous prince who ruled Jerusalem and Nablus and was appointed guardian of the pilgrimage (*hajj*) in Syria in the early 11th/17th century. Unfortunately nothing has survived of the building except for some rooms on its first and second floors, which are currently used as shops; the ruins are hardly representative of the place in its original form. As Ihasan al-Nimr mentions, the *wikala* hosted the Syrian pilgrimage caravan after it joined the Egyptian one in the south on the way to Hijaz.

M.A.K.

VI.1.g **Great Mosque**

The mosque lies to the east of the Old City at the corner where Shari' (avenue or large street) *al-Nasir meets with Shari' al-Khan. The mosque is open to visitors all day, except during prayer times.*

Being the largest and most important mosque in the city, the Jami' al-Kabir (Great Mosque) was the centre where all governmental, political and administrative decrees were announced and displayed.
The current building, as indicated by its architectural components and decorations, is the composite of many styles and developments that took place over the centuries. Its early beginnings can be attributed to the Byzantine period, when the Roman Emperor Justinian (527–565) built a church on this site. The mosque, mentioned by al-Muqaddasi as being

Suq of Khan al-Tujjar, interior, general view, Nablus.

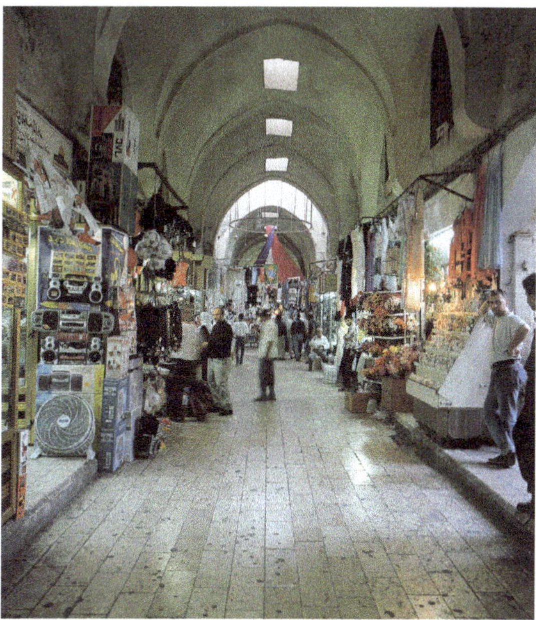

Great Mosque, main entrace, Nablus.

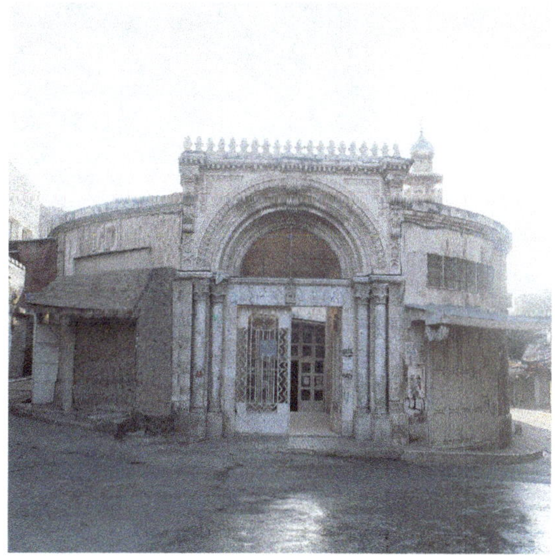

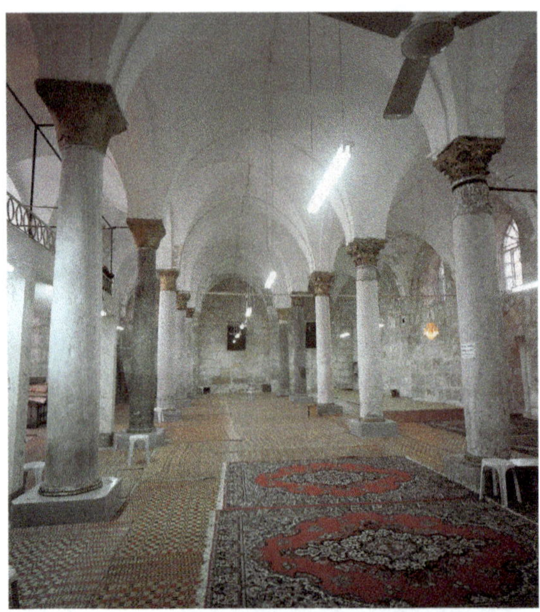

Great Mosque, interior, Nablus.

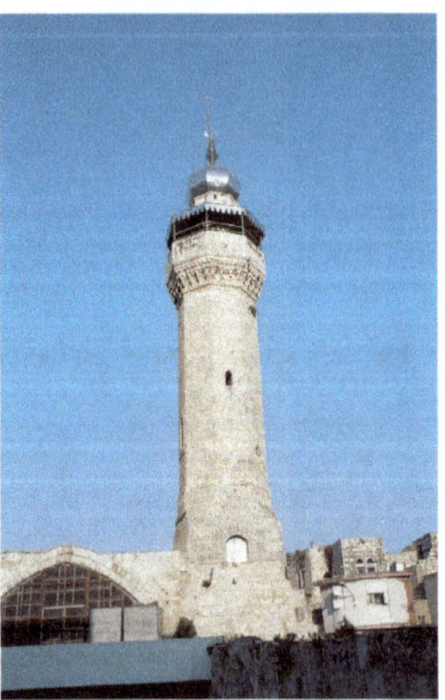

Great Mosque, minaret, Nablus.

located in the centre of the city, was probably built over the ruins of the Byzantine church. However, during Crusader rule over the city, the mosque was expropriated and a church was built on the site using much of the earlier Byzantine architectural elements. Later, following the reconquest of the city from the Franks in 583/1187, Saladin ordered the church to be converted into a mosque, later known as Jami' al-Salahi al-Kabir (the Great Salahi Mosque). The mosque was renovated in the Mamluk and Ottoman periods. A new ceiling was also built in the Mamluk period.

The mosque was not restricted to religious rituals. Many scientific seminars and classes were held there, especially on the science of the Qur'an, jurisprudence and Arabic grammar.

The mosque is a large rectangular complex that has two entrances: one to the east and one to the north. Both entrances lead into an open courtyard that in turn leads to a rectangular prayer hall, measuresing 61 m. east–west, and 16.55 m. north–south. There are three *mihrab*s on the southern wall, the central one being the largest, and facing the northern entrance. To the west of the *mihrab* lies a marble *minbar*, which is ascribed to the Mamluk *amir* 'Izz al-Din al-Amiri (713/1313). Two rows of marble columns and stone pillars divide the prayer hall into three aisles, each covered by a cross vault.

The minaret lies to the centre of the northern wall above the entrance. It has a square stone base that carries an octagonal shaft, which in turn ends in a stone gallery that is carried on rows of stone *muqarnas* decorations, all crowned by a small dome in the centre.

M.A.K.

VI.1.h **Maqam of Rijal al-'Amud**

Located at the foot of Mount Garizim to the south-west of the city and near the police station. The site can be visited during the day after permission has been granted by the shaykh *of the* maqam.

The shrine is associated with the number forty, which is closely connected to different religious rituals and doctrines of the three monotheist religions in Palestine. More than 50 shrines associated with this number are found in Palestine. Many local folk stories have been generated about this place, not least that of the Samaritans that connect it to Emperor Zeno, who sought the conversion of the Samaritans to Christianity and killed 70 of them on this site.

The *sufi* traveller, 'Abd al-Ghani al-Nabulsi described the site in 1101/1679 as follows: "*We went to visit the site of the forty prophets called the Rijal al-'Amud* [the men of the column]. *When we arrived, we saw a magnificent mausoleum. A grotto was inside it, in which a grave was built. It had an opening leading to it called Magharat al-Arba'in* [The

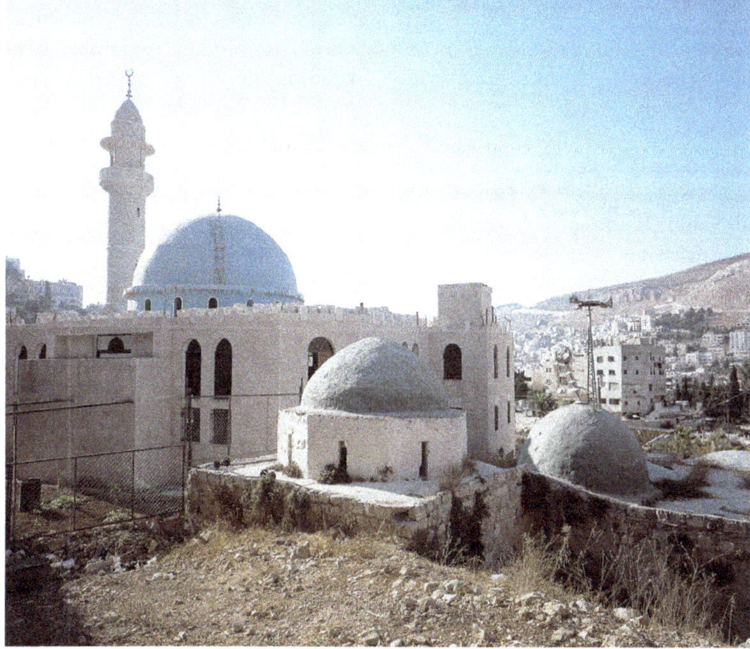

Maqam Rijal al-'Amud, general view, Nablus.

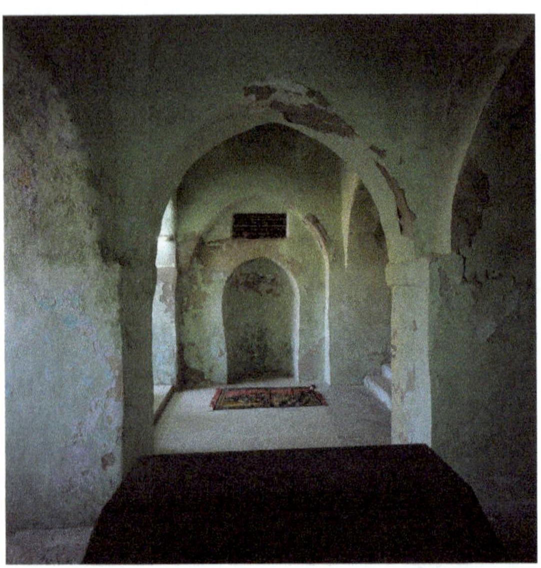

Maqam Rijal al-'Amud, interior, Nablus.

Grotto of the Forty]. *In it was a column and hence the name."*
At the shrine there are some tombstones upon which are the names of the *shaykh* Muhammad 'Amud al-Nur, his son the *shaykh* Salih and *shaykh* Sa'd al-Din. Ihsan al-Nimr, a historian of Nablus, believes that the mausoleum was built in honour of the martyrs that fell during the fight against the Crusaders. It probably dates back to the Ayyubid period ($6^{th}/12^{th}$ century), while many alterations and additions took place in later periods.
The mausoleum consists of an imposing courtyard that is surrounded by an exterior wall through which an imposing mountain can be seen. The tombs are found in the rooms, some of which were used to lodge guests and the inspector of the site. Other rooms have been converted into a mosque. As can be clearly seen, the 'Amudi family chose it as their burial ground, while many of the villagers are buried in the surrounding landscape.
There is hardly a shrine or a mausoleum in Palestine that does not have some symbolic meaning and to which many people come to seek help. This shrine was the site to which the inhabitants of Nablus and the surrounding area came to pray for rain whenever there was a drought. The building has been renovated over the last decades, especially as it serves as the main mosque for the surrounding area.

N.J.

SOAP MANUFACTURE

Marwan Abu Khalaf

Soap manufacture is an old and important industry in Nablus. No exact date of its beginning is available, but it dates way back to the time when olive oil was first used in the manufacturing process. The first recorded date of the industry is the $4^{th}/10^{th}$ century, when soap was mentioned as being one of Palestine's exports in the writings of al-Muqaddasi (380/990). Even though he did not identify the place in which it was manufactured, it is widely believed that Nablus was the city in question. This is because it had raw materials in abundance and had long-held a reputation for manufacture of the product. In the Crusader period, Nablus was so famous for its soap that the king monopolised the industry. Both Shaykh al-Rabwa (d. 727/1300) and Mujir al-Din al-Hanbali (900/1495) referred to it, which indicates that this famous industry continued into the Mamluk period and was associated with Nablus.

In the Ottoman period, it became an important traditional industry. Statistics show that 15 factories existed in Nablus by 1257/1842, and that this was increased to 30 in the early 20th century. Soap factories are found in six quarters of Nablus (al-Gharb, al-Yasmina, al-Qaryun, al-'Aqaba, al-Qaysariyya and al-Habla). There is a street in the Old City called Soap Lane that connects both al-Yasmina and al-Qaryun Quarters.

Soap manufacture helped to establish an economic relationship between the urban and rural areas of Nablus. The production was divided between the city of Nablus and its surrounding villages. While the villages provided the raw material (olive oil), the city manufactured and distributed the soap. The best soap is that made of olive oil; the purest oil is used to produce pure white soap; next in line is the yellow soap, while the oil squeezed from the olive kernels themselves is used to make green soap. The soap industry attracted many workers as it relied largely on manual labour. The manufacturing process is as follows: cooking, spreading, cutting, drying and finally packing.

The owners of the soap manufacturies in Nablus were among the ruling class of aristocrats, scholars and big traders. They advertised and marketed their products abroad, exporting them, especially to Egypt and Syria, and to other Arab countries. Even today, most factory owners pride themselves on the fact that their manufactories do not smell

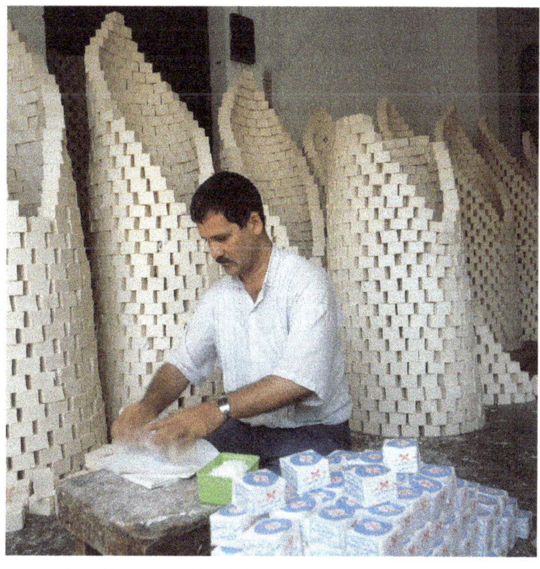

Tuqan Family Soap Factory, a worker packing pieces of soap, Nablus.

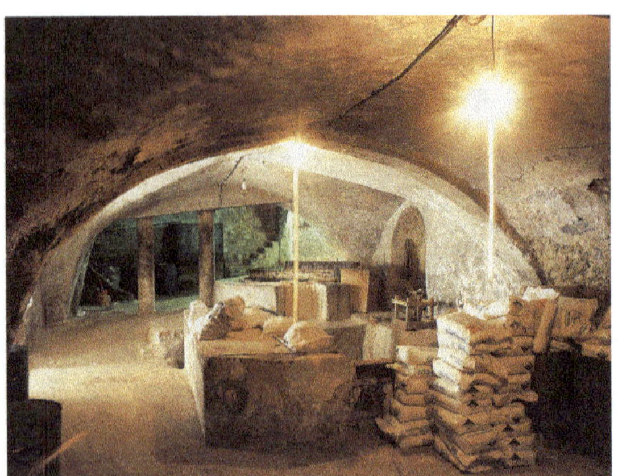

Tuqan Family Soap Factory, ground floor, baking room, Nablus.

– unlike those that use animal fats to produce soap.

The trade registers teach us that Hajj 'Abd al-Rahim Efendi al-Nabulsi was sent to London with samples of Nablus soap to make them known to the markets of Britain. We also know through a book published later, on the production of Nablus soap, that the merchandise was particularly appreciated in England and that a British company ordered a quantity of best-quality Nablus soap.

In addition to using it for washing and cleaning, Nablus soap is used in alternative medicine and in the preparation of some prescriptions, for instance, in plaster. It is also favoured as an ingredient in the manufacture of silk.

Most soap manufactories have the same architectural design: usually two-storey buildings, the first storey is used for cooking the soap and it generally has a long hall with a high ceiling and small windows; the second storey is where the soap is spread, dried and prepared in a vast covered structure that has many windows. The factory has large entrances to facilitate the admission of oil deliveries and the exit of soap carriers. At the entrance is a room, which serves as the owner's office. Also, one or more cisterns that store oil are found inside each factory, in addition to a furnace, a big pot and many basins filled with water.

THE PALACES OF NABLUS

Naseer R. Arafat

The palaces (or mansions) of Nablus's oldest families are considered among the most important architectural monuments in the city, built in a similar style to those in Damascus. Usually large, some of them were part of a huge complex that included a soap manufactory and a private *hammam*. The Palace of the *qadi* 'Abd al-Wahid al-Khammash, which lies in theYasmina district, is a good example.

These palaces can be divided into two categories. The first included the family houses of soap factory owners and rich merchants, such as 'Ashur, 'Arafat, Soufan al-Nabulsi, Kan'an and al-Khamash. These houses were distinguished by their large rooms, the high quality of the materials used in construction, the lavish interior furniture, the particular decorations on the entrances, the ironwork and the coloured interior ceilings, which were made of wood or stucco. The second category of houses looked rather like fortresses. Their owners were the rulers of the city or the *walis* during the Ottoman period who were responsible for tax collection and hence became more affluent. Among these palaces are those that belong to the Tuqan, al-Nimr and 'Abd al-Hadi families.

The experience of roaming through the various sections of one of these palaces is accompanied by a desire to unveil the secrets behind its high, thick walls. Entering the building, if permitted, is through a very small door that lies in front of the palace's huge wooden door; this is called a *khukha*, and the visitor would hardly guess that a palace lies behind it. To enter the palace, the visitor has to bend his/her head in reverence as if entering a holy place. The feeling of being insignificant continues until the visitor has passed through a narrow corridor and reaches an open courtyard.

A fountain lies in the centre of the courtyard together with a charming garden full of flowers, jasmine, and fruit trees, such as pomegranate and lemon. Stables, cor-

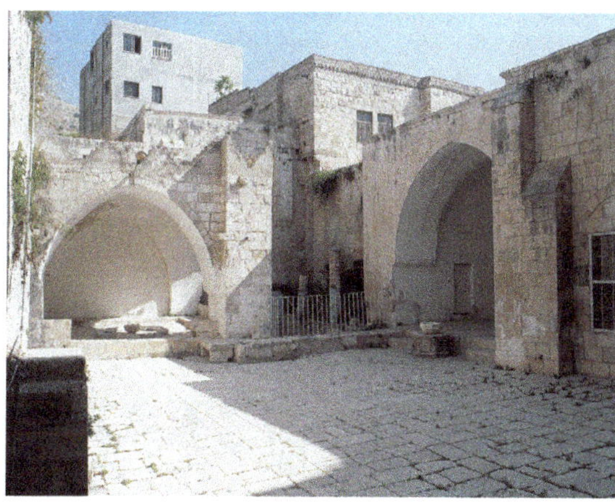

Interior courtyard and iwan of a palace, general view, Nablus.

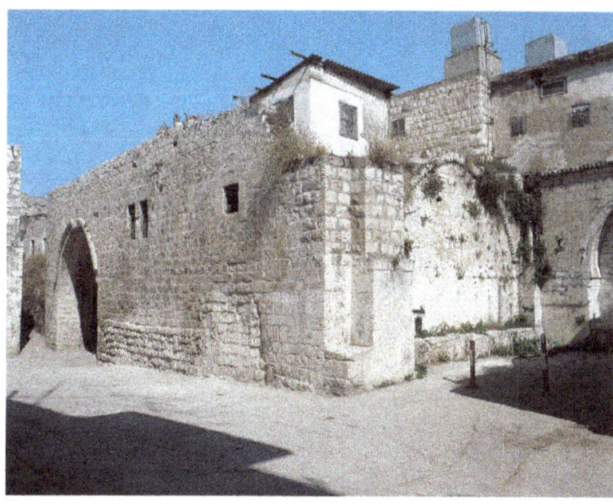

External façade of a palace, Nablus.

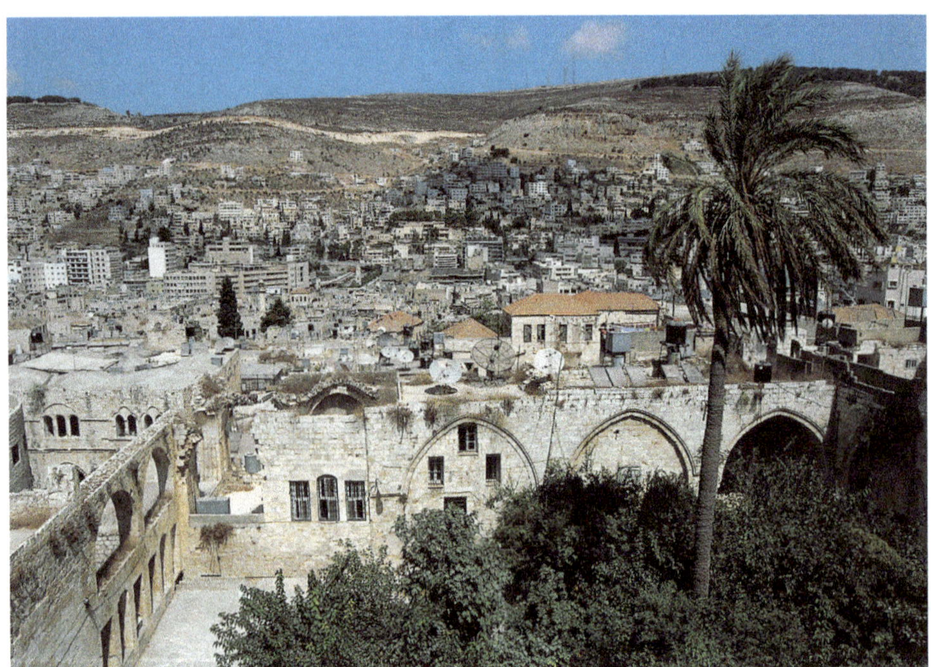

Palace of the 'Abd al-Hadi family, aerial view of the courtyard with the town of Nablus in the background (© Sonia Halliday Photographs, photograph: D. Silverman).

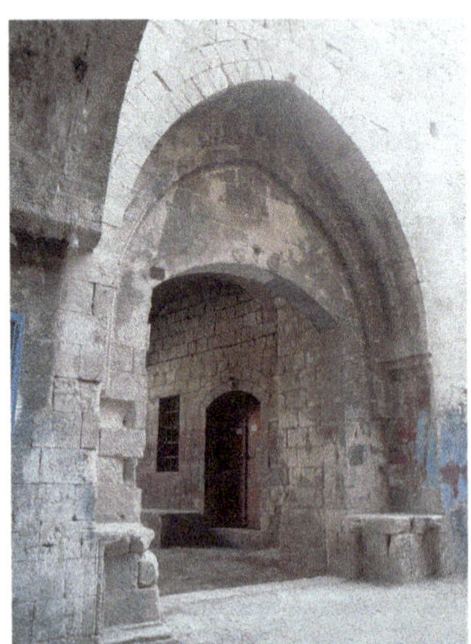

Main entrance of a palace, view from the outside, Nablus.

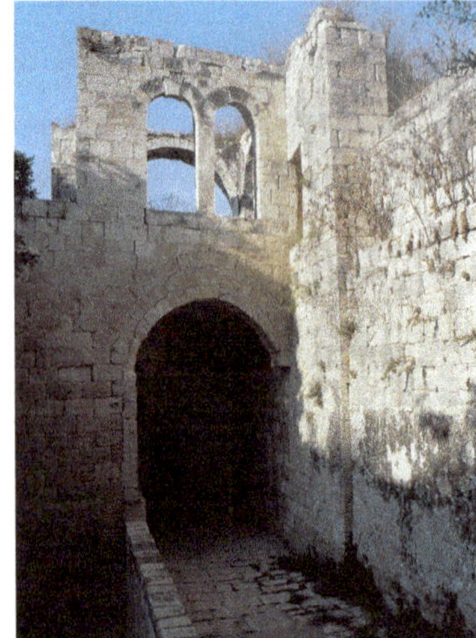

Internal courtyard of a palace, partial view, Nablus.

ridors and staircases surround the courtyard and lead to an upper level, which is separate from the entrance and is the residential area. It has many rooms and *iwans* that surround the courtyard and provide privacy. A third upper level is reached through other corridors and staircases. It consists of a courtyard that has many rooms around it, where the son will live with his own family after marriage; in effect, this provides a private and separate residence for the son's family, while allowing him still to remain in touch with his parents through the main entrance. This helped to sustain what is known as the extended family. The design of the palace echoed both its social and private functions and reflected the values and taste of the owners. It started with the public area, then the private, and the more private immediately after. When building the house the architect would also consider the geographical and atmospheric conditions of the area. The palaces were built so as to adjust with human body temperature, providing warmth in the winter and coolness in the summer.

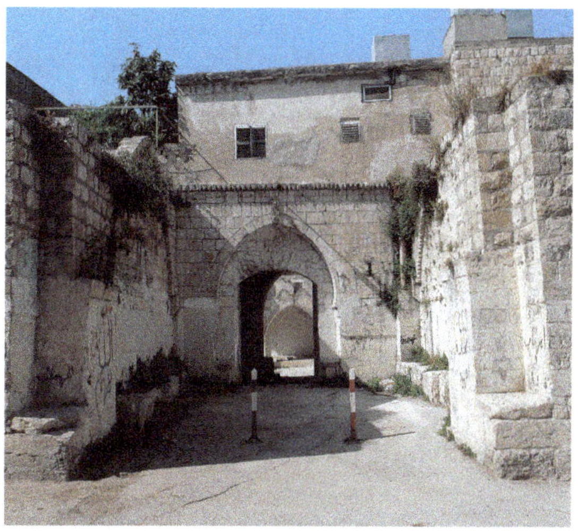

Entrance to a palace, view from the outside, Nablus.

The wooden *mashrabiyyas* (lattices) on the windows allowed those inside to see outside, while also providing privacy from outsiders seeing in. The geometric and vegetal decorations above the entrances to these buildings, the windows, the interior doors and furniture, the fountains and the coloured wooden ceilings never fail to captivate the viewer.

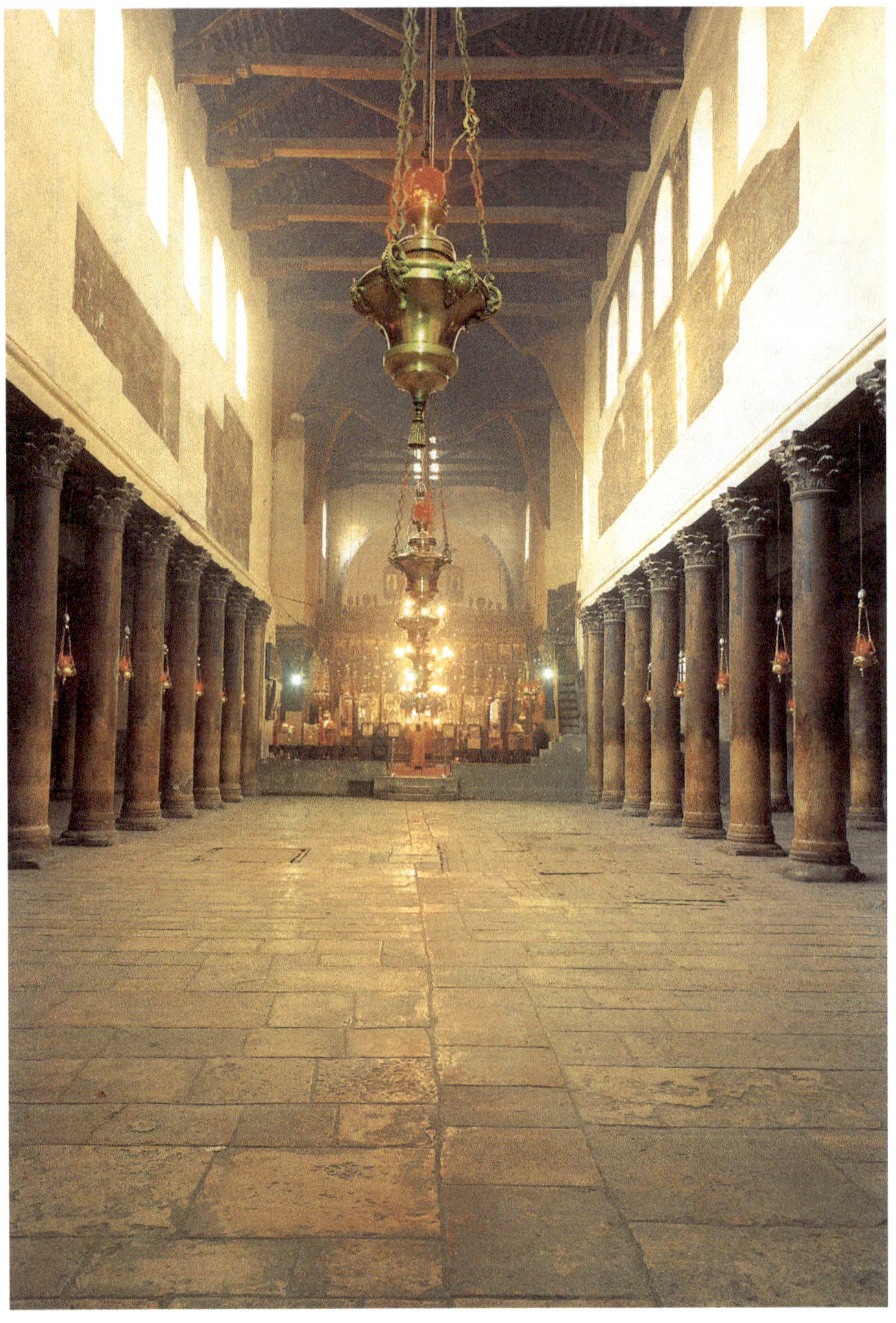

The Pilgrimage Road between Jerusalem and Hebron

Nazmi al-Ju‘beh

VII.1 BETHLEHEM
- VII.1.a The Tomb of Rachel
- VII.1.b The Church of the Nativity

VII.2 SOLOMON'S POOLS
- VII.2.a Solomon's Pools
- VII.2.b Qal‘at al-Birak

SCENIC OPTION
- Wadi Artas: A Typical Rural Landscape in Palestine

The Water-Supply System to Jerusalem

VII.3 HALHUL
- VII.3.a Mosque of Nabi Yunis

VII.4 SA‘IR
- VII.4.a Mosque of Nabi al-‘Is

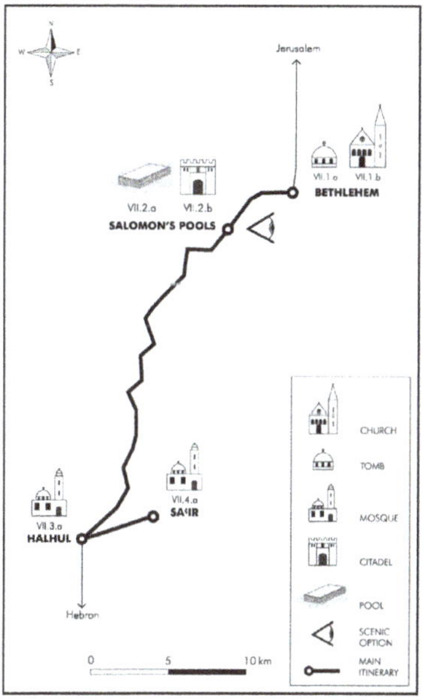

Church of the Nativity, central nave, Bethlehem.

Throughout the ages, Jerusalem and Hebron have been interconnected as a result of their religious, political, social and scientific interaction, and for being generally under the same administrative system. In the Ayyubid period, the post of Inspector to the two holy *harams* of Jerusalem and Hebron was appointed, emulating the post in Mecca and Medina. Having developed during the Mamluk period, this position became an integral and highly respected religious post. The person was directly appointed by the Sultan in Cairo and was responsible for managing the two religious sites and their *waqfs*.

This itinerary will follow the mountainous road that stretches for a disance of 40 km. and connects Jerusalem to Hebron. Many pilgrims have taken this road since time immemorial, as did the *caliphs* and sultans who visited these holy sites, and all the trade caravans on their way from Syria to Egypt and vice versa.

On our way from Jerusalem to Hebron we will visit some of the sites that played a vital role in shaping the Islamic history of Palestine. The visitor will also enjoy the natural and magnificent landscape, including the terraces that protected the soil from erosion throughout the ages, and the watchtowers scattered along the road. The area is famous for its vineyards and some of communication routes have hardly changed since the Islamic conquest.

We will start this itinerary with Rachel's Tomb, which is revered by Muslims, Christians and Jews alike, and is the first holy site on the road from Bethlehem to Hebron. Then, we will visit Bethlehem, the birthplace of Christ and the holiest spot on earth for Christians. Following that, we continue southwards to Solomon's Pools, where we will observe one of the most curious and complicated water projects in the world. Here a scenic option will also be proposed namely that of the river and the Village of Artas, one of the most beautiful valleys in Palestine. The itinerary will continue to the town of Halhul to visit the Mosque of Nabi Yunis (Prophet Jonah) and the Maqam and Mosque of Nabi al-ʻIs, in Saʻir, two sites that have been visited throughout the ages by many thousands of *sufis*.

VII.1 BETHLEHEM

Bethlehem is approximately 10 km. South of Jerusalem, situated on the watershed line of the Jerusalem–Hebron hills, like both Hebron and Jerusalem. For Chistians it is the holiest city in the world, being the birthplace of Christ. A good part of the old city has survived, and a number of buildings were restored for the Millennium celebrations in 2000. Although very little information is available regarding the dates for the majority of these buildings (except for those built in the 19th and 20th centuries), it is believed that a significant number of the buildings in the Old City date to the Mamluk and Ottoman periods, as indicated by their traditional architectural fabric.

VII.1.a **The Tomb of Rachel**

Situated just before the entrance to Bethlehem, 7 km. south of Jerusalem on the right-hand side of the Jerusalem–Hebron road. It is open all day.

Rachel was the wife of Jacob and mother of Joseph and Benjamin. She died after giving birth to Benjamin (Jacob's 12th child) and it is widely believed she was buried in this spot, which bears the name Qubba of Rachel. Rachel's Tomb was mentioned in the early travel literature of Palestine dating to 4th century, and is still mentioned in various travel and geographical books, whether written by Muslims, Christians or Jews. Al-Idrissi (d. 560/1165) mentioned the site, saying: *"Midway to Bethlehem lies the Tomb of Rachel, the mother of Joseph and Benjamin, Jacob's sons. The tomb has 12 stones and a dome on top, which is carved in the rock."* The date and the name of the founder of the building are unknown, but it was probably built in the early Islamic period.

The travellers' sources all agree that the tomb consisted of 12 stones, corresponding to the number of Rachel's sons. The tomb, which is surmounted by a dome, was regularly visited. Muhammad Pasha, the Governor of Jerusalem, commissioned the building of the current structure in 1033/1623, and it was renovated during the Egyptian rule in the early 13th/19th century. The square building has a dome and a long room to the east. In the eastern courtyard is a *mihrab*, in addition to a large number of Muslim tombs,

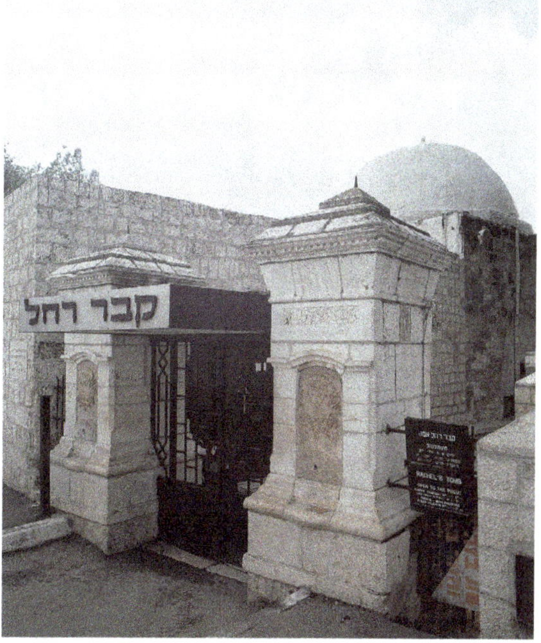

Tomb of Rachel, main entrance, Bethlehem.

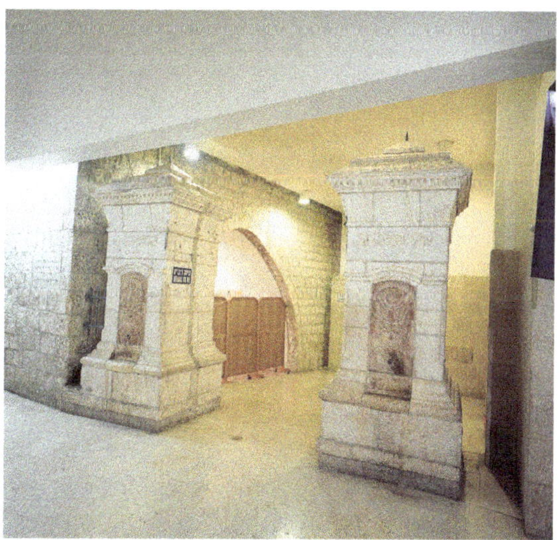
Tomb of Rachel, interior, Bethlehem.

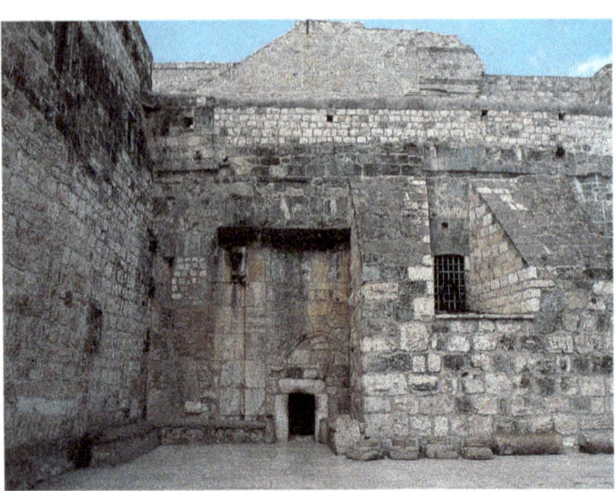

Church of the Nativity, access, Bethlehem.

belonging to those who sought Rachel's blessing.

Lately, high walls and defence towers have been added to the site, which has been under Israeli control since 1967 and been transformed into a military fort.

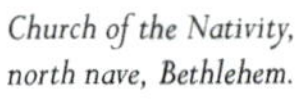

Church of the Nativity, north nave, Bethlehem.

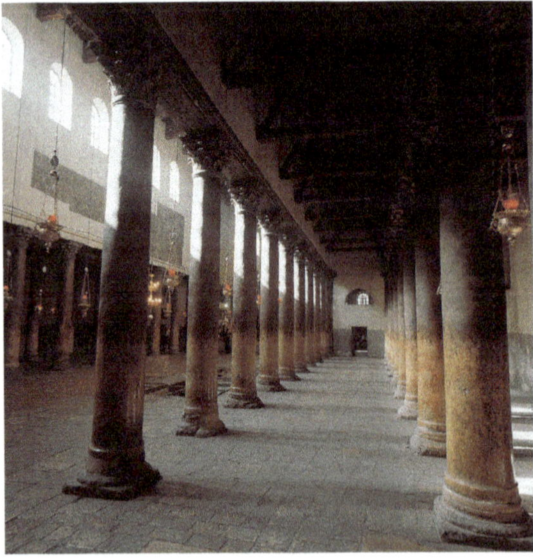

VII.1.b The Church of the Nativity

The Church of the Nativity is considered to be the most important and distinguished monument in Bethlehem. The church is open to visitors daily from 05.30–18.00.

It might cause some astonishment to find this Christian building as a stop in the middle of our Islamic itinerary. The reason is that the town of Bethlehem, as the birthplace of Jesus, occupies a revered place for Moslems, and let us recall indeed that Mary and Jesus are very present in the Qur'an, which recognises Jesus as the last prophet before Mohammad, and whose presence is in many episodes of the life of the Prophet: for example during Mohammad's famous nocturnal journey, when the Prophet recognises the symbolic union of all the different envoys of God, among which is Aïssa (Jesus). On the other hand, the Christians of Bethlehem, the same as their representatives in Jerusalem, and particularly during the Mamluk period, profited under the Islamic dynasties with privileged status. A certain number of decrees guaranteed exemption from taxes for them, and protection for the clergy as well as for the visitors to the basilica and its pilgrims. Others adjudicated to them the right to restore the Nativity whenever it was necessary. This important Christian site appears also in a position of high regard within the most important Islamic travel narratives, which provide detailed descriptions of both the site and of the personality of Jesus within the Islamic tradition.

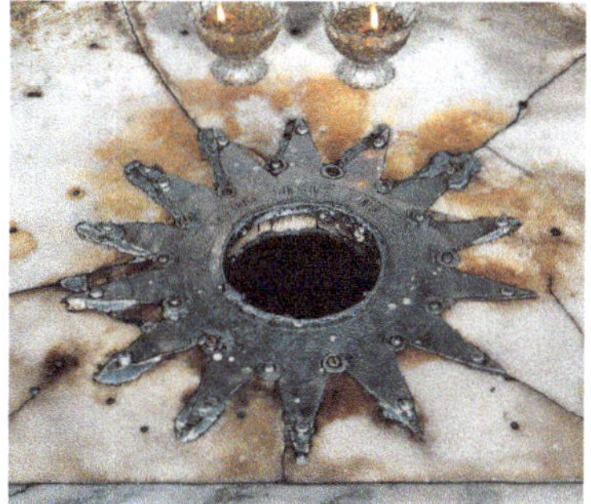

Church of the Nativity, star of the nativity, Bethlehem.

The Church of the Nativity is built over the cave (grotto) where it is believed Jesus was born. Queen Helena, the mother of Emperor Constantine (r. 306–337), commissioned the original church in 329, after Christianity had been officially declared as the religion of the Roman Empire. However it was demolished in 529 and rebuilt soon after by Emperor Justinian (527–565). Apart from the roof and the floor, which have been replaced several times, the basic structure of Justinian's basilica has survived.

Tens of churches and monasteries can be visited in the vicinity of the Church of the Nativity, most of which were important during the Islamic period, including the Milk Grotto Chapel, the Church of St Joseph and the Church of the Shepherds' Fields.

VII.2 SOLOMON'S POOLS

VII.2.a Solomon's Pools

Lies 3 km. south-west of Bethlehem, east of the road leading to Hebron. It is possible to visit the site at all times.

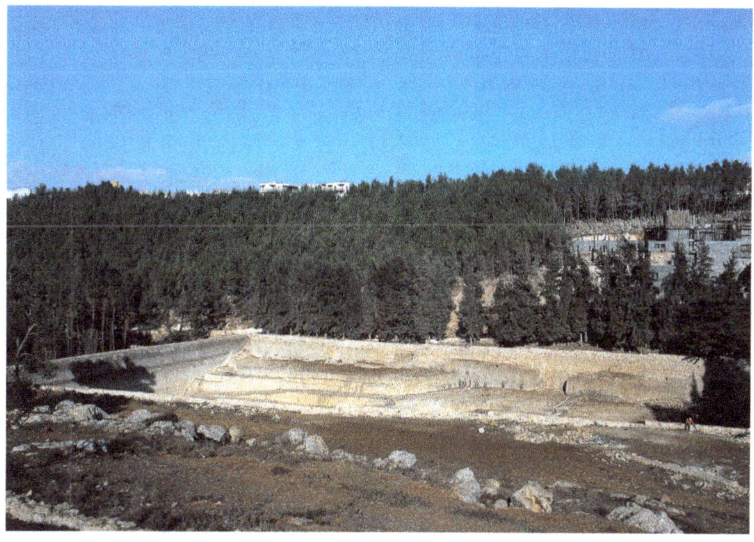

Solomon's Pools, general view.

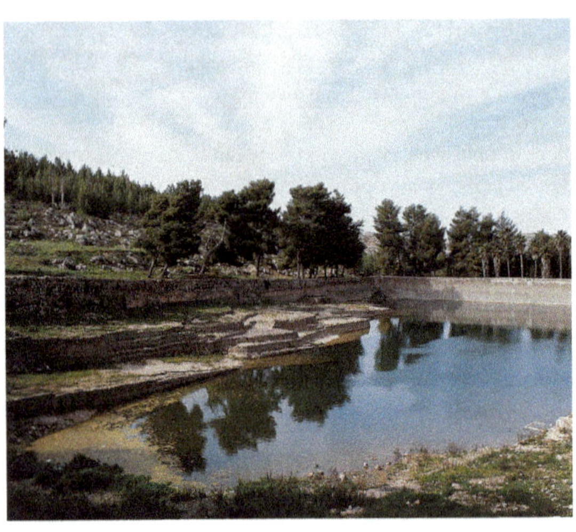

Solomon's Pools, general view (© Sonia Halliday Photographs).

The three pools lie amidst captivating pinewoods within a beautiful landscape, just at the outset of Wadi Artas, which is covered by vegetation and fruit trees. It is not known when the pools were first constructed, but both the middle and upper pools existed during Herod's time (37–4 BC). The third, lower pool was built during the reign of the Mamluk Sultan Khushqadam (865/1460–872/1467), who also ordered the renovation of the whole water system. Nevertheless, the most important rebuilding work on the pools was carried out in 943/1536–1537, during the Ottoman Sultan Sulayman the Magnificent's time; hence these pools still bear his name. He completed the water system and linked it to Jerusalem, adding a series of fountains that can still be seen today in the Old City of Jerusalem.

The pools served as reservoirs that collected rain and water from nearby springs, while the aqueducts carried the water over on bridges and through tunnels inside the hills and along their slopes to Jerusalem, right up until 1922 by means of pumping engines. Some of the water was collected from areas 15 km. away. The longest aqueduct at 68 km. had to follow a natural zigzag course along hillsides using gravity, with a straight of only 21 km. Today the visitor can enjoy the full view of the pools, the remains of the aqueducts and the surrounding tunnels.

The first pool is 116 m. long, 70–72 m. wide and 6–12 m. in depth, in volume it is 85,000 m^3. The middle pool is 129 m. long, 70–76 m. wide and 12 m. in depth, in volume it is 90,000 m^3. The lower Mamluk pool is the largest at 177 m. long, 86–95 m. wide and 15 m. in depth, in volume it is 113,000 m^3.

VII.2.b **Qal'at al-Birak**

Lies 3 km. south-west of Bethlehem, east of the road leading to Hebron and opposite Solomon's Pools. It is possible to visit the site at all times.

This well-built fortress, as the foundation inscription above the entrance portal indicates, was built to defend the vital water supply in 1027/1617–1618 by the Ottoman Sultan 'Uthman II. He assigned 40 soldiers to the site and provided them with canons, weapons and ammunition. The fortress has been popularly called Qal'at al-Birak ("the fortress of the pools") or Qal'at Murad ("the fortress of [Sultan] Murad").

The fortress lies a few meters north of the first pool. It is a rectangular building

(70 m. × 45 m.) and the entrance portal lies in the centre of the west wall. There are four towers on each its corners and arrow slits on top of the walls. The fortress comprises a series of rooms running along the west and east sides. Outside the south-west corner a small mosque once stood. To the south is a spring, which provided the inhabitants of the fortress with water.

Renovated in 1998, preparations are underway to turn it into a centre for Palestinian crafts and popular heritage.

Qal'at al-Birak, main façade, Solomon's Pools.

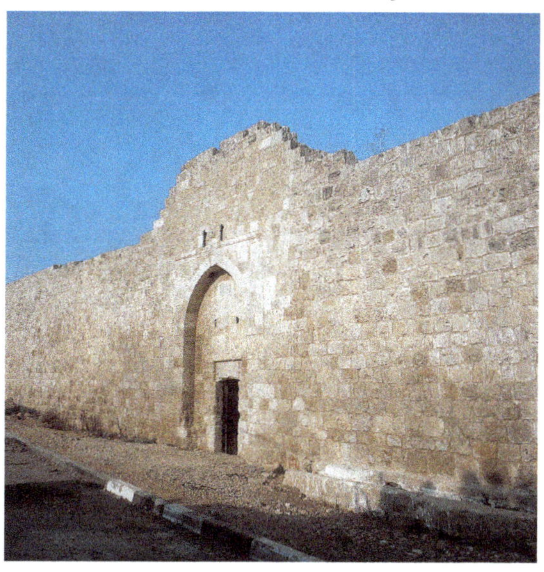

SCENIC OPTION

Wadi Artas: A Typical Rural Landscape in Palestine

The Palestinian landscape, and the rural hillside in particular, is determined by the characteristics of Mediterranean topography. The marks of the extensive human use in this part of the world can be clearly observed throughout the different ages, in which a tradition of harmony and compliance with nature and the environment was achieved. It is, therefore, relatively easy to comprehend the love with which the land has been cultivated by humans. Wadi Artas is one example where the natural conditions coincided with the needs and efforts of human settlers in order to establish a continuous settlement for thousands of years.

In the east of the valley, where it becomes steeper and is more fertile, there are many springs, while on the northern bank lies the historic village of Artas. The valley is renowned for its various vegetables and pulses, the fields remaining green all year round. As a result of the increase in the village's population, inhabitants reclaimed two sides of the valley, and built terraces there to stop the soil from

Wadi Artas, general view of the valley.

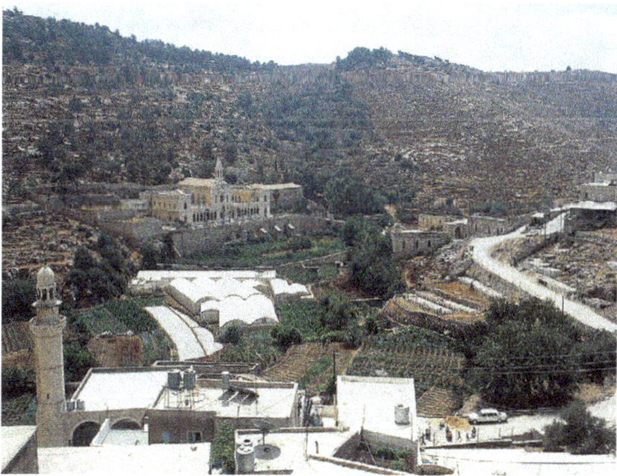

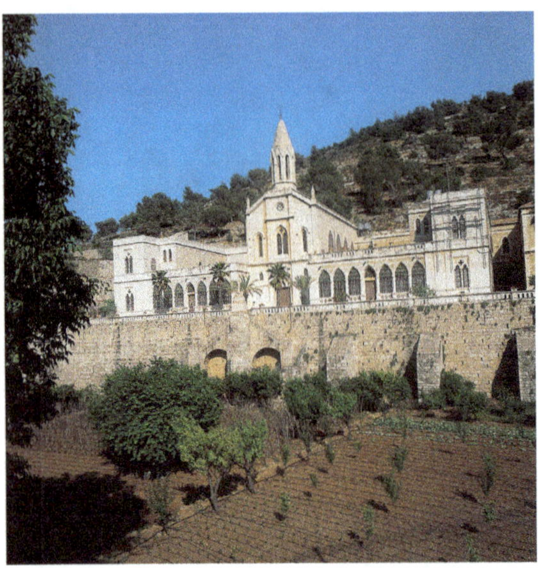

Wadi Artas, monastery, general view.

eroding. They made retaining walls of natural stone that was collected from the fields, which blend beautifully with the natural contours of the hills. Having planted the terraces with almond, plum, cherry and olive trees, they turned the hillsides into an evergreen marvel. During the springtime the terraces look like a surrealist picture. The olive trees also render evergreen scenery that is uniform to the rest of the Palestinian hill landscape from Galilee to Hebron.

Looking towards the east of the valley, the visitor can see the mosaic-like structure of the fields, which have been divided throughout the history of the area, and which still form a picturesque view of the different areas and plantations in this region.

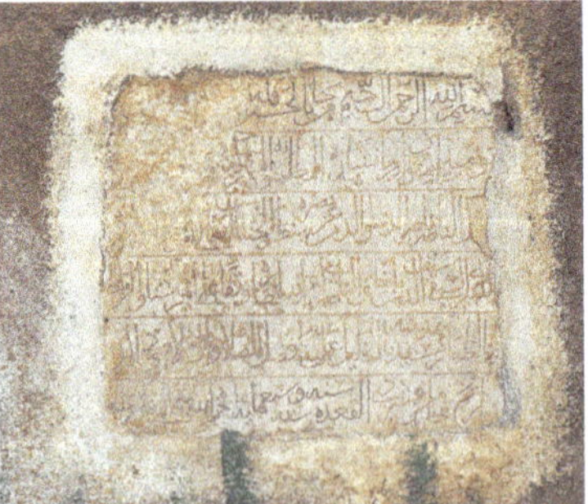

Wadi Artas, inscription on stone in the Mamluk style (removed from its original place).

VII.3 HALHUL

VII.3.a **Mosque of Nabi Yunis**

Halhul lies 32 km. south of Jerusalem and 5 km. north of Hebron. The mosque is open to visitors all day except during prayer times.

The mosque, which also serves as a *maqam*, is situated in the centre of the village and was built by al-Malik al-Mu'addam 'Issa, son of the Ayyubid Sultan al-Malik al-'Adil in 623/1226. The Mamluk sultans continued to look after the *maqam* and visited it when they came to Hebron, this has brought the mosque unparalleled fame since the Ayyubid period as one of the *sufi* centres of note. The *maqam* and the adjoining mosque were mentioned in most of the chronicles of travellers and *sufi*s on their way to Hebron. 'Abd al-Ghani al-Nabulsi records in 1011/1689–1690: *"We continued until we reached Halhul village to visit the tomb of the Prophet Yunis Ibn Matta, peace be upon him! We saw the mosque and a cave and we visited the tomb."* It is worth mentioning here that eight regions in Palestine have a tomb or a *maqam* for Nabi Yunis, the most famous of which is that in Halhul.

The *maqam* or tomb is entered through the main entrance portal of the modern two-storey mosque, which has recently been built on top of the Ayyubid mosque. To explore the remaining parts of the old mosque, one has to walk towards the *qibla* and the centre of the mosque.

The old part of the *maqam* is a square building surrounded by porticoes on all sides except the north. Each portico consists of three pillars that carry impressive and well-built cross vaults. Below the porticoes are windows that look into the commemorative tomb chamber, which is square and covered by a barrel vault.

The cenotaph is covered in green cloth, as is customary in cenotaphs. Above the western window of the tomb chamber there hangs a cloth fragment that has Yunis's name woven in silk. It looks similar to those found in the Ibahimi Mosque in Hebron and probably dates back to the late Ottoman period (probably to Sultan 'Abd al-Hamid's reign). The cenotaph is only commemorative and does not face the *qibla* as other Islamic tombs do; rather, it is turned towards the south-west. This can be explained by the fact that it may be dated to pre-Islamic times, as a series of old tombs found during expansion work on the mosque indicates. The burial chamber lies beneath it in the cave below the mosque, and cannot be reached or visited. To the inhabitants of the village, this *maqam* is the source of blessing for their vows and constitutes a local centre for religious celebrations and folk heritage.

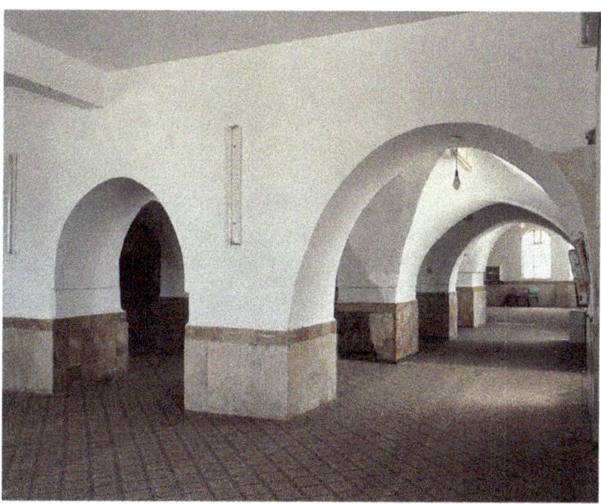

Mosque of Nabi Yunis, interior, general view, Halhul.

If some time is left, it is recommended that the visitor walk about 100 m. south of the mosque to see the historical nucleus of the village. The forsaken houses are densely built up and reflect traditional rural architecture in its most beautiful light.

VII.4 SA'IR

VII.4.a Mosque of Nabi al-'Is

Sa'ir is situated 7 km. north-east of Hebron. The mosque is open to visitors all day, except during prayer times.

The village of Sa'ir stretches today over a vast area; to reach its Mamluk mosque, therefore, one has to go through the modern parts of the village, toward the centre, where the Mosque of Nabi al-'Is (Esau), the son of Isaac, son of Jacob, son of Ibraham, lies.

Sa'ir

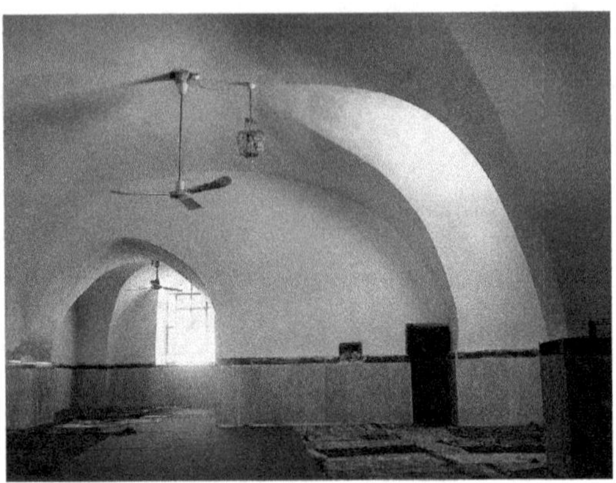

Mosque of Nabi al-'Is, interior, Sa'ir.

The historical sources refer to a mosque that was built in the Mamluk period to commemorate the prophet, who holds an important place in the local Hebron heritage. The first two generations of Abraham's descendants were buried in Hebron, while the grandson was buried here in Sa'ir. The exact date of construction of this *maqam* is not known, but it is almost certain that it is the first mosque to be built here and probably dates back to the early Islamic period.

A large, modern mosque was recently built on top of the Mamluk one to accommodate all the worshippers of the village. Nothing is left of the Mamluk building except for the southern and western façades, but these remains are negligible when the impressive architecture of the period is considered. Rather, these two parts of the façade were built in the local traditional style: the masonry was crudely cut, no coloured stones were used, and no decorations or inscriptions were employed. The cenotaph and the tomb chamber were left untouched.

The shrine is reached from the west via a small door on the second floor of the mosque. There is a rectangular room (approximately 20 m. × 7 m.) just before it, which consists of a portico that has three cross vaults to the north of the tomb chamber. A simple and small *mihrab* is found inside it, which is likely to be the original one. The western side of the room is semi-closed and provides a retreat for *sufis*.

In this hall, prayers are held and Qur'anic verses read whilst looking into the cenotaph through a window. The cenotaph chamber can also be seen from the mosque that lies to the east. At the centre of the chamber – covered by a 10 m. long flattened barrel-vault – the cenotaph is also covered in green cloth.

THE WATER-SUPPLY SYSTEM IN JERUSALEM

Nazmi al-Ju'beh

Jerusalem has hardly any natural water sources: all it has is a very small spring. Throughout the ages its inhabitants sought to collect rainwater in cisterns dug within their houses or in reservoirs that were built in different parts of the city. Despite all this, there was always a shortage of water due to the increase in population and the flow of tourists and pilgrims to the city.

The situation became critical during the Roman period, when many efforts were made to solve the problem. The area of Solomon's Pools was a natural place to get water as it had abundant springs and was at a higher altitude than Jerusalem, which would help the water flow by the power of gravity into Jerusalem.

This huge project depended on gathering water from tens of aqueducts constructed on different levels and in various directions. They would collect the rain and water from the surrounding springs, the furthest of which was 15 km. away. The aqueducts, whether covered or uncovered, were dug through mountains, passed along the slopes or carried on bridges, until they reached Jerusalem and the water that they carried flowed into the fountains and reservoirs. The water would sometimes run for about 65 km. Successive ruling powers from the Roman period until the Ottoman, paid special attention to this system of aqueducts and reservoirs, the last renovation was carried out in 1901. Apart from the three pools, and tens of adjacent aqueducts, the visitor can still follow part of the Ottoman aqueduct on the hillsides between Jerusalem and Bethlehem.

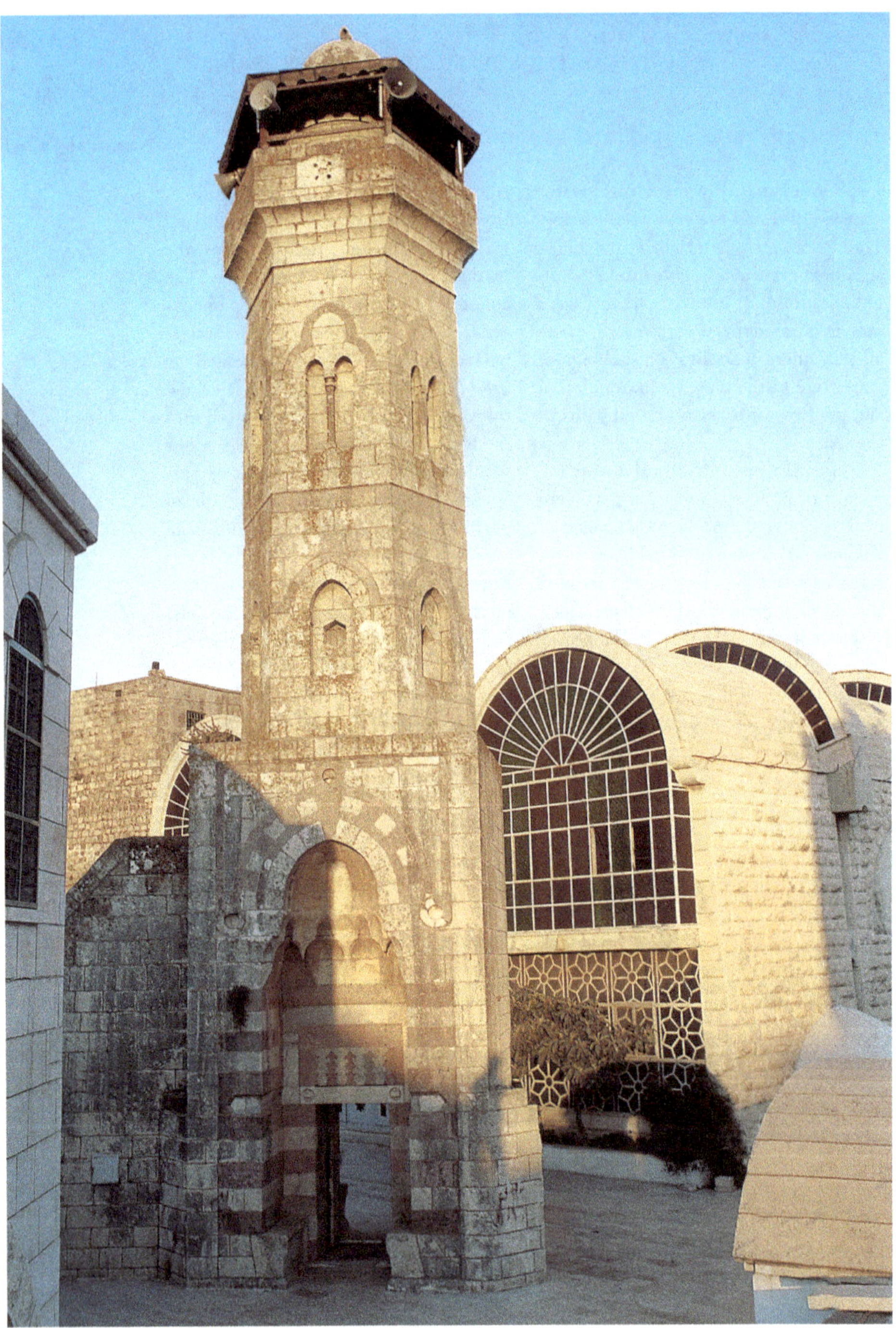

Hebron: the City of Abraham

Nazmi al-Ju'beh

VIII.1 HEBRON

- VIII.1.a The Haram al-Ibrahimi Mosque
- VIII.1.b Mosque of al-Jawali
- VIII.1.c Zawiya al-Ja'abira
- VIII.1.d Zawiya al-Maghariba and the Tomb of Joseph
- VIII.1.e Zawiya of Shaykh 'Ali al-Bakka'
- VIII.1.f Hammam al-Khalil (Hebron Museum)

The Old Quarters
Glass Production

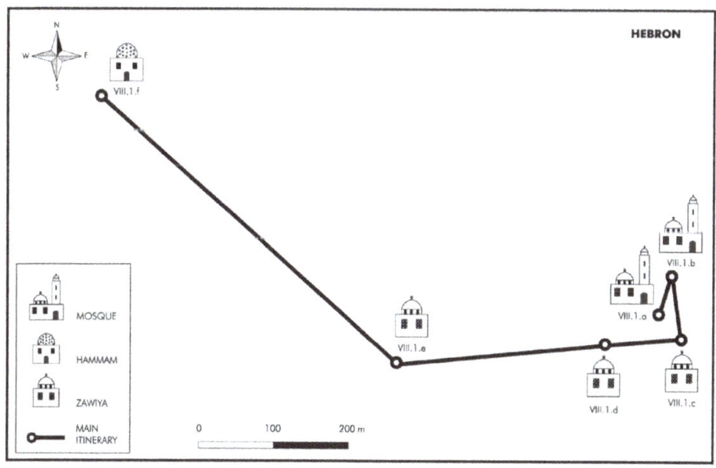

Zawiya of Shaykh 'Ali al-Bakka, main entrance and minaret, Hebron.

Hebron is situated south of Palestine's central mountain range, 30 km. south of Jerusalem and 900–950 m. above sea level. A direct road links the two cities, which passes through Bethlehem and takes around 40 minutes, with regularly available and fast transportation.

Hebron is considered one of the oldest cities and has been continuously inhabited for nearly 3,500 years. Ancient Hebron, dating to the Middle Bronze Age (about 2000–1500 BC), lies on top of al-Rumayda Mountain to the west of the present day city. The walls and gates of the ancient city have been excavated, uncovering many archaeological finds and architectural remains that date back to various periods until the Umayyads (41/661–132/750).

The city is named in Arabic after Abraham's title "al-Khalil" (beloved of God), whose tomb and those of his wife, sons, and their wives, are found in the centre of the city. The presence of Abraham's tomb – who retains a special status in Islam – made Hebron the fourth holiest city in Islam after Mecca, Medina and Jerusalem, and one that has been regularly frequented by Muslim pilgrims throughout all the Islamic periods. During the Ayyubid and Mamluk periods, it became more prominent as it was closely linked to Jerusalem through the introduction of an important administrative post: that of inspector of the two *harams* (holy sanctuaries) of Jerusalem and Hebron, who also managed both their *waqfs*. Enhanced by its status in Islam, building activity during the Mamluk period increased. Many structures were erected, especially *sufi zawiyas*, which became a characteristic feature in Hebron. Many buildings and *zawiyas* were built because a large number of *sufi* Orders sought solitude close to Abraham's tomb.

It seems that Abraham's tradition of hospitality made an impact on the Islamic tradition in Hebron. Following the Arab conquest of the city, a form of guesthouse named "Simat Ibrahim" appeared. Visitors were offered food and drink upon arrival, a tradition that was further developed during the Mamluk period and which is still characteristic of the city today. It was only interrupted during the Crusader period.

It was usual during the Mamluk period for the sultan to exile his opponents to places far away from the capital, the centre of political power. Many Mamluk princes were banished from Cairo and settled in Jerusalem and Hebron. In the latter, they enjoyed the intellectual climate and contributed to the development of its scientific, religious and *sufi* institutions, and bestowed *waqfs* upon them.

Today the city of Hebron, which has a predominance of Mamluk architecture, is one of the few Islamic cities to have preserved its original character. The Old Quarters, the urban fabric with its buildings and markets and traditional way of life, still reflects the original spirit of the Islamic City. Recently, a wide-reaching national campaign has succeeded in renovating and rehabilitating the old city, providing it with a new splendour as an important dimension of

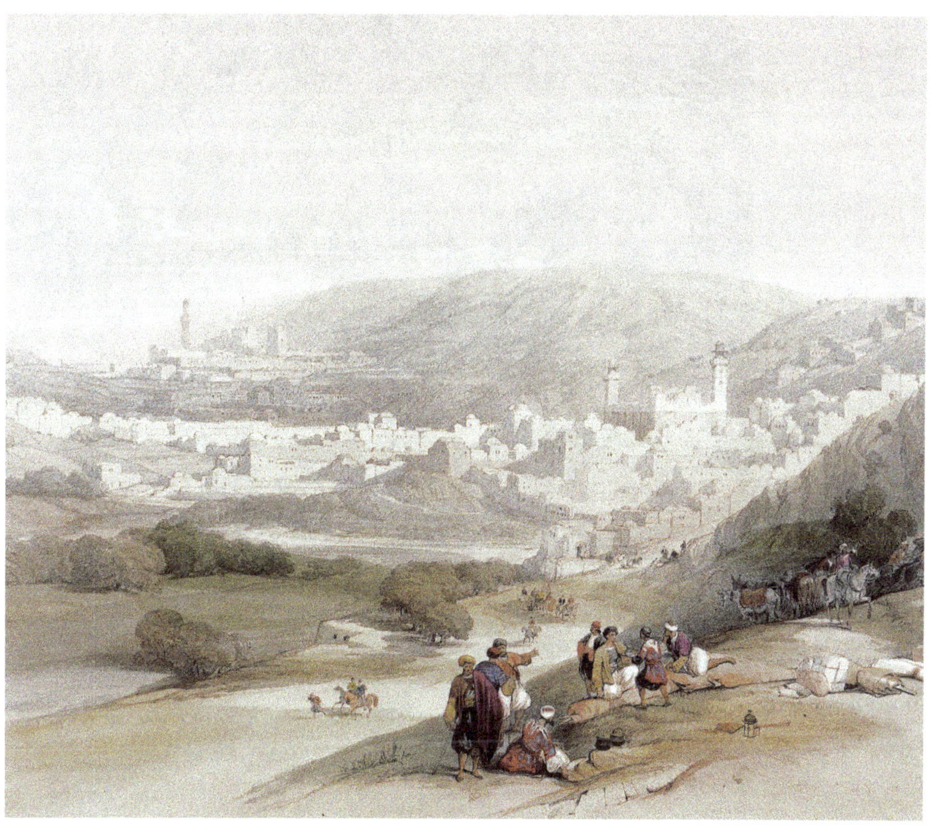

Hebron, general view of the town, lithography by D. Roberts (© Victoria & Albert Museum, London).

the Islamic architectural heritage in Palestine.

This itinerary consists of a visit to the Haram al-Ibrahimi Mosque, the oldest shrine of Palestine that is still in use, despite the religious changes that have occurred during the last two Millennia. Having bestowed such importance upon Hebron, it is the place where the Tombs of the Prophets lie. As a result of the increased *sufi* activity around the Tomb of Abraham, many *sufi zawiyas* were established all over the city and many *shaykhs* and devout Muslims were buried there. Thus this itinerary will include three *zawiyas,* in addition to the city's main *hammam,* which currently houses the Hebron History and Heritage Museum. A "window" will shed light on Hebron's Old Quarters, its history, religious and ethnic fabric, and architectural characteristics. Another "window" looks at the

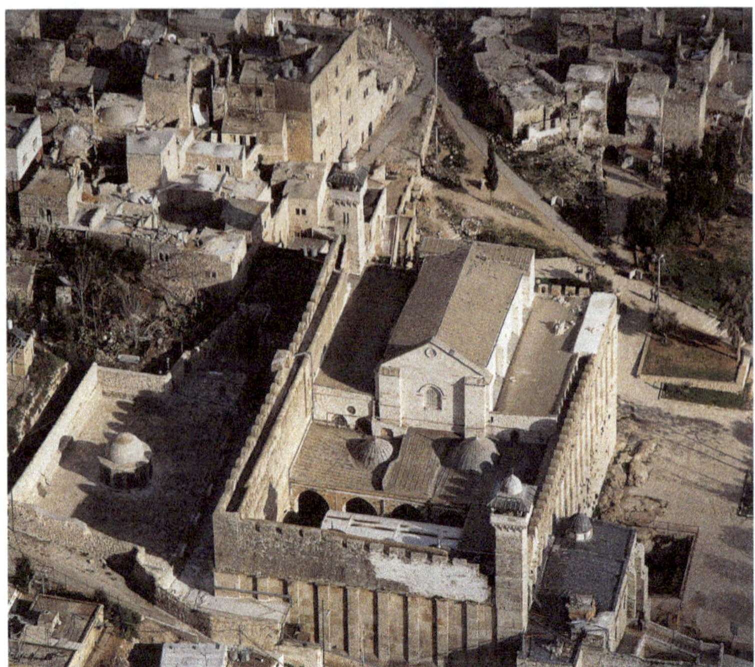

Al-Haram al-Ibrahimi Mosque, aerial view (Tomb of the Patriarchs), Hebron (© Sonia Halliday Photographs).

well-known traditional glassworks in Hebron. While visiting the various sites, the visitor will have the opportunity to walk around the Old City and its markets, observing the architectural fabric and some of the city's economic and social characteristics.

VIII.1 HEBRON

VIII.1.a The Haram al-Ibrahimi Mosque

Lies on the south-west border of the Old City. Open: 08.00–15.00, closed during noon prayers and on Fridays. Parking available. Entry is free and visitors go through a strict security check. A decent dress code is expected from visitors.

This itinerary starts with the Haram al-Ibrahimi (Abraham's Santuary) whose colossal building and two minarets dominate the city's views. The structure has a long history dating from the Roman period (c. 20 BC) until the end of the Ottoman period (1336/1917).

The Haram al-Ibrahimi is the fourth holiest site in Islam and the second holiest place in Palestine after the Aqsa Mosque. Pilgrims, who have visited the Tombs of the Prophets to seek blessing from the early Islamic period until the present day, have maintained the sanctity of the place.

The structure consists of an external wall of large, well-cut masonry blocks, each of which is more than 10 m. in length. The wall forms a huge enclosure that was built during the Roman period to protect the Tombs of the Prophets. In the early 2nd/8th century, the Umayyads erected a mosque inside the enclosure, only to have it destroyed by the Crusaders in 492/1098–1099. They built a Gothic church in its place, which still survives in its general layout until today. When Saladin restored Hebron in 583/1187, he transformed the building into a mosque by only adding a *mihrab*, which can also still be seen today. The wooden *minbar* to the right of the *mihrab* is dated to the Fatimid period and was commissioned by the commander of the Fatimid army, the *amir* Badr al-Jamali, in 484/1091–1092. Saladin brought this sumptuously carved and lapis-inlaid *minbar* from Asqalan and it is one of the oldest wooden *minbars* still in use.

The Mamluks carried out a series of architectural activities in the structure, beginning with general renovations in 667/1268. The *amir* Tankiz, the Viceroy of the Sultanate in Syria (see III.1.f), had work done on the mosque in 733/1332–1333. He ordered that the walls be decorated in coloured marble, in typical Mamluk fashion. Then, al-Nasir Nasir al-Din Hassan (who ruled twice), on the other hand, converted the citadel on the west wall into a *madrasa* that carried his name. However it was destroyed during Ibrahim Pasha's campaign to Palestine (1246/1831–1256/1840). Only the northern wall and tower have survived.

It is said that Sultan Barquq (784/1382–801/1399) ordered the building of the

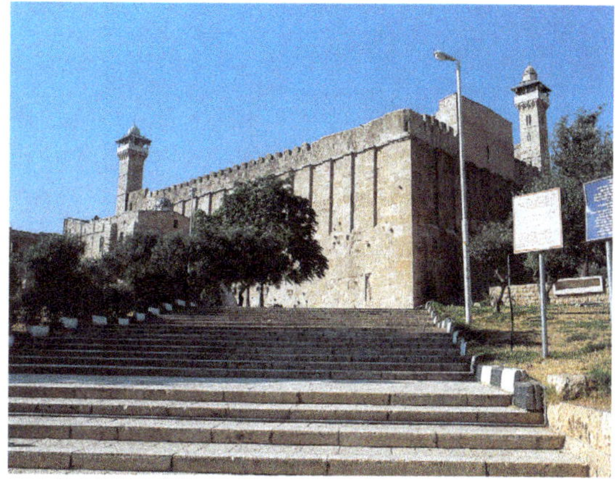

Al-Haram al-Ibrahimi Mosque, general view, Hebron.

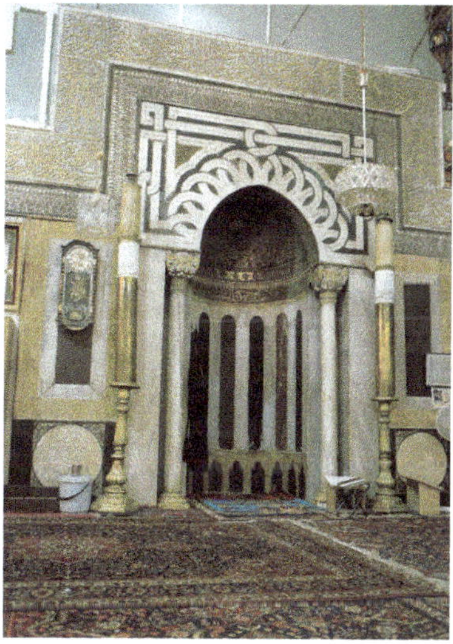

Al-Haram al-Ibrahimi Mosque, mihrab, Hebron.

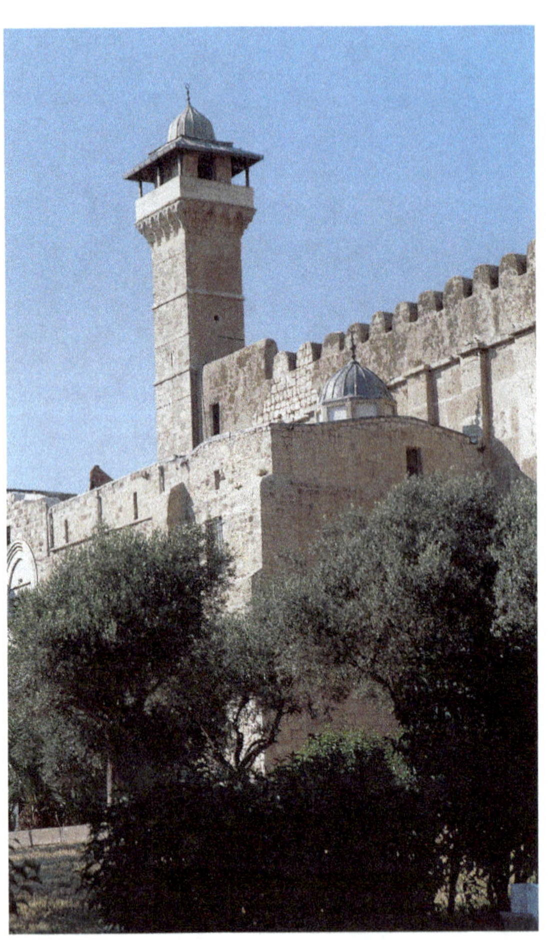

Al-Haram al-Ibrahimi Mosque, minaret, Hebron.

mihrab that lies to the right of the covered area. Then in 796/1393–1394, Shihab al-Din al-Yaghmuri, the guardian of the two holy sites in Jerusalem and Hebron and a representative of the sultan, added a portico along the western wall of the covered area, which is now called Jami' al-Nisa' (the Women's Mosque). Among the most remarkable additions is a platform for prayer leaders (*dikkat al-muballigh*) to the south, parallel to the *mihrab*. Built in 732/1331–1332, it is distinguished by various columns and marble capitals. The Mamluks added the cenotaphs of the six commemorative tombs, which are representative of the craftsmanship and remarkable ironwork techniques of the Mamluk artisans.

To the north of the mosque's courtyard are a number of rooms that were also built during the Mamluk period. One of them is used as a library, which has a collection of manuscripts, some of which date back to Mamluk times. Wonderful Mamluk golden calligraphy can also be seen along the eastern façade of the mosque, and the colourful stones built in the *ablaq* style date back to the same period. On the south-eastern and north-western corners of the enclosure are two Mamluk square minarets, each 15 m. in height.

VIII.1.b Mosque of al-Jawali

The mosque is open to visitors from first thing in the morning until around 15.00. It is closed during noon prayers and on Fridays.
Entry is free and visitors go through a strict security check. A decent dress code is expected from visitors.

The Mosque of al-Jawali shares a corridor with the Haram al-Ibrahimi and looks as though it is joined with it. From the outside the walls of the two buildings can hardly be distinguished from each other.

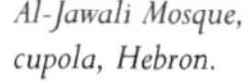

Al-Jawali Mosque, cupola, Hebron.

Al-Jawali Mosque, mihrab, Hebron.

The west wall of the al-Jawali Mosque is in fact the eastern wall of the Haram al-Ibrahimi building, while the east wall of the mosque, hewn from the rock, cannot be seen from the outside at all. The same applies to the northern and southern walls, which are also hewn from the rock. Built in 720/1320–1321 by the *amir* 'Alam al-Din Sanjar al-Jawali, the inspector (*nadir*) of the two *harams* of Jerusalem and Hebron, it can be reached through the Mosque's south-east portal. The first thing one encounters after walking through the marble double door is a hall. A marble inscription stone is seen above the second of these doors, which bears the name of the founder and the date of construction. This door leads to both mosques. Some bands of Qur'anic writing are found on marble stone plaques on the façades of the two portals. The Mosque of al-Jawali can also be reached through the door situated to the north-east of the Haram al-Ibrahimi.

The mosque consists of three aisles covered by cross vaults that are carried on gigantic stone pillars. A fine stone dome covers the centre of the mosque, whose corners are decorated by *muqarnas*. Many windows are found on the drum of the dome. On the *qibla's* side is a *mihrab* cut into the rock and covered in coloured marble. The mosque rises above the level of the corridor leading to the Haram al-Ibrahimi, especially from the eastern side, in order to separate the women's section from the men's, lately the northern (rear) part of the mosque has been elevated by three steps.

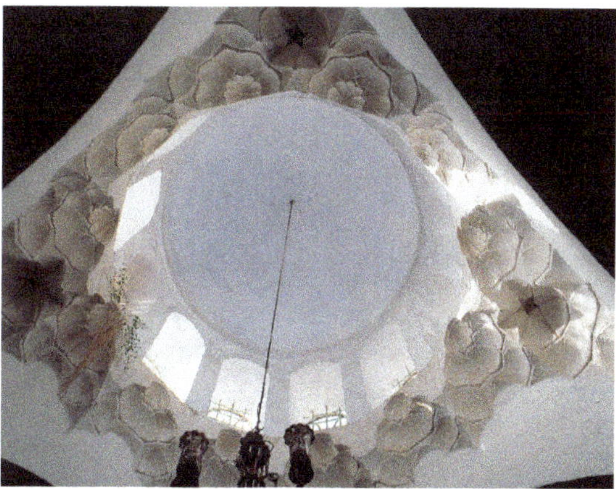

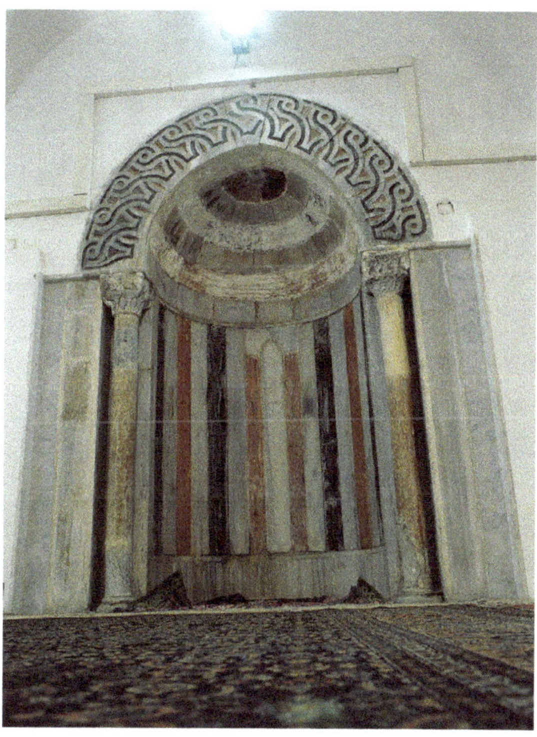

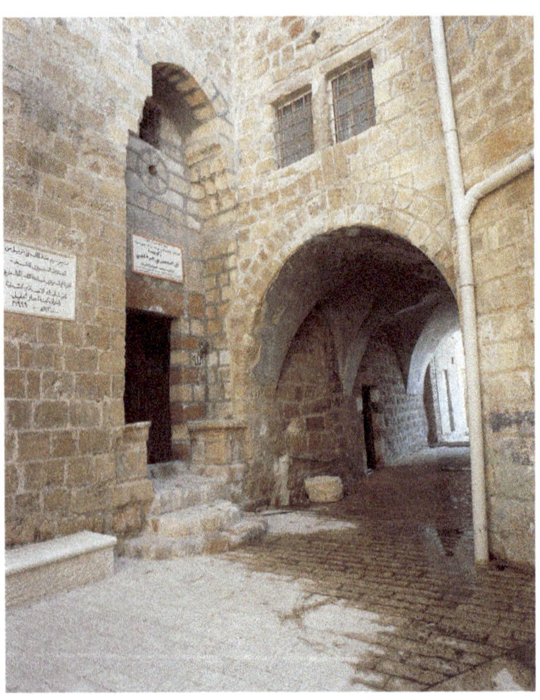

Zawiya al-Ja'abira, main façade, Hebron.

VIII.1.c Zawiya al-Ja'abira

Lies 20 m. south-east of the Haram al-Ibrahimi. Visiting is by prior arrangement with the shaykh *of the* zawiya.

Zawiya al-Ja'abira is one in a series of *zawiyas* built in Hebron during the Mamluk period. The Ja'bari family originated from the Qal'at Ja'bar, a fortress on the Euphrates in Syria. The head of the family, Ibrahim Ibn 'Umar al-Ja'bari (d. 732/1332), came to Hebron at the end of the $7^{th}/13^{th}$ century after he had been appointed the *shaykh* of the Haram of al-Ibrahimi. Many descendants of this family were jurists and religious men who took up administrative and religious posts, some of whom are mentioned in the historical sources.

This *zawiya* played a vital part in the lives of Hebron's *sufis*, and the Ja'baris led one Order. It was still active until recent times, as it still contains the flags, cups and drums that the *dervishes* used during festivals and special prayers. Although the foundation date and the name of the founder are unknown, its architectural style indicates that it dates to the end of the Mamluk period.

Built on a tiny piece of land due to the lack of space around the Haram al-Ibrahimi area, the building consists of one, very high storey. Its western façade contains the usual components of other *harams* of the Mamluk period. Rising to the height of the whole structure, it is built in alternating cream and red stones, and on top of it is a tiny receding *muqarnas*, typical of the late Mamluk and early Ottoman periods. The inscription plaque above the entrance is illegible.

One enters the building through a portal that leads to a small, square vestibule, where another door leads to the southern wall of the *zawiya*. It comprises a large, rectangular hall divided by a pointed arch into two other smaller halls: a western and an eastern. The ceiling of the western hall is covered by a cross vault that is surmounted by a shallow dome decorated in geometrical and vegetal motifs. In this room are two stairs that lead up to the vaulted western hall, the floor of which is covered in stone tiles that may belong to the period of its foundation.

VIII.1.d **Zawiya al-Maghariba and the Tomb of Joseph**

Lies west of the Haram al-Ibrahimi. Visiting requires prior arrangement with the Islamic Waqf Department.

The *zawiya*, which is also known as *zawiy-at* al-Ashraf, lies to the left of the main entrance portal to the *haram,* which in turn leads into the Old City and the mar-ket. It was probably built in around 652/1254–1255 in the early Mamluk period, as the date on one of its tombs indicates. However, its founder remains unknown.

It is worth mentioning that the Maghribi community, who originated from North Africa and al-Andalus, have formed part of Hebron's population since the 6th/13th century. It seems that the Zawiya al-Maghariba was built to lodge the Maghribi pilgrims who came to Hebron to visit the Tombs of the Prophets. Shaykh Muhammad Ibn 'Abd Allah al-Hussayni al-Saqawati (d. 652/1254) is believed to have commissioned the building. In 795/1392–1393, the Maghariba erected another *zawiya,* the Zawiya of 'Umar al-Mujarrad, which was named after the founder. His descendants, members of the al-Sharif family, still live in Hebron today.

Entry to the *zawiya* is through the portal in the eastern wall. This has lately been rebuilt, thus erasing original features of the old façade, which was unfortunately never documented. The stairs lead to an open courtyard that leads to the *zawiya* in the south, and to the cenotaph in the west.

The *zawiya* has a prayer hall and a large, square tomb chamber, which is covered by a cross vault. The chamber is jammed with tombs that belong to the al-Sharif family, who are believed to have been followers of the *sufi* Khalwati Rahmani Order, that was led by the family and widespread in Hebron. In fact, this Order still practices its *sufi* rituals in the historical location of the *zawiya*. The large number of tombs in the chamber reveals how important it was to be buried close to the founder of the Order, the *shaykh* 'Abd Allah al-Saqawati. The prayer room, on the other hand, is rectangular and covered by a cross vault; a simple *mihrab* is found in the *qibla* wall. The *Sufi* Order

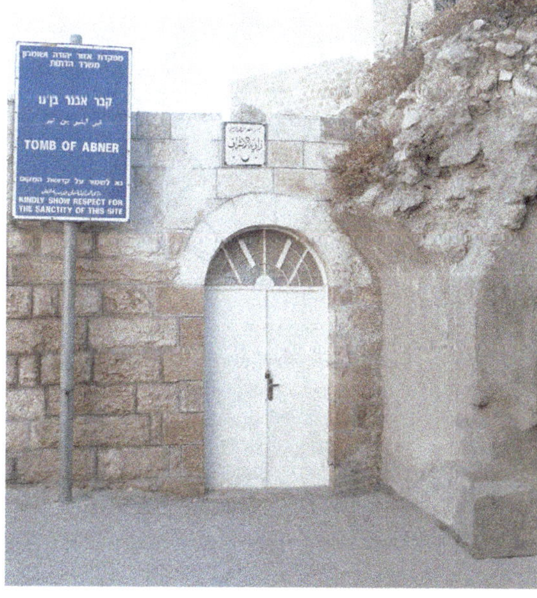

Zawiya al-Maghariba, entrance, Hebron.

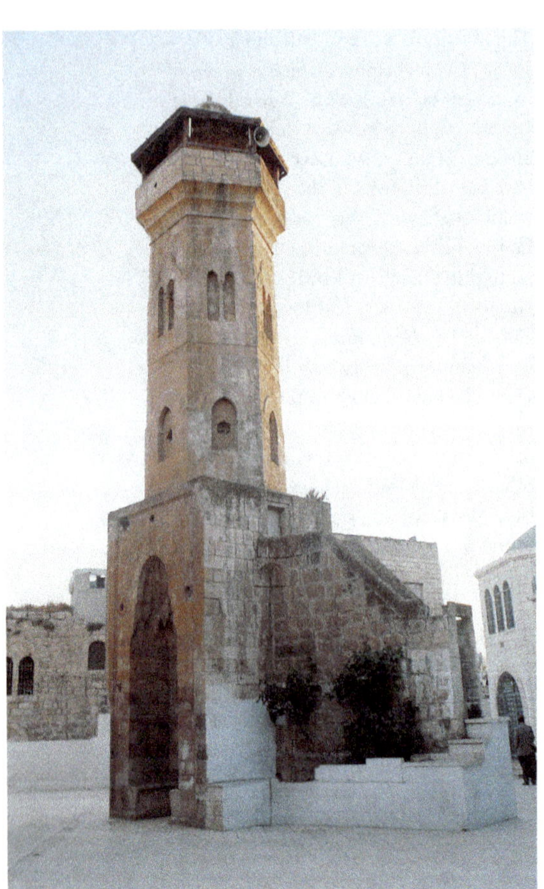

Zawiya of Sheikh 'Ali al-Bakka', main entrance and minaret, Hebron.

as well as the al-Sharif family meet in this room.
The Tomb of Joseph is below the courtyard and is accessed by stairs that lead to a barrel-vaulted chamber containing the tomb in the southern corner. No one knows exactly whose tomb it is, whether it is Joseph's, or just a commemorative shrine built to honour him. The Jews believe that it is the tomb of Avner Son of Ner.

VIII.1.e **Zawiya of Shaykh 'Ali al-Bakka'**

Lies north-west of the city in the 'Ali al-Bakka' Quarter.
It is open all day except during prayer times.

Situated on the north-western outskirts of Hebron, this *zawiya* attracted a large number of people during the Mamluk period, many of whom came to live in the neighbourhood due to the services it provided. Many of the followers of the *shaykh*'s Order resided in the adjacent area, and so a Quarter gradually developed carrying the name of the founder of the *zawiya*. Later on the name was shortened to that of the "*shaykh*'s Quarter", and became an integral part of the city's architectural fabric. The *zawiya* is one of the most celebrated in Hebron, playing a vital role in the history of Sufism. Endowed by generous *waqf*s, many Hebron *shaykh*s, most of whom were descendants of the Ja'bari family and were related to the *shaykh* al-Bakka', looked after it.
The *zawiya* is attributed to the *shaykh* 'Ali al-Bakka', the famous *sufi* who came from Iraq. Renowned for his crying whilst returning to God, he was called *al-Bakka'* (the crying person). Paying special attention to Sufist tradition like all Mamluks, Sultan Baybars commissioned the construction of a whole complex in honour of the *shaykh* 'Ali al-Bakka' in 668/1269. The complex incorporated a mosque, a shrine, a mausoleum, a garden, three rooms, three caves, an oven, a shop and two halls.

In the 20th century many alterations were made to the building that changed its original architectural components. All the same, the *zawiya* still has the city's most beautiful Mamluk minaret, built by the Amir Sayf al-Din Salar, by order of Sultan Muhammad Ibn Qalawun in 702/ 1302–1303. Hexagonal in shape, it stands on a square base, in which a portal leads to the interior courtyard; handsome *muqarnas* carvings decorate the top of the portal and a commemorative inscription surrounds the base. On the ceiling of the portal is the signature of the architect Sulayman. The minaret has all the elements of Mamluk architecture and ornament: *muqarnas*, *ablaq*, cartouches, inscriptions, carved stone decorations and star medallions, among other details.

In 1978 the new mosque was built on top of the ruins of the Mamluk one. The *shaykh*'s tomb chamber was rebuilt and a room for the teaching of the *Hadith*s was added to it.

VIII.1.f **Hammam al-Khalil (Hebron Museum)**

Situated in the Dariya, the oldest Quarter in Hebron. Leaving the courtyard of the Haram al-Ibrahimi, one enters the suq *of the Old City from the gate opposite the Haram. After about 250 m., turn right, and you are there.*
Open: 06.00–14.00.

The *hammam* can be reached through a narrow and winding alleyway covered by a vaulted ceiling, which forms the present *suq* of the Dariya Quarter, built in the 2nd/8th century. During this time, the idea of the *haram* evolved when the city grew around the Tombs of the Prophets and away from its original location on the Rumayda Mount. The *hammam* is 150 m. from the *suq*, north-west of the Ibrahimi Mosque.

The precise date and name of the founder of this *hammam* are unknown, but according to its architectural style, it can be dated to the late Mamluk period. It currently houses the city's history museum,

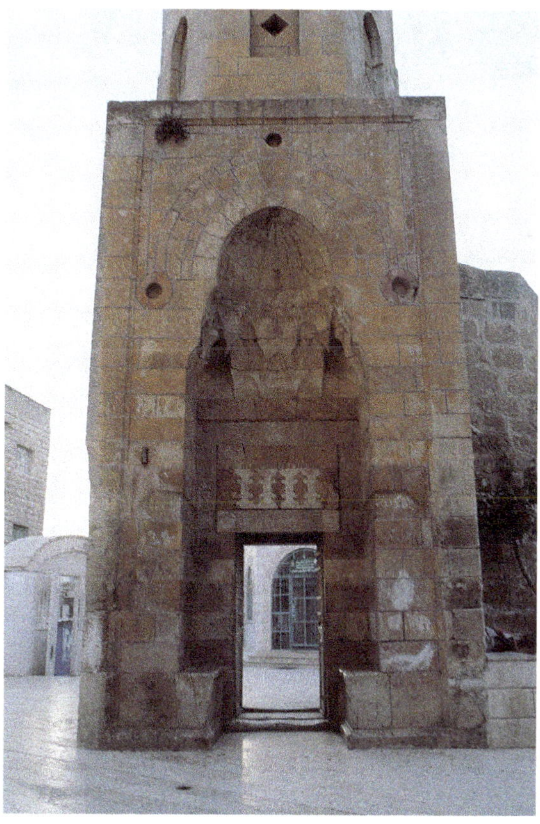

Zawiya of Sheikh 'Ali al-Bakka', main entrance, Hebron.

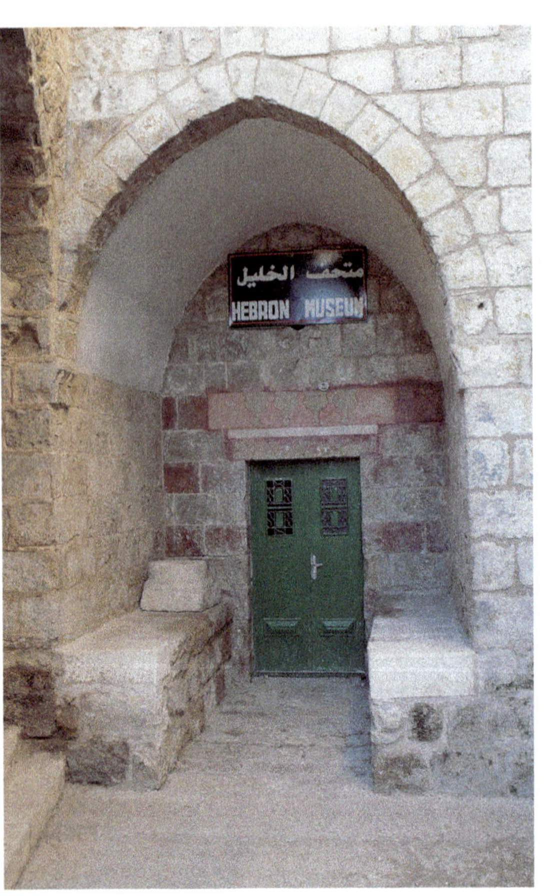

Hammam al-Khalil, entrance, Hebron.

which has a simple exhibitioin of artefacts, among which are stone inscriptions, coins and glassware, manuscripts, stone- and marble-relief decorations dating to different periods, especially the Mamluk era.

The façade of the *hammam* reflects the general architectural style of the building. Relatively small due to lack of space, it has a rectangular entrance portal at the centre, which has a bench on either side. Simple and plain, the façade is built in the *ablaq* style, with alternating cream, red and black stones.

The bath comprises two main halls: an external hall and an interior hot hall. The external hall is square in plan and covered by a fan-vault that has a small polygonal lantern in the centre, with four recesses; concave squinches resting on pointed arches are found in its corners, and together they add a special harmonious atmosphere to the hall. As in other *hammams*, there are cushion-strewn platforms all around on which visitors can recline and drink tea, socialise, or puff on a narghile; at the centre is a charming marble fountain.

A low, narrow corridor leads to the interior octagonal hall, which is covered by a shallow dome. The dome has various coloured-glass skylights for ventilation, and rests on triangular corner *muqarnas*. The hall has four recesses covered by pointed arches that function as separate bathrooms. The floor tiles of these bathrooms are heated by hot water that runs underneath them, and they are steam rooms as a result. The building also has other public utilities.

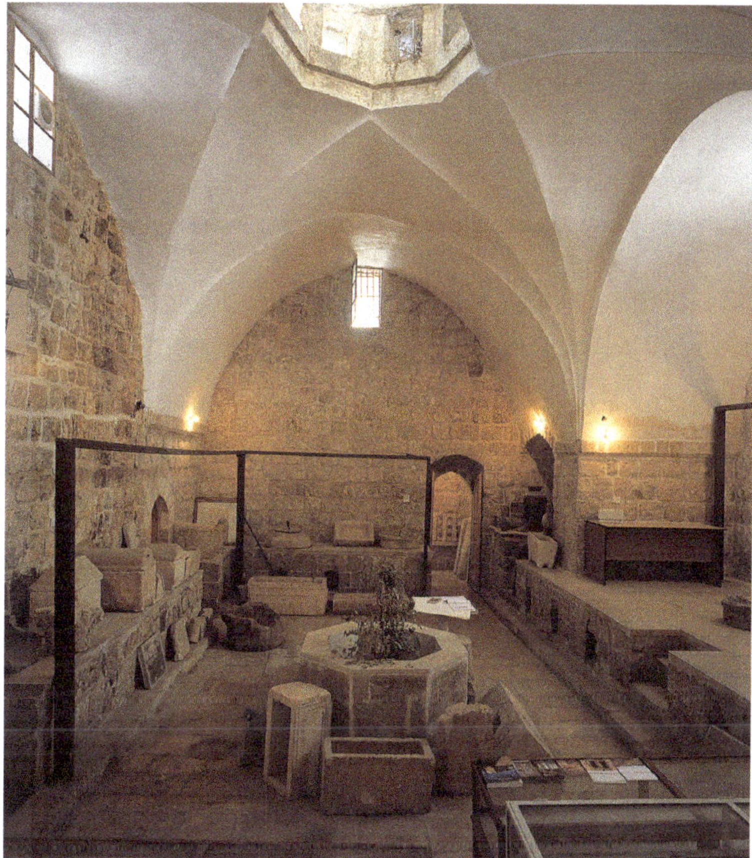

Hammam al-Khalil, reception hall with central fountain, Hebron.

THE OLD QUARTERS

Nazmi al-Ju'beh

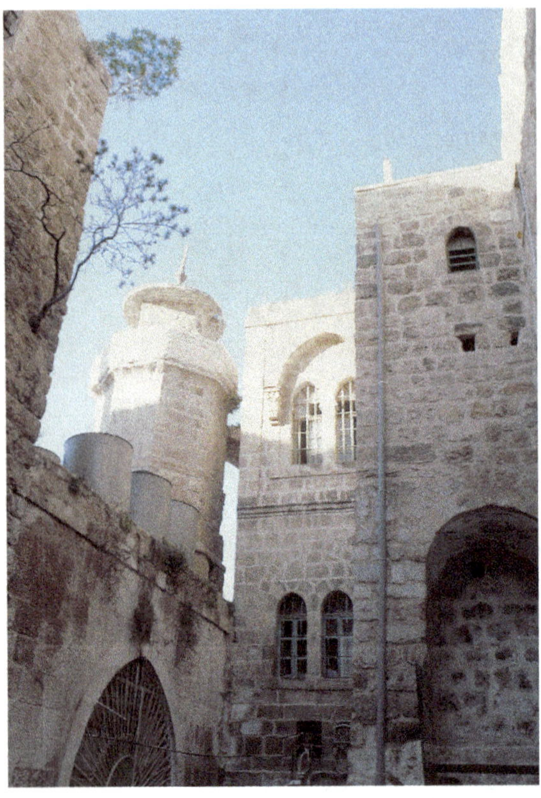

The Old Quarters, Ibn 'Uthman Mosque, Hebron.

The Old Quarters in the City of Hebron are among the few in the Islamic world that still bear the spirit of the Mamluk period. Although some of these quarters were established in the Crusader and Ayyubid periods, most of them evolved and developed during the Mamluk period. It is feasible to state that the architectural fabric of Hebron is Mamluk, with a touch of the local characteristics. In fact, historical descriptions of the city dating to the late Mamluk period still reflect to a large extent the current reality.

Three categories of quarters existed, depending on their function. The first encompassed religious communities: examples of these are the Jewish and the Christian Quarters (the latter ceased to exist in the $10^{th}/16^{th}$ century and became part of the Dariya Quarter). The second type housed specific ethnic groups such as Kurds, Ja'baris (from Ja'bar fortress on the Euphrates), the *shaykh* Quarter, the Tamimiya or the Dariya Quarter (of Arab origin and the oldest in the city). The third was the vocational quarters, such as the Qazzazin Quarter (glass manufacturers) and al-'Aqaba Quarter (leather manufacturers).

Due to this division, local conflicts erupted between the different communities, who competed over political and religious power. An example of this is seen in the devastating feud between the Dariya, their Arab and Bedouin allies, and the Kurds during late Mamluk times; it was so fierce that the sultan had to come from Cairo to end it.

Bordered from the south and east by the Desert Bedouins, Hebron had to fortify itself against repeated attacks from them. Due to the lack of a city wall, the houses, of two storeys or more, were crowded together all along the city's outer perimeter. Few external openings were left, except for those in the high windows (mostly on the second floor) and a few secure and tightly controlled gates. Each quarter had its own gate that connected it to the outside world without the need to pass through other quarters, and gates that connected it to other parts of the city.

Moreso, every quarter took precautions to protect against internal strife by building separate entrances and gates that were locked at night. This continued until the early 20th century. Despite the relative internal harmony, each quarter was divided into a series of independent architectural units, which accommodated the structure of private family spaces within a larger family residence. So although the quarter was formed of many connected families, each family occupied a certain fortified part of the quarter and protected it for social and safety reasons. In each unit, an independent courtyard is found in which the families held their private celebrations and various ceremonies. Each family unit is called *hawsh*, which consisted of an integral architectural complex that had many smaller units (apartments) for the sons of the families. The complex extended with the growth of the family, to the degree that sometimes the family had more than one *hawsh* to accommodate all its different branches.

Walking through any of these quarters, the visitor gets a good idea about this system. For even though the social fabric of the city has changed, the architectural structure has remained the same since the Mamluk and Ottoman times.

GLASS PRODUCTION

Nazmi al-Ju'beh

It is recommended that the visitor stop at the glass factory, which is situated on the outskirts of the city, on the Hebron–Halhul road, before visiting Hebron.
Open: 08.00–22.00.

Travellers of the Mamluk period reported that caravans carrying Hebron glass were seen on the road linking Cairo to Hebron, and also heading towards eastern Jordan. The origins of glass manufacture in Hebron, and how it came to be established there is unknown. However, we are told that since the 7th/13th century the local economy of Hebron largely depended on glass manufacture and on its famous grapes. The glass was exported to Egypt and Syria and to eastern Jordan in particular, with Hebron's merchants establishing commercial centres in Cairo and Karak (Jordan) in order to market huge amounts of glassware.

Although no official statistics are available on the number of glass factories, or the scale of production during the Mamluk period, it is believed that there were a large number of factories and that the production was enormous. For example, during the recession that hit Hebron in 1222/1808 the number of factories reached 26. These produced different household wares and large quantities of glass jewellery such as bracelets, rings and earrings, which were popular in the area.

Today only three factories produce glassware in the traditional way, using the same glass-blowing techniques and traditional tools. While the furnace is still built of clay and mud, the fuel used has been changed from wood to oil. The raw material is no longer the sand and components brought from the Negev region in the south of Palestine; the current manufacturing process depends on recycling by melting the glass down and then reforming it.

Concerning what is produced these days; the popularity of glass jewellery has decreased while the demand for general household glassware and souvenirs has increased. The colours used range from dark blue, turquoise, brown, pale blue, honey yellow and green – the very same colours as the Mamluk artefacts that are still exhibited in museums. Glassware is now once again decorated in gold and enamel, exactly as it was during the Mamluk period

Ceramic production (glazed pottery) is another industry that is still in existence today. This particular tradition, developed in Palestine during the 19th century, is still in high demand particularly within the tourist sector. Made in the Armenian tradition, the designs represent Palestinian decorative themes such as those depicting religious places and scenes, as well as those that replicate ancient ornaments.

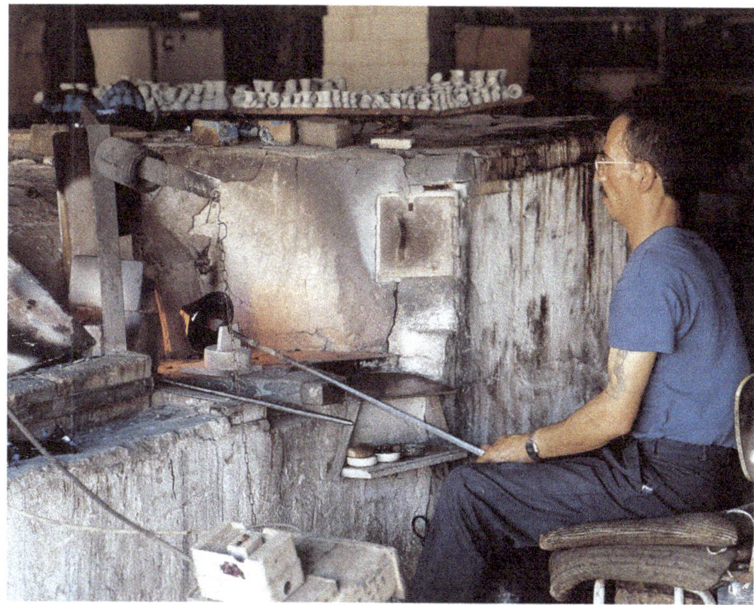

Glass production, a worker using the oven.

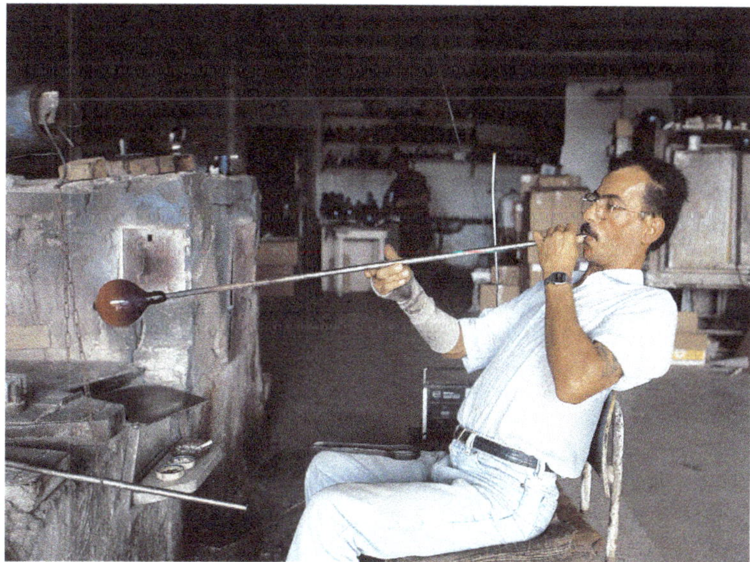

Glass production, glass blowing.

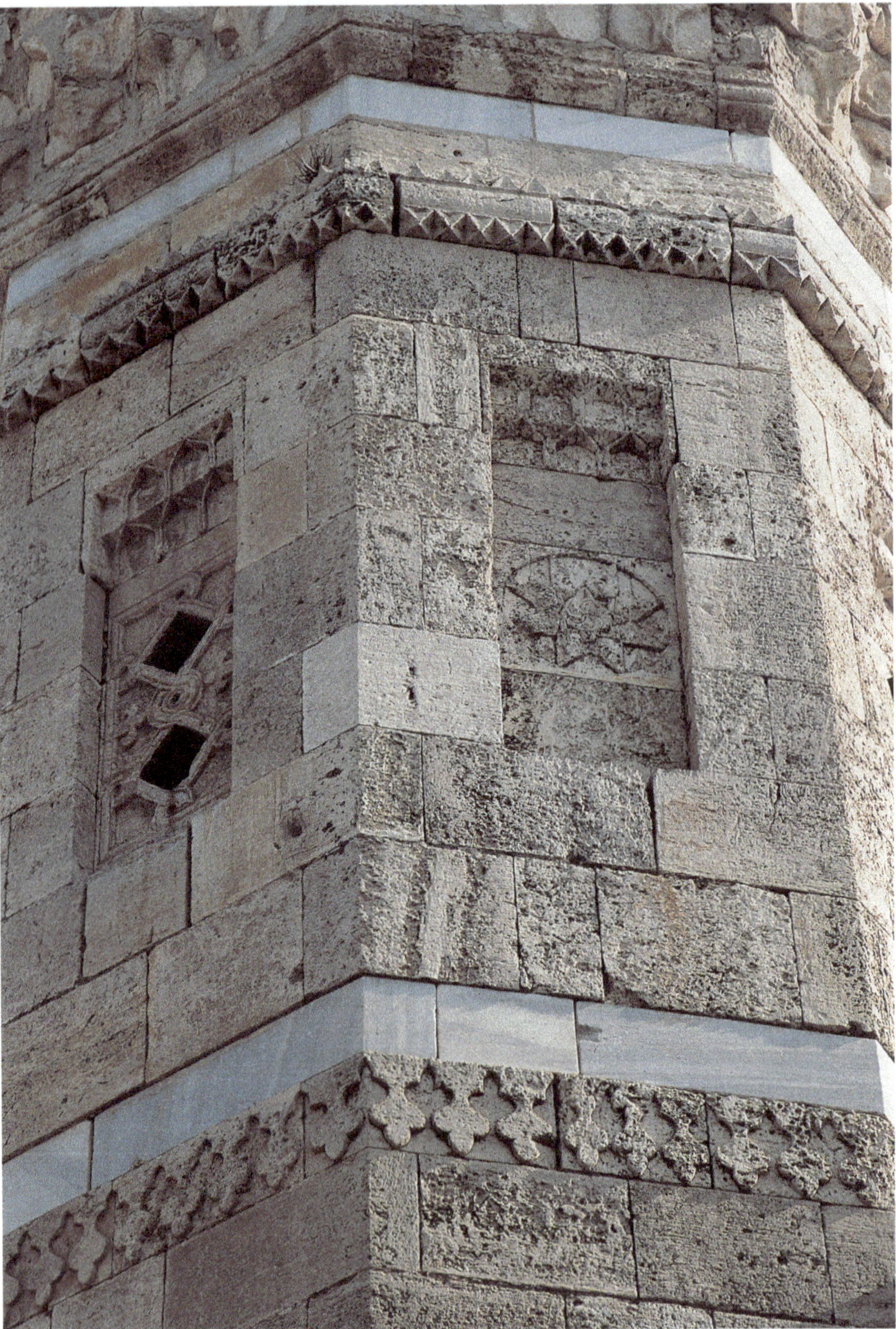

Gaza: the Gate to Africa

Mu'en Sadeq

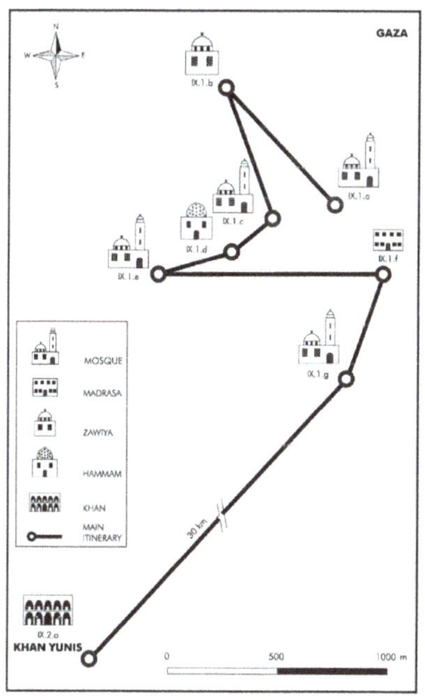

Madrasa of Amir Bardabak, minaret, detail of shaft, Gaza.

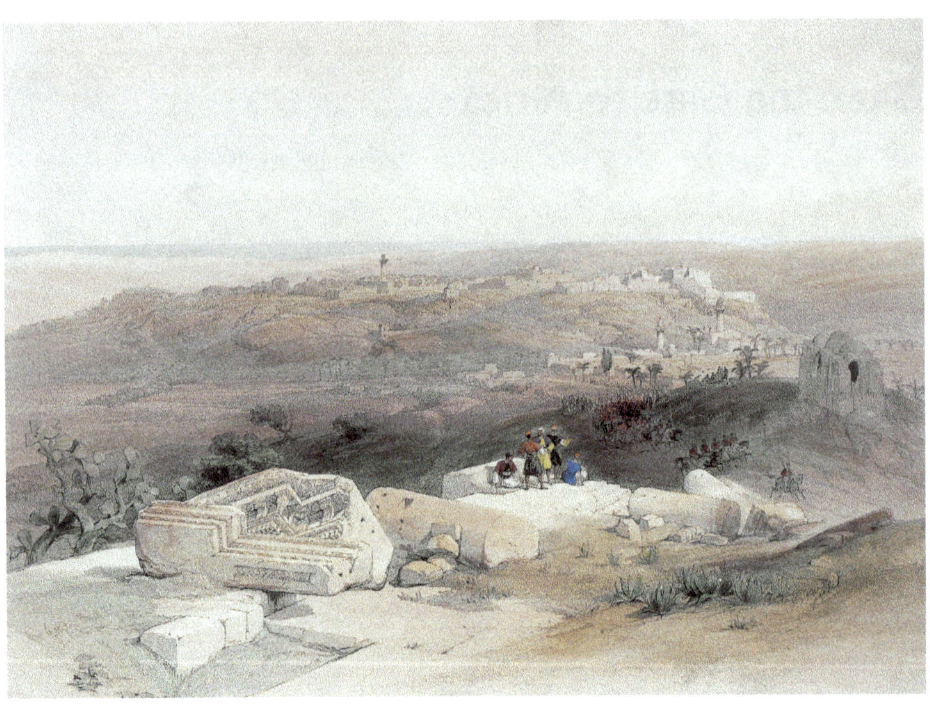

Gaza, 1843, lithograph by D. Roberts (© The Art Archive).

IX.1 GAZA

The City of Gaza has enjoyed a unique geographic position since the dawn of history. It was located on one of the most important military and trade routes in the ancient world, linking Egypt to Syria. Thus many Egyptian kings sought to conquer it in order to take control of the entire area, including the trade routes. The Assyrians and Babylonians assembled their forces in Gaza before invading Egypt. Indeed, it became a gate to Africa and an entrance to Asia.

Although far away from the capitals of successive Islamic states, Gaza held a special position, becoming a renowned centre for Islamic Studies. It was also the place in which the *imam* al-Shafi'i (150/767–204/820), the greatest Muslim scholar and the founder of the Shafi'i School, was born.

Many Arab historians and geographers emphasised Gaza's role as a centre of agriculture and trade during the Fatimid period (358/969–492/1099). Geographers described Gaza as an important city that extended to the desert. They described its well-built Great Mosque and the fact that it was located one mile from the sea, surrounded by orchards and vineyards; the old Roman harbour, *Maioumas,* prospered until Byzantine times.

The Crusaders succeeded in occupying Gaza 50 years after they had conquered Jerusalem and they renovated what had been demolished by the war. Following their defeat in the Battle of Hittin by Saladin in 583/1187, Crusader rule over Palestine, including Gaza, came to an end. In 691/1291, the Mamluk Sultan al-Malik al-Ashraf made Gaza an independent province (*niyaba*) headed by a viceroy.

During the Mamluk period (648/1250–922/1517), Gaza became the most important town in the region and enjoyed a peaceful era. Many buildings were erected such as mosques, *madrasas*, *zawiyas*, *ribats*, *khans* and *suqs*, some of which still survive today.

This itinerary aims to highlight the history of some of the most renowned Islamic buildings in the city and their functions during successive Islamic eras. It comprises eight monuments and contains two "windows". While the first window deals with pottery production in Gaza, the second explores the manufacture of traditional textiles in the region. Four mosques are included (the Mosque of 'Ali Ibn Marwan, the Great 'Umari Mosque, the Mosque of Katib al-Wilaya and the Mosque of Shihab al-Din Ibn 'Uthman), in addition to the *sufi* Zawiya al-Ahmadiyya, Hammam al-Samara, the Madrasa of the Amir Bardabak al-Dawadar (Jami' al-Mahkama Mosque) and the *khan* of Amir Yunis al-Nawruzi.

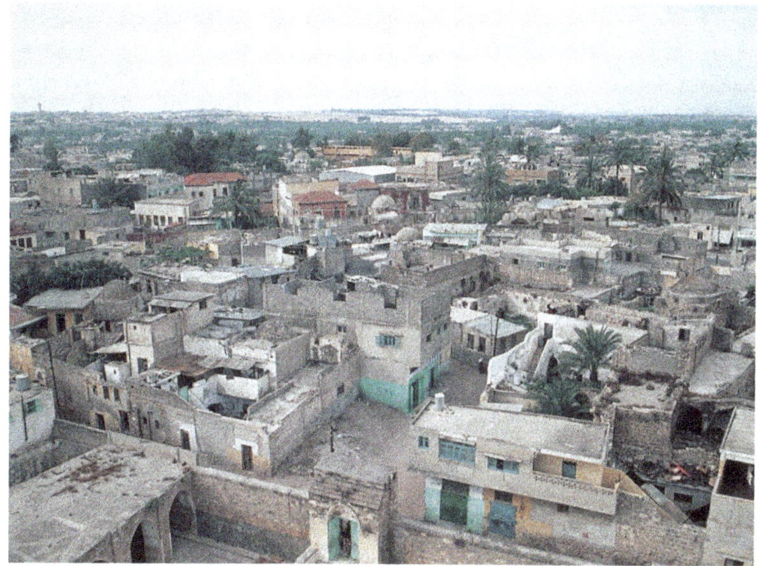

Gaza, aerial view from the minaret of the Great Mosque (© M. Hamilton Burgoyne).

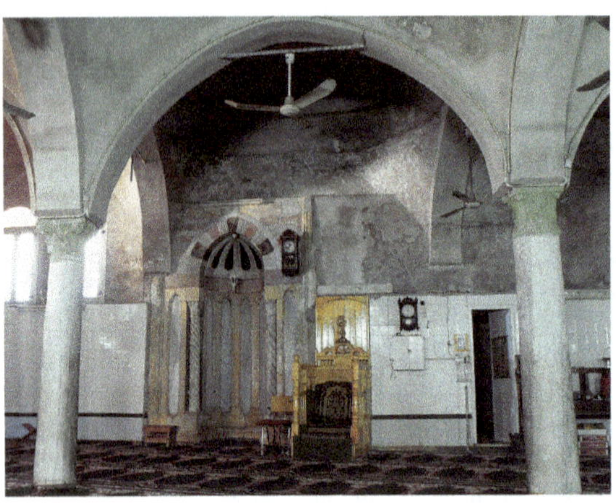

'Ali Ibn Marwan Mosque, mihrab and minbar, Gaza.

IX.1.a Mosque of 'Ali Ibn Marwan

Located in the Tuffah Quarter on Jaffa Street, just before arrival at the Old City. The site is open to visitors all day except at prayer times.

The mosque is attributed to the *shaykh* 'Ali Ibn Marwan, a leading Muslim figure in Gaza during the Mamluk period. When Shaykh 'Ali died in 715/1316, he was buried in an adjacent dome-covered chamber. Today, this chamber is part of the historical cemetery known as the "Cemetery of Ibn Marwan".

The precise date of construction for this mosque is unknown, but it is believed that it existed in the early 8th/14th century. Early historical sources refer to it as being renovated and enlarged in 772/1370–1371 by Muhammad Ibn Buktumur. He expanded the *iwans* of the prayer hall, renovated its minaret and constructed six shops. The revenue from the shops covered the salaries of the *muezzin* and the *imam* of the mosque and also the cost of looking after the mausoleum. In 1217/1802–1803, the *amir* Yahya, the Governor of Gaza, renovated parts of the mosque and opened up a door on the west wall of the prayer hall.

The mosque consists of a prayer hall of 200 sq. m. that is divided into three aisles by marble columns, which have re-used Corinthian capitals; each aisle is divided into nine vaults covered by shallow domes. To the right of the *mihrab* there is a marble *minbar* built by Amir Shamsi Safar who served as a chamberlain in the 8th/14th century. It is one of the most beautiful Mamluk *minbars* in the city, distinguished by its elaborate geometrical and arabesque motifs. The dome, richly decorated on the outside by geometrical and vegetal ornaments, is one of the most unique of the Mamluk period. The minaret which was renovated in 772/1370–1371, rises to 11.60 m. and its square base stands to the south of the mosque's façade. Its octagonal shaft has recesses that carry numerous arches decorated in vegetal and geometrical carvings. The gallery of the minaret is also octagonal and stands on stone corbels. The mausoleum consists of a square chamber that is covered by a dome, situated 10 m. to the south-west of the current mosque. Shaykh 'Ali's marble tomb lies to the south-

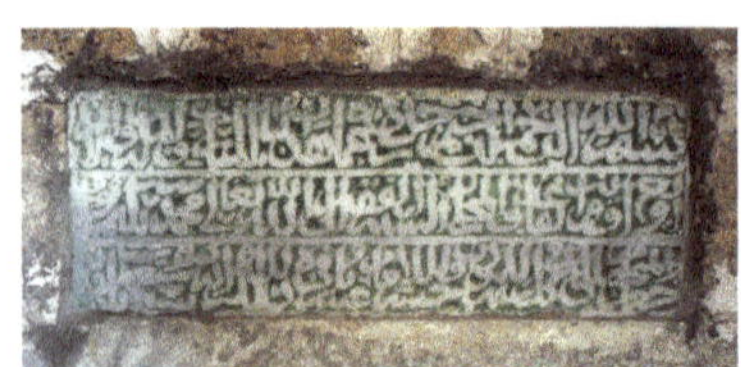

'Ali Ibn Marwan Mosque, foundation inscription, Gaza.

east; there is no tombstone. The circular triangles on the corners of the room give this square-shaped room a circular shape.

IX.1.b **Zawiya al-Ahmadiyya**

Lies in the Daraj Quarter on al-Wahda Street, south of the Pasha Palace.
It is open all day except at prayer times. Visitors should seek permission from the attendants before visiting.

The *zawiya* is attributed to the *shaykh* Ahmad Ibn Ibrahim Ibn Muhammad Ibn Bakr, known as al-Badawi (d. 675/1276). He was a famous *sufi* who lived in Tanta, Egypt, with many followers both inside and outside the area. The foundation inscription above the entrance portal reveals that the Amir Tarantay al-Yukandar the *wali* of Gaza, constructed the *zawiya* in 731/1330–1331, during the reign of the Amir Tankiz al-Nasiri.
The *zawiya* consists of two main sections: the prayer hall and the lodging wing. The square-plan prayer hall lies in the southern part of the building, and its side is 8.5 m. long. A stone dome that stands on a polygonal drum, pierced by many windows for ventilation, covers the prayer hall. The *mihrab* is in the Mamluk style. The lodging wing consists of a large, square interior courtyard, covered with a cross vault. In the centre is an octagonal fountain, used for ablutions. The water for the fountain was supplied from the neighbouring rivulet, which also sup-

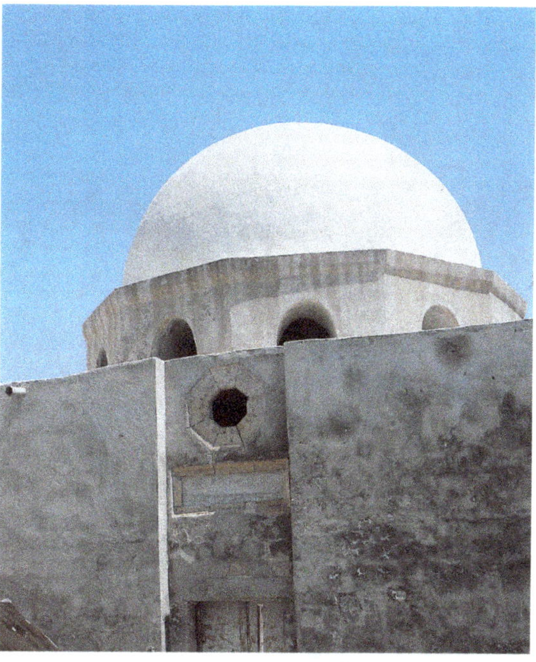

Zawiya al-Ahmadiyya, main façade, Gaza.

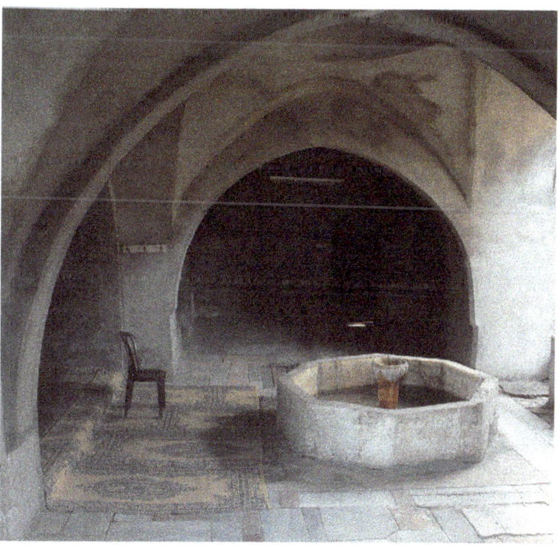

Zawiya al-Ahmadiyya, interior, Gaza.

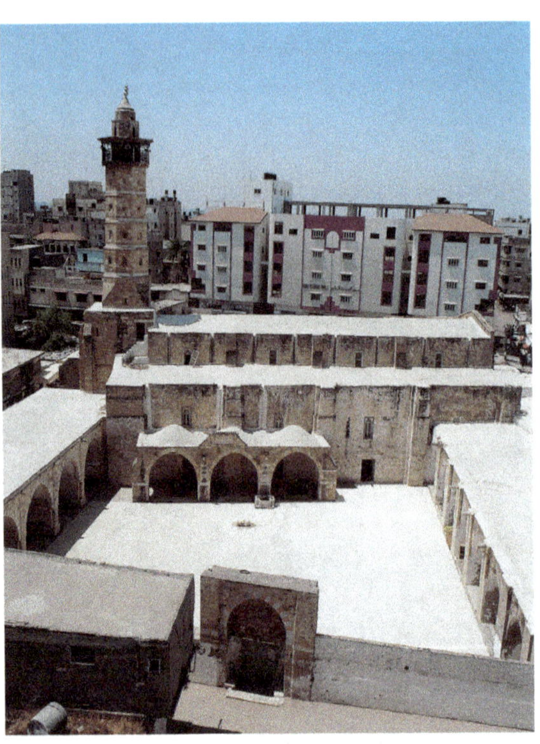

Great Mosque of 'Umar, general view of the courtyard, Gaza.

plied water for the air-cooling system. The hall overlooks the front courtyard from the west through two pointed arches. Three rectangular vaulted *iwans* surround it and each overlooks the external courtyard through a double-vaulted window.

IX.1.c **The Great 'Umari Mosque**

Lies in the Daraj Quarter in the centre of the Old City.
Visitors are usually allowed in between daily prayer times.

The Great 'Umari Mosque measuring 66.5 m. × 65.5 m., is a composite of several architectural styles that developed during various successive periods; the most important of which was the Mamluk period. The mosque was largely ruined during the Second World War, although the Supreme Islamic Council renovated it in 1924.

The oldest part of the mosque, which has a basilica plan, dates to the Crusader period. This was the Cathedral dedicated to St John the Baptist, which was built on the site of the Friday Mosque, and was in the city centre during the early Islamic period. It consists of a central nave flanked by two aisles, all covered with cross vaults. The main entrance portal is on its west wall, above which is a circular window. The design of the portal with its columns, capitals and arches are in the Gothic style. On either side of the nave is a row of pillars and composite Byzantine marble columns crowned with what seem to be re-used Corinthian capitals.

After the Crusaders departed the city in 583/1187, the building was converted into a Friday Mosque, and thus regained its old name: the "'Umari Mosque". In the Mamluk period, Sultan al-Mansur Husam al-Din Lajin (696/1297–698/1299) added to the mosque the eastern portal, which leads directly into the central nave of the early building (the basilica), and a minaret. The latter collapsed as a result of an earthquake, but was rebuilt before the First World War. The *amir* Sunqur al-'Ala'i, the Viceroy of Gaza in 697/1297–1298, supervised the renovation works. He

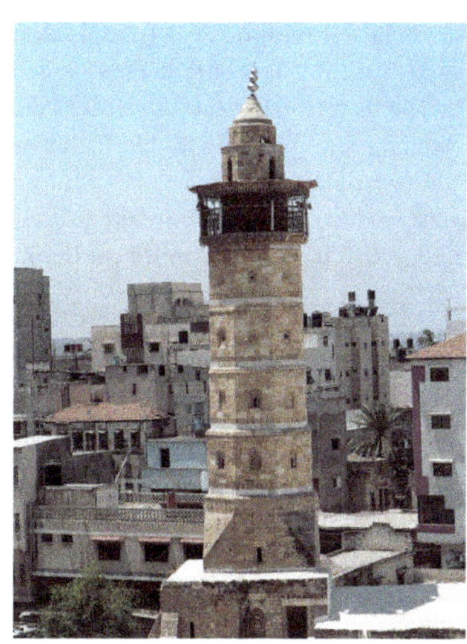

Great Mosque of 'Umar, minaret, Gaza.

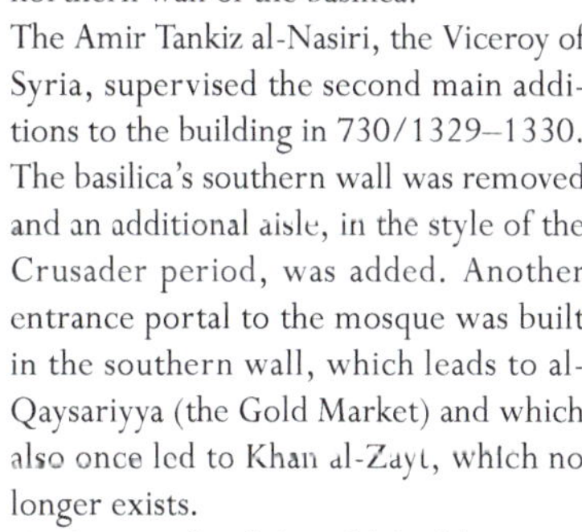

added a window and a portal to the northern wall of the basilica.

The Amir Tankiz al-Nasiri, the Viceroy of Syria, supervised the second main additions to the building in 730/1329–1330. The basilica's southern wall was removed and an additional aisle, in the style of the Crusader period, was added. Another entrance portal to the mosque was built in the southern wall, which leads to al-Qaysariyya (the Gold Market) and which also once led to Khan al-Zayt, which no longer exists.

To the north of the old building is a courtyard surrounded by porticoes from the east, west and south. The southern portico, which was built in the 11th/17th century, faces the courtyard through a triple-arched colonnade, and is covered by three cross vaults with shallow domes. The eastern and western corridors were built at the end of the 12th/18th century. In the southern portico, there is a Mamluk-period *minbar* and a *mihrab*, both of which were moved from the Mosque of Sultan Qaytbay. The western entrance portal, and a number of the porticoes that lie behind it, were constructed at the end of the 13th/19th century.

IX.1.d **Hammam al-Samara**

Located in the al-Zaytun Quarter in the Old City. The hammam *is open daily: for men until noon, and for women after noon.*

The Hammam al-Samara is one of six antique *hammams* that served Gaza's inhabitants and visitors. According to the foundation inscription, it dates back to the Mamluk period. Built of well-cut stone, its floor drops 3 m. below street

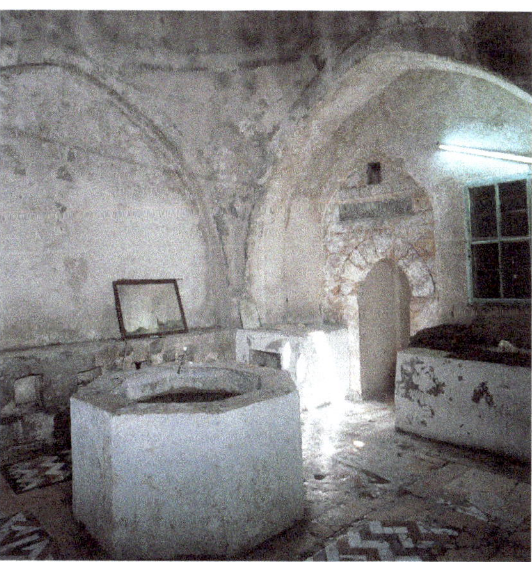

Hammam al-Samara, reception hall, Gaza.

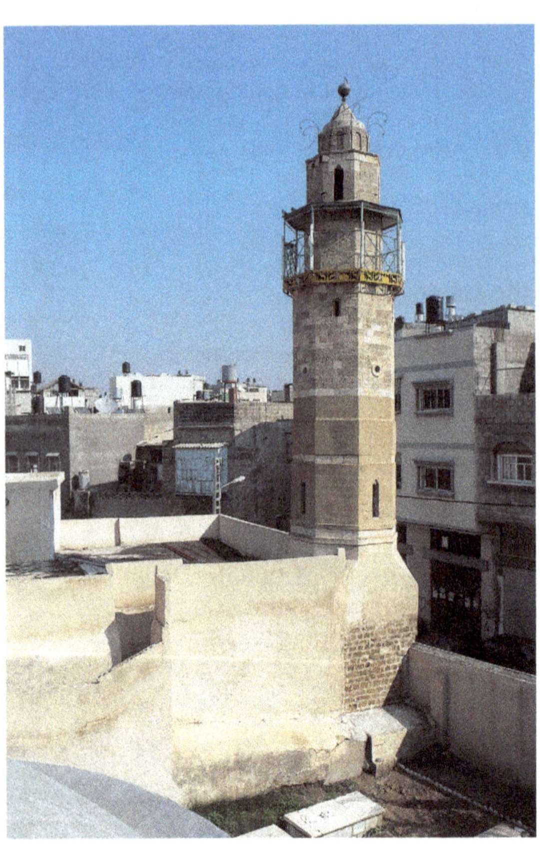

Katib al-Wilaya Mosque, minaret, Gaza.

level. Like all public *hammams*, it also served social functions.

The *hammam* consists of three main sections: the reception hall, the bathing hall and a general utilities area. Its entrance door is situated on the northern wall towards the city centre. A vaulted corridor leads into the square reception hall, the floor of which is paved with coloured and geometrically designed pieces of marble. An octagonal fountain, covered by a dome, is found in the centre. Two *iwans* surround the reception hall from the east and south; this is where people sit and change their clothes. This hall leads to the bathing room through a middle hall. The *hammam* itself is covered with coloured marble tiles, and heated by the hot-air system that passes underneath the floor.

IX.1.e **Mosque of Katib al-Wilaya**

Lies on the Ra's al-Tali' situated in the Zaytun Quarter in the Old City of Gaza. Visitors are usually permitted between prayer times, but permission needs to be granted from the attendant of the mosque.

Although it dates back to the Mamluk period, the mosque is attributed to the Amir Ahmad Bek, secretary of the district (Katib al-Wilaya), who commissioned the expansion of the mosque during the Ottoman period. From a historical and architectural point of view, the mosque is divided into two main parts: the first is the rectangular Mamluk prayer hall and the minaret on top of its eastern wall. Today the prayer hall can be reached through a door in the *qibla* wall, although it is believed the door was previously on the northern wall, in the place of one of the two existing cabins. The prayer hall is rectangular in plan and is divided into six cross vaults by a row of

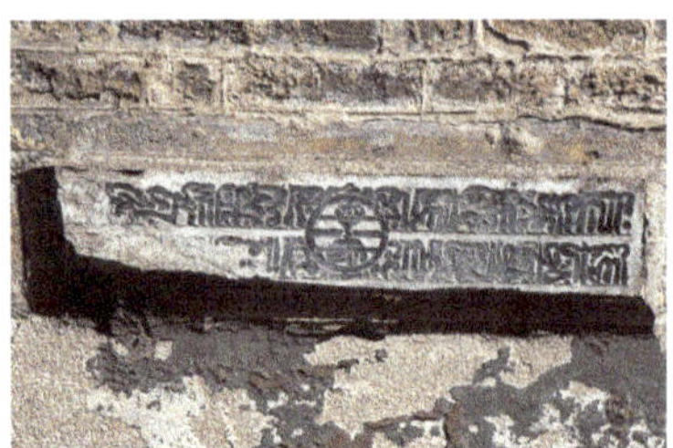

Katib al-Wilaya Mosque, foundation inscription, Gaza.

marble Corinthian columns that carry pointed arches. A semicircular *mihrab* is found in the middle of the southern wall and next to this is a marble *minbar*; some of its stone, marble and decorative features came from another Mamluk building.

The minaret was built in 835/1431–1432 by the Amir Inal al-'Ala'i, the Viceroy of Gaza who later became a Mamluk sultan in 857/1453–865/1461. In the centre of the inscription plaque is a coat of arms that comprises three parts: an inkwell that refers to the post of the *Dawadar* (secretary); a carved cup that refers to the post of cupbearer (*saqi*) and a fleur-de-lis, which refers to the earliest post he held, which was, perhaps, a military one.

The minaret has a rectangular base that carries an octagonal shaft and a *muezzin*'s gallery on top, supported by corbels. Originally 17.55 m. high, the minaret was partially damaged during the First World War, and when later it was re-built the minaret was given more height.

The second part of the mosque lies to the west of the prayer hall, and was built by the Amir Ahmad Bek, the district secretary, in 995/1586–1587. It consists of a double-dome portico which faces the courtyard, with two pointed arches carried on three square stone pillars. The pillar at the side has inscriptions on it written in *naskhi* script, and it was removed from a ruined mosque.

IX.1.f Madrasa of Amir Bardabak (al-Mahkama Mosque)

Lies on Baghdad Street in the historical al-Shuja'iyya Quarter near the main west entrance. The site is open throughout the day.

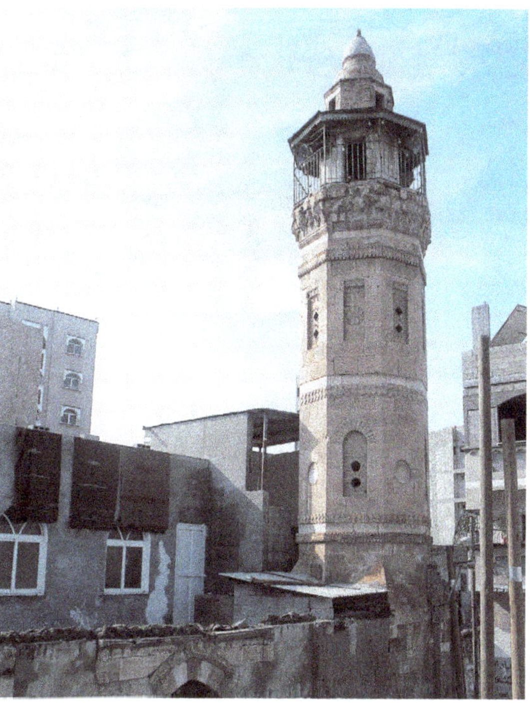

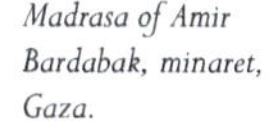

Madrasa of Amir Bardabak, minaret, Gaza.

Built in 859/1454–1455 by the Amir Bardabak al-Dawadar (as revealed by the inscription plaque above the entrance), the major function of the *madrasa* was education, although it also

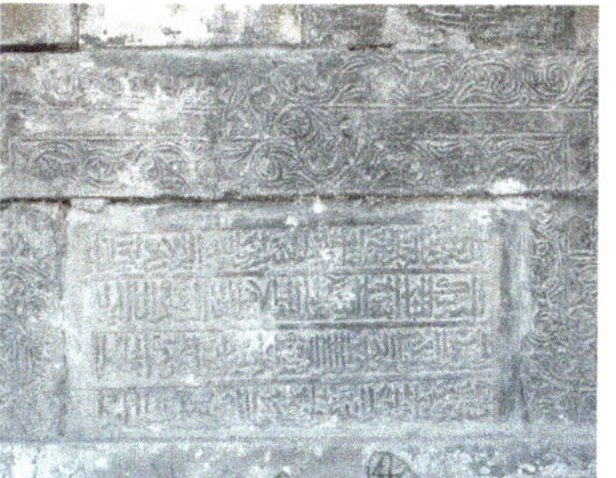

Madrasa of Amir Bardabak, foundation inscription, Gaza.

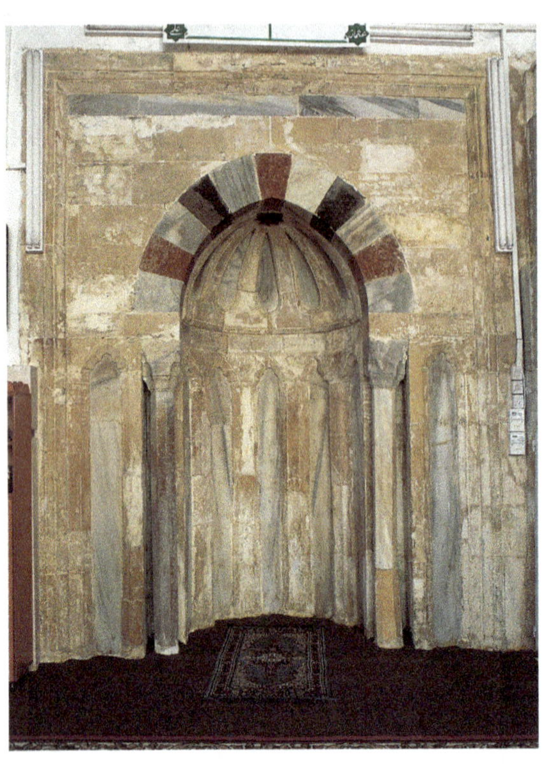

Madrasa of Amir Bardaback, mihrab of the mosque, Gaza.

held prayers, including those held on Fridays. This accords with the function of a *madrasa* during the Mamluk period and explains why it has a minaret, a *mihrab* and a *minbar*. During the Ottoman period the mosque was used as the religious court, hence its name al-Mahkama Mosque. However, during the British Mandate it was used as a boy's *madrasa* and called the Madrasa al-Shuja'iyya al-Amiriyya.

The main entrance portal is on the northern façade; above it is a pointed arch that has vegetal decorations. The *madrasa* consists of a central open courtyard that drops 1.2 m. below street level; to the south-west lies the *qibla*'s *iwan*. This is the largest part of the building and it is divided into three sections: the main, middle section contains the *mihrab* and the *minbar*, and it is covered by a fan-shaped cross vault; the two outer sections of the *iwan* have barrel-vaults, and pointed arches that connect them to the middle section. At one time a smaller *iwan* faced the *qibla*'s *iwan* from the north-west, but it has not survived. The other two sides of the courtyard, namely the northern and southern parts, held the lodging rooms for the *shaykh* and student's, as well as other service rooms. Nothing has survived of these parts except the northern side, which consists of four small, domed rectangular rooms (the entrance hall being one), each measuring 3.77 m. × 3.69 m. It is the only remaining *madrasa* in this style in Gaza.

The minaret of the *madrasa* stands in the north-west corner. In the sides of the rectangular base are placed niches, alleviating the austerity of the structure. The two octagonal levels are pierced with embrasures – covered by translucent vegetal and geometric ornaments – that both ventilate the spiral staircase and allow light into the interior. At the top of the minaret, the *muezzin*'s gallery, which is also octagonal, rests on stone *muqarnas*.

IX.1.g **Mosque of Shihab al-Din Ibn 'Uthman**

Located in the Shuja'iyya area, on Suq Street that is part of the Turkman Quarter. Visitors are welcome all day except at prayer times.

The mosque is attributed to its founder, the Shaykh Ahmad Ibn Muhammad Ibn 'Uthaman Ibn 'Umar Ibn 'Abd Allah al-Nabulsi al-Maqdisi (also known as al-Khalili). He died in Mecca in 805/1402–1403. It is the second largest old mosque in Gaza, measuring 45 m. × 36.5 m. Its plan follows the traditional layout of mosques, consisting of a central courtyard surrounded by porticoes on all four sides. The current building is a composite of different projects carried out in three stages during the Mamluk period, as indicated by inscriptions and its architectural characteristics. The first structural phase of the mosque includes the earliest components of the building, namely, the western façade with its two entrances, a minaret and the rooms behind it. All these components were built under the auspices of the *amir* Aqbugha al-Tulutumari in 802/1399–1400. The western façade has two entrance portals; on top of each an inscription plaque is found stating the date of construction. Above the southern portal is an inscription plaque that recites the works of the *amir* Aqbugha, while on the northern portal there is a record of the buildings that the *amir* Arzamak endowed to the mosque in a *waqf* in 797/1394–1395.

The minaret is built above the west façade, between two portals. Three chambers are found behind it, one of which contains the tomb of the *amir* Sa'd al-Din Yalkhuja, the Vice-sultan to Gaza in 849/1445–1446. He requested burial there shortly before his death in 850/1446–1447. The rest of the chambers are used for the various other functions of the mosque.

The mosque's courtyard (measuring 30.80 m. × 27.90 m.), and the portico in front of the *qibla* represent the second construction phase of the building. The current *qibla* portico was rebuilt at the time of Sultan al-Mu'ayyad Shaykh in 821/1418–1419, under the supervision of the Amir Abu Bakr al-Yaghmuri (Head of the Guards in Gaza). The main *mihrab* is a unique masterpiece that consists of a semicircular niche inlaid with marble. Both the *mihrab* and the dome that precedes it were the work of 'Alam al-Din Sanjar carried out in 834/1430–1431. The mosque's *minbar* is made of marble.

Shihab al-Din Ibn 'Uthman Mosque, entrance and minaret, Gaza.

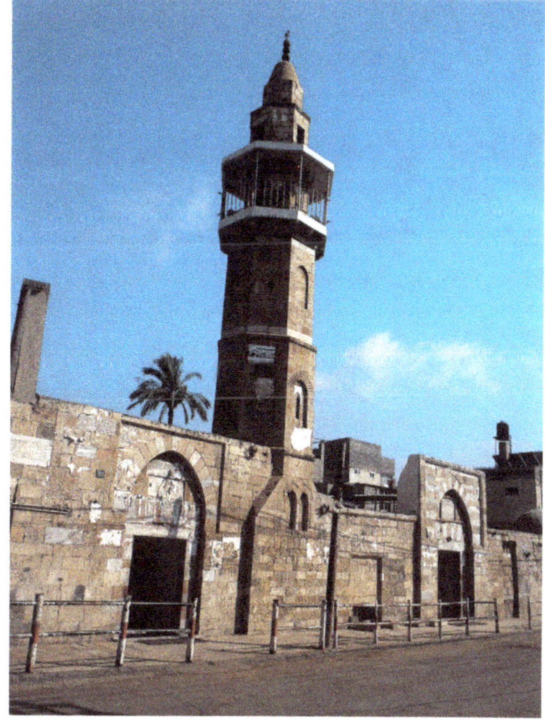

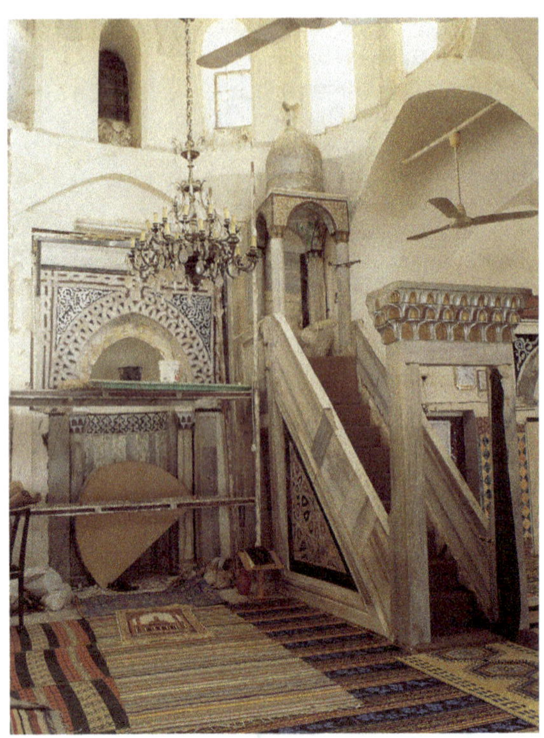

Shihab al-Din 'Uthman Mosque, mihrab and minbar, Gaza.

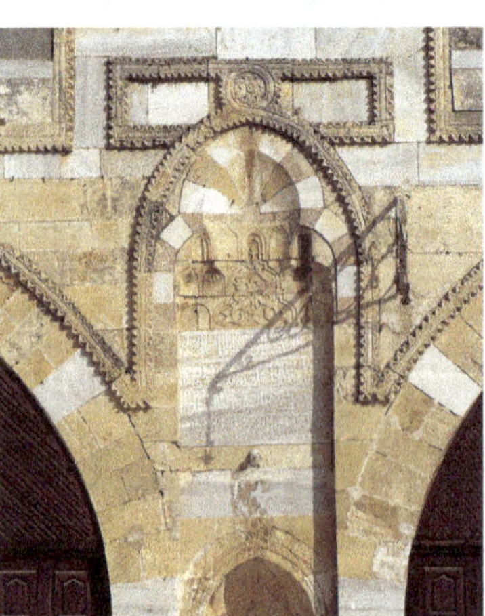

Shihab al-Din 'Uthman Mosque, *mihrab* of the courtyard, Gaza.

The final construction stage includes the north and south porticoes, which were built some time after 821/1418–1419. They face the mosque's courtyard and have pointed arches that rest on square pillars. Each portico is divided by a row of pillars into two parts; all in turn are covered with cross vaults.

IX.2 KHAN YUNIS

IX.2.a Khan of the Amir Yunis al-Nawruzi

Lies in the centre of Khan Yunis City. It is possible to visit the site at any time of the day.

Situated on the old road linking Egypt in the south, and Palestine, Syria and the Fertile Crescent in the north, the *khan* formed the centre of Khan Yunis City and was its architectural nucleus. Its strategic location, the fertility of its soil, the abundance of ground water and, finally, the existence of many quarries to the east, all contributed to the selection of this area for such a building.

This well-fortified *khan* was built to function as a stopping-off place for caravans as well as a commercial exchange centre, postal station and military stronghold for the armies located between the Mamluk Capitals of Cairo and Damascus, the centre of the Mamluk Viceroy. The place continued to play a commercial role until the end of the Mamluk period, when trading activity between Egypt and Syria waned. Soon after this it became an Ottoman military barracks to protect the road, and the site since then has been known as a fortress.

According to the three commemorative inscriptions, the *amir* Yunis built the *khan* during the reign of the Mamluk Sultan al-Dahir Barquq in 789/1387. The longest of these inscriptions is found on both sides of the entrance portal, above which is the *amir* Yunis's coat of arms in the form of a chalice, a large cup and an inkwell with two pens, all of which are symbols referring to the different posts he held. The coat of arms is repeated several times on the façade. Between each pairing of these coats of arms is an almond-shaped plaque that is divided into three parts and carries words of prayer for Sultan al-Dahir Barquq.

Nothing has survived of the *khan* except for the west façade, the remains of several rooms behind it, and the ruins of the mosque's minaret and dome. It degenerated gradually during the First World War. New constructions began to encroach upon it during successive periods of the British Mandate, the Egyptian administration, and also under Israeli occupation.

Based on the remains of the *khan* and available historical information, a reconstruction of the main components of the building has been possible. It was a two-storey building that measured 75.5 m. sq. with a courtyard in the centre. The first storey was allocated as the store, while the second was for lodging merchants and guests. It had a mosque that was a square chamber covered by a dome; parts of it can still be seen today. Both the mosque's *mihrab* and *minbar* have been ruined, only part of the minaret, which lies on top of the façade, still survives. The central courtyard was used for utilities and stables.

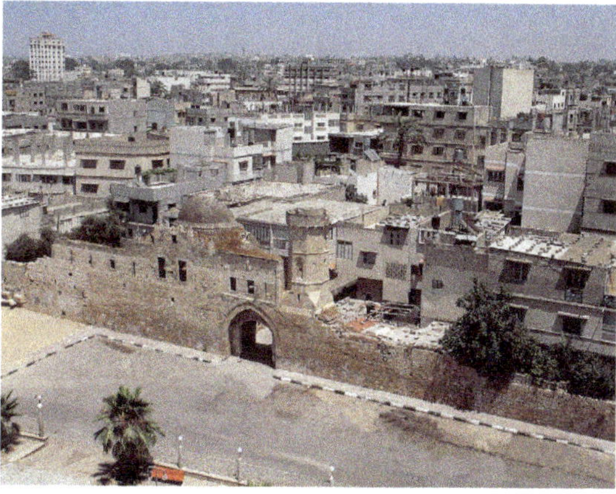

Khan of Amir Yunis al-Nawruzi, general view, Gaza.

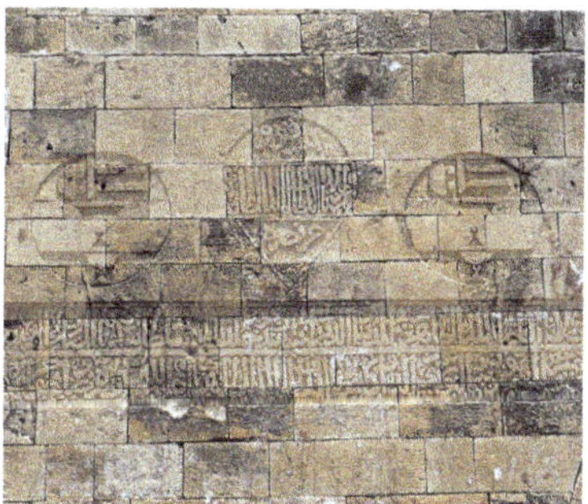

Khan of Amir Yunis al-Nawruzi, minaret, detail of the shaft, Gaza.

Due to its location on a country road before the town was established the *khan* was provided with defensive structures such as thick exterior walls and towers, arrow slits and machicolations above the entrance portal, from which hot oil was poured from above onto the enemy.

POTTERY PRODUCTION

Mu'en Sadeq

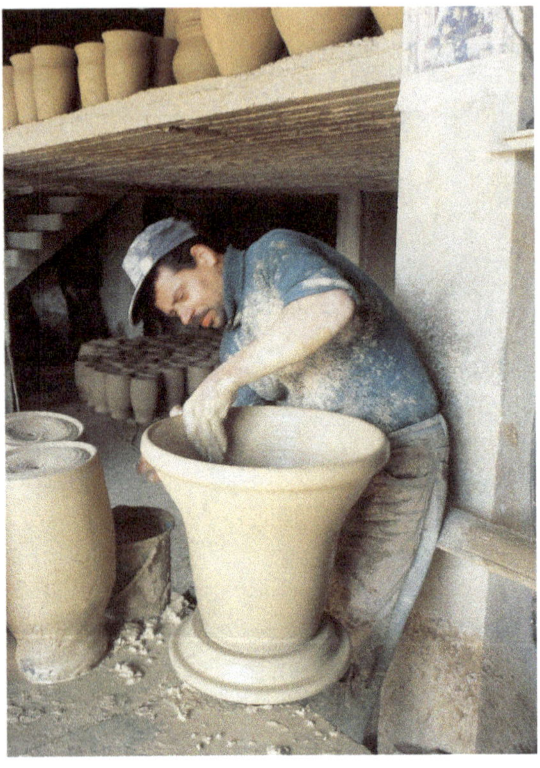

Production of pottery, potter modelling a jar on the hand lathe.

Evidence has shown that Pottery production has existed in Gaza since the 5th millennium BC. This is probably due to the fact that it was influenced by Egypt, the earliest known place to have started this industry, as a result of its contacts with the civilisations of the north and south along the international highway that went through it. The abundance of clay in the area definitely contributed to the establishment and development of this industry in Gaza and its surrounding areas.

From the Iron Age to the Islamic era, Gaza exported its ceramics – distinguished by its brown and redish colours – to all the neighbouring regions and the Mediterranean cities from its ancient harbour Anthedon. The ruins of the harbour can be seen today on the city's north-west coast.

The Gaza pottery centres produced large red-coloured storage jars that were used to export wine, oil and other products to Mediterranean cities, particularly during the Roman and Byzantine periods. Known as "Gaza jars", they reached France, Britain, Greece, Italy and North Africa in large quantities. During the Islamic period, Gaza further developed its pottery production. The Potters Quarter (Hay al-Fukhari) in the Old City was the production centre for this distinguished industry for many centuries.

Pottery production was not limited to various domestic wares, but also included water pipes, sewage systems and other construction materials, especially for domes, floors and walls.

Many Gazans still use ceramic utensils for general purposes, particularly as jugs, storage jars, vessels, and plant pots. Various items of pottery, sometimes painted, or with relief and three-dimensional decorations on them, in various colours, are produced for both the local and tourist markets.

Mu'en Sadeq

Gaza has been a centre renowned for its traditional textile industry since time immemorial, especially for the type of rugs known as *Kilim*, and silk or woollen textiles woven by manual looms. Today, many Gazans especially in the Shuja'iyya area still use manual wooden looms to produce different designs from the cony of camels and sheep, which are cleaned and dyed prior to the weaving process. The shapes, designs, calligraphy and colours reflect the local culture, Palestinian heritage and the artist's personal taste.

Although the traditional textile industry has witnessed a decline in the last few decades, efforts are being made today to preserve it from extinction. The Municipality of Gaza is seeking ways to market the textiles made on manual looms in the area, to become part of the tourist industry for the region. The Arts and Crafts Village is one of these initiatives, where local textiles are exhibited to help promote and preserve one of the city's most important traditions.

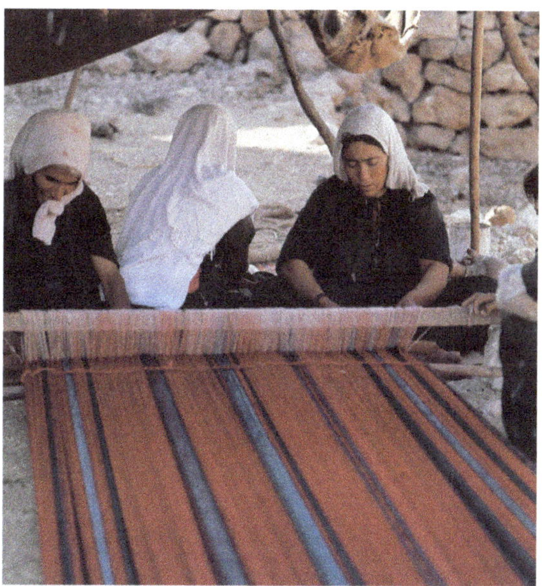

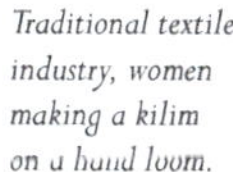

Traditional textile industry, women making a kilim on a hand loom.

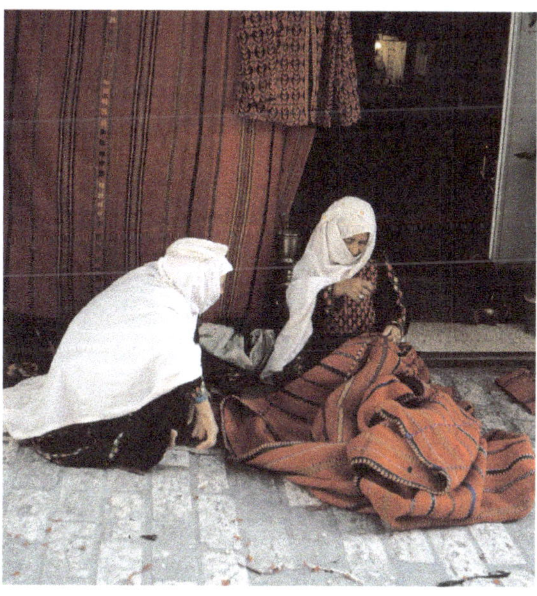

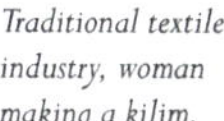

Traditional textile industry, woman making a kilim.

GLOSSARY

Ablaq	(From the Turkish *iplik*, "rope" or "thread"). Building technique consisting of alternating courses of black and white masonry.
Amir	Governor, Prince, dignitary.
Arabesque	Arabic design of intertwined leaves and geometric shapes developed during the Islamic era.
Bahri	Connected to the Nile (al-Bahr). The *Bahri* Mamluks owe their name to the fact that their barracks were in the Island of Rawda on the Nile.
Burj	Fort, bastion. Tower, sometimes surrounded by an outer wall.
Burjide	(From *burj*). The *Burjide* Mamluks or circassians owe their name to having been formed in the towers (singular *burj*) of the citadel in Cairo.
Caravanserai	Hostel along main travelling routes to accommodate travellers and safeguard their goods.
Dawadar	Post occupied by the Secretary of State. *Dawadar kabir* literally "Great Secretary".
Dervish	Member of the religious fraternity renowned for their devotional practices.
Dikkat al-muballigh	Platform from which prayers of the day were recited for all the worshippers to hear.
Diwani	Calligraphy, close in style to that of *farsi*; very sought after, this writing was used in the letters of the Ottoman chancelleries.
Durqa'a	In mosques and *madrasas*, a central space from which access is obtained to adjacent quarters, flanked by two or four *iwans* and generally covered by a wooden roof bearing openings for ventilation and zenithal lighting.
Farsi	Originating from or an inhabitant of Persia. Cursive, particularly elegant calligraphic style which emphasises the curves of the Arabic letter by reducing the angular figures.
Fatwa	Decree, legal adviser's reply to a consultation on religious law.
Funduq	In North Africa, a hostel for merchants and their pack animals; store for merchandise and a commercial centre, equivalent of a *caravanserai* or *khan* in Oriental Islam.
Habus	A gift of real estate given under certain conditions in favour of a mosque or other religious institution, such as the *madrasa* or *khanka*, or a civil institution such as the *sabil*, or even a house.

Hadith	(Lit. "sayings"). Body of traditions related to the sayings and actions of the Prophet Muhammad and his companions.
Hajj	The "fifth pillar of Islam", the great pilgrimage to Mecca and holy places, which every believer must accomplish at least once during his lifetime if he has the means to do so.
Hammam	Public or private bathhouse.
Hamza	The diacritical mark used to represent the glottal stop.
Hamzat al-qat'	*Hamza* to pause, always pronounced, followed by one vowel, and written above the *alif* (first letter of the Arabic alphabet).
Hamzat al-wasl	*Hamza* of connection which allows, the subduance of the voice, helping the transition with the last syllable from the preceding word; feature of union and connection.
Hanafi	One of the four *Sunni* legal schools (Orthodox Islam). Abul Hanifa al-Nu'man (79/699–149/767) began the school, which became the chosen school of the Ottomans, who "exported" it to their provinces.
Hanbali	One of the four *Sunni* legal schools (Orthodox Islam).
Haram	(Lit. "sacred", "forbidden"). Sanctuary. Thus it also indicates an illicit and reprehensible act from the religious point of view.
Harem	(From *haram*). Women's quarters.
Ijtihad	(Same etymological root as *jihad*). A personal effort of interpretation of Islamic law.
Imam	One who presides over Islamic prayer; a guide, a chief, a spiritual model or cleric, and sometimes, also a politician in Muslim society.
Iwan	Vaulted hall walled on three sides with a large opening arch and vaulted recess.
Jami'	Mosque where daily prayers and Friday Prayers are celebrated.
Jihad	Striving towards moral and religious perfection. It can lead to fighting "on the path to God" against dissidents or pagans.
Jund	Military and administrative province.
Ka'ba	(Lit. "cube".) Temple in Mecca, centre of Islamic religion.
Khalwa	A Small room or cell with few or no windows to which *Ssufis* retreat. In Jerusalem, it is an independent architectural unit.
Khan	Inn, lodgings for travellers and merchants on the main caravan routes. A store and hostel in large centres. (See also *funduq* and *caravanserai*).
Khanqa	Monastery or hostel for *sufi* travellers and *dervishes*.
Kilim	A general term for rugs that are woven rather than knotted.
Kufic	Type of Arabic calligraphy of angular and stylised characters, often highly decorated, used both in early Qur'ans and in foundation inscriptions. Its name is probably due to the city of Kufa in Iran.

Laura	Desert-based Monastic Order, which was characterised by solitary living and occasional group meetings.
Madhhab	Islamic juridical school. The four great orthodox or Sunnite Islamic submissions are the *shafi'i*, *malikite*, *hanafi* and *hanbali*.
Madrasa	Islamic school of sciences (theology, law, Qur'an, etc.) and lodgings for students.
Maghribi-Andalousi	Cursive calligraphic style, which was widespread in Muslim Spain and North Africa.
Maktab	School where orphans are taught to read, write and recite the Qur'an.
Maliki	One of the four *Sunni* legal schools (Orthodox Islam). Emerged through the Imam Malik (94/713–178/795) and his disciples and spread throughout western Muslim world, including al-Andalus, Spain.
Maqam	Building of one or more architectural units, usually with a dome that contains the tomb of a important religious figure. A place of worship, and a place to which pilgrims come.
Maristan	Hospital.
Mashrabiyya	Wooden lattice screens made of turned wood assembled together to form a window grille.
Mastaba	Long stone bench against an outer wall on either side of the entrance to a building. In the times of the Pharaohs, the *mastaba* was the tomb of nobles and court dignitaries. It was a truncated pyramid shape with a rectangular base, and communicated with a funerary *hypogeum*.
Mawsim	(Pl. *mawasim*). Festival dedicated to a saint.
Medina	City. In North Africa, the ancient part of a conglomeration, as opposed to the European extension of the city.
Mihrab	Niche in the *qibla* wall, indicating the direction of Mecca. Worshippers face this direction when praying.
Minbar	Pulpit in a mosque from which the *imam* addresses the sermon (*khutba*) to the faithful.
Muezzin	Muslim religious functionary, with responsibility for announcing from the minaret of the mosque the five daily prayers.
Mufti	Muslim sage whose religious knowledge allows him to pronounce *fatwa*s about new situations on the basis of his personal interpretation.
Mujawir	Person who settles in one of the three Islamic holy cities (Mecca, Medina and Jerusalem).
Muqarnas	Stone or wooden stalactite or honeycomb ornament that adorns the cupolas or corbels of a building.

Naskhi	(Lit. "copied"). One of the most widespread styles of calligraphy used in the Arabic script; it combines the flexibility of the *farsi* style with the harmony of the *kufic* script.
Nasta'liq	Cursive Arabic writing (alternative to *ta'liq*) worked out by Persian calligraphers at the end of the 14th century, especially used for the transcription of poetry or prose. It is characterised by its rounded forms, its clarity and its geometrical purity.
Niyaba	Administrative region, province.
Qadi	Muslim judge.
Qaysariyya	A covered market.
Qibla	Direction of the *Ka'ba*, towards which believers orient themselves for prayer. Wall of the mosque in which the *mihrab* is situated.
Qubba	Dome. By extension a monument or chamber built over the grave of a saint.
Ribat	A fortress built in frontier zones, from where religious warriors who lived there fought the holy war (North Africa); a hospice for pilgrims (Mamluk Egypt, Palestine and Syria).
Ruq'a	Calligraphic Style used by the Ottoman administration. Nowadays, it is generally used in the Arab daily newspapers for the headlines.
Sabil	Building designed to provide drinking water. Public fountain.
Sanjak	(Turkish word, lit. "flag"). Old territorial subdivision of a pasha's domain in Turkey.
Saqi	A distinguished post during the Mamluk period whose holder was the sultan's cup-bearer.
Shadda	A diacritical mark placed over a consonant to indicate a double pronounciation.
Shafi'i	One of the four *Sunni* legal schools (Orthodox Islam).
Shari'a	(Lit. "route", "road"). Islamic precepts that the believer must follow in order to be on the right road which leads to God. The *Shari'a* rules the behaviour of the faithful in the spiritual, legal, social and political spheres, and also in the concrete aspects of daily life.
Shaykh	An elder, respected for his knowledge and age. Learned man instructed in the religious sciences; member of a religious brotherhood; *sufi* master.
Spolia	(Latin word, sg. *spolium*). Stones taken from earlier monuments.
Sukun	End of syllables; pause at the end of a syllable.
Sunna	(Lit. "tradition"). For Orthodox Islam, group of traditions of the Prophet in which legal advisers and theologians find support and foundations to establish the content of Islamic law arising from the Qur'an.

Sunni	Follower of *Sunna*. "Sunnism", a political and religious system opposed to "shi'ism". *Sunnis* are divided into four schools: *maliki, hanbali, hanafi, shafi'i.*
Suq	Market place.
Sura	Chapter of the *Qur'an*.
Takiyya	(From Turkish *tekke*). Centre for *dervishes* to meet, pray and live; architectural typology introduced by the Ottomans. Synonym of "place where food is served free of charge".
Ta'liq	Persian calligraphic style elaborated in the 14th century, and used especially in letters from chancelleries.
Thuluth	Cursive calligraphic Style usually used in the decoration of Muslim religious buildings. Extremely codified, the prolongation of its letters allow for very complex decorative compositions.
Turbe	Private burial place; architectural practice introduced by the Turks.
Wali	Title of the governors of Muslim provinces.
Waqf	Endowment in perpetuity (usually land or property) from which revenues were reserved for the upkeep of pious foundations (see *habus*).
Wikala	One of a type of commercial building (see *caravanserai*).
Zawiya	Establishment reserved for religious teaching designed for training *shaykhs*; includes the mausoleum of a saint, built on the site where he lived.
Zellij	Small enamelled ceramic tiles used to decorate the exterior or interior of buildings.

HISTORICAL PERSONALITIES

'Abd al-Ghani al-Naboulsi (d. 1143/1731)
Sufi, poet, voyager and *ulema*.

'Abd al-Hamid II (1293/1876–1327/1908)
Ottoman Sultan.

'Abd Allah al-Saqawati (d. 652/1254)
Shaykh, thought to have built the Zawiya al-Maghariba in Hebron.

'Abd al-Malik, Ibn Marwan (r. 65/685–86/705)
Fifth Umayyad Caliph, who built the Haram al-Sharif.

'Abd al-Qadir al-Jilani (470/1077–561/1166)
Eminent *sufi imam*, founder of the al-Qadiriyya Order, who was one of the most popular saints in Islam, and whose sanctuary is in Baghdad City, where he taught the esoteric sciences over many years.

Abu Bakr al-Yaghmuri, Amir
Chief of the Guard of Gaza, who carried out some work on Shihab al-Din Mosque (821/1418).

Ahmad Ibn Ibrahim Ibn Muhammad Ibn Bakr, called al-Badawi
(598/1199–675/1276)
Celebrated *sufi* of Tanta (Egypt). As a young man, he was characterised by his devotion and his spirituality. In 634/1236, he had a vision telling him to visit the tombs of different *sufi*s in Iraq. On his return to Egypt, he gathered around him a group of disciples within Tanta, and the brotherhood of Badawiyya was born, as well as the reputation of mysticism and holiness of the founder, to whom many miracles are attributed.

Ahmad Ibn Radwan, Pasha (d.1015/1606)
Governor of Gaza for three decades.

Ahmad Ibn 'Uthman, Shaykh (d. 805/1402)
Commissioned the first building of a mosque in Gaza that was named after him.

Al-'Adil Zin al-Din Katbugha (r. 694/1294–696/1297)
Emissary of the sultan for the first period of al-Nasir Muhammad's government, whom he subsequently deposed.

'Alam al-Din Sanjar al-Jawali
He occupied various posts in Egypt and in other provinces during Mamluk Sultan al-Mansour Qalawun's time, and that of his son, Muhammad. Under the reign of this last, he was appointed as Delegate of the Sultan and Governor of Jerusalem, Nablus, Galilee and Gaza cities where he built many mosques, among others that which bears his name in Hebron (720/1320). He was also Guardian of Honour of the two holy places of Jerusalem and Hebron.

Al-Ashraf Salah al-Din Khalil (r. 689/1290–693/1293)
Son of Qalawun, he recovered the City of Acre 690/1291 from the hands of the crusaders followed by the remainder of the towns of Syria under Christian domination, which after practically 200 years, were returned to Islam.

Al-Ashraf Sayf al-Din Barsbay (825/1422–842/1438)
With Sultan Barsbay came a period of stability during which Egyptian sovereignty was extended into a vast area of the Mediterranean, stretching from the port of Jeddah to the Red Sea ports. Cementing his policy of monopoly on the import and export of trade, Barsbay re-routed the Canal of Alexandria, with the aim of facilitating better river navigation and thus improving communications between the various cities. Although prejudicial to the interests of the Egyptian people, this monopoly won the sultan the essential resources to pay his mercenary Mamluk guard, and to prepare a military academy and equipment for the defence of the country.

Al-Ashraf Sayf al-Din Qaytbay (872/1467–901/1496)
The longevity of his government, which extended 29 years, is regarded as exceptional taking into consideration both its military victories and its duration, and given that previous sultans reigned for only a short time. Under the reign of Qaytbay, many buildings characterised by their elegance, construction, smoothness, beauty and decoration were built in Cairo and in the Egyptian provinces of Syria and Hijaz. He also built a *madrasa* and a *sabil* in Jerusalem.

Al-Awza'i Sufyan Thawri (88/707–157/774)
Celebrated *imam*, founder of a *madrasa* that bears his name.

Al-Dahir Rukn al-Din Baybars I al-Bunduqdari (r. 658/1260–676/1277)
Considered the true founder of the Mamluk State, his reign was noted for the buildings and renovations he patronised and his victorious military campaigns. He installed the Abbasid Caliphate in Egypt and remained in power for 17 years. He was the first sultan to send the *Mahmal* (decorated palanquin to carry the Black silk, covering the outer walls of the Ka'ba) to Mecca to prove himself the defender of the Caliphate.

Al-Dahir Sayf al-Din Barquq (784/1382–801/1399)
Named *barquq*, "plums", because he had the protruding eyeballs of a monkfish, Barquq came to the post in 784/1382, and was the first of the Mamluk Circassian Sultans, or the Burji of Egypt, which he remained until his death.

Al-Dahir Sayf al-Din Khushqadam al-Ahmadi (865/1460–872/1467)
He was a Greek native unlike other Mamluk sultans of Circassian origin.

Alexander the Great (356–323 BC)
Successor of King Philippe of Macedonia (r. 336–323 BC), and one of the most renowned conquerors in history, he defeated the Persian Empire and then occupied Syria and Palestine in 332–331 BC. He Hellenised the East and founded the City of Alexandria in Egypt (the second most important metropolis of antiquity after Rome).

Al-Ghazali Abu Hamid Imam (435/1058–505/1111)
This well-known *sufi* philosopher known as "Hujjat al-Islam" ("Witness of Islam") taught the law in Baghdad, where an encyclopaedic knowledge and remarkable approach to teaching offered him vast notoriety; the influence of his theories had a considerable impact on the evolution of Islam. While refuting rationalist philosophy, his writings manage to reconcile theology, philosophy, law and mysticism. Among other major works, we owe to him the celebrated *Ihya' 'Uloum al-Din* (*Revivification of the Sciences of Religion*). In the Latin world of the Middle Ages he was known under the name Alghazel; some of his treaties were adapted in the Catalan language by Raymond Lulle.

Al-Ghazi Abu Su'ud (952/1545–981/1174)
Renowned scholar of Jerusalem at the end of the 10th century/16th century.

'Ali al-Bakka', Shaykh (d. 670/1271)
Sufi renowned for crying whilst praying; he is buried in Hebron.

Al-Idrissi, 'Abd Allah Muhammad (493/1100–560/1165)
Celebrated traveller, geographer and Moroccan chronicler: he lived at the court of King Roger II of Sicily, for whom he wrote a detailed description of the world, *Kitab Rujar* or *The Book of Roger* in 549/1154.

'Ali Ibn Marwan (d. 715/1316)
Leading Mamluk *shaykh* in Gaza, originally from Morocco. He is buried in Gaza in the mosque given his name.

Al-Mansur Husam al-Din Lajin (696/1297–698/1299)
Delegate to Sultan al-'Adil Zin al-Din Katbugha throughout his reign. The sultan's assassination put an end to his reign allowing the return of Sultan al-Nasir Muhammad.

Al-Mansur Sayf al-Din Qalawun (r. 678/1279–689/1290)
Considered the second father of the *Bahri* Mamluk State. His family held power for nearly 100 years. He died during the Siege of Acre.

Al-Mu'addam 'Issa, Amir (d. 625/1227)
Governor of Syria and Palestine during the Ayyubid period.

Al-Mu'ayyad Sayf al-Din Shaykh (r. 815/1412–824/1421)
Circassian Mamluk Sultan.

Al-Muqaddasi, Muhammad Ibn Ahmad (d. 380/990)
Geographer, originating in Jerusalem (*al-Bayt al-Muqaddas* in Arabic) as his nickname indicates, this true globetrotter visited all the areas of Islam, with the exception of al-Andalus. He is the author of the largest geographical encyclopaedia: *Kitab ahsan al-taqasim fi-ma'rifat al-aqalim* (*The better distribution for the knowledge of the provinces*), published in 375/985 and translated in Leyde in 1906.

Al-Nasir Nasir al-Din Muhammad (first reign: 693/1293–694/1294)
Son of Qalawun, he succeeded to the throne at the age of seven and governed for over 40 years. He reigned over several periods for he was twice deposed. His era is considered among the most splendid periods of Islamic architecture, witnessing intense building activity and the increasing popularity of *muqarnas*-decorated façades. He directed a number of architectural projects in Palestine.

Al-Shafi'i, Abu 'Abd Allah Muhammad Ibn Idris (150/767–204/820)
Born in Gaza, *imam* Al-Shafi'i was one of the most eminent authorities on theology and Muslim law. Responsibility was also allocated to him in medicine and physiognomy. Although he is not the founder, he gave his name to one of the four legal schools of Sunnite Islam.

Al-Thawri, Sufyan Abu 'Abd Allah (97/715–161/778)
Originating in Kufa, this famous Iraqi *imam* is regarded as one of the great scholars of his time. An Ascetic with a deep religiosity and an exceptional intelligence, he is the author of a large body of work of mystical and legal comments which influenced a number of other *ulemas*.

Al-Walid I Ibn 'Abd al-Malik (48/668–96/715)
An exceptionally active patron of architecture, the sixth Umayyad Caliph (r. 86/705-96/715) who is especially well known as the person responsible for the building in Damas of the primary chronological masterpiece of Islamic architecture: the Mosque of the Umayyads. We owe to him also the rebuilding of the Large Mosque of Medina and that of the Aqsa Mosque, opposite the Dome of the Rock; highly regarded in Jerusalem and built by his father, 'Abd al-Malik. He continued the powerful working practices of his father, introducing certain Byzantine and Persian practices into the Caliph's administration. Under his reign, Islam continued to expand increasingly to the East, reaching Transoxiana in the West, with the conquest of al-Andalus.

Al-Walid II Ibn Yazid (125/743–126/744)
Aesthete and a man of culture, before he became Caliph he was an original poet, an amateur of pleasures, and when he succeeded his uncle Hisham, encountered the hostility of the Yemenite tribes, and was forced to turn back, hit by exhaustion, the Yemenites made a *coup d'etat*. Pursued by his enemies, he died at the age of 35 years in one of the castles he had built in the desert steppes of Palmyrène.

Badr al-Jamali (404/1014–486/1094)
Of Armenian origin, he was first the Governor of Acre, and later contributed to the consolidation of the Fatimid dynasty by answering to the call of Caliph al-Mustansir (427/1036–486/1094) to restore order in Egypt, where he led his army from Syria in 466/1074. Having soon stabilised the entire country, he was named *vizier* and chief in charge of the armies.

Evlia Çelebi (1021/1611–1092/1682)
As with all the other very many areas he visited, this great Turkish traveller brought back from his two stays in Palestine (1059/1649 and 1080/1669–70) extremely precise written accounts concerning the urbanisation, customs and habits, the beliefs and the legends in force during

the Ottoman period. He also had occasion to meet some great political figures during official missions on behalf of the Sultan Murad.

Farrukh Ibn 'Abd Allah al-Sharkasi
Local *amir* who ruled Jerusalem and Nablus and who instituted the organisation of pilgrimage (Hajj) for the first time in Syria in the 11th / 17th century.

Heraclius I (r. 610–641)
Born in Cappadoce in around 575, he was Byzantine Emperor of the Eastern Roman Empire, victorious over the Sassanids (a Persian tribe), but overcome by the Arabs.

Hisham Ibn 'Abd al-Malik (105/724–125/743)
Tenth Umayyad Caliph, under whose reign, the Arabs found themselves impeded by Charles Martel (in the Battle of Poitiers). It is during this time the Umayyad Empire saw its greatest expansion. Less than ten years after his death, the Umayyad Caliphate disappeared.

Ibn al-'Arabi, Muhammad Ibn 'Abd Allah (d. 543/1148)
This Sevillian lawyer and orator relocated to Jerusalem where his expressed opinions about what was and was not allowed to the Muslims outside the territories of Islam were greatly respected and listened to. He recommended, for example, emigration to the Andalusians, remaining in the Iberian Peninsula after the "reconquest", as well as living faithfully under a dangerous hegemony with regard to his health, his person, his goods and his close relations.

Ibn al-'Arabi, Muhyi al-Din (560/1165/638/1240)
Originating from al-Andalus, he is the author of a colossal philosophical and metaphysical *oeuvre* of more than 400 works. This immense figure of Sufism is notable for his influence both on his partisans and detractors; all the subsequent Muslim thinkers have made mention of his Gnostic terminology, which largely transcends solely Islamic mysticism. A theorist of Ontological uniqueness, his visionary doctrines shook the world of both *sufi* thought, and esoterical Muslim thought in general, and continue to promote reflection on the nature and meaning of the Divine.

Ibrahim Ibn 'Umar al-Ja'bari (d.732/1332)
Shaykh of the Haram al-Ibrahimi, founder of the Ja'bari family in Hebron, a line that originates in Qal'at Ja'bar (Syria); several of his descendants left their names to posterity, to the cause and to the religion.

Ibrahim Pasha (1204/1789–1264/1848)
Under the orders of his father Mohammed Ali, Governor of Egypt, he invaded Palestine and Syria, and demolished the Ottoman army. He then governed these two countries for ten years, from 1246/1830 to 1831, and from 1256/1840 to 1841. His reign saw the cultural flowering of Arabic life, and centres for the arts and many schools were founded.

'Izz al-Din al-Amiri, Amir
Built the marble *minbar* in the Great Mosque in Nablus (713/1313).

Jalal al-Din al-Rumi (604/1207–672/1273)
Persian *sufi* Poet, born in Khorasan, Iran. After having spent several years studying in Aleppo and Damascus, where he undoubtedly met Ibn al-'Arabi, he moved to Konya, where he taught jurisprudence and canonical law, thus succeeding his father, an eminent theologist, who had been invited by the Seljuk sultan to direct a *madrasa*. He founded the order of dancing dervishes. His main work being *Mathnavi (The spiritual Distich),* which cemented his celebrity, and which is a collection of religious reflections and morals which exerted a deep influence on Iranian spirituality, while its musical designs marked the flavour of Turkish music.

Justinian I (482-565) **Byzantine Emperor** (r. 527–565)
He selected the ablest Generals, Belisarius and Narses, who fought the Vandals and Persians, and reconquered Africa and Italy. He published a digest of Roman law, called the *Digeste*, followed by the *Institutiones*, the *Novellea* and the *Codes*, which together make up what is known as the *Corpus Juris Civilis*. He also constructed admirable monuments (Saint Sophie of Constantinople).

Muhammad al-Khalili, Shaykh (d. 1147/1734)
Sufi based in Jerusalem, originally from Hebron.

Muhammad Tahir al-Hussayni
Mufti of Jerusalem who was in charge of the Maqam of Nabi Musa (1303/1885–1886).

Mujir al-Din al-Hanbali al-'Ulaymi (860/1456–928/1522)
Judge and historian of Jerusalem. The near total of our knowledge on Jerusalem and Hébron in the 15th century are due to his two volumes: *Al-khalil bi-tarikh al-Quds wa-l-khalil*, published in 901/1496. He is buried at the foot of the Mount of Olives.

Nasir al-Maqdisi, Shaykh (d. 490/1096)
Jerusalem-based scholar. The construction of the first *madrasa* in Jerusalem is attributed to him and bears his name.

Rabi'a al-'Adawiyya (95/713–185/801)
Responsible for introducing the notion of Divine Love into Sufism, and one of the great figures of Islam; through his acts, words and poems the praises of God were best expressed.

Safronius (d. 17/638)
Patriarch of Jerusalem from 634 to 638, during the period when the Arabs conquered the city; the damascene monk Safronius is distinguished by his asceticism and his piety, but also by his love of sciences and philosophy. He left, together with the monk Jean Moskhos, descriptions of monastic life in Palestine and collections of stories and morals, which were highly appreciated by the 7th-century ecumenical council.

Saint Helena (*c.* 247–327)
The greatest part of the celebrity of Saint Elena is due to the discovery or Invention of the True Cross (the one on which Jesus was killed, found through a vision in a well). This dis-

covery was made during the pilgrimage out of Holy Land. It is said that she discovered the Invention of the True Cross, with the course of the pilgrimage out of Holy Land, accomplished in around 326 when she was 80 years of age. The mother of Emperor Constantine, with whom she played a fundamental role in the official recognition of the Christian church, and a fact to which she owes the greatest part of her celebrity. But, between political action, religious piety and devotion towards the poor and oppressed, her whole life was a novel: from very modest origins, she received the title of Augusta in 324, founded many institutions, and was sanctified after her death which took place in Rome, with a funeral and pageantry previously unequalled.

Salah al-Din al-Ayyubi (Saladin) (531/1137–589/1193)
Founder of the Ayyubid Dynasty (567/1171–648/1250), he is one of the great figures of the Muslim Middle Ages. Essential to his prestige was his victory over the Francs established in Syria-Palestine after the crusade of 1097–1099. This hero of the Battle of Hittin was also an accomplished administrator and his dignified behaviour, particularly with respect to the Christians, was worthy of him, breaking down the denominational barriers, and earning him the esteem and respect of his contemporaries as well as posterity.

Shams al-Din Muhammad al-'Alami (10th /16th century)
Sufi of Jerusalem the *shaykh* of the Zawiya al-S'adiyya, who was also buried there.

St John the Baptist (d. 28)
We know about the life of Yahya, the prophet, through various interpretative presentations of the Gospels and the Acts of the Apostles, and by the more neutral testimony of Flavius Joseph. Precursor of Christianity, this Jewish prophet carried out an ascetic life in the desert and, accompanied by some disciples, preached the path of virtue, justice and personal conversion, while announcing the imminent arrival of the Messiah. He baptised himself by immersion in the River Jordan, where he also baptised Jesus.

Sulayman al-Qanuni (Sulayman the Magnificent, r. 926/1520–974/1566)
Born in Trébizonde in about 900/1494, he died in Szeged in Hungary on September 6 974/1566. Sulayman is the tenth sultan of the Ottoman dynasty, and also the most famous. Called the "Legislator" (*al-Qanuni*) by his own people, and "the Magnificent" by the West, he led the Ottoman Empire to its territorial, political, artistic and intellectual heights. A great conqueror and organiser without equal, he intervened in European policy by taking sides with the party of Francis I against Charles V, and was the first sultan to grant the Europeans, in this case the French, commercial "capitulations" (modalities of trading) in the Ottoman Empire.

Tamim Ibn 'Aws al-Dari
A devout companion of the Prophet Muhammad he was the first inhabitant of Palestine who converted to Islam; he was also the first holder of the tradition of the *waqf* in the Holy Land. Well before the construction of Islamic Palestine, the Prophet Muhammad gave *Al-Dari,* his brothers and his successors a large piece of land in Hebron "until the Day of the Judgement", thus asserting also the legitimate right of Islam on the property of Palestine.

Tankiz al-Nasiri (712/1312–740/1340)
Like many other Mamluk *amirs*, the founder of the Madrasa al-Tankiziyya in Jerusalem, he began his life as a slave, before becoming the most eminent military and administrative figure of Syria under the reign of al-Nasir Muhammad Ibn Qalawun. A generous patron, he financed, thanks to his immense fortune, a considerable number of architectural projects (hydraulic systems, *madrasas*, *caravansarais* and *hammams*) in Damascus, Jerusalem and throughout Palestine. During his brilliant career, he exerted also the functions of *saqi*, an extremely sensitive station in the Mamluk hierarchy.

Tashtamur al-'Ala'i
This Mamluk *amir* was the founder of the *madrasa*, which bears his name in Jerusalem. He was a great amateur musician, and an admirer of poetry and theology, who occupied eminent administrative and military stations. In particular, he was *Dawadar kabir* to Sultan al-Ashraf Sha'ban, governor of the province of Safad and head of the armies of Egypt. He was buried in 138/786 in his own *turbe*, within the Madrasa al-Tashtamuriyya.

Tuqan (family)
We owe to this rich family of Nablus the construction (1149/1736–1737) of Hammam al-Jadida in a palace belonging to him. At the end of the 13th/19th century, he founded one of the most significant soap manufactories in the city.

'Umar Ibn 'Abd al-'Aziz (61/681–101/720)
Eighth Umayyad Caliph (r. 99/717–101/720). His administrative reforms were among his greatest achievements.

'Umar Ibn al-Khattab (r. 13/634–23/644)
Second Orthodox Caliph renowned for his fairness. During his reign, the Islamic armies defeated both the Sassanid and Byzantine Empires.

Yunis al-Nawruzi, Amir
Built a *Khan* (789/1387) which later became the core of the Khan Yunis.

FURTHER READING

ADDAS C., *Ibn Arabi and the Voyage of No Return*, Cambridge, 1999.

ADLER E. N., *Jewish Travellers*, New York, 1966.

AL-ISFAHANI I. D., *Conquête de la Syrie et de la Palestine par Saladin*, translated by H. Massé, Paris, 1972.

AL-SAYYAD N., *Cities and Caliphs: on the Genesis of Arab Muslim Urbanism*, New York, 1996.

AL-SHAFI'I M. I., *Al-Shafi'i's Risala: treatise on the foundations of Islamic jurisprudence*, translated by Majid Khadduri, Cambridge, 1996.

BAEDEKER K., *Palestine and Syria*, Leipzig, 1912.

BAGATTI B., *The Church from the Gentiles in Palestine*, Jerusalem, 1971.

BLAIR S., BLOOM J. M., *The Art and Architecture of Islam 1250-1800*, London, 1994.

BOSWORTH C. E., *The Islamic Dynasties*, Edinburgh, 1980.

CAHEN C., *Orient et Occident aux temps des croisades*, Paris, 1983.

CANAAN T., *Mohammedan's Saints and Sanctuaries in Palestine*, London, 1927.

CHEVALIER J., *Le soufisme ou l'ivresse de Dieu dans la tradition de l'Islam*, Paris, 1974.

CHEVALIER J., *Le soufisme*, Paris, 1984.

CLOT A., *Suleiman the Magnificent: the man, his life, his epoch*, London, 1992.

Collective, *L'Orient de Saladin. Le temps des Ayyoubides*, Paris, 2001.

CONDER C. R., *The Survey of Eastern Palestine*, London, 1889.

CRESWELL K. A. C., ALLAN, J. W., *A short Account of Early Muslim Architecture*, Cairo, 1989.

CRESWELL K. A. C., *Early Muslim Architecture* (2 vols.), Oxford, 1969.

DUSSAUD R., *Topographie historique de la Syrie antique et médiévale*, Paris, 1928.

ELISSÉEFF N., *Nur al-Din, un grand prince musulman de Syrie au temps des croisades (511–569/1118–1174)*, Damascus, 1967.

ETTINGHAUSEN R., GRABAR O., *The Art and Architecture of Islam: 650–1250*, New Haven, 1994.

GRABAR O., *The Formation of Islamic Art*, New Haven-London, 1987.

HAYES J. R. (ed.), *The Genius of Arab Civilization: Source of the Renaissance*, Cambridge, Massachusetts, 1983.

HILLENBRAND R., *Islamic Art and Architecture*, London, 1999.

HOURANI A., STERN M. (ed.), *The Islamic City*, Oxford, Pennsylvania, 1970.

IBN AL-ARABI, *Le Livre des contemplations divines*, translated and edited by St. Ruspoli, Paris-Arles, 1999.

IBN BATTUTA, *The travels of Ibn Battuta, A.D. 1325-1354*, translated with revisions and notes by C. F. Beckingham, from the Arabic text edited by C. Defrémery and B. R. Sanguinetti, London, 1994.

IBN MUNQIDH U., *Des enseignements de la vie, souvenirs d'un gentilhomme syrien du temps des Croisades*, translated by A. Miquel, Paris, 1983.

JAUSSEN A., SAVIGNAC R., *Mission Archéologique en Arabie* (3 vols.), Geuthner, Paris, 1909-1922.

KURAN A., *Mimar Sinan*, Istanbul, 1986.

LAPIDUS I., *Muslim Cities in the late middle Ages*, Cambridge, Massachussets, 1967.

LE STRANGE G., *Palestine under the Moslems, a description of Syria and the Holy Land from A.D. 650 to 1500*, Beirut, 1965.

LINGS, M., *What Is Sufism*, London, 1981.

MEISTERMANN B., *Guide to the Holy Land*, London, 1923.

MOUTON J.-M., *Saladin, le sultan chevalier*, Paris, 2001.

MURPHY-O'CONNOR J., *The Holy Land*, Oxford, 1992.

OTTO-DORN K., *The art and architecture of the Islamic world*, Berkeley, 1996.

PAPADOPOULO A., Islam and Muslim art, London, 1980.

ROBERTS, D., *Yesterday and Today. The Holy Land. Litographs and Diaries by David Roberts R.A.*, Cairo, 1996.

SARTRE M., *Trois études sur la Syrie Romaine et Byzantine*, Bruxelles, 1982.

SAUVAGET J., *La poste aux chevaux dans l'Empire des Mamelouks*, Paris, 1941.

SCHICK R., *The Christian Communities of Palestine from Byzantine to Islamic Rule: A historical and Archaeological Study*, Princeton, 1995.

SÖNMEZ Z., *Başlangıcıdan 16 Yüzyıla Kadar Anadolu Türk Islam Mimarisinde Sanatçılar*, Ankara, 1995.

SOURDEL D., *Histoire des Arabes*, Paris, 1985.

VEINSTEIN G. (ed.), *Les usages du Livre Saint dans l'islam et le christianisme*, Paris, 2001.

WALKER J., *A Catalogue of the Muhammadan Coins in the British Museum*, Vol. 2: *A Catalogue of the Arab Byzantine and Post-Reform Umayyad Coins*, London, 1956.

AUTHORS

Walid Sharif (Head of the Project)

He graduated from the Archaeology, Sociology and Anthropology faculty from the University of Birzeit in 1982. Walid obtained his MA degree in environmental archaeology at the University of Durham, England in 1986 and is currently working on his Ph.D. in archaeology at Université Lumière, Lyon, France.

He served as a lecturer and academic assistant at the Institute of Archaeology, Birzeit University from 1983 – 1993. During this period he participated in numerous excavations and surveys in Palestine. Since 1994 and until the present time he has been serving as the Acting Director General of the Cultural Heritage Directorate. In this capacity, he became a member of ICOMOS, ICROM and ICOM. He is currently an active member in the cultural heritage unit of Bethlehem 2000 project. In addition, he took part in a number of international courses and conferences on architectural conservation.

Mahmoud Hawari

He graduated in archaeology from the Hebrew University of Jerusalem in 1978. He obtained his MA and Ph.D. degrees in Islamic Art and Archaeology from the School of Oriental and African Studies, University of London, England in 1986 and 1998 respectively. His Ph.D. thesis was titled "Ayyubid Jerusalem: an Architectural and Archaeological Study".

He has taught in the Palestinian Universities of Birzeit, Bethlehem and Al-Quds. His work at the Department of Cartography and Geography, at the Arab Studies Society, Jerusalem (1986-1991) has gained him experience in map making and illustration. In addition, he worked on a number of film documentaries and acquired considerable experience in tourism. As a field archaeologist, he has worked on numerous excavations and architectural surveys. He has published numerous articles in Islamic archaeology. He participated in numerous local and international conferences.

Marwan Abu Khalaf

He graduated in archaeology from the University of Jordan in 1973. His MA degree in Prehistoric Archaeology was obtained from the Sorbonne University, Paris in 1975, and his Ph.D. in Islamic Art and Archaeology from Oxford University in 1985. Since then, he has served as Director of the Islamic Museum of the Haram al-Sharif in Jerusalem. He has been teaching Islamic archaeology and history at Birzeit University, Hebron University (West Bank), King Sa'ud University, Riyadh (Saudi Arabia). Since 1992 he became Director of the Institute of Islamic Archaeology at al-Quds University, Jerusalem, a position he is still presently holding. He has participated in numerous archaeological excavations, local and international conferences and seminars. His publications include various articles concerning Islamic art and archaeology in Palestine. His last publication is an illustrated catalogue of the Islamic Museum of the Haram al-Sharif in Jerusalem.

Nazmi al-Ju'beh

He graduated in Middle Eastern Studies and Archaeology at Birzeit University in 1979. He served as Director of the Islamic Museum of the Haram al-Sharif, Jerusalem, between 1981 and 1985. His MA degree in Oriental Studies and Archaeology and Ph.D. degree in Archaeology and History of Planning was obtained from University of Taebingen, Germany, in 1988 and 1991 respectively. He has been working as an assistant professor at the Department

of History, Birzeit University and is the Chairman of the History, Archaeology and Geography department of the university.
In 1994 he became Co-Director of RIWAQ-Centre for Vernacular Architecture, al-Bireh (West Bank), a position he still presently holds. In the course of his work with RIWAQ, he supervised the listing of vernacular architecture in Ramallah and al-Bireh. In addition, he is an active member in various Palestinian academic and public bodies. Between 1992-1994 he served as delegate in the Palestinian Team to the Bilateral Peace negotiations. Dr. Jubeh has written various books and articles on Palestinian history and archaeology. He has also participated in numerous local and international conferences and seminars.

Yusuf Natsheh
He obtained his BA and MA degrees in Islamic Archaeology from Cairo University in 1975 and 1982 respectively. He has obtained his Ph.D. in Islamic Archaeology from the School of Oriental and African Studies, University of London in 1997. His Thesis was titled "Ottoman Public Buildings in Jerusalem during the 16th Century". In addition, he has a diploma in tour guiding.
Since 1977 until the present day he has been serving as Head of the Department of Islamic Archaeology of the Waqf Administration in Jerusalem. As part of his current post, he took numerous training courses in documentation, preservation and restoration of archaeological sites and buildings. He has been teaching on a part time basis at the Palestinian universities of Birzeit, Bethlehem, Hebron and al-Quds. He also participated in numerous local and international conferences. He has published numerous books and articles in Islamic Archaeology.

Mu'en Sadeq
Ha graduated in archaeology from Cairo University in 1979, and did his MA and Ph.D. degrees in archaeology at the Federal University of Berlin, in 1987 and 1990 respectively.
Since August 1994 he has been Director of the Department of Antiquities at the Ministry of Tourism and Antiquities, Gaza.
Between 1980 and 1984 he worked as an archaelogist in the French archaeological mission in Doha (Qatar) as Co-Director of the French-Palestinian, Swedish-Palestinian and British-Palestinian archaeological excavations in the Gaza Strip. In 1991 he was a lecturer in Archaeology at the High Institute of Archaeology at al-Quds University in Jerusalem. Between 1991 and 1994 he was Vice-Dean in the Faculty of Education in Gaza, and Professor of the "Archaeology of Palestine". Between 1994 and 2000 he was part-time Professsor of Archaeology at al-Azhar University in Gaza, and Director of several archaeological excavations by Palestinian teams in the Gaza area. He also conducted a survey of archaeological activity in the Gaza area.
He has participed in local, regional and international conferences and wokshops and has published numerous books, articles and papers on Islamic archaeology.

Naseer R. Arafat
Graduated in Architecture from Birzeit University in 1995, he continued his studies focusing on restoration of old buildings and documentation of Vernacular Architecture in Palestine. He participated in a number of local and international courses on conservation and rehabilitation of historic buildings, most importantly an intensive course titled Restoration and Urban Rehabilitation in Islamic Countries at the Institute of Advanced Architectural Studies at York

University in the UK Naseer worked in Riwaq Center for Architectural Conservation for a number of years on restoration projects, his main task was the supervision of the project's documentation of traditional buildings in various cities and villages in Palestine. As a continuation of his specialty, he is currently coordinating the architectural survey of the Cultural Resources Management Project. He is also the head of the Old City of Nablus Conservation Committee. He presented several papers in a number of local and international conferences in the field of Palestinian Vernacular Architecture.

Sa'd al-Nimr (Production Manager)
He obtained his BA. Degree in Sociology and political science from al-Najah National University – Nablus. He continued his higher education at Exeter University in the UK to obtain MA degree in Politics – Middle Eastern Studies; he is currently working on his Ph.D. in the same field. He worked as the manager of International Relations at the Arab and International Relations Department / PLO. He joined the MWNF team as Production Manager in 1999.

Jihan Barakat (Assistant Production Manager)
Was Given her first Diploma in Jerusalem on July 1993 in Hotel Reception from the Notre Dame of Jerusalem Center – Professional Promotion Section, and was given her second Diploma at Bethlehem on July 1995 in Tourism and Travel Agency Management. Recently working with Museum With No Frontiers as Assistant Production Manager.

ISLAMIC ART IN THE MEDITERRANEAN

This cycle of Museum With No Frontiers Exhibition Trails permits the discovery of secrets in Islamic Art, its history, construction techniques and religious inspiration.

ALGERIA

*LEGACY OF ISLAM IN ALGERIA: The Art and Architecture of Light** introduces the varied and richest forms Islamic art assumed in Central Maghreb (Algeria), an important artistic heritage related to crucial events that marked the country's history, from the rise of dissident religious movements to the influence of great dynasties, and the roles played by trade and pilgrimage routes and by the Ottomans in the Mediterranean cities. The synthesis of Arab and Berber, African, Andalusian and Eastern influences shaped the artistic and architectural models, the purity and harmony of Ibadid architecture, Almoravid mosques, Ziyanid monuments and Ottoman palaces on the Mediterranean shore.

Five itineraries invite you to discover 70 museums, monuments and sites in Biskra, Ghardaia, Bani Isguen, Algiers, Tlemcen, Nedroma and Tamentit (among others).

EGYPT

MAMLUK ART: The Splendour and Magic of the Sultans tells the story of almost three centuries of political security and economic stability achieved by the sultans' successful defence against Mongol and Crusader threats. The intellectual, scientific and artistic currents that flourished then are manifest in Mamluk architecture and decorative arts, almost modern in their elegant and lively simplicity, bearing witness to the vitality of Mamluk trade, to their cultural exuberance and to their military and religious strength.

Eight itineraries invite you to discover 51 museums, monuments and sites in Cairo, Alexandria and the Nile Delta.

ITALY

SICULO-NORMAN ART: Islamic Culture in Medieval Sicily illustrates how the great artistic and cultural heritage of the Arabs who ruled the island in the 10th and 11th centuries was assimilated and reinterpreted during the Norman reign that followed, achieving its acme in the resplendent age of Ruggero II in the 12th century. Spectacular coastal and mountain landscapes provide the backdrop for visits to villages, castles, gardens, churches and Christianised old mosques.

Ten itineraries invite you to discover 91 museums, monuments and sites in Palermo, Monreale, Mazara del Vallo, Salemi, Segesta, Erice, Cefalù and Catania (among others).

JORDAN

THE UMAYYADS: The Rise of Islamic Art presents a journey through the great artistic and cultural flourishing that gave birth to the formative phase of Islamic art during the 7th and 8th centuries. The Umayyads unified the Mediterranean and Persian cultures and developed an innovative artistic synthesis that incorporated and immortalised Classical, Byzantine and Sassanid heritage. The elegant architecture of desert castles and the frescoes, mosaics and masterpieces of figurative and decorative art still evoke the strong sense of realism and the great cultural, artistic and social vitality of the centres of the Umayyad Caliphate.

Five itineraries invite you to discover 43 museums, monuments and sites in Amman, Madaba, Al-Badiya, Jerash, Umm Qays, Aqaba and Humayma (among others).

MOROCCO

ANDALUSIAN MOROCCO: Discovery in Living Art tells the story of the exchanges between the furthest frontier of the Maghreb and Al-Andalus for more than five centuries. Political and social circumstances gave birth to a crossroads of cultures, techniques and artistic styles revealed by the splendour of Idrisid, Almoravid, Almohad and Marinid mosques, minarets and madrasas. The influence of Cordoban architecture and Andalusian decorative models, horseshoe arches, floral and geometric motifs and the use of stucco, wood and polychromatic tiles, display the continuous interchange that made Morocco one of the most brilliant homes of Islamic civilisation.

Eight itineraries invite you to discover 89 museums, monuments and sites in Rabat, Meknès, Fez, Chefchaouen, Tétouan and Tangier (among others).

PALESTINIAN TERRITORIES

PILGRIMAGE, SCIENCE AND SUFISM: Islamic Art in the West Bank and Gaza explores a period during the reigns of the Ayyubid, Mamluk and Ottoman dynasties when numerous pilgrims and scholars from all quarters of the Muslim world came to Palestine. The great dynasties commissioned architectural and artistic masterpieces in the most important religious centres. Attracting the most learned scholars, many centres enjoyed considerable prestige and encouraged the spread of a rarefied art that still fascinates today. The Islamic monuments and architecture of this Exhibition Trail clearly reflect the connections between dynastic patronage, intellectual activity and the rich expression of people's devotion, rooted in this land for centuries.

Nine itineraries invite you to discover 70 museums, monuments and sites in Jerusalem, Jericho, Nablus, Bethlehem, Hebron and Gaza (among others).

PORTUGAL

IN THE LANDS OF THE ENCHANTED MOORISH MAIDEN: Islamic Art in Portugal uncovers five inspired centuries of Islamic civilisation that shaped the people of the former Gharb al-Andalus. From Coimbra to the furthest reaches of the Algarve there are palaces, Christianised mosques, fortifications and urban centres, all of which bear witness to the splendour of a glorious past. This artistic recollection is the expression of a very delicate symbiosis that determined the particularities of vernacular architecture and still permeates the cultural identity of Portugal.

Ten itineraries invite you to discover 76 museums, monuments and sites in Lisbon, Sintra, Coimbra, Evora, Mertola, Faro and Sesimbra (among others).

SPAIN

MUDEJAR ART: Islamic Aesthetics in Christian Art uncovers the fascinating richness of a genuinely Hispanic cultural and artistic symbiosis that became a distinctive element of Christian Spain after the end of Arab rule. Mudejars were Muslims who were allowed to stay in the reconquered territories and Mudejar artists and craftsmen strongly influenced the culture and art of the new Christian kingdoms. Beautifully decorated brick-built churches, monasteries and palaces in Aragona, Castile, Estremadura and Andalusia provide a unique example of the creative preservation of Islamic forms within Christian art in Spain between the 11th and 16th centuries.

Thirteen itineraries invite you to discover 124 museums, monuments and sites in Madrid, Guadalajara, Saragossa, Tordesillas, Toledo, Guadalupe and Seville (among others).

SYRIA

THE AYYUBID ERA: Art and Architecture in Medieval Syria[*] focuses on the unique artistic and architectural development in 12th–13th century Syria, when Atabeg and Ayyubid military resistance to the Crusaders coincided with a great cultural and artistic revival in the most important Syrian cities. The Ayyubid patrons provided educative, religious and charitable institutions; their intense activity left its mark in the sober elegance of mosques, madrasas, citadels, mausoleums and hospitals, embellished with Eastern architectural and decorative motifs, muqarnas, Kufic inscriptions, carved stucco and wooden minbars, beautifully illuminated manuscripts, pottery, metalwork and textiles.

Eight itineraries invite you to discover 95 museums, monuments and sites in Damascus, Bosra, Homs, Hama, Tartus, Aleppo and Raqqa (among others).

TUNISIA

IFRIQIYA: Thirteen Centuries of Art and Architecture in Tunisia is a voyage through the history of the Islamic architecture of the Maghreb, to uncover a millenary civilisation that made works of art of its most important spaces. The great Islamic dynasties – Abbasids, Aghlabids, Fatimids, Zirids, Almohads, Hafsids, Ottomans – and Islamic religious schools and movements left the mark of their artistic expression over the centuries. Islamic art in Tunisia is a cultural crossroads, widely influenced by local artistic customs, by Andalusian and eastern architectural and decorative elements, by Arab, Roman and Berber traditions and by the variety of its natural landscape.

Eleven itineraries invite you to discover 108 museums, monuments and sites in Tunis, Sidi Bou Saïd, Bizerte, Testour, Al-Kef, Kairouan, Mahdia, Sfax, Tozeur and Gabès (among others).

TURKEY

EARLY OTTOMAN ART: The Legacy of the Emirates presents the artistic and architectural expressions in Western Anatolia and the emergence of the Ottoman dynasty in the 14th and 15th centuries. The Turkish Emirates developed a new stylistic synthesis by blending Central Asian and Seljuq traditions and the legacy of the Greek, Roman and Byzantine past. The architectural schemes of mosques, hammams, hospitals, madrasas, mausoleums and the great religious complexes, columns and domes, floral and calligraphic decoration, ceramics and illumination testify to the richness of styles. The cultural and artistic flourishing that matched the rise of the Ottoman Empire was deeply marked by the distinctive legacy of the Emirates.

Eight itineraries invite you to discover 61 museums, monuments and sites in Milas, Selçuk, Manisa, Bursa, İznik, Karacabey, Çanakkale, Gelibolu and Edirne (among others).

[*] Under preparation.

www.ingramcontent.com/pod-product-compliance
Lightning Source LLC
LaVergne TN
LVHW010857110826
845149LV00005B/1418
* 9 7 8 3 9 0 2 7 8 2 1 0 6 *